GLOBALIZATION AND INFRASTRUCTURAL DEVELOPMENT IN INDIA

J.G. Valan Arasu

ATLANTIC
PUBLISHERS & DISTRIBUTORS (P) LTD

Published by

ATLANTIC

PUBLISHERS & DISTRIBUTORS (P) LTD

B-2, Vishal Enclave, Opp. Rajouri Garden,
New Delhi-110027
Phones : 25413460, 25429987, 25466842

Sales Office
7/22, Ansari Road, Darya Ganj,
New Delhi-110002
Phones : 23273880, 23275880, 23280451
Fax : 91-11-23285873
Web : www.atlanticbooks.com
E-mail : info@atlanticbooks.com

Branch Office
5, Nallathambi Street, Wallajah Road,
Chennai-600002
Phones : +91-44-64611085, 32413319
E-mail : chennai@atlanticbooks.com

ISBN 978-81-269-0973-5

Printed in India
at Nice Printing Press, Delhi

This book is dedicated
with deepest love and affection to
my father
Late Mr. J.G. Gaspar,
my mother
Mrs. R. Thresammal
and to my uncle
Rev. Fr. J.G. Jesudas.
Their love, encouragement,
wisdom and strength have
inspired me to be the best I can be.

Acknowledgements

This work would have remained unaccomplished if it were not encouraged, guided and supported by my research guide Dr. A.D.N. Bajpai, former Vice-Chancellor, A.P.S. University, Rewa, M.P. He has been my professor, guide and inspiration. Long hours of discussions with him, his spiritual and economic insights and critical analysis of my work helped me immensely to clarify the concept of globalization, and its impact on infrastructural development in India. He has been the best research guide and the most tolerant and encouraging person that one could ever aspire to work under. I am deeply indebted to him for his appreciation, guidance, prayers and love.

I am also thankful to Gerald Almeida, Bishop of Jabalpur and Chairman of St. Aloysius College Governing Body and Foundation Society, for his encouragement and motivation. His positive attitude and confidence expressed in me made it easier to complete this research work. His efficient leadership and keen interest in my work have been a source of great inspiration and support. I also extend my heartfelt gratitude to Theophane O. Praem, Bishop Emeritus of Jabalpur and the former Chairman, St. Aloysius College Foundation Society and Governing Body, for encouraging me to complete this work. His generous consent, loving inquiry and keen interest in my work have been a source of guidance and encouragement. His love and fatherly concern shown towards me cannot be forgotten at any point of my life.

I am deeply indebted to Rev. Dr. Davis George, our Principal, guide, philosopher, friend and brother. He has been a source of inspiration and encouragement. Without his timely and loving guidance, advice, encouragement and help, this work would have remained merely a desirable object rather than an achievable goal. His constant motivation to reach the unreachable and to dream impossible dreams continued to ring into my ears, mind and heart constantly. His brotherly motivation and guidance cannot be forgotten.

Dr. Shailesh Choubey, Head, Department of Economics, R.D.V.V., Jabalpur and Dr. Neelkanth Pendse, Reader, Department of Economics, R.D.V.V., Jabalpur need to be thanked for their timely encouragement, appreciation and guidance. Sincere thanks are due to Dr. Mrs. Elena Philip and Dr. Mrs. Neelanjana Pathak for their patience while reviewing the manuscript. I extend my special thanks to the staff and students of St. Aloysius College, Jabalpur, in particular faculty members of Economics Department. I am indebted to the scholars and biographers named in the Bibliography and I acknowledge all of them with profound gratitude. University Grants Commission, New Delhi needs to be acknowledged and thanked for granting me this research project. I express my special thanks to Dr. K.R. Gupta, Chairman, Atlantic Publishers & Distributors (P) Ltd., New Delhi for his confidence in me.

It is unfortunate that my father late Mr. J.G. Gaspar is no more now to acknowledge and to see my dream come through. His unseen encouragement is felt at every moment of my life. My beloved departed father is remembered and thanked for his heavenly blessings. I am ever grateful to my loving mother Mrs. Thresammal Gaspar, and my ideal loving uncle J.G. Jesudas and my beloved brothers J.G. Cuthbert, J.G. Kolaso, J.G. Peppin, J.G. Dhanam, J.G. Green and my loving sister Mrs. J.G. Gunaseeli Rajendran and their family members. Their prayers and sacrifice have been behind this endeavour and their pride in my work has been my motivation and encouragement.

Above all, I am grateful to Lord Jesus Christ, my source of spiritual and moral strength who said: "... do not be afraid for I am with you till the end of this world." At the end I am grateful to all my friends and all who have encouraged and helped me, and prayed for me in one way or the other.

J.G. Valan Arasu

Preface

Infrastructural development in India started during the British rule but remained woefully inadequate looking at the size, population and development requirements of the country. The initiation of Five-Year Plans marked the milestone in the process of infrastructural development as a sizeable part of the plan expenditure was earmarked for the development of roads, railways, power generation and distribution, irrigation facilities, marketing and services networks, etc. With the introduction of economic reforms in the 1990s India's economy was put on a high growth path. More emphasis started being laid on infrastructural development to draw maximum benefit from the booming economy and attract foreign capital to take up higher projects for fast socio-economic progress.

Although significant improvements have come about, deficiencies do exist in the development of infrastructure. Regional imbalances have not been corrected. Inadequate infrastructural facilities—still a major constraint in the development of many remote areas—are responsible for keeping them backward. Elsewhere, the quality of infrastructure has remained poor, and the escalating costs of inputs have played a prohibitive role. Thus, the development of infrastructure in India has raised certain pertinent issues which call the attention of government officials, planners and experts while drawing plans, and of policymakers while framing, revising and implementing policy. Thorough studies need to be made to throw light on the inadequacies of infrastructural development in the country, identify causes thereof and suggest viable solutions.

The study in *Globalization and Infrastructural Development in India* is a sincere attempt to understand and comprehend the unique contribution and development—both positive and negative—towards the infrastructural sector in India. This work is undertaken to create awareness about the effect of globalization on Indian economy, in particular the infrastructural sector. In this pursuit a number of recommendations have been suggested to the policymakers of India, so that they could take necessary steps to implement the suggestions. As a result, India could improve upon its ability to withstand shocks, remove difficulties and become stronger than ever before by adjusting to the realities of globalization and thereafter play its part as a major economic player in terms of infrastructural development in a globalized world economy.

The book is an in-depth study of various ingredients of infrastructure in India—power, telecommunication, railways, roads, ports, civil aviation and financial network. The importance of power, which is a key infrastructure and the prime mover of the economic development of any country, has been highlighted. The impact of globalization on telecommunication, one of the prime support services needed for rapid growth and modernization of various sectors of the economy, has been studied in the light of recent policy changes. Inadequate transport infrastructure is a major deterrent to diversification of trade, distribution of production and it slows down the pace of growth. Various roadblocks in this sector have been analysed and suggestions made to clear them. The effect of globalization on various sectors involving infrastructural development has been deeply studied.

This work would not have been accomplished without the encouragement and guidance of Dr. A.D.N. Bajpai, former Vice-Chancellor A.P.S. University, Rewa, MP. I am deeply indebted for his support and blessings. I am also thankful to Gerald Almeida—Bishop of Jabalpur, Dr. Davis George, Dr. Shailesh Choubey and Dr. Neelkanth Pendse for their guidance and support. Finally, the unseen encouragement of my late father Mr. J.G. Gaspar was felt at every moment of writing this book. I remember him and thank for his heavenly blessings. I extend my sincere thanks towards Atlantic Publishers and Distributors (P) Ltd. for bringing out this book in an elegant form.

The book has been written in a cogent style and lucid manner for easy understanding by the readers. The text has been supplemented with tables and figures. Bibliography has been provided at the end to suggest further reading on the subject. The book will prove highly beneficial to students and teachers of Economics and all those concerned with the infrastructure development in India. It will be equally helpful to policymakers, planners and researchers in this field.

J.G. Valan Arasu

Contents

Abbreviations

AAI	Airports Authority of India
ADB	Asian Development Bank
AVSEC	Aviation Security
BCAS	Bureau of Civil Aviation Security
BOLT	Build-Own-Lease-Transfer Scheme
BOO	Build-Own-Operate
BOT	Build-Own-Transfer
BSNL	Bhart Sanchar Nigam Ltd.
BU	Billion Units
CASE	Commission for Additional Sources of Energy
CBC	Centre Buffer Couplers
CDMA	Code Division Multiple Access
C-DoT	Center for Department of Telematics
CEA	Central Electricity Authority
CERC	Central Electricity Regulatory Commission
CMTS	Cellular Mobile Telephone Services
COAI	Cellular Operators Association of India
CPSUs	Central Public Sector Undertakings
CRAR	Capital to Risk-weighted Assets Ratio
CRR	Cash Reserve Ratio
DEL	Direct Exchange Line
DFHI	Discount and Finance House of India
DFIs	Development Finance Institutions
DLD	Domestic Long Distance

DNES	Department of Non-Conventional Energy Sources
DoT	Department of Telecommunications
DPA	Directly Productive Activities
DSL	Digital Subscriber Line
DTS	Department of Telecom Services
EFT	Electronic Funds Transfer
EOI	Expressions of Interest
EPW	Economic and Political Weekly
FERA	Foreign Exchange Regulation Act
FIIs	Foreign Institutional Investors
FIMMDA	Fixed Income Money Market Dealers Association of India
FIPB	Foreign Investment Promotion Board
FSO	Free Space Optics
FTS	Fixed Telephone Services
Gbps	Gigabyte per seconds
GDP	Gross Domestic Product
GMPCS	Global Mobile Personal Cellular Services
GRIDCO	Grid Corporation of Orissa
GRT	Gross Registered Tonnage
GSI	Geological Survey of India
GTA	Global Technical Advisors
IA	International Access
IAMAI	Internet and Mobile Association of India
IATA	International Air Transport Association
IBA	Indian Banks' Association
ICT	Information Centered Technology
IDFC	Infrastructure Development Finance Corporation
IFC	International Finance Corporation
IFC	Indian Financial Consultants

IGRUA	Indira Gandhi Rashtriya Uran Akademi
ILD	International Long Distance
IMRB	Indian Market Research Bureau
IPP	Independent Power Projects
IPPs	Independent Power Producers
IRC	Indian Railways Corporation
IREB	Indian Railways Executive Board
IRRA	Indian Rail Regulatory Authority
ISDN	Integrated Services Digital Network
ISP	Internet Service Provider
IT	Information Technology
IWT	Inland Water Transport
JV	Joint Venture
JVCs	Joint Venture Companies
KCC	Kissan Credit Card
LCCs	Low Cost Carriers
LED	Light Emitting Diode
LEO	Low Earth Orbiting Systems
LMA	Last Mile Access
LSS	Line Sharing System
MARR	Multi Access Rural Radio System
MNC	Multi-national Company
MNP	Minimum Needs Programme
MOEF	Ministry of Environment and Forests
MOST	Ministry of Surface Transportation
MoU	Memorandum of Understanding
MSEB	Maharashtra Electricity Board
MTNL	Mahanagar Telephone Nigam Ltd.
MTS	Mobile Telephone Service
NABARD	National Bank for Agricultural and Rural Development

NASSCOM	National Association of Software and Services Companies
NHAI	National Highway Authority of India
NHDP	National Highway Development Project
NIT	Notice Inviting Tenders
NITs	Notice Inviting Tenders
NLD	National Long Distance
NLDA	National Long Distance Access
NLDC	National Load Dispatch Centre
NPAs	Non-Performing Assets
NTKM	Net Tonne Kilometer
NTP	National Telecom Policy
OFC	Optical Fiber Cable
OTL	Omnibus Telephone Line
PCO	Public Call Office
PDAI	Primary Dealers Association of India
PFC	Power Finance Corporation
PLF	Plant Load Factor
PMGSY	Pradhan Mantri Gram Sadak Yojana
POPs	Points of Presence
PSBs	Public Sector Banks
PV	Photovoltaic
R&M	Renovation & Modernization
RBI	Reserve Bank of India
RCT	Rural Cordless Telephone
RGGVY	Rajiv Gandhi Grameen Vidyutikaran Yojana
RIDF	Rural Infrastructure Development Fund
ROR	Rate of Return
RTGS	Real Time Gross Settlement
SBI	State Bank of India
SEBI	Securities and Exchange Board of India

SEBs	State Electricity Boards
SERC	State Electricity Regulatory Commission
SLR	Statutory Liquidity Ratio
SOC	Social Overhead Capital
SONATA	Son-Narmada-Tati
SPV	Solar Photovoltaic
SPV	Special Purpose Vehicle
SRSF	Special Railway Safety Fund
SRTUs	State Road Transport Undertakings
SSIs	Small Scale Industries
STP	Software Technology Park
SWOT	Strengths Weaknesses Opportunities Threat
TAMP	Tariff Authority of Major Ports
T&D	Transmission and Distribution
TDSAT	Telecom Disputes and Settlement Appellate Tribunal
TEFS	Techno-Economic Feasibility Study
TELCOS	Telephone Companies
TEU	Twenty-foot-equivalent Units
TRAI	Telecom Regulatory Authority of India
TRC	Telecom Research Center
VPT	Village Public Telephone
VSAT	Very Small Aperture Terminal
VSNL	Videsh Sanchar Nigam Ltd.
VTMS	Vehicle Traffic Management System
WILL	Wireless in Local Loop
WOS	Wholly Owned Subsidiary
WTO	World Trade Organization

Introduction

0.1. INTRODUCTION

Infrastructural development plays a key role in the economic development of a country. It forms the foundation of the superstructure of the development process. A strong foundation is almost a guarantee for rapid and continuous development of a nation provided its people are properly motivated and equipped with technological knowledge and managerial skills. Weak and inadequate infrastructure leaves the country backward and allows its people to stagnate in poverty and lower standard of living. As K.C. Pant rightly said, "Infrastructure sectors may not always be an engine of growth directly but they are essential rails on which the wheels of economic progress can proceed with sustainable speed. Without a strong and viable infrastructure, it is difficult to achieve rapid and sustained growth ... which is necessary for progressively eradicating poverty."[1]

Infrastructural development in India started during the British period, but it remained inadequate looking to the size of the country, its population and developmental requirements. Inadequate infrastructural facilities have remained a major constraint in the development of the country and have been responsible for keeping it backward. Several regions of the country remained backward and poor because they lacked adequate infrastructural facilities. The initiation of Five-Year Plans for economic development in the country marks a threshold in the process of infrastructural development. A large part of the plan expenditure was diverted towards the development of roads, railways, telecommunication, power and irrigation facilities and various kinds of social infrastructure. As a consequence infrastructural imbalances and gaps were corrected to some extent and foundations for long-term economic and social development were laid.

Despite all this development of infrastructure during the various plans it is not possible to say that all has gone well with the development of infrastructure in the country. Deficiencies do exist and regional imbalances could not be corrected. Quality of infrastructure has remained poor and charges for infrastructural facilities have sometimes been prohibitive. Thus the development of infrastructure in India raises certain pertinent questions and poses some problems before the research workers for study and enlightenment. Thoroughly researched studies of infrastructural development in India during the plan period are very much needed to throw light on the inadequacies of infrastructural development in the country even after six decades of planning, to identify its causes and suggest viable solutions for the existing problems. This can be of immense help in laying a strong foundation for rapid economic development in future.

0.2. GLOBALIZATION—ITS MEANING AND DEFINITIONS

After World War II human consciousness desired to attain a level of internationalism in which everyone is interrelated to each other. This awareness is gradually growing in the minds and hearts of people because the entire world feels that no nation would be safe without its commitment to international obligations. "No man is an island", it is this consciousness that has led people to "Think global, and act global". As a result the different economies have given a practical shape to the concept of a "global village".

The word Globalization was thus currently spoken, used, and discussed at large, like socialism. The collapse of socialist economies has to a great extent enhanced the prestige and value of 'globalization'. Today, economies are interlinked in such a way that the economic life has become competitive and interdependent. "The national markets have virtually turned into a world market and economies have partially or fully, willy-nilly been globalized or are moving towards globalization."[2]

Globalization, liberalization, and privatization have thus become the three powerhouses of the modern world which is interested in everyone living in this world. "It has become the focal point of attention in the social sciences since the late 1980s, and appeared as a paradigmatic concept in analyzing the economic, social, political, environmental, ecological, and cultural metamorphoses occurring across the modern world."[3]

0.2.1. The Origin of Globalization

The concept of globalization dates back to the voyages of discovery in the 15th century. The capitalist economic foundation was laid in the 16th century. Wallerstein[4] analyzes his "World System Theory" in terms of the power play which the center or core extends and links to the periphery, i.e. extension of power from the "metropolis" to the "satellite." This image of exercised influence in the idea of global culture gives impetus to those who identify culture as an independent factor in the creation of one world. Robertson[5] develops a paradigm to denote the historical-temporal aspects of globalization, apparently intellectually inherited from Rostow. Considering political inputs, Robertson directly analyzes the canvas of development in terms of the globalization process, which binds it to reality. This is linked to the growth of communication, on which globalization depends. Robertson claims that globalization refers both to the compression of the world and the intensification of the consciousness of the world as one whole.

Globalization, a term first used by Theodore Levitt is the latest buzzword and the most misleading and ambivalent in the dictionary of capitalism. "It is an integration of world markets for goods, services, and accumulation of profits for the richest few. It is marked by a phenomenal increase in the private capital flow across the world, aided by information and communication technology, spread out of production and capital across the nations of the world, by transnational corporations, spreading a culture of consumerism and the Western popular culture, spread of market tentacles to every nook and corner of the world."[6] It also connotes pervasiveness, inclusiveness and sweepingness with significant implication in international trade and financial relations. The 'doable' part of globalization signifies[7] that it widens the frontiers of economic activities across political boundaries of nations and helps the process to increase economic integration and growing economic interdependence between countries onto the world economy.

Globalization is a continuation of four centuries of colonialism. The current phase of globalization was shaped by the strategies initiated by the seven richest countries (known as the G-7, now G-8, with the inclusion of Russia), through international financial institutions and the liberalization of trade and capital flow. Such a shift in macro-economic strategies was on the one hand prompted by the Oil crisis in 1973 and 1979, and, on the other, by the need for capital accumulation in the rich countries, primarily through economic expansion. In the 1970s, oil price rise helped most OPEC countries to amass enormous wealth. But the ruling elite of these kingdoms survived under the military and political patronage of the West, especially the USA. Hence, the 'petrodollars' were recycled back to the West to purchase armaments as well as for investment in the international banks located there.

The World Bank and the IMF stepped into the scene when the oil importing developing countries began to face a Balance of Payment crisis. They were willing to lend the 'petrodollars' to the poor countries, mainly Africa and Latin America, knowing that a large part of the money would be recycled back to the West for purchasing armaments for the ruling military regimes. After a few years, when these banks smelt trouble, all of a sudden they stopped lending and wanted to get back their money with interest. In this volatile financial situation, the Reagan regime induced an increase in the international interest rate. As a result of which many underdeveloped countries got entangled in the debt trap, Mexico being an example.

This provided an opportunity for the international financial institutions, controlled by the G-7, to use the Balance of Payment crisis to force open their national economies to serve the long-term economic and political interests of the rich countries. The IMF conditionalities and the structural adjustment programme of the World Bank paved the way for the free market. IMF disproportionately protected the interests of creditors and investors and forced millions of people to bear the brunt in the form of inflation, unemployment, and wage cut. In 28 of the 32 Sub-Saharan countries, foreign debt exceeded their annual GNP. They were forced to cut down on education, health, and nutrition to repay this debt.

This process of forcing open the national economies to integrate them into a global market was accompanied by the spread of transnational corporations. Under the protective political and economic hegemony of the US, powerful American Corporations, later on joined by Japanese and Europeans, began to look for markets and cheap labour in the developing world. To legitimize this system, the demise of statism and authoritarianism in Eastern Europe was projected by the media as the failure of socialism and as the ultimate victory of capitalism. The institutional exercises started by the IMF and the World Bank were followed-up by the establishment of the World Trade Organization. Globalization thus, became synonymous with the economic hegemony of the rich.

0.2.2. Origin and History of Globalization Process in India

During the time of Buddha (3rd Century BC) Indian sailors could go to places now called Myanmar, Malaysia, Philippines, Indonesia, Laos, Vietnam, Campuchea and Sri Lanka. The emergence of the Roman Empire in the Western world and the invasion of Alexander in the West of India gave momentum to Indian trade in the West. Mauryan policy of friendship with the Hellenistic world during Chandragupta rule and his son's facilitated this process. In the early centuries of the Christian era maritime trade with West became vigorous when people of the Roman Empire demanded the luxuries of the East in great quantities. These included not only spices, perfumes, jewels and fine textiles but also ivory, sugar, rice, ghee, Indian iron,[8] dyestuffs, live animals—buffaloes, lions, tigers, elephants and birds etc. Both land and sea trade flourished at that time.

Against these exports, India imported from the West items like pottery, glassware, wine, tin, lead, coral and slave girls. But there was distinct adverse balance of trade for Rome as there was drain of gold leading to financial difficulties after the emperor Nero. This is evident from the discovery of a large number of Roman coins in several cities of India. All these evidences clearly prove that India in the initial centuries of the first millennium gained considerably from the globalization process of international trade where India played a leading role.

India's leadership in the international trade thus extended both to the West extending up to Rome and to the east to Bali via Sri Lanka in the south. It is quite conceivable that India enjoyed a major share in the global trade (about 20%) which was largely free in those days barring some tariffs at the ports and entry points.

In trading with the West, Indians had to face stiff competitions from Arab and Roman merchants. To meet such competitions India established a trading centre in the island of Socotra in the Arabian Sea. Palmyra in Syria was another principal centre of trade though not colonized by India like Socotra. The expansion of India's globalization process in East Asia may be traced through different periods like pre-Christian era, early Christian era, Gupta era and post-Gupta era. While India's international trade connections reached its peak during the Gupta era, it started to decline from the 8th century AD and became insignificant in the course of the next three hundred years.

Thus the internal development of transport system, discovery and maintenance of river and sea ports all over the country helped Indian merchants to promote their goods to West Asia, Africa and Europe. Economic and political obstructions came in their way on many occasions but India's foreign trade was strong enough to sustain such losses. The most important advantage that India enjoyed was the highly superior quality of their products. The spread of Indian culture and civilization in the east through the globalization process that India led in the past is evident in the language, literature, religion, society, art and sculpture that is still practised in the east Asian countries. Through the cultural exchange between the trading countries permanent imprints were made by the dominant culture on others.[9]

The benefits of the Indian globalization process in the past gradually declined as her share in the global trade slowly declined due to economic, political and geographic. Benefits of globalization process in the past also declined due to loss of competitiveness of Indian products and India's inability to protect its trading infrastructure from foreign invaders. The production technologies of a number of exportable items were lost in India as the techniques were not disclosed outside the family. As a result, by the middle of the 2nd millennium, the outward-looking and commercially vibrant Indian economy became agricultural, inward-looking, poor and underdeveloped.

0.2.3. Globalization in the Present

In the 19th century globalization started around 1907 in a global context and came to an end with the outbreak of the First World War in 1914. In the 20th century globalization in India started since 1985 and is continuing till now with varying pace in its successive phases and is expected to continue further under the unipolar economic world. It has been seen that the 19th century globalization could be identified by the expansion of international finance in the global economy.

For India it was more appropriate to consider the beginning of the new globalization process only at the fag end of the 2nd millennium when there was constant pressure from the lending countries and institutions to open up the economies of the borrowing countries as a precondition for obtaining loans. Since the beginning of the aid-led or loan-tied economic development strategy from the early planning era, India experienced gradually increasing stringent conditions to obtain foreign loan. As Indian economy always suffered an adverse balance of payments from the sixties, she had to take loan from different countries and agencies in different forms under different conditions. The foreign loan was always tied with some conditions which were sometimes not disclosed by the Government to avoid public criticism. There are a few instances when India did not even take the last instalments of such loans. Such foreign loans were also conditioned in those days by the cross currents of cold war very much felt by the low-income countries and specially by those like India which decided to remain neutral or non-aligned. However, the conditions attached with loan gradually became more stringent and explicit with the strengthening of the international financial institutions like the IMF and World Bank, which are always dominated by the rich countries of the world.

While planning resulted in many benefits for the economy, it could not fulfil the aspirations of the people for rapid all-round economic development. With a new regime at the helm of the Central Government in India, an import-liberalization policy was substituted in 1985 initiating the second phase of globalization in India in the true sense. But in 1990, India had to confront a major balance of payments crisis which required India to take drastic measures to correct the situation.

It may be said that 1991 was the official year for initiation of this phase of globalization for India as the Economic Reforms policies consisted of LPG strategies.[10] But this globalization was never a full-fledged one as it did not allow free movement of labour though it emphasized on the absolutely free movement of financial capital, freedom for foreign direct investment in all sectors, import liberalization without any restriction and lowering of tariffs in foreign trade.

0.2.4. Meaning and Definition of Globalization

The word 'globalization' has been misinterpreted and made to assume many different meanings ever since it was propounded. Globalization means different things to different people. Many economists and scholars look at it from different angles and define it from their own perspective. Some people consider globalization as a magical word that takes a country on the road to paradise, while some others consider globalization as a more romantic word indicating the desire to interrupt nation-states within the overall framework of the World Trade Organization.

0.2.4.1. Generic Classes of Meaning to Globalization

We can distinguish between two different generic classes of meanings attributed to globalization. One is the spread of human civilization, artifacts, institutions, patterns of living, information and knowledge to span the planet earth and the stratosphere surrounding it. The other is a policy deliberately aimed at spreading certain institutions, modes of doing business, production and trading commodities, services and information across all the states of the world. An analyst can trace the process of globalization in the various senses of the first generic class. We can also distinguish the following sub-classes included in 'globalization' in its analytical sense.

Firstly, there is a spread of international trade in goods and commodities. These are produced with the help of inputs traded in the market and are destined primarily for sale. Secondly, people migrate from one country or region to another temporarily or permanently. Thirdly, money or means of payments are exchanged on an increasing scale between different countries or regions within the same country. Fourthly, capital flows from one country to another to help produce goods and services. Fifthly, finance—not necessarily linked to the production of goods and services—flows between different countries. Sixthly, transnational companies arise which increasingly engage in the activities listed so far. Seventhly, technology is traded as between different countries. Increasingly, with the spread of the provisions of the World Trade Organization, frontier technologies take an increasingly proprietary form. The eighth aspect of globalization is the spread of print and electronic media. The ninth aspect is the growth in international trade and production of services of all kinds—shipping, insurance, banking, health care and finance.[11]

0.2.4.2. 'Open Pluralism' and 'Structured Pluralism'

'Open pluralism' and 'structured pluralism' are the two approaches to those who explain globalization as a process. Persons with 'open pluralism' approach define globalization "as a process that is contingent and multi-centred in such a way that there is no single site of power and transformation that serves as a mechanism to drive it." In 'structured pluralism' globalization is attributed to approaches based on historical materialism and these school of thought generally agree upon the proposition that the driving mechanisms of globalization are to be found in the logic and structure of capitalism as a world-system. Economic globalization is thus, "perceived not as a self-induced or natural process but as a process driven by mechanisms of capitalist expansion. These mechanisms could be either direct exercise of political power of domination and control as in the past or indirect imposition of a set of policies that would bring out structural transformation to facilitate easier penetration of capital."[12]

In the present era of fundamental reorganization of international relations, globalization is regarded as the mother of all ideologically charged contemporary expressions.[13] In this context globalization is seen as "another word for the reach of American imperialism, the power of financial markets, the spread of capitalist social relations, the intensification of exploitation and a vast growth in social inequality."[14] The above list reveals the multifaceted nature of globalization as a process. The multifaceted nature of globalization, therefore, calls for multi definitions and meanings given by different economists. The following are some well-known definitions:

According to the dictionary, the term globalization means "to extend to other or all parts of the globe or make worldwide." Globalization thus in simple terms means 'integrating' the economy of a country with the world economy. But in current economic literature, the term globalization is used to mean a more liberal and "Outward-oriented" policy, which includes eliminating anti-export biases, lowering of very high import tariffs and placing lesser reliance on quantitative restrictions and imports. According to the World Bank, globalization means gradual abolishment of import control over all items, reducing the rate of import duty and privatizing public sector enterprises.[15]

Deepak Nayyar has defined globalization "simply as the expansion of economic activities across political boundaries of the nation. More important perhaps, it refers to a process of increasing economic integration and growing economic inter-dependence between countries in the world economy. It is associated not only with an increasing cross-border movement of goods, services, capital, technology, information and people, but also with an organization of economic activities which straddles national boundaries. This process is driven by the lure of profit and threat of competition in the market."[16] More or less in the same words Russi Mody in his article titled "Globalization Efforts with Accent in Export" views globalization as a two-way thing. First, globalization envisages free competition, high productivity using the state-of-the-art of technology and second, selling in one single marketplace of the whole world.[17] But Prof. C.T. Kurien views global economy, "as a collection of heterogeneous units with different agendas interacting with one another in a variety of ways and thus changing its character over time."[18]

According to Malcolm S. Adiseshiah, "Globalization of the economy may be defined as the global dimension of the evolving world economy." This term covers all facets of life—economic, political, social, and cultural. It means not merely looking at every problem internationally, not merely looking at issues from a world point of view, but it means that the global dimension is emerging and has emerged as a reality today.[19] According to Ruddra Datt and K.P.M. Sundharam, "Globalization is nothing but a modern version of the 'Theory of Comparative Costs Advantage' which was propagated by the classical economists to provide the theoretical foundations of unrestricted flow of goods from Great Britain to other less developed countries."[20] For, Devendra Awasthi, the idea of globalization has emerged from market-oriented development strategy and it refers to integration of the national economy into an international competitive environment. It assures relatively liberalized economic relations among nations. This is designed to generate culture of competition and to promote high efficiency in production, technology transfer and mutual sharing of the fruits of research and development.[21] However, to Nowel M. Tichy globalization is "the capacity to treat the world as one market while paradoxically dealing with it as many culturally diverse merchants."[22] The term "global" is an indicator of change. In the 1960s, this came to be used to mean "belonging to the world" or "world worldwide." Marshall McLuhan (1994) uses the term "the global village," capturing a property of the modern culture, like the possibility of global communication and suggests that the instant reception of far-off lights and voices has changed the very concept and content of culture.

For Samir Dasgupta globalization is "a process which denotes a transformation in the spatial organization of social relations and transactions. The prime features of this process is associated with several historical trajectories, such as universal adoption of the state system and emergence of a globally interdependent economic, political, cultural, technological, and communication system. But, simultaneously, it is also associated with the feeling of powerlessness and economic depression.... Globalization is like an American child whose glittering eyes are fixed on the enchanting Disneyland but also presents a tragic picture of a dejected child beggar."[23] The European Commission defines globalization as the process by which markets and productions in different countries are becoming increasingly interdependent due to the dynamics of trade in goods and services and flows of capital and technology. This indicates a new type of capitalism known as "flexible accumulation."

Contemporary social scientists discuss globalization as a process by which the world is becoming increasingly interconnected and unified, subject to homogeneous and uniform process of culture, technological and economic unification. It is a process through which an increasing free flow of ideas, people, goods, services and capital leads to the integration of economies and societies. This process replaces the concept of modernization, which mainly depends on the dualistic interpretation like "center-Periphery", "North-South", "Developed-Third World" distinctions. Theoretically, the concept of globalization may be viewed as the expansion of the world system, accompaniment of modernity, creation of a single world market and a resultant of modernity.

0.2.4.3. Dimensions of Globalization

According to P.S. Alluwalia, globalization should be viewed from three important dimensions, that is time, distance and volume. There is always a time gap between the designing, making and selling of a product. Two hundred years ago it took many years for a product to move from the laboratory to the firm. For example, it took 200 years to move gunpowder from the laboratory to the artillery. But today it takes only a few months to move the same from the laboratory to the firm. Some years ago the dominating factors were trail and error. But today the watchwords are innovation, speed, service, and quality, to serve the global market. Thus globalization has brought down the time factor considerably.

Another dimension of globalization is the distance between national economies. Reduction in the distance between national economies has resulted in the setting up of integrated production facilities around the world. This has enlarged the scope for research and development and widened the scope for production and marketing facilities. As a result of the fast diminishing boundaries, borders and controls between countries, the traditional notion of "Nation and State" has become obsolete and has been replaced by globalization.

The final dimension of globalization is volume. Under globalization, every service, every capital investment, every plant capacity, every production begin to grow bigger in volume and size to meet global demands. For example, earlier power plants of 200 MW were considered as giant size, but today 1000 MW turbo sets are considered as normal. Automobile production has increased 100 times compared to the plant capacities.[24]

0.2.5. Characteristics of Globalization

While describing the comprehensive nature of the recent wave of globalization, Riccardo Petrella provides an insight into the different characteristics of the globalization process. He writes, "the principal characteristics of globalization consists of the following: the globalization of financial markets; the internationalization of corporate strategies, in particular their commitment to competition as a source of wealth creation; the diffusion of technology and related Research and Development and knowledge worldwide; the transformation of consumption patterns into cultural products with worldwide consumer market; the internationalization of the regulatory capabilities of national societies into a global political economic system; the diminished role of national Governments in designing the rules of global governance."[25]

The term liberalization has four parameters. They are reduction of trade barriers, free flow of capital among nation-states, free flow of technology and free movement of labour force in different countries of the world. Developed countries who are the advocates of globalization define the term globalization in terms of only the first three parameters of liberalization, that is, unhindered trade, capital flow and technology flow. But several economists in the developing world reject this definition as incomplete and define it in terms of all the four parameters of liberalization. That is unhindered trade, capital, and technology flow as well as the free movement of labour force as an essential component of globalization.[26]

0.3. CONCLUSION

Globalization can be defined simply as the expansion of economic activities across political boundaries of nation-states. It is associated not only with an increasing cross-border movement of goods, services, capital, technology, information and people, but also with an organization of economic activities which straddles national boundaries.[27] Thus, the fundamental attribute of globalization is the increasing degree of openness. To sum up, one can say that globalization is nothing but the adoption of a market-friendly approach thereby making the economy more open rather than close. In order to be more market-friendly, privatization and economic liberalization are used as means to attain the various objectives of globalization.

But in the context of India, globalization means opening up the economy to foreign direct investment by providing facilities for foreign companies to invest in the different fields of economic activity. This is done by scrapping restrictive laws, removing constraints and obstacles to the entry of multi national companies in India. It also means allowing domestic companies to enter into foreign collaborations and also encouraging them to set up joint ventures abroad; and a restructuring of Indian economy with a view to making Indian industries internationally competitive.[28] This is also done by carrying out massive import liberalization programmes by switching over from quantitative restrictions to tariffs in the first place and bringing down the level of import duties considerably; and instead of a plethora of export[29] incentives opting for exchange rate adjustments for promoting exports.

In all recent discussions globalization has been identified with the Industrial Policy Reforms of July 1991 and the subsequent extension of these reforms carried out in later years. This is because the real thrust to the globalization process was provided by the new economic policy introduced by the Government of India in July 1991 at the behest of the International Monetary Fund and the World Bank. But a close look at the Trade Policy of the Government of India, Foreign Capital and Aid, Multinational Corporations and FERA clearly shows that the seeds of the globalization and liberalization process had been sown in the early eighties itself.

This is true because in the early eighties many concessions and much freedom were granted to foreign capital. Multinational companies were also allowed to enter a number of crucial sectors to which their entry was previously restricted or banned. Dalip S. Swamy in his book, *The Political Economy of Industrialization* noted the above point and said, "A number of committees in the 1980s had advocated substantial liberalization of the industrial trade and other sectors of the economy. A powerful public opinion in favour of liberalization had also emerged within the economy. As a result, wide ranging changes in industrial and trade policies were introduced in the eighties.... However, the real opening up of the economy and attempts at integrating it with the world economy came up only in 1991 consequent upon the adoption of the structural adjustment programme. In all subsequent years the process was carried still further by the Government."[30]

With the objective of globalization of the Indian economy since 1991, India too has initiated a wide range of economic liberalization and reforms. Successive Governments carried through the reforms undertaken in 1991 and implementation of the second round of reforms is an indication of the all-round political consensus in India about the need for economic dynamism and growth. India embarked on reforms in every sector of the economy like capital, money, real estate and labour markets, debureaucratization, privatization of state enterprises, maintaining fiscal discipline and curbing deficits, cutting subsidies and financial sector reform and opening of the insurance sector. These reforms are thought to be absolutely essential in order to optimize the advantages of the globalization process because most economists who favour the globalization process suggest that it is needed to implement stronger domestic policies and reforms mainly "to consolidate macro-economic stability, enhance human resource development, improve basic infrastructure and spur agricultural development, accelerate trade liberalization and regional economic integration, promote a sound banking system, foster private investment, and ensure good governance."[31]

END NOTES

1. K.C. Pant, *India's Development Scenario Next Decade and Beyond...*, Academic Foundation, New Delhi, 2003, Vol. I, p. 149.
2. Shridhar Pandey, "Liberalization, Globalization and the State in Indian Economy", K.R. Gupta (ed.), *Liberalisation and Globalisation of Indian Economy*, Atlantic Publishers and Distributors (P) Ltd., New Delhi, Vol. II, p. 60.
3. Samir Dasgupta, *The Changing Face of Globalization*, Sage Pubiications, New Delhi, 2004, p. 15.
4. Immanuel Wallerstein, "The Modern World System", Academic Press, New York, Samir Dasgupta (eds.), *The Changing Face of Globalization*, Sage Publications, New Delhi, 2004.
5. Ronald Robertson, "After Nostalgia?" Bryan Turner (ed.), *Theories of Modernity and Post-Modernity*, Sage London, in Samir Dasgupta (eds.), *The Changing Face of Globalization*, Sage Publications, New Delhi, 2004.
6. John Samuel, "The Deceptive Globalization", *Caritas India Quarterly*, Vol. 49, No. 1, January-March 1999, p. 2.
7. R. Annapoorani and K. Nirmaladevi, "Impact of Globalization on Export Performance of Manufactured Goods in India", *The Indian Economic Association 85th Conference Volume*, Thiruvananthapuram, 2002, p. 352.
8. For its purity, hardness and probably of stainless nature.
9. Entire idea regarding origin and history of globalization process in India has been taken from *The Indian Economic Journal*, Vol. 51 and exact details regarding the title and author's names are not known to me.

10. Liberalization, Privatization and Globalization.
11. Amiya Kumar Bagchi, "Globalization, Liberalization and Vulnerability: India and Third World", *Economic and Political Weekly*, Vol. 34, No. 45, November 6-12, 1999, p. 3219.
12. D. Narasimha Reddy, "Globalisation and Decentralised Development Bringing Back the Nation-State", *The Indian Economic Association 85th Conference Volume*, Thiruvananthapuram, 2002, p. 258.
13. C.T. Kurien, *Global Capitalism and the Indian Economy*, Orient Longman, Hyderabad, 1994.
14. L. Panitch, "Reflections on Strategy for Labour", L. Panitch and Colin Leys (eds.), *Working Classes – Global Realities: Socialist Register*, Merlin Press, London, as quoted by Ibid., p. 259.
15. S.K. Patel and R.C. Talati, "Globalization of the Indian Economy", K.R. Gupta, (ed.), *Liberalisation and Globalisation of Indian Economy*, Atlantic Publishers and Distributors, New Delhi, Vol. I, p. 85.
16. Deepak Nayyar, "Globalization: The Past in Our Present", *Indian Economic Journal*, Vol. 43, No. 3, January-March 1996,
17. Russi Mody, "Globalization Efforts with Accent in Export", *The Economic Times*, April 21, 1992.
18. C.T. Kurien, "Indian Economic Reforms in the Context of Emerging Global Economy", *Economic and Political Weekly*, 10 April 1993.
19. S. Adiseshiah, Malcolm, "Globalization of the Economy", *Indian Association of Social Science Institution*, Vol. 11, No. 1, July-September, 1992.
20. Ruddra Datt and K.P.M. Sundharam, *Indian Economy*, S. Chand & Company Ltd., Ram Nagar, New Delhi, 1999, p. 719.
21. As quoted by S.K. Patel and R.C. Talati, 'Globalization of the Indian Economy", R.K. Gupta (eds.), Vol. I, *op. cit.*, p. 86.
22. Nowel M. Tichy, "Glee and Gloom of Globalization", *Indian Currents*, July 12-18, 1999, p. 20.
23. Samir Dasgupta, *The Changing Face of Globalization*, Sage Publications, New Delhi, 2004, pp. 15-16.
24. S.K. Patel and R.C. Talati, "Globalization of the Indian Economy", R.K. Gupta, (eds.), Vol. I, *op. cit.*, p. 90.
25. As quoted by V.R. Panchamukhi, "Globalization, Competition and Economic Stability", *Disarmament and Development*, Vol. 2, No. 2, March-April 1999, pp. 12-13.
26. Ruddra Datt and K.P.M. Sundharam, *op. cit.*, p. 719.
27. Leena George and M.S. Vijayakumary, "Reflection on the Globalization of Indian Economy", *Southern Economist*, Vol. 38, No. 14, November 15, 1999, p. 3.

28. S.K. Misra and V.K. Puri, *Indian Economy: Its Development Experience*, Himalaya Publishing House, June 1999, p. 727.
29. Plethora of exports like duty drawbacks, cash compensatory support replenishment licenses and other fiscal incentives etc.
30. S. Dalip Swamy, *The Political Economy of Industrialization*, New Delhi, 1994, pp. 234-249.
31. Md. Abdus Salam, "Globalisation: A Myth of the Indian States", *The Indian Economic Association 85th Conference Volume*, Thiruvananthapuram, 2002, p. 326.

Infrastructure and its Meaning

1

1.1. INTRODUCTION

The prosperity of a country depends directly upon the development of agriculture and industry. Agricultural production, however, requires power, credit, transport facilities, etc.; industrial production requires not only machinery and equipment but also skilled manpower, management, energy, banking facilities, marketing facilities, transport services which include railway, roads, shipping, communication facilities, etc. All these facilities and services constitute collectively the infrastructure of an economy. Provision and maintenance of adequate infrastructure facilities are absolutely necessary if rapid economic growth is to be achieved and sustained. The availability of infrastructure like power telecommunication and transport is absolutely vital for accelerated development and modernization of a country. "Infrastructure sectors may not always be an engine of growth directly but they are essential rails on which the wheels of economic progress can proceed with sustainable speed. Without a strong and viable infrastructure, it is difficult to achieve rapid and sustained growth of the order of 7 to 8 per cent, which is necessary for progressively eradicating poverty."[1] The absence of a dependable infrastructure can impose severe barriers to economic development.

According to Dr. V.K.R.V. Rao, "The link between infrastructure and development is not a once for all affair. It is a continuous process and progress in development has to be proceeded, accompanied and followed by progress in infrastructure, if we are to fulfil our declared objectives of a self-accelerating process of economic development."[2] Rostow, in the stages of economic growth includes social overhead capital as one of the preconditions for an accelerated growth. Similarly, Myrdal in his Asian Drama regards the existence of infrastructure as a necessary condition for development of an economy.

In recent years, much research has been devoted to estimating the productivity of infrastructure investments. "Many studies examining the link between aggregate infrastructure spending and GDP growth show very high returns in time-series analyses.... Research indicates that total infrastructure stocks increase by 1 per cent with each 1 per cent per capita GDP, household access to safe water increases by 0.3 per cent, paved roads by 0.8 per cent, power 1.5 per cent and telecommunications 1.7 per cent."[3]

World Bank also in its study has established that 1 per cent increase in investment in the infrastructure culminates in a corresponding 1 per cent increase in the GDP of the nation.[4] The indispensability of a sound infrastructure for reaping the benefits of industrialization has been realized. Also as proper infrastructure facilities have become a muse for attracting foreign investment, therefore pointing out need for rapid improvement in infrastructure. Bimal Jalan, former Governor, Reserve Bank of India says, "India needs to rapidly improve its infrastructure for trade, such as ports, airports, communications, and transportation. Growth in exports requires high quality infrastructure for rapid and timely delivery of goods and services.... It is more important for the state to provide a conducive environment for exports than the promotion of specific commodities."[5]

The Indian Government has traditionally been well aware of this and has accorded high priority to investment in sectors such as railways, roads, power, telecommunications, ports, water supply, sanitation and sewerage and airports. This is evident from the allocation of over 50 per cent of total plan outlay to infrastructure development in the successive Five-Year Plans right from the First Plan. However, the efforts of the successive Governments in creating better infrastructure in India did not yield results at the desired speed. The Global Competitiveness Report of the World Economic Forum ranked India last in a list of 53 counties surveyed in terms of the quality of their overall infrastructure. Therefore, in the year 1991, our planners were forced to adopt a strategy, which attached high priority to the development of efficient infrastructure and towards creating an enabling environment for private participation in the infrastructural sector.

1.2. MEANING AND DEFINITION OF INFRASTRUCTURE

According to renowned economist Prof. Rosentien Rodan the term infrastructure originated as a military term during World War II. It was applied to such items as oil pipe-lines and subsequently broadened to include various other capital items. The term was adopted in a general terminology as preferable to "Social Overhead Capital" in the early days of Marshall Plan to avoid confusion with hospitals, schools and similar welfare oriented facilities.

Irrespective of the genesis of the term, it is commonly used in the context of the economics of industry, agriculture, development, etc. With no precise definition, many experts use the term infrastructure and social overhead capital interchangeably. Another view is that the infrastructure indicates the basic services on public utilities, which are necessary to the commodity producing sectors of the economy.

Further, the term infrastructure or social overhead capital may be defined as "the foundation underlying a nation's economy[6] upon which the degree of economic activity depends. It may include such tangible assets as the population's educational level and social attitudes, industrial skills and administrative experience."[7]

Infrastructure is an umbrella term for several activities referred to as 'social overhead capital' by development economists such as Paul Rosenstein-Rodan, Ragnar Nurkse and Albert Hirschman. Neither term is precisely defined, but comprise activities that share technical features (such as economies of scale) and economic features (such as spill-overs from users to non-users). Social overhead capital (SOC), by definition, includes all those which are not directly productive activities (DPA), but are necessary for the development of directly productive activities such as agriculture and industry.

Infrastructure is often described as social overhead capital in economics. However, the term infrastructure has not been defined very rigorously. As a result one is not sure as to what services are to be included in infrastructure. According to Albert O. Hirschman, "SOC (infrastructure) is usually defined as comprising those basic services without which primary, secondary and tertiary productive activities cannot function. In its wider sense, it includes all public services from law and order through education and public health to transportation communications, power and water supply, as well as such agricultural overhead capital as irrigation and drainage system. The hard core of the concept can probably be restricted to transport and power."[8]

Rakesh Mohan Committee has defined infrastructure "as the physical framework of facilities through which goods and services are provided to the public. Its linkages to the economy are multiple and complex, because it affects production and consumption directly, creates positive and negative spillover effects (externalities), and involves large flow of expenditure."[9]

According to Hirschman an activity can be included in the category of social overhead capital (infrastructure) provided it satisfies the following conditions:

- The services provided by the activity facilitate, or are in some sense basic to the carrying on of a great variety of economic activities.
- The services are provided in practically all countries by public agencies or by private agencies subject to some public control; they are provided free of charge or at rates regulated by public agencies.
- The services cannot be imported.
- The investment needed to provide the services is characterized by lumpiness (technical indivisibilities) as well as by a high degree of capital-output ratio (provided the output is at all measurable).[10]

In a narrow sense, infrastructure is defined to include economic infrastructure.[11] Economic infrastructure includes broadly three categories of services:

- Public utilities including power, telecommunications, drinking water supply, sanitation and sewerage, solid waste collection and disposal, gas supply and storage and warehousing.
- Public works including roads, dams, canal works and tanks for irrigation and drainage.
- Other transport sectors including roadways, railways, ports and waterways and airports.

In a broader sense, infrastructure encompasses what is referred to as the social sector which includes services such as education, health and housing which are basic to human development.[12]

1.3. EVOLUTION OF GROWTH OF INFRASTRUCTURE IN INDIA

Even before the advent of the British rule, the Indian economy had an infrastructure of some sort. We had a good canal irrigation system in Gangetic areas. In South India Hindu and Muslim rulers built most of the roads. Yet transport and communication were quite underdeveloped at that time. Animals were the main source of transport in rural India. Pathshalas and Madarsas gave traditional education to a small segment of people. Some charitable dispensaries of the Aruvedic or Unani type of public health system was prevailing, which included a very small segment of the population.

For the first time, Lord Dalhousie laid down the foundation of a long-range policy of building a countrywide network of railways and developed the modern infrastructure sector. The first railway line from Bombay, Calcutta and Madras were laid in 1850, whose aim was to serve the interests of Britain rather than that of India. Most of the lines started from three ports. At the end of the British rule, they had built some 65,000 kms railway line in undivided India. Due to the partition, about 11,000 kms of railway lines went to Pakistan and the Indian union was left with about 54,000 kms of railway lines. The railway network, which the free India inherited from the British, was reasonably good. The same holds for introduction and development of posts and telegraphs and other modern means of communication. But the growth rate was low. However, historic educational dispatch of 1854 did lay at least some workable foundations of modern educational system.

After independence, we concentrated in development of infrastructure. There are bright signs of development in road, transport, communication, education, banking and insurance, water supply, etc. But the development of the infrastructure sector is too far from satisfaction. After 1991, the Government has given top most priority to this sector. Many fiscal incentives were declared in various budgets from 1992 to 2002. The 2002-2003, 2003-04, 2004-05, 2005-06, 2006-07 and 2007-08 Union Budget also gave a renewed threat to sectors such as power, petroleum, roads, ports and telecom.

1.3.1. Inadequate Infrastructure

The Indian economy is suffering from inadequate infrastructure. Power shortages are common in all parts of this country. Transportation facilities are poor and inadequate. Communication facilities are poor and they are being developed due to the participation of private companies. Bank and Finance companies are not progressing due to several reasons. There is no encouraging signal from Science and Technology and other sub-sectors. According to the World Bank Country Study 1997, the Indian states are caught amidst three major crises viz., fiscal crisis, infrastructure crisis and human resource development crisis. This study made it obvious that "By the second half of the 1980s, it became evident that the states were experiencing considerable fiscal difficulties. Implicit and explicit subsidies for goods and services, which are not of a public nature rose to reach about 7 per cent of GDP. They also expanded public employment to the point that in most states wage and pensions absorb between 4-5 per cent of the state GDP and 9-10 per cent is not infrequent. They contracted debt without establishing the financial base for its servicing. As a result, fiscal stress became evident. In particular, there was deterioration in the quality of spending. While the state's fiscal deficit remained relatively stable at around 3 per cent of GDP. Social capital, education, health operations and maintenance expenditure started declining from the mid-1980s and interest expenditure tended to increase. Resources for operation and maintenance became insufficient and infrastructure began to exhibit signs of decay.... Most states found themselves unable to play their control role in India's development; to provide key infrastructure for health and education."[13]

1.3.2. Reasons for Inadequate Infrastructure

India's infrastructure is up to the mark. Simultaneously, India is upgrading its infrastructure. Unfortunately, India is till not on the fast path. For Shubhashis Gangopadhyay there are three reasons why the movement in infrastructure is so slow in India. "First, long periods of inaction have got us into a state where the problem is huge and hence large amounts of resources needed simply to overcome the backlog and you can forget about planning for the future. Second, we spend too much time debating on how it should be done—private, public or through public-private partnership. This obviously has strong political connotations in India. For many of us, ideological postures on growth and poverty alleviation are most important than actually achieving them. Ideologies define the method of solution independent of the problem solving itself has never been a national objective. Third, it took us a long time to understand that good infrastructure coupled with free enterprise is a great substitute for all the leaky targeted programmes for the poor."[14] Major reasons for inadequate infrastructure are as follows:

- The main reasons for inadequate infrastructure are inadequate investment. The Government has no money to spend on infrastructure development.
- Different sections of the infrastructure do not earn adequate profit to encourage other entrepreneurs.
- Infrastructure industries have long gestation period.
- Private entrepreneurs are not interested in investing in this type of industries.
- People's participation in safeguarding the infrastructure is low.

1.3.3. Problems of Infrastructure Development

Infrastructure is the base of development of modern economy and society. The Government has not succeeded in achieving higher growth rate in infrastructure sector. The average annual growth rate of transportation, power, gas and water supply came down. The Indian private sector and foreign sector do not give proper and sound response towards Government encouragements and incentives. There are many problems in the development of infrastructural sector. Some of the main problems can be narrated as under:

- Huge and giant financial requirement is a major problem. Rakesh Mohan Committee too recognized the problem of the huge financial requirement. Neither the Government nor the private sector can fulfil this huge financial requirement. For example, Bharti Enterprise plans to enter a long distance service and its project cost is Rs. 20-25 million. For a road project between Delhi-Calcutta and Chennai-Tiruchirappalli the project cost is $1.2 billion.
- Less profitability is another obstacle in the development of infrastructure. It is rather less profit motive sector. Private and multinational enterprises are less interested in this sector because they want profit maximization.
- We are in an age of liberalization, privatization and globalization. But still there are lots of prevailing administrative hurdles, controls and regulations. Scams and scandals become public everyday. India is considered as one of the most corrupt countries of the world.
- Resource allocation and management in this sector are very poor. Problems of infrastructure are not only quantitative but also qualitative. Mismanagement of this sector is responsible for these problems.
- We have no proper, balanced and efficient planning and implementation for the development of the infrastructure sector.
- Higher growth rate has been the main object of every five-year plan, due to which we neglected this crucial infrastructure sector.

- Infrastructure sector involves long gestation period. Previously, whenever the Government made any investment, they did not consider the Return on Investment as well as gestation period. The projects are evaluated on the basis of social cost benefit analysis rather than on the basis of quick return. It takes more than 30 years to get the return. Private companies want to get the return at the earliest.
- Majority of the projects are incurring heavy operating losses. This is mainly because of overheads. Establishment overheads alone constitute 50-55 per cent of their revenue. This is mainly because of excess manpower.
- Furthermore, the traditional organizational framework for the delivery of infrastructure has shown serious weaknesses in the planning and implementation of projects. Non-availability of funds on a timely basis and lack of proper evaluation and implementation of projects have led to major time and cost overruns.

Problems of infrastructure are more serious. There is an urgent need to think about this. There is a need to change the whole strategy, direction and nature of economic development. Infrastructure services are often monopolistic in nature. In the past, infrastructure services have been predominantly provided by the public sector and the responsibility for providing infrastructure services was vested with the Government. This was due to a number of reasons including lumpiness of capital investments, long gestation periods, externalities, high risks and low rates of return.

But fiscal constraints and technological innovations have challenged the old paradigm of infrastructure being a public sector monopoly. Limits on budgetary allocations and public debt, and the dismantling of the allocated system of credit have catalyzed encouragement of private entry in infrastructure provision. Technological and organizational innovations have also made it possible to unbundled different segments of infrastructure services and reduce the level of public monopoly.

1.3.4. Change in the Old Paradigm of Infrastructure

A wave of privatization and deregulation has been sweeping the infrastructure sector around the globe over the last decade or so. These bold new approaches promote improvement in efficiency and service quality. There are five basic pragmatic and non-ideology-related factors that are leading economies all over the world to consider enhanced commercialization of infrastructure provision:

- The massive investment requirements arising from sharply rising economic growth rates are pushing countries to look for additional sources of financing against the backdrop of fiscal stringency.
- The rising awareness of the importance of efficiency in investment and delivery, in the context of tight fiscal conditions, is leading to rethinking on the ability of Government-owned entities to supply infrastructure services in a business like manner.
- Changes in technology now make it easier to change for marginal use of infrastructure services. Such technological changes are making possible the introduction of competition horizontally and unbundling of services vertically.
- The increasing need for countries to compete in the global marketplace is putting additional pressure on countries to provide efficient infrastructure services to their businesses in a cost efficient and competitive manner. Higher infrastructure costs in terms of both price and time delays can make the difference between firms being globally competitive or otherwise.
- The new dynamism and integration of world capital markets have vastly increased the possibility of raining large funds for infrastructure investment on a commercial basis whereas, earlier, it was the Government, which had better access to resources. In many cases, it is now the private sector, which has the capability of souring large funds internationally.

1.3.5. The Government as a 'Facilitator'

The abovestated reasons forced the Government to change its old paradigm of infrastructure and have recognized that private sector participation including foreign investment is required to supplement the public sector efforts. Various reforms have been made in infrastructure sectors, and rules and procedures for investment have been liberalized in order to provide an enabling environment conducive for private participation. The possibility of commercialization of infrastructure investment and services thus has increased tremendously over the last decades.

Speaking about reforms undertaken by the Indian Government, the World Bank country study on India in 1997 has observed that, "The reforms underway since 1991 have radically changed the framework within which state's development policies are implemented. States can attract private capital in such sectors as power, irrigation, ports, roads and all areas of manufacturing and it is its ability to attract private capital, which now determines a state's growth performance. Development spending, therefore, needs to be more narrowly focused on the state's areas of comparative advantages, where it complements rather than substitutes for the private sector. This is a radical departure from the pre-1991 period, when the volume of public development spending was a key determinant of a state's growth performance."[15]

Yet the role of the public sector in investment, delivery of services and in regulation of the Government will continue to be vital however with a difference. That is, "the role of the Government has changed from the 'owner' and 'sole provider' to that of a 'facilitator' and of safeguarding the interests of the vulnerable sections of the community by legal and institutional framework."[16]

In this direction Rakesh Mohan Committee has recommended the following changes:

- Existing sector-specific enactments be unified into a single statute.

- An autonomous regulatory body be set-up for each infrastructure sector, on the lines of SEBI.
- The role of the regulator and the operator must be separated in every sector.
- Mechanisms to settle disputes quickly must be set up.
- An overarching legislation be made for project formats such as BOT, BOO and the like governing projects across all sectors, on the lines of the BOT Law of the Philippines.
- An infrastructure Coordination Committee be constituted on the same lines as the Foreign Investment Promotion Board which will clear projects on a national level based on broad principles.
- The present restrictions in FII guidelines be removed for investment in infrastructure projects, or separate guidelines similar to FII guidelines without investment limits be issued. Similar guidelines and tax regime should govern any offshore fund set up by a domestic asset management company registered with the SEBI, or by a domestic institution.
- Special Purpose Vehicles (SPVs) be used for funding infrastructure projects. Such SPVs should be able to vary their capital with ease; they should be easy to wind up; they should be tax-transparent.[17]

1.4. CURRENT POSITION OF INFRASTRUCTURE IN INDIA

Analysis of the infrastructure sector in India reveals that despite significant reforms and incentives in the infrastructure sector, performance of infrastructure during 1992-93 to 1999-2000 has been disappointing. Table 1.1 reflects a slowing down in the average growth of some of the infrastructure sectors for the period 1992-93 to 1999-2000 as compared with the period 1980-81 to 1991-92.

Table 1.1. Performance of the Infrastructure in 1980-81 to 1999-2000

(Average Annual Growth Rates)

Per cent

Sectors	1980-81 to 1991-92	1992-93 to 1999-2000
1. Power		
Electricity generation	8.8	6.7
2. Railways		
Railway revenue-earning goods traffic	4.8	3.9
Passenger Kilometers	3.9	4.1
3. Ports		
Cargo handled at major ports	6.1	7.1
4. Civil Aviation		
Cargo handled at AAI Airports	6.5	15.1
Passengers handled at AAI Airports	6.0	10.2
5. Roads		
Length of roads	3.6	0.7
Length of National Highways	0.5	0.6
6. Telecommunications		
New telephone connections provided (New Exchange Lines)	19.0	27.1

Source: Economic Survey 2000-2001, p. 171.

- Power sector performance during the period 1992-93 to 1999-2000 has been disappointing despite significant reforms in the sector. It is found that the annual average growth rates of power sector has declined from 8.8 per cent during 1980-81 to 1991-92 to 6.7 per cent during 1992-2000.
- The annual average growth rate of railway revenue-earning goods traffic has declined from 4.8 per cent during 1980-81 to 1991-92 to 3.9 per cent during 1992-2000. But the growth rate in railway passenger kilometers has increased from 3.9 per cent to 4.1 per cent during the same period.
- Performance of major ports has improved, in terms of the indicator 'cargo handled at ports' during the period 1992-93 to 1999-2000 compared with the growth in 1980-81 to 1991-92.

- Performance of civil aviation sector has improved both in terms of cargo and passengers handled at AAI airports during the period 1992-93 to 1999-2000 compared with the performance during the period 1980-81 to 1991-92.
- There has been a rapid growth in the telecommunications sector in terms of new telephone connections over the last decades.
- Table 1.1 reveals that after the Economic Reforms the performance of the infrastructure sector in India is quite mixed in nature.

1.5. CONCLUSION

According to a census, nearly 20 per cent of the urban population is deprived of safe drinking water and 52 per cent without sanitation and basic facilities. This is of an indication that India needs massive investment on infrastructure. Many beginnings have been made in this direction, during the early and the Post-Economic Reform's period. The transport sector witnessed a flurry of activity. This could have major positive effects on the economy, because this would facilitate improvement of infrastructure and reduction in transport time. Since Railways is caught in the cross-connections of vested interests it has not yet responded positively. Power remained in the limelight, without being any physical improvement in the sector. But it is generally accepted that for the power sector to see any improvement, adequate user charges have to be levied, billed and collected. In the telecommunication sector, investment made by the private sector has been quite impressive. There are 22 private companies offering cellular telecom services. A total of six privately financed independent power projects are in operation. There has been some private investment in the roads and ports sectors, and a privately funded airport is also being developed.

Above all it is also agreed that the role of the Government has to diminish if the infrastructure sector is to see any improvement. Before that a strong regulatory body should be in place before any privatization takes major chunks of utilities and other infrastructure facilities. However, this does not mean that the public sector stop investing in infrastructure rather the public sector will have to continue to fund a greater part of fresh investments taking place in infrastructure. It is possible only if the Government manages to discipline its expenditures.

"The telecom sector has demonstrated that competition can do what regulation and state control cannot. Deregulation brought cellular tariffs to nearly a tenth of what they were two years ago."[18] In this given situation a monopoly situation is thus undesirable. It is necessary to have both the private and the Government sector in building up of infrastructure facilities so that an alternative system of public-private partnership is possible in infrastructure development in India. For this, "rulers and administration would have to mend their ways to move forward. All State Governments have to realize that there is no alternative to competition and public-private partnership in infrastructure."[19] There is also need to broaden the base for institutional investors for infrastructure investment by adding the insurance companies, pension funds and endowment funds with mutual funds and fills.

END NOTES

1. K.C. Pant, *India's Development Scenario Next Decade and Beyond…*, Academic Foundation, New Delhi, 2004, Vol. II, p. 149.
2. V.D.R.V. Rao, "Infrastructure and Economic Development", *Commerce Annual*, 1981, as quoted by P.K. Dhar, *Indian Economy,* Its *Growing Dimensions*, Kalyani Publishers, New Delhi, 2001, p. 510.
3. Rakesh Mohan Committee, "India Infrastructure Report," Rakesh Mohan Committee, p. 48.
4. M.V. Srinivasa Gowda and Susheela Subrahmanya (eds.), *Infrastructure Development for Economic Growth*, Deep & Deep Publications, New Delhi, 1997, p. 4.
5. Bimal Jalan, *India's Economic Policy: Preparing for the Twenty-first Century*, Penguin Books, New Delhi, 1996.
6. Transportation and communications system, power facilities and other public services.

7. *Mc-Graw-Hill's Dictionary of Modern Economics*, as stated by Anil Gupta and Rajya Shree Arora, *Growth of Infrastructural Sectors in India*, Radha Publications, New Delhi, 1991, p. 2.
8. Albert O. Hirschman, *The Strategy of Economic Development*, Yale University Press, p. 83, as quoted by S.K. Misra & V.K. Puri, *Economic Environment of Business*, Himalaya Publishing House, Mumbai, 2002, p. 323.
9. Rakesh Mohan Committee, "India Infrastructure Report", p. 47.
10. Albert O. Hirschman, *The Strategy of Economic Development*, Yale University Press, pp. 83-84, as quoted by S.K. Misra & V.K. Puri, *Economic Environment of Business*, Himalaya Publishing House, Mumbai, 2002, p. 323.
11. It is also referred as physical infrastructure.
12. M.V. Srinivasa Gowda and Susheela Subrahmanya, (eds.), *Infrastructure Development for Economic Growth*, Deep & Deep Publications, New Delhi, 1997, pp. 3-4.
13. The World Bank Country Study on India, 1997, xvii.
14. Shubhashis Gangopadhyay, "Gram By Kilogram", *Outlook*, April 3, 2006, p. 74.
15. The World Bank Country Study on India, 1997, xvii-xviii.
16. Uma Kapila (ed.), *Indian Economy Since Independence*, Academic Foundation, New Delhi, 2002, p. 506.
17. *Ibid*., pp. 505-506.
18. Anupam B. Rastogi, *The Infrastructure Sector in India*, 2000-01, *op. cit*., 3iNetwork (2002), p. 53.
19. *Ibid*., p. 54.

Role of Power Sector in Economic Development of India

2

2.1. INTRODUCTION

Power is a key infrastructure, which is the backbone and prime mover of the economic development of any country because power is required for all the sectors of economy which include agriculture, industries, service, information and technology, transport and others. The term energy has been employed to designate not only chemical energy, but also kinetic energy, mechanical energy, electrical energy, radiant energy and thermal energy. These six energy sources play a vital role in the economic development of a nation, because energy facilitate to grow food; keep people alive; transport people and goods; fuel economic development and sustain the economic system.

Economic growth too is driven by energy in the form of finite resources such as coal, oil and gas or in renewable forms such as hydroelectric, wind, solar and biomass, or its converted form, electricity. Modern economists believe that an index of energy could be used as an index of capital because in "economic parlance, energy caters both to the direct consumption and the production of goods: as consumer goods, their consumption tends to vary with changes in income and consumer preferences; as an input in production, their availability and increasing quantity are a *sine qua non* of rising national income."[1]

2.2. POWER AND ECONOMIC DEVELOPMENT

Energy is considered to be the prime mover of economic development and growth. A comprehensive energy regression analysis will indicate a positive relationship between aggregate economic performance and total commercial energy consumption. According to Anil Kakodkar, thus "Energy is the engine for the growth. It multiplies human labour and increased productivity in agriculture, industry as well as services. Easy access to modern energy services holds the key to development."[2] Therefore, the availability of quality power in the required quantity is one of the most important determinants in the success of the country's development because the national income energy elasticity coefficient reflects the relative responsiveness of the energy sector for any change in the national income figures. Energy demand is thus projected in terms of likely growth of future national income. "If national income is expected to grow by a particular growth rate, demand for energy too would grow in response to the elasticity coefficient estimated, the underlying assumption here is that these coefficients would be able to bring out the actual two-way linkages between the energy sector and the rest of the economy."[3] In addition providing adequate and affordable electric power is essential for economic development, human welfare and higher standard of living. India being a developing country with increasing population makes power the critical infrastructure for India.

The draft of Fifth Five-Year Plan thus stated "Electricity is the most versatile form of energy and provides an infrastructure for economic development. It is a vital input for industry and agriculture, and is of particular importance to a developing rural sector, which needs more power for its agricultural operations, for its small scale and agro industries. All sectors of the economy need electricity for their common needs of water supply, transport, communication and domestic lighting. Given the large scale dependence on lift irrigation for food production, food processing and preservation industries, the increase in the power-intensive industries such as aluminium, fertilizer, petrochemicals, etc., and the increasing dependence on electric traction for transport, there is hardly any community or sector which is not affected by a power shortage today. The future development of the country, therefore, will depend upon the rate of growth of power generation capacity."[4]

The draft of Ninth Five-Year Plan once again reinstating the need for power for the future development and growth of the country said, "Electricity is the most versatile form of energy and provides an infrastructure for economic development. It is a vital input for industry and agriculture, and is of particular importance to a developing rural sector. The future development of the country, therefore, will depend upon the rate of growth of power generation capacity."[5] As a result India has taken rapid strides since Independence in the Power sector both in terms of enhancing power generation and in making available power to widely distributed geographical boundaries. The total installed electricity generation capacity has increased from a mere 1,363 MW in 1947 to about 1,36,970 MW in 2002-03. The average growth rate over the entire period has been 8.6 per cent per year. The annual generation is now over 530 BU. The power transmission and distribution network has also grown substantially. Allthough sixty years have passed since Independence a large percentage of the population in India, yet have no access to electricity and a number of villages are still out of reach of electrical power. Per capita energy consumption is still very low. In addition, share of non-commercial energy resources continues to be much higher than what is in the developed countries. India is still not in a position to overcome the power crisis. Power cuts and load shedding has become the order of the day in a number of States.

Restructuring, privatization, liberalization and globalization being the worldwide phenomenon in the power sector, the energy sector in India has witnessed rapid shift in financial and political ideologies. That is why even in India many began to comment that power sector reforms were an absolute necessity because "the nation should not be left behind while the rest of the world is galloping full steam ahead towards prosperity."[6] Speaking on the same level a few years back when Jack Walch first came to India he said, "Infrastructure is the biggest bottleneck here...India does not have the infrastructure. The power requirement of the digital world will blow your mind.... You have sent so many people back who came to set up power plants. You just do not have a chance if you do not wake up."[7]

The general driver for this transfer has been stated as 'efficiency' in resource mobilization and enhancement of supply.[8] The logic for this argument is that private sector involvement and competition would lead to better resource allocation and eventually improve services for end-users of electricity services. In developing countries, according to 'Washington consensus' only privatization would raise capital for power sector investments, reduce political interference, address the problems concerning non-performing public investments and public sector corruption, establish more efficient pricing[9] and reap efficiency gains[10] to enhance economic development.

At present in developing countries, reform efforts are focused on privatization of the publicly owned sector and establishment of an independent regulator. They also envisage market competition in the sector in the longer run. Here privatization efforts are partly justified on the basis of future potential gains from competition. India too has been influenced by the worldwide changes that are taking place in the power sector. Dr. Manmohan Singh presiding over the conference on "Rajiv Gandhi for Contemporary Studies" organized in Delhi justifying power sector reforms undertaken by the Government said, "Experts found that power sector needed structural reforms, equipment change, mindset change, efficiency, cost reduction, competitiveness and quality to serve the economy needs."[11] In response to this the reforms were conducted in technical and financial performance and capital availability. That is why the Electricity Act, 2003 has been passed in the parliament.

In spite of reforms in the power sector, from the year 1991 onwards many states have persistent power shortages. In many states scheduled power cuts, unscheduled outages and fluctuating voltages are common. Also power shortages, both in terms of peak capacity as well as electrical energy, have been common in most of the states. As a result of which every consumer is forced to purchase voltage stabilizers, inverters, small diesel generator sets and burnt-out motors. Consequently, all these impose large economic costs.

To understand why this has been the case, it is necessary to critically examine the power sector in India. Till 1991, the power sector was mainly in the public sector. With a few exceptions, electricity distribution and supply, was the prerogative of state electricity boards (SEBs) of the state Governments. SEBs also set up and operated generating plants. There were also Central Government agencies that set up and operated large generating plants that served more than one State. The Ministry of Power is responsible for policy and planning in India's power sector. The Central Electricity Authority and the new Central Electricity Regulatory Commission share regulatory responsibilities. Eleven State Electricity Regulatory Commissions have been established. Two State-owned corporations play key roles in India's power sector: National Thermal Power Corporation, India's largest generator, and Power grid, which operate the national transmission system. State-level generation, transmission, and distribution is largely in the hands of state electricity boards, most of which are in poor physical and financial health. The power sector depends heavily on Coal India Ltd., Indian Railways, and the Gas Authority of India Ltd. for fuel supply.

2.3. FIVE-YEAR PLANS AND GROWTH OF POWER SECTOR IN INDIA

Power generation and development is a joint responsibility of both the States and the Central Government in India. In the First Five-Year Plan 19.7 per cent of the total Plan outlay was allocated for power development. The power outlay has increased steadily since then in absolute terms. However, its percentage share reduced to 12.4 per cent in the Second Five-Year Plan, and then increased 25.2 per cent in the Sixth Five-Year Plan, 28.1 per cent in the Seventh Five-Year Plan and 26.5 per cent in the Eighth Five-Year Plan. But the Ninth and Tenth Five-Year Plans allocated the largest allocation which is 23.3 per cent during Ninth Five-Year Plan and 26.5 per cent of the total outlay has been kept for the energy sector in the Tenth Five-Year Plan. It indicates that a major thrust was given to the development of energy and power by enhancing the public expenditure in this sector. So the share of energy sector in the total public sector outlay has been increasing over the various Plan periods with the power sector accounting for the major part.

2.4. PHYSICAL PERFORMANCE OF POWER SECTOR

2.4.1. Electricity Requirement and Availability

India's installed capacity for power generation has tripled over the years and now exceeds 1,01,000 MW. However, "the total demand is expected to increase by another 3.5 times in the next two decades, even under a best-case scenario that envisions intensified efforts to modernize power plants, improve transmission and distribution efficiency and adopt more efficient generation technologies."[12] The soaring demand for power will necessitate a tripling of the installed generation capacity from 1,01,000 to 2,92,000 MW over the next two decades.

Table 2.1. Electricity Requirement and Availability

Year	Requirement (million kWh)	Availability (million kWh)	% Change in Requirements	% Change in Availability	Energy Deficit
1981-82	120118	113928	7.6	9.8	-11.9
1982-83	136849	121311	5.9	6.5	-11.4
1983-84	145284	130122	6.2	7.3	-10.4
1984-85	155432	145393	7.0	11.7	-6.5
1985-86	170746	157301	9.9	8.2	-7.9
1986-87	192356	173803	12.7	10.5	-9.6
1987-88	210993	187873	9.7	8.1	-11.0
1988-89	223194	206326	5.8	9.8	-7.6
1989-90	247762	228784	11.0	10.9	-7.7
1990-91	267632	246941	8.0	7.9	-7.7
Total			**83.8**	**90.7**	**-91.7**
1991-92	288071	260136	8.0	9.0	-6.9
1992-93	305266	282384	5.6	4.9	-7.5
1993-94	323252	303681	5.9	7.5	-6.1
1994-95	352260	329255	9.0	8.4	-6.5
1995-96	389721	356441	10.6	8.3	-8.5

1996-97	413490	371395	6.1	4.2	-10.2
1997-98	436258	394989	5.5	6.4	-9.5
1998-99	446584	421488	2.4	6.7	-5.6
1999-2000	480430	453205	7.6	7.5	-5.7
2000-01	507216	470777	5.6	3.9	-7.2
Total			**66.3**	**66.8**	**-73.7**

Source: Energy, Centre for Monitoring Indian Economy, Mumbai, May 2003, p. 128.

Table 2.1 shows how the sizable shortages of both capacity and energy have persisted from the years 1981-82 to 2000-01 even after economic liberalization. From table it is clear that in the year 2000-01, the total percentage of power shortage was only 7.2 per cent. Over the Eighth Five-Year Plan the shortage of power percentage is increased to 7.8 per cent. In the year 2000-01, total power requirement was 4,96,266 million units but the total availability of power was 4,57,557 million units and the total shortage was 38,709 million units. The power shortages reflect inadequate investment in building generating capacity and transmission network. With regard to the change in the availability of electricity in 2000-01, it was just 3.9 per cent which is much lower in comparison to the change in the availability of electricity in the year 1981-82. In the year 1981-82, the total change in the availability of power is 9.8 per cent.

From the year 1981-82 to 1990-91, the total change in the availability of electricity is 90.7 per cent, but from 1992-93 to 2000-01, the total change in the availability of electricity is just 66.8 per cent. This is much lower than what was achieved before the liberalization process. However, total energy deficit during post-liberalization period was -73.7 per cent whereas during pre-liberalization period energy deficit was -91.7 per cent. This means that during post-liberalization period Government has succeeded in reducing power deficit by 9 per cent. But this cannot be considered as a considerable achievement during post-liberalization period.

2.4.1.1. Power Shortages

The indigenous production of commercial energy in India increased from 74 million tonnes of oil equivalent in 1980-81 to about 219 million tonnes of oil equivalent in 1999-2000, registering an average rate of growth of about 5.9 per cent per annum. Despite the resource potential and the significant rate of growth in energy supply over the last few decades, India faces serious energy shortages. In 1990-91, the country faced peaking shortage of about 8 per cent. The position has worsened with peaking shortage of 18 per cent and energy shortage of 12 per cent at the end of Eighth Plan and Ninth Plan. The electricity sector has been experiencing severe shortages for almost two decades now. Table 2.2 provides an indication of the magnitude of shortages in the last decade.

It has been projected that electricity demand would grow at approximately 6 per cent per annum over the period 1997-2012.[13] The magnitude of the challenge in meeting this demand is shown in Table 2.2. Table 2.2 also compares the capacity additions that would be needed in this period to meet supply targets with actual capacity achievements achieved in the last five plan periods. The shortages in energy and peak demand are well known, but the deficiencies in transmission also continue to limit the ability of regional dispatch operations to transfer the bulk power from one region to another region and to operate the transmission network in a secure condition

Table 2.2. All India Energy Peak Demand and Supply and Power Shortages

Year	Peak Demand (MW)	Peak Supply (MW)	Deficit (MW)	Deficit Per Cent
1992-93	—	—	—	20.5
1993-94	54,875	44830	10045	18.3
1994-95	57530	48066	9464	16.5
1995-96	60981	49836	11145	18.3
1996-97	63853	52376	11477	18.0
1997-98	65435	58042	7393	11.3
2000-01	79856	69475	10381	13.0
1-1-2005	86446	75732	10714	12.4

Source: Ministry of Power (2005).

at the lowest possible cost. For this purpose, it is essential that transmission should be planned in an integrated manner so as to obtain the maximum economic benefits from scarce financial resources.

During the year 1998-99, the country faced an energy shortage of 5.91 per cent and a peak shortage of around 13.91 per cent. Therefore to reduce India's dependence on imported fuels and the strain on the environment, some forms of renewable energy such as biomass power production and ethanol motor fuel.[14] These strategies should not be regarded from the narrow perspective of energy alone, but from the wider perspective of national development and this requires conducive national polices and programmes designed to attract active participation from the private sector.

Over and above the demand side management measures have a key role to play in eliminating power shortages to a considerable extent. According to Tenth Five-Year Plan, demand side management would result in saving of electricity in keeping with the concept of energy conservation and recommends reducing the peak load and shifting demand to off-peak hours in the following way:

- Introduce differential pricing according to time of day, thus giving incentives to users to shift their demand to the off-peak period....
- Institute a two-part tariff for all categories of consumers in which the consumers have to pay an amount that depends on the maximum demand for power, plus a charge for each unit of energy consumed.
- Segregate irrigation feeders so as to allow power to the agricultural load at off-peak hours.
- Staggering of office timings.
- Create incentives and commercial arrangements for the transfer of power between regions to take advantage of different peak times....[15]

While emphasizing the need for proper management of power to overcome the crisis of the growing gap between supply of power and demand for power, Dr. Manmohan Singh in his address at the Tata Energy Research Institute in December 1996 said, "India today is facing with the crisis of energy management. For the past five years we had a mistaken belief that somehow the growing gap between India's requirements of power and the supply of power will be made good by the entry of the private sector...."[16]

2.4.2. Financial Performance

The financial performance of the power sector in India has not improved substantially even after reforms incited in the power sector. Over the years the gap between user charges and the cost of supply has worsened despite reform efforts. According to 'Economic Survey' reports the gap between the cost of supply and average tariff has actually worsened over recent years. For all the SEBs in India, the unit cost for supply of electricity in 1974-75 was 22.5 paise per unit, which increased to 41.9 paise per unit in 1980-81 and further to 108.6 paise per unit in 1990-91. The post-reforms period saw sharp rise in the unit cost of supply, from 116.8 paise per unit in 1991-92 to 227.89 paise per unit in 1997-98[17], 243 paise per unit in 1998-99 and 303 paise per unit in 2000-01. As far as the financial performance of any sector is concerned, minimum supply cost is considered to be a prerequisite. When the supply cost of electricity itself is witnessing sharp increase over the years, how can we expect the SEBs to perform better in respect to finance?

Table 2.3. Recovery of Cost through Tariff

Year	Average Cost/Unit (paise)	Average Tariff/Unit (paise)	Per cent Recovery of Cost
1992-93	128.2	105.4	82.2
1993-94	149.1	116.7	78.3
1994-95	163.4	128.0	78.3
1995-96	179.6	139.0	77.4
1996-97	215.6	165.3	76.7
1997-98	239.7	180.3	75.2
1998-99	263.1	186.8	71.0
1999-2000	305.1	207.0	67.8
2000-01	327.3	226.3	69.1
2001-02	349.9	239.9	68.6

Source: Ministry of Power.

From Table 2.3 it is clear that "the gap between the cost of supply and average tariff has worsened over the years from a level of 23 paise in 1992-93 to about 110 paise in 2001-02. Also revenues dropped from 82.2 per cent of costs in 1992-93 to 68.6 per cent in 2001-02."[18] This suggests that reforms in the power sector have not yielded the desired results with regard to recovery of cost through tariff. The State Electricity Board's financial performance continues to deteriorate over the period. The commercial losses without subsidy increased from Rs. 4560 crore in 1992-93 of Eighth Plan to Rs. 13808 crore at the end of 1998-99. Agriculture and domestic sectors continued to be subsidized heavily. The average tariff charged from these categories of consumers was projected to be 30 paise and 131 paise respectively in 1998-99 compared to an average cost of supply of 243 paise per unit.[19] Part of the subsidies is recovered by cross subsidization from commercial and industrial consumers. Because of the poor financial health, the SEBs is unable to raise the resources for the funding of their ongoing schemes.

Most of the State Electricity Boards have incurred huge amount of losses due to irrational tariff. They cannot even meet the day-to-day expenditures. Table 2.4 reveals the financial conditions of the State Electricity Boards. Financial health of SEBs has been deteriorating over the years. According to Economic Survey 2002-03, barring Himachal Pradesh State Electricity Board and Maharashtra State Electricity Board, all other SEBs have recorded losses between 1992-93 and 2001-02 ranging from Rs. 4 crore to Rs. 3682 crore. A highly disturbing feature is that losses have been rapidly increasing over the decade of the 1990s.[20] As a result the Government is forced to sustain the SEBs by providing subsidies. The gross subsidy was Rs. 7449 crore for the year 1991-92, however over the decade of the 1990s the gross subsidy provided increased and for the year 2000-01 it amounted to Rs. 34428 crore. It further increased to Rs. 36187 crore for the year 2004-05. Ever growing subsidy given to SEBs itself indicates the poor financial performance of the power sector in India.

The Planning Commission has estimated that during the financial years of 2002-03, 2003-04 and 2004-05 the commercial loss excluding subsidy was to the order of Rs. 21382 crore, 21517 crore and 23558 crore respectively. Together the states of Bihar, Delhi and Uttar Pradesh reportedly account for more than 50 per cent of total outstanding dues.[21] These heavy financial losses are the result of tariffs that do not cover costs and also because of poor management and operational practices.

Table 2.4. Financial Performance of the State Power Sector

	1991-92	2000-01	2001-02	2002-03	2003-04	2004-05 *	2005-06 RE
Gross Subsidy	7449	34428	36713	30568	31941	36187	35652
Commercial Losses							
Commercial Losses (excluding subsidy)	4117	25395	27306	21382	21517	23558	22569
Commercial Losses (including subsidy)	N.A.	16575	17207	8386	10090	13080	11007
Revenue Mobilization							
Rate of Return %	-12.7	-41.8	-39.5	-31.64	-30.86	-31.94	-26.13

Notes: RE: Revised Estimates, %: In per cent, *: Provisional.
Source: Various Economic Surveys.

In 1999-2000 only seven SEBs had a positive rate of return. The number of SEBs with a positive rate of return of more than 3 per cent has also fallen. In 1999-2000 only two SEBs had a positive rate of return of more than 3 per cent. The hidden gross subsidy for agriculture and domestic sectors has increased from Rs. 7,449 crore in 1991-92 to Rs. 34,428 crore in 2000-01 and in 2002-03 it increased to Rs. 38,426 crore.

Table 2.5. Financial Performance of SEBs

Particulars	1996-97	1997-98	1998-99	1999-2000	2000-01
1. Cost of supply (paise / kWh)	215.60	239.70	262.50	283.80	303.80
2. Average tariff (paise / kWh)	165.60	180.30	180.50	199.00	212.00
3. Percentage of recovery	76.70	75.21	70.70	70.10	69.80
4. Average agriculture tariff*	21.20	20.22	20.62	21.09	28.48
5. Commercial losses&	4674.31	7597.95	12396.77	18266.11	20220.50
6. Commercial losses$	11305.00	13963.00	19972.00	23028.11	13092.50
7. Net internal resources.	2090.70	6209.00	11401.70	11531.60	13092.50
8. Subsidy for domestic consumers	4386.00	5258.40	6433.00	8671.00	10061.80
9. Subsidy for agriculture consumers	15585.20	17706.67	20685.43	24598.77	27083.47

10. Gross subsidy @	20209.96	23422.23	27672.09	33081.47	37037.11
11. Subvention received	6630.60	6364.80	7574.80	4801.80	5792.80
12. Uncovered subsidy	5800.41	8046.61	12255.85	20031.33	23638.35
13. Gross subsidy unit of sages*	75.40	82.60	92.70	103.40	108.40

Notes: @: Gross subsidy includes subsidy for domestic consumers, agricultural consumers and on interstate sales, *: (paise / kWh), &: (with subsidy), $: (without subsidy)

Source: Planning Commission.

Thus, the restoration of the financial health of SEBs and improvement in their operational performance continue to remain a critical issue even today in the power sector. The deteriorating financial health of the State utilities has been one of the major factors for the slow pace of development in the power sector.

Table 2.6. Rate of Return (ROR) of SEBs on Capital Employed

Year	With Subsidy	Without Subsidy
1992-93	—	-12.8
1993-94	—	-12.2
1994-95	—	-13.0
1995-96	—	-15.4
1996-97	-7.93	-19.57
1997-98	-12.30	-22.94
1998-99 (prov.)	-18.78	-30.84
1999-2000 (RE)	-26.34	-33.78
2000-01 (AP)	-27.13	-35.06

Notes: Numbers indicate negative return, i.e. loss; RE: Revised Estimate; AP: Advance Projection.

Source: Planning Commission, June 2001, Annual Report on Working of SEBs.

The commercial losses of State Electricity Boards are expected to be Rs. 20,707 crores in 1999-2000 (RE) against Rs. 9,978 crores at the beginning or the Ninth Plan. The Rate of Return on the net fixed assets was (-) 17.9 per cent in the beginning of Ninth Plan and (-) 31 per cent in 1999-2000. Before the State Electricity Regulatory Commission (SERC) was set up, the SEBs had to set tariffs for the final consumers under the recommendation of periodically set up ad hoc tariff commissions and guidance of the State Governments. There was no compulsion to set tariff in a commercial manner. The

SEBs did not retain profits. The State Government appropriated the profits and bore the losses. Political considerations of the State Governments have played increasing roles in the management of SEBs. Over the years the SEBs became financially sick. Table 2.5 and Table 2.6 shows the financial performance of SEBs. The annual losses reached Rs. 20,220 crores in 2000-01 even after accounting for Rs. 5,793 crores provided by the State Governments towards subsidies.

2.4.2.1. Causes of Sickness

2.4.2.1.1. Subsidies

The sickness of the power sector is directly attributable to the financial sickness of SEBs, which is a consequence of various political power lobbies like farmer subsidies, etc. One of these is agricultural lobby. Electricity is provided to agricultural users at highly subsidized rates. Initially, electricity demand by agriculture was a small part of the total demand. It was 3.9 per cent in 1950-51, 6 per cent in 1960-61 and had grown to 30.75 per cent in 1997-98. Net subsidy in the year 1991-92 was 5,404 crores but over the year this has acquired an upward trend.

Table 2.7. Power Sector Subsidies

(Rs billion, Current Prices)

Year	Agriculture	Residential	Total
1992-93	51.4	20.3	71.7
1993-94	67.4	21.3	88.7
1994-95	85.4	25.4	110.8
1995-96	109.9	31.6	141.5
1996-97	12912	3897	16809
1997-98	15987	4295	20282

Source: Ministry of Power, 1997.

Residential and especially agricultural consumers are heavily subsidized (Table 2.7). These groups enjoyed a subsidy of Rs. 20,282 billion in 1997-98, equivalent to around 1.4 per cent of GDP. About 80 per cent of the Rs. 20,282 billion went to agriculture. Average revenue per unit was estimated at about Rs. 1.7 per kilowatt-hour in 1996-97, compared to average costs of just over Rs. 2 per kilowatt-hour that year.

The rationalization of tariffs continues to be a distant and illusive goal even today. Every State Government is in competition with other State Governments with regard to subsidized tariffs for agriculture. For example in case of Haryana Government, the subsidy payable in 2001-02 was as high as Rs. 1,355.8 crore. In the same year the Government of Madhya Pradesh had paid a subsidy of Rs. 560.27 crore. Maharashtra Government gave a subsidy of Rs. 745 crore for subsidized tariffs for agriculture. This was in addition to compensating the SEB for the huge loss of Rs. 1,986 crore during the year.[22]

As a result the net subsidy estimated in the year 2003-04 was Rs. 23,803 crores. It means that the net subsidy increased five times in comparison to the year 1991-92. Also in the year 1991-92 only Rs. 5,938 crores of gross subsidy was involved in agriculture sector. In the year 2002-03, it increased to Rs. 24,759 crores. Within 11 years gross subsidy provided has increased fourfold. There is substantial increase in the subsidy provided to the agriculture sector over the years because the political parties consider farmers' vote as substantial for their political future. Thus the political parties, which obtained their support to remain in power, had to concede their demands for various agricultural subsidies.

K.P. Pant says that in normal situations "low agricultural tariffs create a vicious circle. They are a consequence of the policy adopted by the Government and a cause of the crisis of the State power sector."[23] The average agriculture tariff which was 49 paise per kWh at all-India level in 1984-85 came down to 25 paise per kWh in 1999-2000. There are some States where power for agriculture is given free of cost. It is generally thought that any increase in power tariff for agriculture will go against the interests of the farmers. A recent study by the World Bank on the supply of power to agriculture in Haryana shows that 50 per cent tariff increased with no improvement in supply conditions. As a result the net farm income is to reduce by less than 4 per cent on an average.

However, "subsequent and sustained improvements in the conditions of power supply, along with phased tariff increases towards full cost recovery would, in fact, increase the net farm income of all farmers, regardless of their size over the medium term."[24] Over a period of about 6 years, the farmers' average net income would more than double as a result of power reforms even if agriculture tariffs were increased to reach a level equivalent to about 2/3rd of the cost of supply. But the study conducted by Shonali Pachauri and Daniel Spreng reveals that "subsidizing energy to the household and agricultural sectors of the economy...in the form of low tariffs for electricity are essentially appropriated by that part of the population which is less poor. This is because...the poorest households do not have access to electricity. An energy policy that takes poverty reduction seriously must subsidize energy infrastructure expansion to poor areas rather than the energy itself."[25]

Subsidy to the agriculture sector has increased from Rs. 15,299 crores in the beginning of the Ninth Plan to Rs. 25,576 crores in 1999-2000(RE). The share of agricultural sector in the total electricity consumed in the country is about 30 per cent, yet the sector accounted for only about 3-4 per cent of the total revenue of SEBs from sale of electricity. Similarly, the share of domestic sector in the total electricity consumption in the country was about 16-17 per cent and the sector contributed about 11-12 per cent of the total revenue of SEBs from sale of electricity. The main reason is that against the average cost of supply of 242 paise per unit in 1998-99, the average tariff charged for agriculture and domestic consumers was 30 paise per unit and 131 paise per unit respectively.

This has resulted in the escalation of commercial losses of the SEBs, as the cross-subsidies are no longer sufficient. At the same time, since cross subsidy is being provided by charging a higher tariff from industry, the cost of industrial production increases. The cost of supply has also increased because of higher establishment charges, poor maintenance and higher fuel consumption. There is need to reduce the cost of supply through better efficiency and management. This becomes all the more important once we realize that in an increasingly globalized world this would in fact lead to more and more industrial units losing their competitiveness due to higher input costs.

2.4.2.1.2. Transmission and Distribution Losses

One of the major points on which there has been a totally disappointing record of SEBs and private sector distribution companies in Orissa is the non-adherence to the targets for reduction in Transmission and Distribution losses. Even more than agricultural subsidies, overstaffing and large transmission and distribution (T&D) losses contribute to the financial sickness of SEBs. It is shocking to see that, in a number of cases, instead of the losses coming down the actual losses have gone up as compared to those of reported loss. In the year 2000-01, MSEB reported 31.87 per cent of T&D loss. In its submission for 2001-02 MSEB has estimated that the actual loss was 39.4 per cent.[26]

Although reported energy losses are about 21 per cent throughout India, closer examination of State Electricity Board losses often shows serious under reporting. Table 2.8 shows T&D losses. These however are only notional numbers as they were mostly assumed figures and the missing electricity was ascribed to users whose consumption was not metered, mostly agricultural users. From Table 2.8 it is clear that T&D losses has increased from 15.2 per cent in 1997-98 to more than 35 per cent in 2001.

In many countries in the world the T&D losses ranged only between 20-30 per cent, but in India in several states the T&D losses are nearly 50 per cent. This is evident from Table 2.8. The Transmission and Distribution loss in the country is nearly 22 per cent and the losses in the States vary from as low as 16.1 per cent to as high as 51.7 per cent. Transmission and distribution losses in 2001-02 were 34 per cent of generation of the country as a whole, whereas all India transmission and distribution losses in 1992-93 was 21.8 per cent. This goes to prove that T&D losses increased during the post-liberalization period. Although Economic Survey 2003-04 claims that processes of measurement of T&D losses have improved over time and the earlier estimates are considered to be biased downwards yet the high T&D loss figures clearly indicate the enormous scope for improvements in transmission and distribution.

Table 2.8. Transmission and Distribution Losses

	1992-93	1995-96	1996-97	1997-98	2001-02
Andhra Pradesh	20.65	18.9	30.1	25.0	26.81
Assam	21.41	26.2	24.9	24.0	42.78
Bihar	17.15	25.9	25.9	23.0	51.70
Delhi	24.02	48.0	45.0	43.0	43.97
Gujarat	22.2	18.3	18.2	18.0	26.87
Haryana	26.78	31.4	31.7	32.2	39.22
Himachal Pradesh	19.98	17.5	17.9	17.4	25.55
Jammu and Kashmir	48.13	48.6	48.0	47.5	48.85
Karnataka	19.62	17.5	18.5	18.4	33.83
Kerala	22.77	20.1	20.0	19.0	32.21
Madhya Pradesh	22.52	19.5	19.3	19.0	44.55
Maharashtra	18.21	15.4	15.3	15.2	37.28
Meghalaya	11.62	17.8	19.3	16.8	22.66
Orissa	25.87	46.9	45.1	39.0	47.34
Punjab	19.61	18.2	18.0	18.0	27.70
Rajasthan	22.71	28.5	25.3	23.0	43.06
Tamil Nadu	17.30	17.0	17.0	17.0	16.06
Uttar Pradesh	24.68	22.8	24.6	23.0	37.62
West Bengal	17.53	20.7	20.1	19.7	31.67
All India	21.8				33.98

Note: In per cent.
Source: Planning Commission (1999).

"T&D losses are caused by a variety of problems including energy sold at low voltage, sparsely distributed loads over large rural areas, inadequate investments in the distribution system, improper billing and theft."[27] Indiscriminate grid extension despite low load densities has resulted in inefficiencies. The Tenth Five-Year Plan attributed the following reasons for the high T&D losses:

- Weak and inadequate sub-transmission and distribution systems due to haphazard growth of demand to meet the short-term objective of extension of power supply to new areas.
- Long transmission and distribution lines.
- Inappropriate size of conductors.
- Improper load management, resulting in overloading of systems.
- Pilferage and theft of energy.

- Unmetered supply.
- Financial constraints to undertake system improvement schemes.[28]

Unless a serious dent is made on this large and overwhelming problem, there is no possibility of any appreciable improvement in the financial viability of the SEBs. The performance of the power utilities can be improved in the short-term through reduction in the T&D losses and increasing productivity through renovation and modernization work. Large investments are required to reduce technical deficiencies and improve the quality of power supply to the consumers. The Tenth Five-Year Plan rightly states that "it is necessary that various electricity supply organizations take up system studies and carry out energy audits for identification of the causes of excessive losses"[29] so that we could reduce T&D losses.

2.4.2.1.3. Labour Productivity and Overstaffing

Even though the number of total employees in all the SEBs together has declined from 0.98 million in 1992-93 to 0.91 million in 1997-98, most of the SEBs are still overstaffed. However, the total manpower in the power sector is expected to reach around one million by the end of Tenth Plan. To some extent overstaffing is the outcome of political compulsions. Very often, this degrades staff quality. Some of the SEBs have, however tried to reduce the number of employees. The number has gone down during the period 1991-2002 to 1997-98 in Assam, Bihar, Uttar Pradesh and West Bengal.

Table 2.9. Indicators of Labour Productivity and Labour Cost per Unit Supply (1996-97)

SEBs	Per Employee			Labour Cost (1994)	
	Sales 000 kWh	Consumer (Number)	Revenue 000 Rs	Rs/kWh of Supply	as % of Sales Revenue
Andhra Pradesh	290	135	479	0.15	16.30
Assam	101	38	208	0.66	38.78
Bihar	204	58	417	0.43	27.73
Delhi	294	88	909	N.A	—
Gujarat	556	128	1000	0.16	12.04

Contd...

SEBs	Per Employee			Labour Cost (1994)	
	Sales 000 kWh	Consumer (Number)	Revenue 000 Rs	Rs/kWh of Supply	as % of Sales Revenue
Haryana	167	63	313	0.30	25.93
Himachal Pradesh	93	45	152	0.57	47.60
Jammu and Kashmir	97	37	37	N.A	NA
Karnataka	333	175	476	0.23	21.22
Kerala	286	200	286	0.30	33.02
Maharashtra	380	103	773	0.28	20.39
Meghalaya	123	108	883	0.65	78.49
Madhya Pradesh	250	26	164	0.23	14.18
Orissa	159	40	370	0.37	24.55
Punjab	217	56	333	0.28	24.21
Rajasthan	250	82	417	0.24	17.27
Tamil Nadu	278	123	588	0.28	18.33
Uttar Pradesh	270	72	526	0.26	20.27
West Bengal	233	74	500	0.24	17.18
USA	4057	110			
China	423	242			

Notes: China's average is better than most Indian SEBs, China is also a labour intensive economy where regional electricity boards are run by the State with a high share of coal-based thermal power.

Source: J. Parikh and A. Das (2000).

Labour performance is relatively better in some of the SEBs (Table 2.9) like A.P., Maharashtra, Gujarat, Karnataka and Kerala. Sales per employee vary from 93,000 kWh in Himachal Pradesh to 4,00,000 kWh in Maharashtra. Similar figures in USA and China are respectively 40,57,000 kWh and 4,23,000 kWh on the average for the whole nation. Labour productivity can be increased and labour cost per unit supply can be reduced over the years provided proper training is available to the manpower involved in the power sector because the success of the process of power sector reforms requires human resource development.

2.4.2.1.4. Arrears

Despite more than 50 per cent employees of the over-staffed SEBs being involved in distribution and consumer-related activities, almost all the SEBs have accumulated a large amount of arrears as shown in Table 2.10.

Table 2.10. Arrears of SEBs as on March 1997

SEBs	Revenue Rs. Crores	Arrears Rs. Crores	Arrears or Revenue	No. of Days
Andhra Pradesh	4236	932	22	81
Assam	414	290	70	255
Bihar	1529	2784	182	665
Delhi	2274	887	39	143
Gujarat	5065	1165	23	83
Haryana	1694	610	36	130
Himachal Pradesh	433	69	16	59
Jammu and Kashmir	69	14	20	75
Karnataka	2743	1289	37	172
Kerala	692	305	44	159
Maharashtra	9242	2495	27	99
Meghalaya	71	102	144	525
Madhya Pradesh	4474	1834	41	149
Orissa	1399	742	53	194
Punjab	2861	486	17	61
Rajasthan	3029	757	25	90
Tamil Nadu	5606	280	5	18
Uttar Pradesh	4813	3754	78	283
West Bengal	1899	931	49	178
All SEBs	37	136		

Source: Ministry of Power, Government of India, New Delhi.

The receivables are due not only from agricultural consumers and Government departments but others as well. The seriousness of the problem of arrears worsening in recent years can be gauged from yet another aspect. During 1981-93 the board wrote-off just Rs. 2.77 crores. But in the year 1993-94, the board wrote-off Rs. 99 crores. This went up to a massive amount of Rs. 371 crores in 1996-97, which is high. During the period 1996-97, the total bad debt write-off amounted to Rs. 931 crores. Debt write-off generates an expectation of future write-off and leads to default in payments. SEBs should take some serious steps towards improving revenue collection. There is a negative correlation of arrears with employees.

2.4.2.1.5. SEBs as Agents to Sub-serve the Social and Economic Policies

True to the spirit of a social-democratic State, India had originally evolved her power development policy, and shouldered that responsibility, in line with the State's professed commitment to honouring and ensuring social security equations. Though the State Electricity Boards were statutorily required to function as autonomous service-cum-commercial corporations, they became in effect agents of the Governments to sub-serve the social, political and economic policies of the State. As a result the power sector "became in effect the translatory channel for the populist policies of the political party in power.... In such a contest of composite interests, accumulation of disfunctioning has been a natural outcome in the power sector."[30] And hence it never felt the need to break even or to contribute to capacity expansion programs. This unaccountability culture in turn led to gross inefficiency at all levels – technical, institutional and organizational as well as financial.

2.4.2.1.6. Gap between User Charges and the Cost of Supply

The basic problem being faced by the sector is the gap between user charges and the cost of supply. Despite reform efforts, Table 2.3 reveals that the gap between the cost of supply and average tariff has actually worsened over the years from a level of 23 paise in 1992-93 to about 110 paise in 2001-2002. Revenues dropped from 82.2 per cent of costs in 1992-93 to 68.6 per cent in 2001-2002. This suggests that as of yet, reforms have not yielded the desired results in the functioning of SEBs and this motivates a prime focus upon the functioning of SEBs in power reforms.

2.4.3. Growth of Installed Capacity

The total installed capacity grew at an average annual compound growth rate of 6.65 per cent during the last four decades. It has grown from approx. 1,300 MW in 1947 to 93,253 MW by the end of March 1999 and 1,07,900 MW by the end of March 2003. Despite the significant progress in capacity addition, the demand for electricity continues to outstrip the supply with the result that energy and peak shortages continue to plague the economy. The best performance was witnessed during the Seventh Plan Period (1985-90) when 21,051 MW were added as against the target of 22,245 MW. However, the capacity addition during Eighth Plan was only 16,423 MW against the target of 30,538 MW. The share of hydel capacity in the total installed capacity is only 24 per cent as compared to 46 per cent at the end of 3rd Plan and that of thermal capacity went up to 76.4 per cent from 62.3 per cent. Out of the total installed plant capacity in 1997-98, 63.3 per cent was owned by the States, 30.7 per cent by the Centre, and 6 per cent was in the private sector.

The capacity addition for power generation during the Eighth Five-Year Plan period was 16,742 MW, which was approximately 54.8 per cent of the planned capacity addition for the period. Of the total capacity addition, the share of hydel energy was 14.5 per cent (2,428 MW) and that of thermal and nuclear energy was 85.5 per cent (14,314 MW).[31] An aggregate capacity addition of 3,239 MW was targeted for commissioning during the year 1997-98 against which the actual achievement was 3,283 MW. Of this hydel energy accounted for 233 MW and thermal and nuclear energy 3,050 MW.

The Ninth Plan programme envisaged a capacity addition of 40,245 MW during the period 1997-2002, out of which 11,909 MW will be in the central sector, 10,784 MW in the State Sector and 17,588 MW from private sector. As against this the actual energy generation has been 515.3 Billion Units. This is a compound annual growth rate of about 5.5 per cent during the Ninth Plan period. The capacity addition proposed in the Private Sector, if materializes fully, would be quite significant in the Ninth Plan compared to earlier plans. As against the average capacity addition programme of around 8,000 MW per year, the capacity addition during the first two years of Ninth Plan was only 7,528.3 MW. The Ninth Plan envisaged a capacity addition of 40,245 MW. But the actual capacity addition was 19,015 MW.

Table 2.11 illustrates total installed plant capacity in the form of hydro, thermal, wind and nuclear over the years. In

Table 2.11. Growth of Installed Generation Capacity

(Thousand MW)

Year	Utilities				Non-	Total	Geothermal/Solar
	Hydro	Thermal	Nuclear	Total	Utilities		Wind/Biomass
1980-81	11.8	17.6	0.9	30.3	3.1	33.4	
1981-82	12.2	19.3	0.9	32.4	3.4	35.8	
1982-83	13.1	21.4	0.9	35.4	3.9	39.3	
1983-84	13.9	24.4	1.1	39.4	4.4	43.8	
1984-85	14.5	27.0	1.1	42.6	5.1	47.7	
1985-86	15.5	30.0	1.3	46.8	5.5	52.3	
1986-87	16.2	31.8	1.3	49.3	5.7	55.0	
1987-88	17.3	35.6	1.3	54.2	6.3	60.5	
1988-89	17.8	39.7	1.5	59.0	7.5	65.5	
1989-90	18.3	43.8	1.5	63.6	8.2	71.8	
1990-91	18.8	45.8	1.5	66.1	8.6	74.7	0.02
1991-92	19.2	48.1	1.8	69.1	9.3	78.4	0.03
1992-93	19.6	50.7	2.0	72.3	10.1	82.4	0.03
1993-94	20.4	54.4	2.0	76.8	10.7	87.5	0.04
1994-95	20.8	58.1	2.2	81.1	11.2	92.3	0.05
1995-96	21.0	60.1	2.2	83.3	11.8	95.1	0.12
1996-97	21.7	61.9	2.2	85.8	12.1	97.9	0.55
1997-98	21.9	65.0	2.2	89.1	13.2	102.3	0.82
1998-99	22.4	68.7	2.2	93.3	14.1	107.4	0.93
1999-2000	23.9	71.3	2.7	97.9	14.7	112.6	1.02
2000-01	25.1	73.6	2.9	101.6	15.4	117.0	1.08
2001-02	26.3	75.9	2.7	104.9	16.1	121.0	1.27
2002-03	26.8	78.4	2.7	107.9			1.51

Source: Buddhadeb Ghosh & Prabir De, *India Infrastructure Database 2005*, Vol. II, Bookwell, New Delhi, p. 1098.

1980-81 total installed plant capacity in the power sector was 30.3 thousand MW and it further increased to 66.1 thousand MW in 1990-91. Percentage of change as on 1990-91 over 1980-81 was 118.15 per cent. Total installed capacity further increased to 101.6 thousand MW in 2000-01 and percentage of change as on 2000-01 was 52.95 per cent. It means there has been shortfall in total installed plant capacity in comparison to pre-reforms period.

Shortfall in new generation capacity addition during the Ninth Five-Year Plan is seen mostly in the private sector, because "Proposals for setting up joint-venture mega projects with American, Chinese, and Austrian power generation companies have either been taken up or are being considered. Also, there are eight fast track projects with independent producers under Government of India guarantees, already approved, although only a minor fraction of them have been taken up for actual implementation."[32] The main reasons for the shortfall in capacity addition according to the Tenth Plan are: "inability to get private sector projects off the ground in the absence of adequate arrangements for ensuring payment security, delay in land acquisition and environmental clearances, unresolved issues relating to fuel linkages, contractual problems, resettlement and rehabilitation problems and law and order problems."[33]

2.4.4. Growth of Gross Energy Generation

In the early 1990s, India embarked on full-scale introduction of economic reforms thus creating way for economic growth. The GDP growth, around 4 per cent in the first half of the 1990s and consecutive years the GDP stayed between 5 to 8 per cent. As a result India's primary energy consumption too expanded considerably. "BP Statistics report that India's primary energy consumption grew by 4.7 per cent per year on an average from 183 MTOE in 1990, reaching 276 MTOE in 1999."[34] It is right therefore to examine the growth of energy generation in India.

2.4.4.1. Hydro Power Plants

Hydroelectric power plant utilizes the potential energy of water stored in a dam built across the river. The potential energy of water is used to run water turbine to which the electric generator is coupled. The mechanical energy available at the turbine is converted into electrical energy by means of the generator. The share of hydel capacity in the total generating capacity has declined from 34 per cent at the end of the Sixth Plan to 25 per cent at the end of the Ninth Plan. The share continued to decline even during post-reforms period.

Table 2.12 illustrates the growth of gross energy generation during pre-reforms period and post-reforms period in the energy sector. In 1980-81, the gross energy generated by hydro plants was about 56.5 billion kWh and in 1990-91 the gross energy generated by hydro plants increased to 71.7 billion kWh. Gross energy generated by hydro plants as on 1990-91 over 1980-81 was 26.90 per cent, whereas in 2000-01 the gross energy generated by hydro plants was about 74.5 billion kWh and its percentage of change as on 2000-01 over 1990-91 was 2.34 per cent. It is 24.56 per cent less than the percentage of change in terms of gross energy generated by hydro pants during 1980-81 to 1990-91.

It means that neither the public sector nor the private sector invested in hydro means of production of energy during post-reforms period. The significantly decreasing role of hydroelectric energy may be noted during post-reforms period. Though the raw material cost of hydroelectricity is insignificant and further is not subject to inflationary pressure, yet significant attention is not given to hydroelectric energy because too much dependence would subject energy supply to fluctuations in rainfall and vagaries of nature. It is stated that Geological uncertainty, contract management, resettlement and rehabilitation, delay in land acquisition and infrastructure development have been stated as the main reasons by the Tenth Five-Year Plan in hydro projects. In order to avoid delays in project implementation and to accelerate the pace of hydro developmental projects the Tenth Five-Year Plan suggests the following:

- Bankable detailed project report based on a detailed survey should be prepared to avoid geological uncertainty.
- Contract monitoring, as distinct from project monitoring, should be emphasized.
- Land acquisition and infrastructure development should be settled and completed before the start of the project.
- Detailed ranking study and preparation of detailed feasibility report based on economic viability needs to be done.

- Adopt a national rehabilitation policy and implement the policy uniformly.
- Streamline clearances for pursuing priority projects.
- Simplify approval procedures.
- Facilitate the early financial closure of projects through a concerted approach towards multilateral agencies and other international funding sources.[35]

2.4.4.2. Thermal Power Plants

Thermal power generated by coal and oil has been the major source of electric power in India. Mostly thermal power is derived from coal and only a small fraction comes from oil. The performance of the thermal power plants registered an overall improvement during the Ninth Five-Year Plan. The all-India average Plant Load Factor (PLF) of the thermal power plants was 64.4 per cent at the beginning of the Ninth Plan and had increased to 69.9 per cent by the end of the Plan period. However, the comparative analysis of post-reforms and pre-reforms period reveals a different picture all together. The energy generated through thermal plants in 1980-81 was about 61.3 billion kWh and in 1990-91 gross energy generated through thermal plants increased to 186.5 billion kWh. Gross energy generated through thermal plants as on 1990-91 over 1980-81 was 204.24 per cent. Whereas in 2000-01 the gross energy generated by thermal plants was about 408.1 billion kWh and its percentage of change as on 2000-01 over 1990-91 was 95.54 per cent. It is 108.7 per cent less than the percentage of change in terms of gross energy produced by thermal plants during 1980-81 to 1990-91. It means that neither the public sector nor the private sector invested much in thermal means of energy production during post-reforms period. However, a thermal power station is liable to cause environmental pollution and air pollution. The major areas of concern are surface and groundwater pollution, noise pollution, change of land-use pattern, impact on green cover and on flora and fauna, etc.

Table 2.12. Growth of Gross Energy Generation

Billion kWh

Year	Utilities				Non Utilities	Total
	Hydro	Thermal@	Nuclear	Total		
1980-81	56.5	61.3	3.0	120.8	8.4	129.2
1981-82	49.6	69.5	3.0	122.1	9.0	131.1
1984-85	53.9	98.8	4.1	156.8	12.3	169.1
1985-86	51.0	114.4	5.0	170.4	13.0	183.4
1987-88	47.5	149.6	5.0	202.1	16.9	219.0
1989-90	62.1	178.7	4.6	245.4	23.0	268.4
1990-91	71.7	186.5	6.1	264.3	25.1	289.4
% of Change over 1980-81	**26.90**	**204.24**	**103.33**	**103.15**		
1991-92	72.8	208.7	5.5	287.0	28.6	315.6
1992-93	69.9	224.8	6.7	301.4	31.3	332.7
1995-96	72.6	299.3	8.0	379.9	38.2	418.1
1996-97	68.9	317.9	9.1	395.9	40.8	436.7
1997-98	74.6	337.0	10.1	421.7	44.1	465.8
1999-2000	80.6	386.8	13.3	480.7	51.5	532.2
2000-01	74.5	408.1	16.9	499.5	55.0	554.5
% of Change over 1991-92	**2.34**	**95.54**	**152.23**	**88.99**		
2001-02*	73.9	422.0	19.3	515.2	58.0	573.2
2002-03	64.0	449.3	19.4	532.7		

*: Provisional, @: Includes Wind

Note: Figures may not add up to the total owing to rounding off.

Source: Buddhadeb Ghosh & Prabir De, *India Infrastructure Database 2005*, Vol. II, Bookwell, New Delhi, p. 1099.

2.4.4.3. Nuclear Power Plants

Nuclear energy is considered an important source of electric power. It is considered that it has environmental advantages and is also likely to be economical in the longer run. As a result comparative study between post-reforms and pre-reforms period on nuclear method of energy generation shows quite different picture altogether in comparison to thermal and hydro method of power generation. Nuclear plants were preferred over other means of energy production during post-reforms period because an expanded programme of energy generation through nuclear method would make it possible to reduce the costs of construction and power generation. Tenth Five-Year Plan therefore states that "aggressive nuclear power development is essential in the context of energy security, environmental advantages and changing perceptions about nuclear power in developed countries...improvements in nuclear technology are likely to make nuclear power more economical and total life cycle costs more competitive in comparison to other fuels."[36]

Energy generated through nuclear plants in 1980-81 was about 3 billion kWh and in 1990-91 it increased to 6.1 billion kWh. Gross energy generated through nuclear plants as on 1990-91 over 1980-81 was 103.33 per cent. In 2000-01 gross energy generated by nuclear plants was about 16.9 billion kWh and its percentage of change as on 2000-01 over 1990-91 was 152.23 per cent. It is 48.9 per cent higher than the percentage of change in terms of gross energy produced by nuclear plants during 1980-81 to 1990-91.

2.4.4.4. Gross Power Generation by All Plants

In 1980-81, the gross energy generated was about 120.8 billion kWh and in 1990-91 the gross energy generated increased to 264.3 billion kWh. The growth of gross energy generated as on 1990-91 over 1980-81 was 103.15 per cent, whereas in 2000-01 the gross energy generated was about 499.5 billion kWh and its percentage of change as on 2000-01 over 1990-91 was 88.99 per cent. It is just 14.16 per cent less than the percentage of change in terms of gross energy generated during 1980-81 to 1990-91. It means that the open invitation rendered to private sector participation in the energy sector did not lead to increase in gross energy generated in the country. The policy of inducting private investment into the power sector was expected to result in the addition of 17,588 MW of power capacity during the Ninth Plan. But the actual addition was 5,061 MW, which is a mere 29 per cent of the target. The main impediments in private sector investment in power sector according to the Tenth Five-Year Plan have been:

- The chronic financial weakness of SEBs.
- Unviable tariffs to IPPs, due to factors such as high cost of liquid fuels, risk factors and slow growth in demand.
- The absence of an enabling regulatory, legislative and market environment.
- The slow pace of reform in the power sector and related sectors such as coal and transport.
- The inability to deliver bankable contractual frameworks.
- The lack of recognition of the fact that the distribution segment would need to be made efficient and bankable before private investment and competition emerges in generation.[37]

According to energylineindia.com the country's total generation capacity stood at 1,24,172 MW as on 17th March 2006. Of this, the thermal and hydro segments accounted for 82,369 MW and 32,335 MW capacities respectively. The renewable energy source-based generation capacity was pegged at 6,158 MW while the rest was nuclear generation capacity. In the thermal segment, coal-fired capacity was put at 68,433 MW.[38] Gas-based capacity accounted for 12,734 MW while the rest was based on costly liquid fuels.

2.4.4.5. Performance of Renewable and Non-Conventional Energy Sources

India's search for alternative fuels that would ensure sustainable development on the one hand and energy security on the other hand forced the search for new and renewable sources of energy as an option. Therefore, the Government of India has initiated a programme for the development of non-conventional energy technologies. For this a Commission for Additional Sources of Energy (CASE) was set up in 1981 and in 1983 the Department of Non-Conventional Energy Sources (DNES) was formed. Now this has been upgraded to the Ministry of Non-Conventional Energy Sources. As a result several specialized centres have been set up and a number of research projects have been taken up to strengthen the generation of non-conventional energy sources. Emphasis to bring about great market orientation by involving non-Government organizations and private entrepreneurs is also being given.

Table 2.13. NRSE Potential and Achievement

	Potential	Achievement As on 31-12-2004
Biogas Plants	120 lakh	32.75 lakh
Improved Chulhas	1200 lakh	338 lakh
Wind	45,000 MW	1507 MW
Small Hydro	15,000 MW	1423 MW
Biomass Power/Co-generation	19,500 MW	358 MW
Biomass Gasifiers		42.8 MW
Solar PV	20 MW/sq km	82 MW
Waste-to-Energy	1,700 MW	17.1 MW
Solar Water Heating	1,400 lakh sq.m. Collector Area	6 lakh sq.m. Collector Area

Source: Annual Report, 2004-05, Ministry of Non-Conventional Energy Sources.

As a result the Ministry of Non-Conventional Energy Sources is also "involved in the development, demonstration and utilization of various renewable energy based technologies, such as, solar thermal; solar photovoltaics; wind power generation and water pumping; biomass combustion/co-generation; small, mini, and micro hydro power; solar power; utilization of biomass-gasifiers, briquetting, biogas, improved chulha (cook-stove); geothermal for heat applications and power generation; energy recovery from urban, municipal and industrial wastes; and tidal power generation."[39]

Over and above this, it also deals with other emerging areas and new technologies, such as, chemical sources of energy, fuel cells, alternative fuel for surface transportation and hydrogen energy, etc. The Ministry also succeeded in creating awareness about the benefits of renewable energy through sustained public awareness generation campaigns, using different media and through demonstrations at exhibitions and fairs across the country. Renewable energy presently contributes about 5,700 MW, which represents about 4.99 per cent of the total installed power generating capacity from all sources. Wind power contributes about 2,980 MW, while biomass power and cogeneration account for 727 MW and the share of small hydro power is 1,693 MW.

2.4.4.5.1. Solar Power

Solar photovoltaic system is a technology that enables conversion of solar energy directly into electricity. But the system will work successfully in areas where sufficient sunny days are available ranging from 150 to 250 days. Most parts of India get 300 days of sunshine a year, which makes it a very promising place for solar energy utilization. So far, photovoltaic (PV) generation has been limited to very small installations. But today "solar photovoltaic (SPV) routes, find several applications like cooking, water heating, drying farm produce, water pumping, home and street lighting, power generation for meeting decentralized requirements in villages, schools, hospitals, etc. Solar water heating systems are becoming increasingly popular among hotels, hostels, hospitals, and other large institutions. Water heating systems with a total collector area of 1,000,000 sq.m. have so far been installed in the country."[40]

During the year 2004-05, about 25,000 box solar cookers and dish type solar cookers were sold resulting in a total of 5.80 lakh cookers being sold in the country. A number of industries have started using solar air heaters to produce hot air at low temperature ranges as process heat for drying. Its use has helped to substitute and supplement conventional heating systems and resulting in lower fuel consumption.

There are more than 7,50,000 of them, generating a total of about 58 MW. Most of these are stand-alone installations, for applications such as pumping water for irrigation, but there are 17 grid-interactive PV installations that supply a total of about 1.4 MW to the electricity grid during daylight hours. Throughout the country the cumulative capacity of SPV modules produced till December 31, 2004 reached 191 MWp of which around 105 MWp capacity products has been exported. A total of more than 12.02 lakh systems with an aggregate capacity of over 86 MWp has been deployed in the country. SPV technology is also being used for water pumping for agriculture and related uses. Number of SPV water-pumping systems has increased to

6780 of which 366 SPV water-pumping systems were installed during 2004-05.

The 140 MW Integrated Solar Combined Cycle Power Project at Mathania in Rajasthan has been in the advanced planning stage after obtaining approval from the Government. This would be the first commercial project of its kind in the world. "The solar photovoltaic power programme aims at providing voltage support in the remote sections of weak grids, on public buildings in urban centres for peak load shedding and as diesel savers on islands. 34 grid-interactive SPV power projects with an installed capacity of 2.80 MWp have been installed. Six projects with an aggregate capacity of 400 KWp are under installation."[41]

2.4.4.5.2. Wind Power

India has abundant wind resources to harness for power generation. Strong seasonal winds blow across the Indian subcontinent April through September. The gross potential of the wind power sector has been assessed as 45,000 MW and has identified more than 200 sites suitable for wind power facilities. The technical potential, at 20 per cent grid penetration, is estimated at 13,400 MW. India has the fifth largest wind power capacity in the world, largely created on account of an enabling and conducive policy framework for commercial wind power projects. The southern coastline has relatively higher wind speeds than the rest of the country as a result Southern India has been identified as excellent wind resources, with the states of Gujarat, Andhra Pradesh, Tamil Nadu, Karnataka, Kerala, Madhya Pradesh, Maharashtra, and Rajasthan having the highest potential.

Wind power farms in India are made up of numerous small units, each generating, in effect, only an incremental amount of electricity. The lone exception is Suzlon Energy Ltd.'s Vankusawade Wind Park, located on a high mountain plain above the Koyna reservoir in Maharashtra State, which uses 350 kilowatt wind generators. The Vankhusawade Wind Park is presently the world's largest wind power facility. However, the problem with our wind mill is that we follow the designs developed in Denmark. But when we consider wind power as a viable alternative to fuel-based power it is important to take following issues into consideration:

- The wind regime in India is quite different from that in the Western countries.
- Wind speed increases substantially, arrangement for its capture is to make at higher and higher heights.
- It is feasible to design wind power engine adopted to function more effectively and efficiently under India's wind regimes.[42]

If these three factors are given due consideration in designing and planning wind power installations, Bani P. Banerjee feels that the ultimate wind power potential in India would be considerably higher than that envisaged today. It is interesting to note that the participation of the private sector in this area is highly encouraging.

2.4.4.5.3. Geothermal Power

There are seven main geothermal regions in India, which contain a total of about 400 thermal springs. The major geothermal area is the Son-Narmada-Tati (SONATA) rift zone, which follows the Narmada river valley from Gujarat into Madhya Pradesh, and then continues into Eastern India. An additional place of interest is Barren Island in the Andaman Islands, which has the only active volcano on the Indian subcontinent. Geothermal energy in India is presently mostly being used for direct heating applications such as heating of bathing pools and drying of agricultural produce. For power generating purposes, the overall geothermal potential of India is about 10,000 MWe. The Geological Survey of India (GSI) has developed an atlas identifying more than 300 potential sites for generating power.

2.4.4.5.4. Biomass

Biomass-based power plants are considered to be for decentralized applications in rural areas where it is either costly to extend the grid or the demand intensity is low because bio resources, such as firewood, agro-residues and animal wastes are the important component of the energy. It is said that it offers a vast potential if it is well-organized. The resource base for all biomass units is agro processing industries such as cigarette factories, cashew processing units, ayurvedic medicine units, etc., which produce large quantities of biomass waste. The potential for power production from captive and field-based biomass resources, using technologies for distributed power generation, is currently assessed at 19,500 MW including 3,500 of exportable surplus power from bagasse-based cogeneration in sugar mills.

Against this potential, the total installed capacity of commissioned projects is 727 MW. Projects of 600 MW capacities are under various stages of implementation. A number of biomass gasification technologies, developed indigenously, find use in the commissioned projects. "During the year up to December 31, 2004, 16 biomass gasifier systems for different end-use applications aggregating to around 4.00 MWe were commissioned while 20 projects had been initiated during the year. A total of 1844 biomass gasifier systems aggregating 62 MW (equivalent) have been commissioned so far in 22 States and the UTs."[43] However, there is scope for further expanding the size of these programmes and they can directly benefit the majority of the rural population and help them to meet their basic daily need for energy.

2.4.4.5.5. Concluding Remarks

The Tenth Five-Year Plan has proposed to "electrify 5000 villages through decentralized energy sources, 4000 of them by solar and the remaining villages by biomass and small hydro plants and to install 10 lakh solar lantern SPV lighting systems, 5 MW of SPV power plants, 8000 SPV pumps and 10000 SPV generators. In addition, solar water systems, etc., are also proposed."[44] However, the current utilization of renewable energy sources is much below their potential. This is evident from Table 2.13 where actual potency of renewable energy in India is much higher but the actual achievement in this area is much below estimated potential of renewable energy sources. In spite of the recognized need for emphasizing the role of renewable energy devices in the total energy scenario, the penetration has been poor and much below the desirable level. This is mainly due to the dispersed nature of these sources, development stage of some of these sources and high initial cost of renewable energy sources. For this the Ninth Five-Year Plan has suggested the major areas of focus for the future and they are:

- Change the structure of the existing programmes from subsidy-driven to gradual commercialization of non-conventional energy sources.
- Gradual phasing out of subsidies in the socially oriented programmes like Bio-gas, improved Chulhas, Biomass and Solar Photo Voltaics programmes.
- Strengthening of research, development and commercialization of non-conventional energy sources.[45]

For this, it is also essential to integrate the objectives of natural resources with the overall development process[46], as it is articulated in Agenda 21 of the United Nation's Conference on Environment and Development.

2.4.5. Financial Investment in the Power Sector

With the focus of private sector investment in the power sector it appears that many State Governments have started giving low priority to the power sector in terms of investment. Investment has come down from 27.2 per cent in 1992-93 to 8.5 per cent in 1998-99. Many States are giving as low priority as 6-15 per cent. This is a short-sighted strategy.

There is a strong case for increasing the investment in the power sector, and within that for transmission and distribution. The financial position of most of the State Governments/State Electricity Boards (SEBs) are in a bad shape and as such they are not in a position to invest in the creation of new capacity, improvement in the T&D system and the required R&M works for improving the financial health of the SEBs.

Table 2.14. Investments in Electricity

Rs. billion at Current Prices

Year	Gross Domestic Investment	Infrastructure	Electricity, Gas, Water Supply	Public Sector Electricity, Gas, Water Supply	Private Sector Electricity, Gas, Water Supply
1980-81	308.8	60.8	31.7	29.5	2.2
1981-82	342.1	80.1	42.1	37.3	4.8
1982-83	363.4	91.9	48.3	44.4	3.8
1983-84	418.1	95.7	50.6	47.6	3.0
1984-85	454.7	112.6	55.5	52.8	2.7
1985-86	581.7	136.5	72.4	69.1	3.3
1986-87	611.6	176.2	96.3	90.9	5.5
1987-88	764.6	184.4	103.8	98.8	5.0
1988-89	969.7	219.4	113.0	105.6	7.3
1989-90	1138.2	251.7	123.4	117.6	5.9
1990-91	1448.5	287.4	144.1	137.7	6.4
1991-92	1449.8	350.5	189.0	174.1	14.8
1992-93	1631.8	387.3	189.8	154.5	35.3
1993-94	1733.3	452.2	213.8	204.4	9.4
1994-95	2381.1	494.1	233.0	222.7	10.3

Source: Infrastructure Developmental Report 1997.

Based on the 15th Electric Power Survey, The Central Electricity Authority (CEA) has prepared a National Power Plan in 1996-97 covering the 15 year period up to the end of the Eleventh Five-Year Plan. In the Plan, projects, totaling to 52,820 MW have been identified as the need-based requirement in the Ninth Plan. The capacity addition needed during the Tenth Plan could be 45,370 MW and the capacity addition needed during the Eleventh Plan would be 55,593 MW.[47] Based on the capacity addition requirements, funds requirement for the generation component of the National Power Plan have been assessed are Rs. 1,60,00,000 millions and in terms of US dollars it is 143 billion dollars. The requirement of funds for the transmission and distribution component would be about 60 per cent of the funds requirement for generation. For T&D components, Rs. 40,00,000 million would be required. So a total amount approximately required is Rs. 20,000,000 million for the power sector in India.

2.4.6. Consumption Pattern of Electricity

Consumption of power by industries in the total utilization of power has come down from 58.4 per cent in 1980-81 to 42.2 per cent in 1990-91. It further declined to 34 per cent in 2000-01. This does not imply that industrialization is coming down nor does it imply that industrial units are shifting to other sources of fuel. Large industries are setting up their own captive power plants, instead of depending upon the inadequate and often undependable public utilities.

However, consumption of power by agricultural sector in the total utilization of power has increased considerably over the years from 17.6 per cent in 1980-81 to 26.4 per cent in 1990-91. It further increased to 26.8 per cent in 2000-01. Increase in energized pump sets over the years and the promise made by most of the State Governments to provide free electricity for the farmers are considered to be the main reason for growth in the consumption of power by agricultural sector.

Table 2.15. Pattern of Electricity Consumption

(Per cent)

Year	Domestic	Commercial	Industry	Traction	Agriculture	Others
1980-81	11.2	5.7	58.4	2.7	17.6	4.4
1981-82	11.6	5.8	58.8	2.8	16.8	4.2
1982-83	12.7	6.1	55.4	2.8	18.6	4.4
1983-84	12.9	6.4	55.8	2.6	17.8	4.5
1984-85	13.6	6.1	55.2	2.5	18.4	4.2
1985-86	14.0	5.9	54.5	2.5	19.1	4.0
1986-87	14.2	5.7	51.7	2.4	21.7	4.3
1987-88	15.2	6.1	47.5	2.5	24.2	4.5
1988-89	15.5	6.2	47.1	2.3	24.3	4.6
1989-90	16.9	5.4	46.0	2.3	25.1	4.3
1990-91	16.0	5.9	44.2	2.2	26.4	4.5
1991-92	17.3	5.8	42.0	2.2	28.2	4.5
1992-93	18.0	5.7	40.9	2.3	28.7	4.4
1993-94	18.2	5.9	39.6	2.3	29.7	4.3
1994-95	18.5	6.1	38.6	2.3	30.5	4.0
1995-96	18.7	6.1	37.8	2.3	30.9	4.2

1996-97	19.7	6.2	37.2	2.4	30.0	4.5
1997-98	20.3	6.5	35.4	2.3	30.8	4.7
1998-99	21.0	6.4	33.9	2.4	31.4	4.9
1999-2000	22.2	6.3	34.8	2.6	29.2	4.9
2000-01	23.9	7.1	34.0	2.6	26.8	5.6

Note: Figures may not add up to 100 per cent owing to rounding off.
Source: Buddhadeb Ghosh & Prabir De, *India Infrastructure Database 2005*, Vol. II, Bookwell, New Delhi, pp.1087, 1088 & 1089.

The same trend too is seen in the domestic sector too. Consumption of power by domestic sector in the total utilization of power has increased from 11.2 per cent in 1980-81 to 16.0 per cent in 1990-91. It further increased to 23.9 per cent in 2000-01. Growth in electronic goods and availability of various electronic goods for a quality living is considered to be the main reason for growth in consumption of power by domestic sector. But the growth seen in the consumption of power by commercial sector was very marginal. Consumption of power by commercial sector was 5.7 per cent in the total utilization of power in 1980-81 and it increased to 5.9 per cent in 1990-91 and 7.1 per cent in 2000-01.

The per capita consumption of electricity is considered to be one of the important and a fair indicator to measure the economic growth of country. Table 2.16 shows the data relating to the growth in per capita electricity consumption of India from 1970-71 to 2000-01 and per capita electricity consumption of developed countries and developing counties in 1992. The per capita consumption of electric power in India in 1980-81 was 132.34 kWh and it rose to 269.98 kWh in 1991-92 thus recording a growth rate of 7.46 per annum.[48]

In 1992-93 and 1994-95, the per capita consumption of electric power in India was 281.48 kWh and 318.84 kWh respectively. It rose to 374 kWh in 2000-01. It is not only quite low but also increasing at a slow rate.

Table 2.16. Growth in Per Capita Electricity Consumption

(kWh)

India		Developed Countries (1992)		Developing Countries (1992)	
Year	Consumption	Country	Consumption	Country	Consumption
1970-71	090.00	UK	5660	Pakistan	435
1980-81	132.34	USA	12990	China	647
1990-91	252.77	Canada	18309	Thailand	1000
1991-92	269.98	France	8089	Mexico	1381
1992-93	281.48	Germany	6693	Singapore	6353
1994-95	318.84	Japan	7211	Brazil	1570
2000-01	374.00			India	374

Source: Bani P. Banerjee, *Handbook of Energy and the Environment in India*, Oxford University Press, 2005, pp. 180 & 181.

India's per capita consumption of electricity in comparison to developed and developing countries is one of the lowest. The per capita electricity consumption in India was only 374 kWh units in 1992. Whereas during the same year USA's per capita energy consumption was 12990 kWh, Canada's per capita consumption of energy was 18309 kWh and France's per capita energy consumption was 8089 kWh. India's per capita energy consumption is also low in comparison to developing countries. In 1992, Singapore's per capita energy consumption was 6353 kWh, Mexico's per capita energy consumption was 1381 kWh and Brazil's per capita energy consumption was 1570 kWh. India's per capita energy consumption was even lower than Pakistan's per capita energy consumption because Pakistan's per capita's consumption was 435 kWh, which is higher than India's.

2.4.7. Rural Electrification

Rural electrification is an important component in rural development, because the availability of power in rural areas will lead to economic development. As a result Indian Government has been making plans and allocating finance for village electrification since beginning of the planning process. Around 86 per cent of the villages have been electrified up the year 2005.

Table 2.17. Progress in Rural Electrification

Year	Villages Electrified in 2000s	Villages Electrifie as % of Total Villages	Pump Sets Energized 2000s
1980-81	272.4	47.3	4330.5
1985-86	390.3	67.7	6152.0
1990-91	481.1	83.1	8909.1
1991-92	487.2	84.1	9391.1
1992-93	490.8	84.8	9851.2
1993-94	494.2	85.3	10276.6
1994-95	497.7	86.3	10619.5
1995-96	501.8	86.7	11104.1
1996-97	498.8	84.9	11565.3
1997-98	502.0		11849.4
1998-99	504.7		12215.1
1999-2000	506.9		12514.2*
2000-01	508.1		
2001-02	512.2@		
2002-03	492.3@		
1-1-2005	497.1	84.7	14290.6

Notes: * Also comprises the latest data as per the Tenth Plan Document.
@ Also comprises the data given in *India Infrastructure Database 2005*, Vol. II, p. 1069.

Source: Bani P. Banerjee, *Handbook of Energy and the Environment in India*, Oxford University Press, 2005, p. 181.

However, Table 2.17 reveals that there has been a deceleration in the rural electrification programme during the Eighth Five-Year Plan and the Ninth Five-Year Plan compared to the Sixth Five-Year Plan and Seventh Five-Year Plans. As a result about 70 per cent of the rural households are yet to get electric connections.

About 80,000 villages remain to be electrified, of these, 18,000 villages are in remote and difficult areas where grid supply may not be feasible. Non-conventional energy sources have to play a critical role in electrifying these villages and meeting their energy needs. The Tenth Five-Year Plan therefore rightly holds that "the actual benefits of the investments made in the rural electrification programme can only be realized if the people are in a position to use electricity for their day-to-day activities as well as for industrial and commercial activity. Therefore ... rural electrification programme ... must also ensure more widespread use of electricity by the rural people in a time-bound manner."[49] For this involvement of the community NGOs and Panchayati Raj Institutions has been envisaged and Rajiv Gandhi Grameen Vidyutikaran Yojna (RGGVY) programme has been incited to achieve this objective. At present, only 44 per cent of the rural households have access to electricity. The services of Central Public Sector Undertakings (CPSUs) have been offered to the States for assisting them in the execution of rural electrification projects as per their willingness and requirement.

2.4.7.1. Progress of implementation of RGGVY

As per Economic Survey 2005-2006, the following programmes had been undertaken and implemented under Rajiv Gandhi Grameen Vidyutikaran Yojna:

- So far 187 projects for 191 districts have been sanctioned covering 22 States at the cost of Rs. 6,241.86 crore covering 51,284 un-electrified villages and 69.29 lakh rural households, of which 45.15 lakh are BPL households.
- Notice Inviting Tenders (NITs) have been issued for projects covering 163 districts.
- Contracts had been placed for projects covering 95 districts covering 41,461 un-electrified villages and 9,379 electrified villages.
- CPSUs are working in 131 districts.
- 1,941 villages had been electrified till December, 2005.[50]

Since around 18,000 villages are located in remote and difficult areas the Tenth Plan has proposed to electrify 5,000 villages through decentralized energy sources.[51]

2.5. PRIVATE SECTOR PARTICIPATION

In 1993, The World Bank made reform an explicit condition of continued lending for electricity and the strategy called on borrower countries was to encourage private investment in the power sector.[52] Therefore, there emerged in the electricity sector "changes in management practices, which may or may not involve changes in ownership from Government to the private sector and restructuring for competition, which is a process of separating or 'unbundling' vertically integrated utilities to progressively introduce competition into the system."[53] Thus at the beginning of the Eight Plan it was realized that Government could no longer finance the incremental capacity requirement of the country. In order to supplement the efforts of the Government and bridge the gap between the demand for and availability of power, a policy to encourage private sector participation was initiated in 1991. The objective was to mobilize additional resources for power generation, transmission and distribution and to introduce competition in the sector to improve the financial health of SEBs thereby enable them to function as commercial entities.

Table 2.18. Private Sector Participation in Power Generation

(MW)

Year	Central Govt.	State Govt. Department	State Electricity Boards	Private Sector	Total
1980-81	2198	1481	23456	1382	30214
1985-86	5781	3111	33614	2165	46769
1990-91	14740	5294	40727	2742	66086
1991-92	16498	4924	42145	2916	69065
1992-93	18763	5301	42569	2904	72330
1995-96	23772	6449	46092	3876	83294
1999-2000	27570	16702	41792	8950	97884
31-1-2005	37935	65314 @		12294	115544

Note: @ All State Government generation of power taken into consideration.

Source: Centre for Monitoring Indian Economy, May 2003, p. 100. While information related to 31-1-2005 are taken from Ministry of Power, Government of India Website.

The reforms initiated in June 1991 were accompanied by a reduced emphasis on the public sector. Thus public sector reforms and privatization were parts of the reform strategy. A lowering of public sector investment was also called for by the need to reduce fiscal deficit. The Government had recognized the problem caused by reduced investment in infrastructure. It had hoped, however that private investment would come forth to take the place of public investment. Thus shortly after the initiation of the reforms process in June 1991, the Government of India opened up the power sector to foreign-private plants in October 1991. The private generators were required to sell only to the SEBs. When one's only customer is financially sick, one would definitely think twice before getting into the business. The experience so far made private producers to think even more before they could plan to invest in the power sector.

However, Table 2.18 indicates that over the year's private sector participation in power generation has increased. In 1980-81 only 1,382 MW electricity was generated by the private sector and it increased to 2,742 MW in 1990-91 and the percentage of change as on 1990-91 over 1980-81 was 98.41 per cent and the average growth achieved during this period by private sector was 9.84 per cent. Private sector participation in power generation further increased to 8950 MW in 1999-2000 and the percentage of change as on 1999-2000 over 1990-91 was 209.93 per cent and the average growth achieved during this period by the private sector was 26.24 per cent. It is clear that the average growth experienced by the private sector in power generation during post-reforms period was greater than the average growth seen by the private sector in power generation during pre-reforms period.

Table 2.19. Additions to Installed Capacity during Five-Year Plans

Type	Target				Achievement (MW)			
	Central Sector	State Sector	Private Sector	Total	Central Sector	State Sector	Private Sector	Total
8th Plan								
Hydro	3260	5860	132	9282	146	794.7	168	2428
Steam	5890	7050	2340	15280	4310	5098	500	9908
Gas	2608	1960	306	4876	1942	942.5	762	3647
Nuclear	1100	—	—	1100	440	—	—	440
Total	12858	14870	2810	30538	8157	6835	1430	16423
9th Plan								
Hydro	3455	5815	550	9820	540	3912	86	4538
Thermal	7574	4933	17038	29545	3084	5538	4975	13597

Nuclear	880	—	—	880	880	—	—	880
Total	11909	10748	17588	40245	4504	9450	5061	19015
Grand Total	**24767**	**25618**	**20398**	**70783**	**12661**	**16285**	**6491**	**35438**

Source: The Ninth and the Tenth Five-Year Plan, Planning Commission.

The higher performance in terms of power generation by private sector during post-reforms period cannot be considered a positive growth because the achievement by the private sector participation in power generation is much lower than the target set for the private sector in terms of creation of additional installed capacity for the private sector during Eighth and Ninth Five-Year Plans. The capacity addition target set for the private sector during the Eighth Five-Year Plan was 2,810 MW of which only 1,430 MW was achieved by the private sector during the Eighth Five-Year Plan and the private sector percentage slippage was 49.4 per cent during the Eighth Five-Year Plan. However, during the Ninth Five-Year Plan target set for the capacity addition in power generation for the private sector was 17,588 MW. But only 5,061 MW of the target was achieved during the Ninth Five-Year plan by the private sector and the private sector shortfall during this period was 71.2 per cent and the actual achievement ratio for the private sector was a mere 28.8 per cent. This goes to prove that during the post-reform period the private sector was not passionate to invest capital in the power sector.

Lack of enthusiasm on the part of the independent power producers (IPPs) is attributed mainly to want of credibility and lack of progress in the power sector reforms by majority of the States. The financial health of the SEBs has been deteriorating over the years. The commercial losses of SEBs have risen from Rs. 1,235 crores in 1984-85 to Rs. 24,920 crores in 1999-2000. The Tenth Five-Year Plan has identified the following as the main impediments for lukewarm attitude of the private sector towards the power sector:

- The chronic financial weakness of SEBs.

- Unviable tariffs to Independent Power Projects (IPPs), due to factors such as high cost of liquid fuels, risk factors involved and slow growth in demand for future power below the expected levels, etc.
- The absence of an enabling regulatory, legislative and market environment.
- The inability to deliver bankable contractual frameworks.
- The lack of recognition of the fact that the distribution segment would need to be made efficient and bankable before private investment and competition emerges in generation.[54]

Private investors will not come forward unless there is a credible move towards restoring the creditworthiness of the power sector. Imposition of economic user charges holds the key to the overall reform process. In fact, unless the financial sickness of the SEBs is taken care of, private-power generators are unlikely to come in. It was realized that adequate private investment will not flow and not many generation plants could come up unless the important issue of commercial viability of SEBs is addressed properly and certain promises made towards the private sector should be maintained, otherwise private sector may not believe in the commitment of the Government towards reforms in the power sector. Speaking on the failure of Ennore Power Project McCormick said, "We were promised by the Central Government, by the ministries and leaders that we would get Central credit support—equivalent to the counter-guarantee—because the state electricity board could not provide the credits for it. But the various authorities have not delivered on their promises in India ... Unless we can get the various Indian authorities to live up to their commitments ... unless that can happen, the project will not go forward."[55]

These problems should be addressed and sorted out with the initiation of another power sector reform. Besides the Malana Power Project which is operational from 2002 has exploded the myth that hydel projects are highly capital-intensive and have a long gestation period. What is thus required is that the State Governments and the Central Government should "involve the private sector in small projects of up to 15MW as these would not displace people and would not affect the environment."[56]

2.6. RECENT INITIATIVES IN ENERGY SECTOR

From the year 1991-92 onwards there has been some effort on the part of the Government to address some of the problems plaguing the sector. It was mainly driven by the recognition that energy shortages were threatening the economic growth potential of the country. The reforms initiated in June 1991 were accompanied by a reduced emphasis on the public sector. Thus public sector reforms and privatization were part of the reform strategy. Given the state of public finances, the Government came to the conclusion that participation by the private sector was essential to address the energy bottleneck. The Government had also recognized the problem caused by reduced investment in infrastructure. It had hoped, however that private investment would come forth to take the place of public investment. Shortly after the initiation of the reforms process in June 1991, the Government of India opened up the power sector to foreign-private plants in October 1991.

In order to attract the private sector to help in building the energy infrastructure, several reforms measures were identified for implementation. Enactment of the new Electricity Act, 2003 on June 10th 2003 was one major step in this direction. This Act represents a new regulatory paradigm for the power sector in India and holds promise of transforming the economics of this sector. It provides a "liberal framework conducive to development of the sector in an open, non-discriminatory, competitive, market driven environment, keeping in view the interest of the consumers as well as those of the suppliers."[57] One of the key reforms introduced is related to a distancing of regulatory functions from those of policy-making by the Government. As a result, "independent regulatory commissions have been established at central level and in several States of India. Other States are being encouraged to establish such institutions. The primary functions of the electricity regulators have defined as rationalizing tariff and encouraging competition."[58]

It also recognized many activities that were included under generation of electricity. It therefore defined captive generation, co-generation, electricity trader and trading. This Act also gave freedom to 'construct, maintain and operate' captive generation plants and dedicated transmission lines. This Bill also provided for open access from captive generation plants to the destinations of their use subject to availability of adequate transmission facility as determined or applicable by the Central or State transmission utilities. The Bill imposes penalties for failure in meeting standards of quality laid down by the commission after due hearing. For greater financial independence Electricity Bill, 2001 provides for the commission to retain all fees and also to receive grants and funds from Government as well as other agencies.[59] This would give greater financial independence and functional autonomy to the functioning of the commissions.

2.6.1. The Electricity Act, 2003

The power sector development has turned out to be one of the most problematic areas of the Indian Economy. The annual losses of State Electricity Boards have been estimated at Rs. 24,000 crore at the end of 2001-02, and the outstanding dues to the connected central public sector undertakings projected at Rs. 35,000 crore, uneconomic power tariffs for agriculture and household consumers with cross-subsidization by the industry and commercial users, transmission and distribution losses officially estimated as much as 24 per cent for the economy as a whole. In some cases transmission and distribution losses have actually been found to be as much as 45-50 per cent charges. Due to operational inefficiencies SEBs are actually able to collect only 80 per cent of the billed electricity. These are the endemic and stark realities of the power sector in India. The Kanungo Committee has rightly concluded that, "The State's power sector is now on the brink of a crisis. It is high time all agencies, namely, the State Government, the Central Government, the World Bank and the aid agency of the United Kingdom got together and took a holistic view on what can be done by each to rescue the reform."

The Tenth Plan Draft Approach Paper proposes that: "as States embark on power sector reforms it will be necessary to deal with the problems of the very large outstanding dues of SEBs and also the medium-term restructuring of the SEBs to bring about viability in operations over a 3 to 4 year period. Substantial financial resources will be needed to help States make the transition."[60] In these critical circumstances, the Government after understanding the seriousness of the situation, drafted 'The Draft: Electricity Bill 2001', and presented in Lok Sabha on August 30, 2001. It is therefore the right time to take a close look at the Bill and examine the extent to which it is going to render useful service to our country. Stating its purpose, objective and reasons the Bill states that it has become "necessary to enact a new legislation for regulating the electric supply industry in the country.... There is also need to provide for newer concepts like power trading and open access. There is also need to obviate the requirement of each State Government to pass its own reforms Act. The Bill has progressive features and endeavours to strike the right balance given the current realities of the power sector in India." The Bill is therefore to be examined with reference to these claimed objectives.

2.6.1.1. The Salient Features of the Bill

The salient features of the Bill are given below:

- Generation of power will be free from licensing, that is, the need to apply and acquire a licence for generating electricity will no more be necessary as long as generation technology would conform to the minimum technical standards laid down by the CEA (Central Electricity Authority).
- Any industry can set up captive generation anywhere and will have the right to transmit electricity to its plant through transmission lines of others.
- Any person can construct or maintain captive generating plants and dedicated transmission lines.

- According to this Bill a captive generating plant will have the right of open access for carrying the electricity to his factory.
- A generating company may supply electricity to any licensee. Due to this the generator need not any more supply only to a single buyer, the SEB.
- Transmission utilities will be solely for wheeling of electricity from generating stations to load centres. It will not trade in electricity.
- Distribution agencies will have their tariff regulated. However, when the supply from the captive plant is through the grid, the concerned commission will regulate the tariff.
- No licence is required for generation and distribution of electricity to a rural area.
- The activities of transmission, distribution and trading require to be licensed by the concerned State Commission.
- To promote the development of a market in power, the Bill enables the appropriate commission with the approval of the Government.
- Creation of a National Load Dispatch Centre that will be responsible for the optimum scheduling and dispatch of electricity among the regional load dispatch centres.
- In order to protect the consumer interest, the Bill requires the licensee to establish a forum for redressal of consumer grievances.
- It will be the duty of the commission to issue draft tariff orders, inviting objections and suggestions and issuing the final order within a specified period.
- The Bill also requires that reimbursement of subsidy amounts by the State Government should be made within 90 days. If the payment is not forthcoming, the subsidy will not be given to the customers.
- The CEA will basically advise Government on national power policy, formulate plans for the development of

the electricity system, specify construction standards, specify safety requirements at all stages, specify grid standards for the operation and maintenance of the transmission lines, etc.

- The functions of the CERC have been expanded to include regulating of the trading margin of electricity traders in interstate transactions, issuing licences to transmission licensees and electricity traders, framing guidelines in matters relating to tariffs for generation and high-voltage transmission, specifying the Grid Code, and a uniform system of accounts for generating companies and transmission licensees.
- The Bill also creates an Appellate Tribunal for Electricity, which will hear appeals against orders of any of the regulatory commissions. The Bill also requires the Tribunal to decide within a given period.

2.6.1.2. Probable Effects of the Electricity Act, 2003

These reforms will lead the electricity sector to an entirely different from the power sector we have known and experienced during the past 50 years of our planned economy. For the first time all social objectives that had been built into the electricity sector for the last 50 years, have been stripped away. This process visualizes to build a power sector that will function on "commercial lines", that is, the power sector will generate sufficient profits to fund its own expansion, research and modernization. The state's role will be limited to regulating the sector and providing explicit subsidies to any group of consumers that it considers economically vulnerable or genuinely in need of such subsidies.

Another proposal of the Bill is to convert electricity into a commodity that can be traded freely. According to the proponents of the Bill, the free trading of the electricity will introduce competition in generation and lead to reduction in prices of electricity. This will lead to improvement in "efficiencies" of the State run electricity sector, or privatization of the State-run electricity sector. In the long run this will result in decline of electricity rates which will ultimately be beneficial to the consumers.

In order to bring about competition among generators and to bring down the prices of electricity, the reform proposes to separate generation, transmission and distribution. The very purpose of separating generation, transmission and distribution is to introduce competition amongst generators so that the price of electricity could be reduced considerably. In reality it was with this end in mind that California introduced large-scale changes in 1996. The recent crisis of the electricity sector in California and the lack of success of the reforms in UK reveal little evidence to show that there is a realistic basis for the consumer benefits in any way from such competition.

Even in Mumbai, open access and power trading has not been beneficial to the consumers in spite of two private licensees operating in the city for many decades. If these reforms thus fail, it is not the larger consumers that are going to bear the brunt of the failure rather it will be the small consumers.

Many Economists say that the claiming of a reduction in losses by the draft of Electricity Bill 2000 is a sleight-of-hand exercise because the Bill deliberately leaves the question of ownership of the transmission company vague. According to the Bill, the State Government owns the Transmission Company, and thus the losses of the Transmission Company too had to be shouldered by the State Government. If such losses are added to the subsidies to be provided by the State, then the losses of the State Governments are likely to increase once the reforms are implemented in the power sector. Hence the statement 'claiming a reduction in losses by the Bill is a sleight-of-hand exercise'.

The Electricity Bill proposed that electricity could be supplied to rural areas through NGOs, Panchayats, Cooperatives and other institutions. But this proposal leaves aside the vital question as to who will take electricity up to the distribution point near a village from where the local community structures can take over. The major cost of the distribution system is providing the high-tension lines and the substation. From a commercial viewpoint, this activity is unlikely to be profitable in reality. As proposed by the Bill, the existing structure has to be dismantled. After dismantling the existing structure there has to be an alternative mechanism in place to satisfy the needs of rural electrification. But the Electricity Bill 2001 does not propose any alternative mechanism but it only suggests that NGOs, Panchayats, Cooperatives and other institutions will supply electricity to rural areas.

Another feature of the proposed Bill is the plan to take away the power of techno-economic clearance from the CEA. Currently any project, above a certain size, needs this clearance. By taking away this power from the CEA, the Central Government wants to ensure that no impediment is left for the private entrepreneurs to invest their capital in the power sector. The Government also wants to guarantee that no serious scrutiny takes place for the private power projects. Through this the Government wants to permit the private power industries to set up captive generation without any kind of restrictions imposed on them.

The provision of captive generation in the Bill is quite harmful for the economy. The setting up of captive generation anywhere, and without any restrictions, means that large industries are allowed to move away from the grid. It is the large-scale industries that are the primary consumers that provide cross-subsidy to others. If large-scale industries are allowed to move away from the grid, then only agricultural and domestic consumers will be left.

Under these conditions, the Government subsidy to agriculture and low-end domestic consumers will only increase. The burden of the Government will increase, due to the increase in low-end domestic consumers. One of the reasons for the current crisis in the SEBs is that industrial consumers are deserting the grid. The Electricity Bill 2001 through its innovative policies is thus actually aiming at accentuating this flight rather than containing it.

The past decade has seen and experienced a sharp reduction in the resources provided for the power sector in the Five-Year Plans. It is because the Government in its over enthusiasm to attract private foreign capital in the power sectors, instead of providing adequate resources for the power sector, offered a large number of concessions to private power producer in particular foreign investors. As a result, the investment in the power sector dropped to 16 per cent in the 1990s. It used to be 19-20 per cent of the total plan allocation in the 1970s and 1980s. Budgetary allocation has also dropped and was only about Rs. 3,000 crore last year. During the Seventh Plan we managed to produce more than 20,000 MW power capacity additions. However, in the Eighth Plan we could add only 17,666 MW power capacity additions and it was likely to be less than 20,000 MW in the Ninth Plan.

Another proposal of the Government is to offer a large number of concessions to the private investors so that it could attract foreign capital into the sector. The major initiatives taken were with regard to fast-track projects, liquid fuel-based power stations, and now unbundling and privatization. Eight Independent Power Producers (IPPs) were identified and concessions were given. The argument offered was that these IPPs would help bring in additional resources and provide more efficient power stations. A stock taking of the IPP route and fast-track projects will show that it has failed completely in bringing additional resources and providing more efficient power stations. The three fast-track projects that have come on-line have taken more than seven years to start. The Enron case has shown that the cost of such IPPs electricity is so high that it has resulted in bankrupting the SEBs. By imposing projects such as Enron on the SEBs the viable boards such as MSEB have been rendered bankrupt, which is an unfortunate event recorded in the history of the power sector in India.

The second initiative was to go in for naphtha or liquid fuel as fuel for power stations. It was planned to add 12,000 MW through the liquid fuel route. The sharp rise in the price of oil in the international market has shown how shortsighted and dangerous this policy was. Today the cost of naphtha required to produce one unit of power, is more than Rs. 3. Therefore, it is time for the Government to stop pursuing a mythical market-driven power sector and focus on the real needs of the people for consistent and affordable power.

The other aspect of the electricity sector that needs to be addressed is the provision of enough resources for renovation and modernization (R&M). Currently, we are unable to meet a peak demand of about 75,000 MW with an installed capacity of 100,000 MW and are only providing a peak supply of 65,000 MW. Even after having an installed capacity of 100,000 MW we are unable to meet the demands of the peak period because our SEBs have not really made sincere efforts for the maximum utilization of the existing installed capacity. If our SEBs decide and implement the use of the available resources for an accelerated renovation and modernization programme, it will definitely help our power sector to improve our ability to meet a higher peak demand with existing resources. Therefore, what is necessary is not Independent Power Producers and inflow of foreign capital in the electricity sector, rather a conscious effort, proper utilization and provision of enough resources for renovation and modernization.

The Electricity Bill 2001 has unfortunately based its reasoning on a wrong understanding of the power sector that has failed not only in India but also elsewhere. It seeks to bring in unbundling, competition and private power including IPP power. In reality the IPP projects have been found not only prohibitively expensive in Maharashtra but also in several countries.

The privatization of essential infrastructure imposes high costs on the consumer, which a poor country such as India cannot afford. A low cost option for the power sector means an active state sector which means establishment of a structure in which state, employees and the public at large actually participate in the development of the power sector with utmost accountability and sincerity. But our planners, instead of creating participatory structures for the employees and public accountability for the sector, are trying to set the people against the electricity employees. These divisive methods are being used with the purpose of diverting the attention of the people from the real problems of the power sector and to privatize its public assets worth Rs. 8,00,000 crore.

The present Bill is based on the World Bank view of unbundling of SEBs and privatization. "It assumes that what has been attempted abroad can be easily, smoothly and painlessly replicated in India, and that too without any loss of time" says

Madhav Godbole. According to him this premises itself has to be challenged in the light of Orissa and other States' experience so far. As far as the Orissa experience is concerned the electricity sector reforms based on this model has been an utter failure. A mind-boggling expenditure of over Rs. 306 crore was incurred on hiring domestic and international consultants to advise the Government on various facets of reforms. Although a number of states like Haryana (in 1997), Andhra Pradesh (in 1998) Uttar Pradesh, Karnataka and Rajasthan (in 1999) and Delhi (in 2001) have passed the power sector reform law, yet there is no progress in terms of privatization. Kanungo Committee therefore has rightly reported that there has been considerable increase in the average tariff at a cumulative rate of 15.5 per cent annually over the last nine years without any perceptible improvement in customer service.

The Bill is too soft and lenient with regard to the rampant menace of power theft. It states that where unauthorized use of electricity is detected it shall be presumed that such unauthorized use was continuing for a period of three months immediately preceding the date of inspection in the case of domestic and agricultural services and for a period of six months immediately preceding the date of inspection for all other categories of services, unless the responsibility is rebutted by the person, occupier or possessor of such premises or place. It is soft because several users who have been taking unauthorized supply of power for years, the biggest punishment if a charge of unauthorized use of power is established would be that such a person could be punished with minimum imprisonment of six months along with being debarred from getting power supply for at least a year. But the Bill has failed to impose such deterrent punishment for failures on matters ranging from theft and non-payment of bills.

The draft Bill envisages that though jurisdiction over generation, transmission and distribution shall vest in independent commissions, the appropriate Government can issue directions to generating companies and to load dispatch centres which means that the generating and transmission functions also come under the appropriate Government when they choose. In case of generation as per the Bill in "extraordinary circumstances" and in case of transmission in normal circumstances also. The need for such provision is difficult to appreciate. This is because even in the extraordinary circumstances the Commission may be quick enough to act in the national interest than the whole Government machinery. This type of dual jurisdiction resulting in overruling the regulator would destroy the root of independence.

Certain instances lead the SEBs to believe that the power sector regulator is considered a Frankenstein. It is because the approval of ERCs is necessary in matters like power purchases, power utility, and circulation of commercial circulars and entering into agreements. SEBs feel that such regulations and conditions will be time consuming as they will require issue of public notice and holding public hearing and they may be bureaucratized.

2.6.2. State-Level Regulatory and Policy Reform

Several states are attempting far-reaching power sector reforms. This involves a combination of divesting existing assets to private operators and establishing a regulatory framework for the sector, which will allow recovery of cost-based prices. Efforts to change the performance of the State Electricity Boards have been pioneered in Orissa. Legislation was enacted in 1995 as the basis for this reform. This legislation established the Orissa Electricity Regulatory Commission (OERC) as an autonomous regulatory body. The OERC regulates transmission and distribution tariffs. The Commission has many other powers, including the authority to license companies that want to engage in transmission and distribution and regulate the quality of the services provided by these companies. The same legislation also provided for the corporatization of the Orissa State Electricity Board and created the Grid Corporation of Orissa Limited (GRIDCO), which is responsible for transmission and distribution. The Orissa Power Generation Company, a state-owned corporation, has since been successfully divested. Forty-nine per cent of the equity was sold to AES Corporation, the highest bidder for the assets.

The states of Haryana and Andhra Pradesh have enacted legislation comparable to Orissa's as the first step in restructuring the power sector. In addition to creating regulatory bodies with similar autonomy and powers, the legislation in both states provides for the corporatization of power sector entities. The Haryana Electricity Regulatory Commission has already held its first hearings.

The experience so far has been disappointing to say the least. The private distribution companies are in financial stress and their operations are not viable. After three years of privatization, T&D losses for the private distribution companies remain at 42.7 per cent whereas they were told at the time of privatization that T&D losses were only 35 per cent. Consumer tariffs fixed by Orissa ERC (OERC) have not fully accounted for these losses. One would have expected privatization to bring about greater efficiency and lower costs. But the consumers thus see no improvement in the quality of supply or a reduction in tariffs.

The lesson one learns is that privatization of distribution, by itself, does not create a competitive market nor does it provide incentives for efficiency. The private-distribution companies, unable to reduce T&D losses, do not pay the state-owned Transmission Company, GRIDCO, on time for the power it supplies. The private companies are able to get away with this as the Government; a majority shareholder of GRIDCO is unwilling to force a shutdown and disruption in power supply. Thus, GRIDCO is also in financial distress and unable to meet its working expenses, let alone service its past liabilities.

2.7. FUTURE FRAMEWORKS SUGGESTED

Energy sector in India has played a significant role in shaping India's desire to progress and development. However, for better future prospects of India the importance of power sector cannot be negated. The implementation of economic reforms in India has resulted participation of private sector to certain extent and growth of power sector in India. However, to sustain the growth achieved over the years following policy recommendations are suggested to energy sector in India:

- The product of power has an ever-increasing demand in the market. So, generate as much as possible and supply power to the consumers at fair price. Corporatise the power sector and apply the concept of productivity—number of employees per 1000 consumers and per million units sold.
- Compared to urban areas consumption of power is less in the villages. Decentralize the use of sources of renewable energy such as solar-thermal, solar-photovoltaic, bio-mass based thermal power or mini and micro-hydropower system in villages where power consumption is less. This would eliminate a large part of the line loss, as also huge investment in setting up of transmission lines meeting the administrative overheads.
- The entry of private investors will be encouraged wherever feasible and possible, which would ensure higher rate of return on investment.
- In India, the per capita power consumption is the lowest in the world but highest in wastage of energy, which is attributed to lack of modern fuel-efficient equipment, operations of energy management and culture of saving and conservation. Hence it is essential to offer and allow the private enterprises to start power-generating availability.
- The efficient management and educational programmes like use of energy efficient bulbs, tube lights, agriculture pump-sets and metering at differential tariff for peak and non-peak seasons are important measures to be implemented on demand side.
- For tariff fixation consider only two slabs—agriculture and non-agriculture in the present seven slabs. For agriculture purpose the tariff is to be charged on the basis of cost of generation of hydropower projects while for non-agricultural purposes the tariff is to be charged on the basis of average cost of generation of electricity from all other generating units. This would fulfil the Government obligation to agriculture on the one hand,

and the commercialization of power tariff for better revenue on the other.

- "Modernization of the work through extensive computerization in power stations both for process control and general management and in distribution system planning, computers are also extensively used for commercial land establishment applications, in the head office. Over and above sufficient attention to human resource development and training for staff at all levels in job-related skills and modern technical and analytical skills and computers right from induction level and all levels."[61] This is the main contributory factor for the good performance of number of Electricity Boards in the World. It is understood therefore that "the solution to the power sector squarely lies on 'Prudent Management with Expertise'—know-how and do-how, which is a guiding and governing principle."[62]
- The provision with regard to the electricity bill payment by 'pay date' should strictly be implemented. If not paid by pay date, a penalty will be imposed at specific rate for the first time and permanent disconnection in subsequent instances.
- Loss in transmission is purely technical which should be brought down to ideal figures by proper planning of transmission at technical and commercial level. Commercial loss means un-metered consumption, which in other words is called as power theft. This should be reduced to nil through means of penalized provisions through the anti-power theft law.
- Energy Audit should be initiated at all substations. Penalty may be imposed for the theft or loss on erring person. Electricity thefts should be eliminated not gradually but speedily. For this it must infuse among the employees a sense of accountability based on a well-devised system of incentives or disincentives. Bill readings of the consumers in the area of the sub-station and

reading at the sub-station through the check meter provided for the purpose should tally. If not the in-charge employee should be made responsible.

- India's power system is divided into five regional systems: eastern, northern, northeastern, southern, and western. Weak or non-existent connections between these regions means that there is little exchange of energy. The east cannot export much of its power surplus to other regions. The Government should plan to increase regional interchanges of power by developing the transmission system and creating the necessary pricing and grid rules for bulk power markets.
- The role of the Government should be focused on and confined to policy level. The regulatory bodies should monitor the regulation of generation, transmission and distribution. So that the functions of generation, transmission and distribution of electricity should segregate with accountability and transparency on the basis of power utility rate with business risk analysis.
- "The heavily subsidized farm and residential sectors should be targeted to achieve major energy savings through a judicious blend of agricultural demand side management and residential energy efficiency, which can be converted into utility flow."[63]
- Privatization of distribution should be done in a way that does not turn consumers away from reforms. For this we should set up a process which ensures that consumers are not required to pay any more for the inefficiency of the system. For this it is necessary to create conditions for competition in the electricity industry, between producers, suppliers, transporters and traders so that the power tariff could be linked to the actual quality of power supplied. They pay a higher price if they get good quality power supply; otherwise they pay what they pay now.
- "For the balance of the poor, the Government's effort should be directed towards facilitation rather than dole.

For this purpose, India needs to start looking at a different set of mechanisms. The poor need to be able to choose from a specially designed set of services tailored to meet their end-use needs in quantities that they can afford."[64]

- We should work out the minimum cost at which an efficiently working power system without pilferage would supply power to different consumers.
- The private Distribution Company should be asked to make a plan for eliminating pilferage over a given period of time.
- Fundamental changes are required in the boards' management and operations. Improving their performance will require the introduction of private management, with a substantial financial incentive to cut losses and increase efficiency. Experience from power privatizations in Latin America suggests that the private sector can minimize losses from theft, inadequate metering, and other factors in systems with high and low loss levels. Corporatization will be an important first step in introducing the private sector, and will require legislation to allow the transfer of state electricity board assets to successor companies.
- The distributors are free to purchase electricity at a mutually agreed price from generators. They are also free to set up their own generating plants. The generators may be permitted to sell power directly to consumers.
- The task of revenue collection can be handed over to the private sector. Prepaid cash system, advance payments or deposits, and remotely readable meters are some of the other new alternatives.
- Measures taken to improve the financial health of the SEBs should aim at efficiency gains and thereby have efficiency pricing. For this the Government should aim at improvement in technical performance so that it could reduce fuel cost, auxiliary consumption, etc., and control the expenses on salary and wages.

- Keep political influence away from employment and wages.
- Unbundle the SEBs and privatize distribution immediately. However, this need not be a pre-condition for taking measures aimed at efficiency gains and levy of economic user charges.
- The establishment of regulatory agencies is necessary. Regulatory agencies could be granted a wider range of powers. These powers could include licensing, resolving disputes among service providers and regulating their quality of service. This authority can be given to regulatory commissions established under the 1998 Act. The need to strengthen the regulatory body arises partly from the need to insulate tariffs from political processes as much as possible. This will enable tariffs to track costs over time. These bodies will also facilitate the process of introducing tariffs that reflect costs and in reducing current levels of cross-subsidies.
- In order to augment power availability in a short period, R&M works should be given priority. It is well known that 1 per cent improvement in plant load factor is equivalent to creation of 600 MW capacities. Similarly, 1 per cent reduction in T&D losses leads to additional revenue of about Rs. 600 crores. Recognizing the importance of R&M works[65] improvement in transmission/distribution system and 100 per cent metering works must be undertaken in a time-bound manner.
- There should be a growing interest in cross-border power trade. The benefits from trading power lie in addressing the mismatch between supply and demand in the region, while using regional natural resources better.
- Encourage captive power generation.
- Encourage decentralized energy production and supply systems, mostly through renewable sources, by private players like NGOs, cooperatives, PRIs, etc.

2.8. CONCLUSION

In India we are at the crossroad of development of the power sector. Since Independence tremendous strides have been made in this sector. Despite this, much more remains to be done. Power has been one of the main drivers of the growth of our economy. It is essential to ensure that lack of power does not become a drag on the accelerated growth which we are aiming at. The estimated capacity addition of 1 lakh MW during the Tenth and Eleventh Plan will need periodic review so that it is in line with the projected GDP growth rate at 9 per cent per annum during the Tenth Plan and explosion of growth in the IT sector. Supply and demand gap is likely to widen, unless capacity addition is more than doubled in each of the next two Five-Year Plan periods compared to the Eighth and Ninth Plans.

The power sector in India therefore needs the concept of an integrated energy strategy. It means a system and process of coordinated decision-making and actions that bring various energy activities and decisions into a common framework. The institutional structure that allows integration of energy decision making would rest on a system of integrated analysis, monitoring and coordinated decision-making. So that it becomes a regular part of policy formulation and implementation.

For example T&D losses comprise both the technical and commercial losses. T&D losses appear significantly in Low-Tension system and High-Tension sectors. Prayas, an NGO, brought this in its study by stating that "the starting point in the battle against excessive T&D losses should be to institute an effective energy audit at the HT level. Such an approach is desirable for many reasons, which include relatively small requirements of investment and managerial efforts, high cost-benefit ratio, higher tariff and small number of consumers."[66]

The second-generation reforms should focus on open access to transmission and distribution system. CERC has already notified grid code for the control and dispatch of power from one system to another system and asked suggestions from those involved in the sector. Open access to the transmission and distribution facilities by various utilities will enable wheeling of power from one region to another region at the lowest cost to the consumers and would further encourage investments in transmission network and generating capacities. This will introduce competition not only among various generating companies but also at the distribution level and will enable improvements in revenue collection and in which the voltage and frequency will be maintained at nominal levels. Only then India will be able to reap the fullest benefits of Power Pooling.

Reforms should aim at allowing freedom to the consumers to get power from any distributor/generating company of his choice and also introduction of differential pricing of power according to the time of the day giving incentives to users to shift their demand to the off peak period. There should be a mandatory provision to encourage use of solar energy for heating, say water heating, in certain categories of buildings.

The power sector today is in need of a holistic approach to reap the potential benefit which various reforms could render. Thus there is a "need for a coordinated movement across all sectors linked to the provision of energy services."[67] The success of reforms in India "will depend upon the existence of some sort of restraining or disciplining mechanism in the sector. In the absence of which, efforts made will likely result in a transition from inefficient public ownership to profit-gouging monopolies or oligarchies."[68] Thus to enable competition, acceleration of economic growth and to raise the comfort level of the common man, the major challenge of the power sector is to continue with the reforms, improve the financial health of the utilities, so that power could be made available at quality and affordable price.

END NOTES

1. S. Ramaswamy and T. Tamizh Chelvam, "Energy and Economic Development", *Infrastructure Development for Economic Growth*, M.V. Srinivasa Gowda and Susheela Subrahmanya (eds.), Deep & Deep Publications, New Delhi, 1997, p. 118.
2. Anil Kakodkar, "Fast Breeding Nuclear Energy", *Yojana*, Vol. 48, No. 1, January 2004, p. 37.
3. Kula Saikia, "Energy Planning: Relevant Issues", *Energy and Energy Resource Management*, V.S. Mahajan, S.K. Agnihotri and R.P. Athparia (eds)., Deep & Deep Publications, New Delhi, pp. 23-24.

4. Government of India, Planning Commission, Draft Fifth Five-Year Plan, 1974-79, Vol. II, p. 117, as quoted by S.K. Misra & V.K. Puri, *Economic Environment of Business*, Himalaya Publishing House, Mumbai, 2002, p. 325.
5. As quoted by C.R. Reddy and others, "Power Sector Reforms", *Southern Economist*, Vol. 42, No. 7, August 1, 2003, p. 5.
6. Amol Phadke and Sudhir Chella Rajan, "Electricity Reforms in India: Not Too Late to Go Back to the Drawing Board", *Economic and Political Weekly*, Vol. 38, No. 29, July 19-25, 2003, p. 3061.
7. As quoted by I.V. Trivedi in "Commerce Education in the New Millennium", RBAS Publishers, Jaipur, pp. 83-84.
8. R. Venkatapathey and R. Rani Geetha Priyadarshini, "Current Status of Power, the Key Infrastructure in India", *Infrastructure Development and Financing*, S. Ganesan, (eds.), Kanishka Publishers Distributors, New Delhi, p. 311.
9. Including the reduction of socially based subsidies.
10. i.e., reduce losses and theft, improve performance and streamline operations.
11. As quoted by C.R. Reddy, *op. cit.*, p. 5.
12. S.P. Gupta (ed.), *India: Vision 2020*, Planning Commission, Government of India, New Delhi, 2004, p. 113.
13. Central Electricity Authority (CEA), 1997, *Fourth National Power Plan 1997-2012*, New Delhi.
14. India has the capacity to generate bio-fuels in massive quantities. Curcas is a plant introduced from Africa, which already grows wild in India. The plant produces large quantities of seeds which contain up to 35 per cent oil that is a substitute for No. 2 diesel and kerosene and can be blended in diesel motor fuels up to 15 per cent. The cost of production is competitive with other fuel oils. It is said that cultivation of 10 million hectares of this crop could generate 7.5 million tonnes of fuel annually. Ethanol is another bio-fuel with enormous potential. Ethanol can be produced from maize, tapioca, sugar cane, sugar beet and other crops. It can be mixed as a pollution-free blend with petrol and diesel. Ethanol-petrol fuel blends are utilized in more than 20 countries.
15. *Tenth Five-Year Plan*, Infrastructure Power, Chapter 8.2., Government of India, New Delhi, p. 917.
16. As quoted by R. Magesh and R. Duraipandian, "Infrastructure Development and India's Power Policies," *Infrastructure Development and Financing*, S. Ganesan (ed.), Kanishka Publishers, New Delhi, 2001, p. 283.

17. K.P. Kannan and N. Vijayamohanan Pillai, *Plight of the Power Sector in India*, Centre for Development Studies, Thiruvananthapuram, 2002, pp. 55-56.
18. *Economic Survey 2002-03*, p. 183.
19. K.C. Pant, *India's Development Scenario: Next Decade and Beyond ...*, Academic Foundation, New Delhi, 2004, Vol. II, p. 156.
20. *Economic Survey 2002-03*, *op. cit.*, p. 182.
21. World Bank & Public-Private Infrastructure Advisory Facility, *India Country Framework Report for Private Participation in Infrastructure*, p. 17.
22. Madhav Godbole, "Electricity Regulatory Commissions: The Jury is Still Out", *Economic and Political Weekly*, Vol. 37, No. 23, June 8, 2002, p. 2199.
23. K.C. Pant, *op. cit.*, Vol. II, 2004, p. 156.
24. *Ibid.*
25. Shonali Pachauri and Daniel Spreng, "Energy Use and Energy Access in Relation to Poverty", *Economic and Political Weekly*, Vol. 39, No. 3, January 17, 2004, p. 277.
26. Madhav Godbole, *op. cit.*, p. 2199.
27. *Economic Survey 2002-03*, *op. cit.*, p. 182.
28. *Tenth Five-Year Plan, op. cit.*, p. 904.
29. *Ibid.*
30. K.P. Kannan and N. Vijayamohanan Pillai, *Plight of the Power Sector in India: Inefficiency, Reform and Political Economy*", Centre for Development Studies, Thiruvananthapuram, Kerala, p. 389.
31. Bani P. Banerjee, *Handbook of Energy and the Environment in India*, Oxford University Press, New Delhi, 2005, p. 176.
32. *Ibid.*, p. 178.
33. *Tenth Five-Year Plan*, *op. cit.*, p. 901.
34. Ken Koyama, *Energy Strategies in China and India and Their Implications*, This report is a part of a study project conducted in FY2000 on behalf of the Agency of Natural Resources and Energy, p. 15.
35. *Tenth Five-Year Plan*, *op. cit.*, pp. 910-911.
36. *Ibid.*, p. 911.
37. *Ibid.*, p. 912.
38. http://www.energylineindia.com, on 10th April 2006.
39. http://www.mnes.nic.in, on 14th April 2006.

40. *Annual Report, 2004-05*, Ministry of Non-Conventional Energy Sources, Government of India, New Delhi, p. 17.
41. *Ibid.*, p. 20.
42. Bani P. Banerjee, *op. cit.*, p. 211.
43. *Annual Report, 2004-05*, Ministry of Non-Conventional Energy Sources, *op. cit.*, p. 21.
44. *Tenth Five-Year Plan*, *op. cit.*, p. 927.
45. *Ninth Five-Year Plan*, Chapter 6, Energy, No. 6.297, Planning Commission, Government of India.
46. As given by Bani P. Banerjee, *op. cit.*, p. 206.
47. P. Ganesan and S. Ratinavel, "Empowering India with Power Sector Development", *Infrastructure Development and Financing*, S. Ganesan (ed.), Kanishka Publishers, New Delhi, 2001, p. 277.
48. V. Anbumani and K. Amuthavalli, "Development of Electric Power", *Infrastructure Development for Economic Growth*, M.V. Srinivasa Gowda and Susheela Subrahmanya (ed.), Deep & Deep Publications, New Delhi, 1997, p. 139.
49. *Tenth Five-Year Plan*, *op. cit.*, p. 914.
50. *Economic Survey* 2005-2006, Government of India, p. 181.
51. *Tenth Five-Year Plan*, *op. cit.*, p. 927.
52. World Bank, *The World Bank's Role in the Electric Power Sector*, Washington, D.C., 1993, as found in "The Changing Global Context for Electricity Reform", Navroz K. Dubash, *WRI: Politics*, p. 18.
53. Navroz K. Dubash, "The Changing Global Context for Electricity Reform", *WRI: Politics*, p. 12.
54. *Tenth Five-Year Plan*, *op. cit.*, p. 912.
55. As quoted by Pooja Kothari and Aditya Chatterjee, "Short-circuit at Ennore Power Project", *Economic Times*, 15 June 2001.
56. Anupam B. Rastogi, "The Infrastructure Sector in India, 2001-02", *India Infrastructure Report 2003*, 3iNetwork, Oxford University Press, 2003, p. 79.
57. V.S. Verma, "Power Reforms: Overview of Power Sector", *Yojana*, Vol. 48, No. 1, January 2004, p. 35.
58. TERI (Tata Energy Research Institute), "Defining an Integrated Energy Strategy for India", 2002, p. 35.
59. S.L. Rao, "Electricity Bill, 2001: Many Shortcomings, but a Step Forward", *Economic and Political Weekly*, Vol. 38, No. 5, February 1, 2003, pp. 463-466.
60. *Tenth Five-Year Plan*, *op. cit.*, p. 899.

61. T.L. Sankar, "Power Sector: Rise, Fall and Reform", *Economic and Political Weekly*, Vol. 38, Nos. 12 and 13, March 22, 2003, p. 1171.
62. C.R. Reddy and others, *op. cit.*, pp. 7-8.
63. R. Ponraj, "Power Sector Reforms: Need for Different Thinking", S. Ganesan (ed.), *Infrastructure Development and Financing*, Kanishka Publishers, New Delhi, 2001, p. 295.
64. TERI (Tata Energy Research Institute), "Defining an Integrated Energy Strategy for India", 2002, p. 38.
65. K.C. Pant, 2004, *op. cit.*, p. 158.
66. 'HT Energy Audit: The Crucial Starting Point for Curbing Revenue Loss', *Prayas Occasional Report*, February 2002, as stated by Godbole, Madhav, *op. cit.*, p. 2199.
67. TERI (Tata Energy Research Institute), "Defining an Integrated Energy Strategy for India", 2002, p. 41.
68. Amol Phadke and Sudhir Chella Rajan, *op. cit.*, p. 3062.

Globalization and Telecommunication Sector in India

3

3.1. INTRODUCTION

Telecommunication is considered as one of the prime support services needed for rapid growth and modernization of various sectors of the economy. Telecommunication is now universally recognized as one of the prime movers of modern day economy because of the enormous growth of Information Technology and its significant impact on the rest of the economy. Telecommunication, Information and Globalization are restructuring every aspect of business and society. Hence its vital importance is experienced even within a developing economy like India. It is also acknowledged that the telecom professionals are the key players, who will play a crucial role as leaders in the changing dynamics of global communications, internetworking, the Internet, e-commerce, mobile and wireless communications strategy.

Modern age is the age of convergence and telecommunication is a key to modern economic development. Telecommunication when linked with computer becomes Information Technology. This is the most dominating technology of today as it influences the entire spectrum of the economy. It covers all aspects of business, technology, manufacturing and other services. Telecommunication is significant for economic development since 1% increase in telephone density leads to a 3% increase in the GDP.[1] Today the networks and companies will no longer be categorized on the basis of only voice, data or video services that they provide rather they have to become info-communication companies providing a bundle of services. The benchmark for any country's communication infrastructure therefore is not tele-density any more, but it is the fancy term "per capita bandwidth."

3.2. BRIEF HISTORY

Indian telecommunication liberalization in the 1990s was driven by a state which has seen its capacity and consensus fritter away over the last fifty years under the weight of pluralistic pressures and personalistic rule. Indian reform efforts in the 1980s were halting and nepotistic even though demands from businesses, urban residential users and Government administrations continued to grow. India was pushed toward further telecommunications liberalization after a severe fiscal and balance of payments crisis in 1991 which weakened the status quo constituencies in the country and empowered many businesses to demand liberalization. India, like many other countries of the world, has adopted a gradual approach to telecom sector reform through selective privatization and managed competition in different segments of the telecom market. To begin with, India introduced private competition in value-added services in 1992 followed by opening up of cellular and basic services for local area to private competition.

The National Telecom Policy (NTP) of 1994 introduced the concept of 'telecommunication for all and telecommunication within the reach of all'. It visualized universal service covering all villages. Under this, out of the nearly 6 lakh villages in the country, about 4 lakh villages have been provided with telecom services. The objective of the Government is to see that before the end of year 2020 all villages are provided with basic telecom services. The 1994 policy announced ambitious goals for provision of telephones (20 million lines by 2000) and also liberalized the telecommunications sector further. The state owned monopoly, the Department of Telecommunications (DoT), could not be corporatized or privatized due to resistance from its 4,80,000 workers. But DoT will now compete with a private player in each of the 21 regions (known as Telecom Circles) announced by the State.

Further in 1995 a multimedia center with video conferencing facility was opened followed by providing commercial ISDN services. As a result of liberalization followed by competition in the telecom services, the Government of India set up the Telecom Regulatory Authority of India (TRAI) in 1997. This was restructured in 2000 and an appellate authority Telecom Disputes and Settlement Appellate Tribunal (TDSAT) was set up. The biggest landmark in 2001 was when MTNL invested U.S. $300 million for operations in Bangladesh and Nepal and now the Government control over the country's telecommunication sector undergoes a change with the privatization of Videsh Sanchar Nigam Ltd. (VSNL) and competition was also introduced in national long distance (NLD) and international long distance (ILD) telephony at the start of the current decade.[2] The privatization of India's largest telephone service provider is being considered a milestone in telecommunication history of India.

Two state-owned public sector incumbents with a large existing subscriber base dominate the fixed line service. As on December 31, 2004, the two Public Sector Enterprises (PSEs), BSNL and MTNL[3] owned 4,48,78,118 Direct Exchange Lines (DELs) against 43,01,891 privately owned DELs. These two PSEs were allowed belated entry into the cellular segment in the beginning of the present decade. Consequently, their cellular subscriber base is tiny compared to the private operators. Out of 48,01,3971 mobile phone subscribers in the country in December 2004, they had only 96,71,810 subscribers whereas private operators owned 3,83,42,161 mobile phone subscribers.[4] The share of private sector in the numbering of telephone sector is of 45.91 per cent whereas the share of public sector is 54 per cent.

3.3. ECONOMIC GROWTH AND TELECOMMUNICATION

It is observed that there is a direct correlation between the availability of telecommunication facilities and access to telecom infrastructure and a country's economic growth. According to International Telecom Union (ITU), the number of main telephone lines has nearly doubled from 546 million in 1991 to 1.12 billion by the end of 2002. Mobile subscribers have grown phenomenally from 91 million in 1995 to 1.5 billion in 2002. In

1991 the total telephone penetration was 49% in developed countries, 3.3% in emerging nations and 0.3% in least developed countries. The above fact indicates a strong association between economic development and growth in telecommunication sector.

Over and above this there are plenty of evidences[5] to show that telecom is improving life chances across the strata of the society. A whole range of information based industry and applications have created new sources of employment and earning with welfare enhancement for the wealthy and the poor. "As a meta-technology, ICT has caused rapid innovations to occur in all other areas of material sciences. As a fabric of information society, ICT has improved access in the fields of education, healthcare, governance and all aspects of business services. It has also improved the abilities of the poor to manage risks and mitigate vulnerabilities through the provision of timely information."[6] Manas Bhattacharya thus has rightly said, "Telecommunications have emerged as a springboard of ICT applications with economy-wide ramifications."

According to former World Bank economist Surjit Bhalla, every 10 million new phone lines add 0.5% to annual economic output. This means increased productivity because these inexpensive phones prove to be a lifeline for business. "Some Indian business owners hope that if allowing private investment improves telecom services, the Government will then surely be encouraged to do the same for India's limping power networks, road system, and airports, all of which are languishing under state control."[7]

3.4. TELECOMMUNICATION POLICIES

India's telecom sector has failed in three measures of performance, namely quantity, quality and price. On quality, the number of telephone connections in India per capita is around one-sixth of that found in countries with a comparable per capita GDP. On quality, telecom facilities in India are noisy and unreliable specially, during monsoon season. As compared with what is easily attainable using contemporary technology India's telecom sector has failed in telecom facilities as well in after sale services. On price telecom services in India are very often hundreds of per cent costlier than the fair prices provided in other countries for these services.[8] As a result there was a widespread consensus for a new policy environment where the Government would play a small role in the economy. In this new era of new paradigm the Government decided to guide the telecom sector with new policies such as New Telecom Policy 1994, 1999 and Communication Convergence Bill, 2001.

3.4.1. NTP 1994

NTP 1994 recognized that basic infrastructure in telecommunication sector would not be made available only out of Government sources but the private investment and involvement of the private sector was required to bridge the resource gap. The Government therefore invited private sector participation in a phased manner from the early nineties. Initially private sectors provided value added services such as Paging Services and Cellular Mobile Telephone Services (CMTS) and thereafter Fixed Telephone Services (FTS).

However, the results of the privatization were not entirely satisfactory. The main reason, according to the cellular and basic operators, was the fact that the actual revenues realized by these projects fell far short of the projections and the operators were unable to arrange financing for their projects. As a result, some of the targets, as envisaged in the objectives of the NTP 1994, remained unfulfilled. The Government viewed these developments with concern as it would adversely affect the further development of the sector and recognized the need to take a fresh look at the policy framework for this sector. This resulted in the New Telecommunications Policy 1999.

3.4.2. NTP 1999

3.4.2.1. Targets of the Policy

The policy has the following targets:

- Telephones available on demand.
- Tele-density of 7 per cent by 2005 and 15 per cent by 2010.
- Affordable tariffs for rural connections.

- Mandatory rural connections for all fixed service providers.
- Rural tele-density to increase from 0.4 per cent to 4 per cent by 2010.
- Telecom coverage of all villages.
- Encourage development of telecom in rural areas making it more affordable by suitable tariff structure and making rural communication mandatory for all fixed service providers. Increase rural tele-density from the current level of 0.4 to 4 by the year 2010 and provide reliable transmission media in all rural areas.
- Provide high-speed data and multimedia capability using technologies including ISDN to all towns with a population greater than 200,000.
- Internet access to all district headquarters.

3.4.2.2. *Market Competition*

- VSNL's monopoly on international services.
- National long distance voice open to competition. Alternative infrastructure providers[9] can provide long distance data services immediately.
- Within cellular segment of telecom sector MTNL and Department of Telecommunications will be third operator, with an additional operator to be added where available spectrum allows.
- Fixed basic services will move toward a liberal entry regime, with potentially open entry, although there will be restrictions initially.

3.4.2.2.1. Spectrum Management

- The National Frequency Allocation Plan 2000 will be made public and updated every two years.
- Defense and security communications will be relocated from commercial frequencies; these forces will be compensated.
- An inter-ministerial group will establish broad allocation policy.

- Spectrum users will pay fees and TRAI will recommend their level.

3.4.2.2.2. Universal Service Obligations

- Fixed service providers will have targets for universal service obligations; all service providers could participate in universal access programs funded by a levy on provider revenues.
- The Department of Telecommunications will refund for cellular license payments because of the burden of universal service obligations.

3.4.2.2.3. New Legislative Framework

The policy recognizes the need for new legislation to replace the Indian Telegraph Act of 1885, but sets no timeline for devising such legislation.

The main objectives of the New Telecom Policy are to:

- Increase the availability of affordable and effective communications.
- Provide universal service to all areas, including remote, hilly and tribal areas.
- Capture the benefits of technology convergence in building an efficient telecommunication infrastructure.
- Provide multimedia facilities nationwide.
- Create a modern and efficient telecommunications infrastructure taking into account the convergence of IT, media, telecom and consumer electronics.
- Introduce competition into telecommunications and create a level playing field for all players.
- Achieve efficiency and transparency in spectrum management.
- Protect the country's defense and security interests.[10]

3.4.2.3. Critical Outlook

- The New Telecom Policy envisions a substantial liberalization in market entry for telecommunications services.

- The New Telecom Policy is a clear step toward modernizing India's telecommunications. The new policy is explicit about new entry and competition. The policy also addresses some of the implications of convergence.
- The New Telecom Policy established the possibility of a revenue-sharing regime with a one-time entry fee.
- The New Telecom Policy acknowledges the costs of universal service obligation by introducing a fund to encourage expansion into non-economic areas.
- The New Telecom Policy reaffirms the government's commitment to a "strong and independent regulator with comprehensive powers and clear authority to effectively perform its functions."

3.4.3. Telecom Regulatory Authority of India (TRAI) Act

The Telecommunications Regulatory Authority of India (TRAI) was established in January 1997 under the TRAI Act as an autonomous body with quasi-judicial powers to regulate telecommunications services in India. The TRAI Act was amended in 2000, following which TRAI's powers to adjudicate disputes have been vested in the Telecom Disputes Settlement and Appellate Tribunal (TDSAT). The regulatory functions of TRAI fall within two broad categories — recommendatory and mandatory. The principal recommendatory functions of TRAI may be exercised either on its own initiative or on request from the licensor. This function mainly covers introduction of new service providers, terms and conditions of licenses to be awarded to service providers, and revocation of licenses. The recommendatory function also covers, "measures to facilitate competition and promote efficiency in the operation of telecommunication services so as to facilitate growth in such services." In 2001-02, regulatory initiatives were taken relating to increased competition, tariff policies, quality of service, consumer protection, and universal service obligations, etc.

3.4.4. TDSAT

The TRAI Act was amended in 2000, following which TRAI's powers to adjudicate disputes have been vested in the

Telecom Disputes Settlement and Appellate Tribunal (TDSAT). As a result TDSAT has been granted powers to adjudicate any dispute between a licensor and a licensee, between two or more service providers, and between a service provider and a group of consumers. TDSAT also has the jurisdiction to hear and dispose off appeals against any direction, decision or order of TRAI. Decisions of TDSAT can be appealed only in the Supreme Court of India.

3.4.5. Communication Convergence Bill, 2001

Keeping in view the rapid convergence of telecom, computers, television and electronics, need was felt to prepare a new comprehensive statute to replace the Indian Telegraph Act, 1885. The Convergence Bill will repeal a number of existing legislations relating to the telecommunications industry, including the Indian Telegraph Act of 1885, the Telegraph Wire Unlawful Possession Act, 1850, the Cable Television Networks (Regulation) Act, 1995 and the TRAI Act. The Convergence Bill proposes significant changes in the organization, functions and structure of the regulatory bodies functioning in the telecommunication sector. It seeks to establish the Communication Commission of India and this Commission will facilitate and regulate all matters relating to carriage and content of communications. It will also issue licenses and allocate spectrum and regulate content, an activity so far dealt with by the normal legal processes.

The Communications Commission of India, while exercising its functions, will be guided, among others, by the following principles:

- That the communication sector is developed in a competitive environment and in consumer interest;
- That communication services are made available at affordable cost to all, especially uncovered areas including the rural, remote, hilly and tribal areas;
- That a modern and effective communication infrastructure is established taking into account the convergence of information technology, media, telecom and consumer electronics;

- That equitable, non-discriminatory interconnection across various networks are promoted;
- That licensing and registration criteria are transparent and made known to the public;
- That an open licensing policy allowing any number of new entrants (except in specific cases constrained by limited resources such as the spectrum) is promoted; and
- That the principle of a level playing field for all operators, including existing operators on the date of commencement of the Act, is promoted so as to serve consumer interest.[11]

Accordingly, the Communication Convergence Bill, 2001, was introduced in the Lok Sabha on August 31, 2001. "It aims at promoting, facilitating and developing carriage and content of communications (including broadcasting, telecommunications and multimedia) in view of the necessity to facilitate development of a national infrastructure for an information based society, provide a choice of services to the people with a view to promoting plurality of news, views and information."[12] The Bill was referred to the Standing Committee on Information Technology for examination. The Committee submitted its report on November 22, 2002.

3.5. PERFORMANCE OF TELECOMMUNICATION

3.5.1. At the World Ranking

The act of opening up of the market unleashed dynamism that was so far latent in the sector. This is evident from a number of performance indicators. First and foremost in terms of overall size of main telephone lines in operation, India ranked 14th in the world in 1995. However, the rank improved to 7th position in the world in 2001. This is mainly due to opening of market in the telecommunication sector for private sector participation.

Table 3.1. Number of Main Telephone Lines in Operation in Terms of the World

Country	No. of lines in 1995 ('000)	Ranks (1995)	No. of lines in 2001 ('000)	Ranks (2001)
USA	159,735.2	1	190,000.0	1
Japan	62,292.0	2	76,000.0	3
Germany	42,000.0	3	52,280.0	4
China	40,705.7	4	179,034.0	2
France	32,400.0	5	34,032.9	9
UK	29,411.4	6	34,710.0	8
Russia	25,018.9	7	35,700.0	6
Italy	24,845.0	8	27,303.0	10
Korea, Rep.	18,600.0	9	22,724.7	11
Canada	17,567.0	10	20,319.3	12
Brazil	13,263.0	12	37,430.8	5
India	11,978.0	14	34,732.1	7

Source: World Telecommunication Development Report 2002, ITU, as given by Manas Bhattacharya, "Telecom Sector in India: Vision 2020", India: Vision 2020, Planning Commission, Government of India, New Delhi, p. 656.

3.5.2. Physical Growth of Telecom Network

Greater and impressive growth has been realized in the telecom sector after 1995. In the year 1997 there were only 148.80 lakh of telephone connections. However, the total telephone connections as in December 2004 increased to 928.92 lakh which comprises 342.67 lakh fixed lines and 480.14 lakh cellular connections provided by the public and private sectors. Table 3.2 Figure 3.1 indicates the significant increase of telephone connections from 1997 to December 2004. In the year 2003-04, 219.20 lakh telephones were added. This is equal to the total number of phones installed as on 1999. During this period the actual growth has been nearly 6.24 fold when we compare this year with 1997.

The structure and composition of telecom growth has undergone a substantial change in terms of mobile versus fixed phones and public versus private participation. In 1999, both mobile phones and private sector separately accounted for 5 per cent of total number of phones. In December 2004, mobile phones accounted for 57 per cent of total phones. The share of mobile has thus surpassed the share of the landlines and this trend is likely to continue. During the same period the private sector accounted for 46 per cent of total phones. Of the 163.52 lakh additional phones provided during 2004-05, major share, i.e. 125 lakh (about 77%) was provided by the private sector. So in the years to come the private sector will continue to play a significant role in the growth of telecom sector.

Table 3.2. Growth of Telecom Network (PSUs & Private)

Year	PSUs Network	Private Network	Total Network
1997	145.40	3.40	148.80
1998	178.00	8.80	186.80
1999	215.90	12.20	228.10
2000	265.10	20.20	285.30
2001	324.40	38.50	362.90
2002	381.58	68.06	449.64
2003	431.71	114.46	546.17
2004 (March)	464.83	300.56	765.40
2004 (December)	502.48	426.44	928.92

Source: Annual Report 2004-2005, Department of Telecommunications, Ministry of Communications and Information Technology, Government of India, New Delhi, p. 97.

3.5.2.1. Mobile Telephone

There has been phenomenal growth in mobile subscribers in the world in the nineties, increasing from 11 million in 1990 to 941 million by the end of 2001. In 1991, less than one per cent of the world population had a mobile phone. The proportion has grown to the vicinity of one phone per every six people by the end of 2001. Similarly, one-third of the total number of countries of the world had cellular network in 1991. The ratio rose to over 90 per cent by end-2001.[13] Considering the fixed telephone lines it is likely that mobile phones would surpass fixed line.

Cellular mobile telephony industry was opened to the private sector in 1992. Initially there were great hopes for profits in this business. Several new entrants have done well, and the industry is quickly moving to maturity, due to the attractive technology, marketing and competitiveness. Stiffer competition, new entrants, and developments in the limited-mobility industry have given opportunities as well as posed challenges, generating appropriate responses. India's cellular phone industry is considered as one of the world's fastest growing markets.

The cellular phone industry market is affected by the hesitation of investors in new technologies and networks. The industry is also affected by the changing telecom and tariff policies on profit prospects and competition. For example: COAI (Cellular Operators Association of India) was recently disappointed at the revision in monthly rentals for WLL (Wireless in local loop) and limited mobility services announced by TRAI. It stated that "by abstaining from prescribing either a ceiling or a floor in the monthly rental, consumer interest has been sidelined, as there is no protection to the consumer from an upward revision in tariffs at any time."[14]

Keeping in trend with the world technology in telecommunication cellular mobile telephones subscribers in India too increased from 77 thousand in 1995 to 3.6 million in 2000. By December 2004, it has grown to 480.14 lakh. However, cellular subscribers in proportion to total number of telephone subscribers have increased from 0.6 per cent in 1995 to 14.6 per cent in 2002. This is still lower than the average of 24.6 per cent achieved by the low-income countries in 2001. Therefore, we can say that India is yet to experience mobile explosion of the scale other countries have seen. However, we can expect a rapid growth in mobile telephony in the years to come. India has also achieved significant quality upgradation of its network.

In spite of all this, the cellular subscribers are growing at an exponential rate. Its growth touched 2.4 crore in March 2005. This means mobile phones would account for 20.5% of total telephone connections in India. The mobile telephone services today cover 480.14 lakh subscribers in 900 cities and 60,000 villages. In addition to this, there are 4,67,131 WLL subscribers in urban areas and 9,98,976 subscribers in rural areas. Today the share of mobile phones has surpassed the share of landlines and this trend is likely to continue. Table 3.2.1 and Figure 3.2 highlights shift towards wireless telephony.

With falling tariff rates for cellular phones, there has been a greater increase in the number of cellular subscribers. From a mere 3.39 lakh cellular subscribers in March 1997, the number increased to 480.14 lakh in December 2004. The share of the cellular subscribers in the total telephone subscribers has gone up from 10 per cent in March 2001 to 21 per cent at the end of December 2002. It shows that there has been rapid expansion in the telecom sector, accompanied by a significant technological change. As a result there has been continuous shift in the technology of access from fixed line to mobile telephony. In 2003-04 fixed lines grew by less than 3 per cent, while mobile telephones grew by 159.2 per cent.

Table 3.2.1. Fixed Line Telephones and Cellular Mobile Phones

Year	Fixed Line Telephones	Cellular Mobile Phones
1997	145.43	3.39
1998	178.02	8.82
1999	216.13	12.0
2000	266.53	18.84
2001	327.02	35.77
2002	385.36	64.32
2003	423.10	129.98
2004	352.93	337.01
2004 (31st December)	342.67	480.14

Source: Annual Report 2004-2005, Department of Telecommunications, Ministry of Communications and Information Technology, Government of India, New Delhi.

BSNL and MTNL alone have provided 90.56 lakh GSM and 6.51 lakh WLL mobile phones as on December 31, 2004. This shows that there is a positive shift in the use of mobile telephony. This is confirmed from the rising share of mobile phones. Use of mobiles has increased from 44% as on March 31, 2004 to more than 52% as in December 2004. Mobile phones once considered a luxury is no more considered to be a luxurious item at all. In recent years due to low price telephony affluent households and middle income groups are going from one fixed line per family to one mobile phone per person.

Table 3.3. Growth of Mobile Phones

Year	Mobile including WLL (in Million)			
	PSUs	Pvt.	Total	% of PSUs
2001-02	0.26	6.28	6.54	3.98
2002-03	2.64	10.35	12.99	20.32
2003-04	5.99	27.70	33.69	17.21
2004-05 (October)	8.99	35.50	44.49	20.21

Source: Annual Report 2004-2005, Department of Telecommunications, Ministry of Communications and Information Technology, Government of India, New Delhi, p. 199.

Table 3.3 reveals that in the mobile phone segment the private sector is having 79.79 per cent of the market share and the PSUs are having only 20.21 per cent of the market share. However, it is interesting to note that the PSUs' actual gain in the market share in mobile telephony increased from 3.98 per cent in 2001-02 to 20.21 per cent towards the end of October 2004. But as in February 2005 its market share decreased to 19.22 per cent. Among the private sector it is Reliance that has the highest market share with 21.92 per cent and Bharti has the second highest with 20.50 per cent of market share of mobile telephony as in February 2005.[15]

The private sector is also providing other value added telecom services that include paging services, VSAT services for providing data services to closed user groups. Government is issuing licenses for opening up of Global Mobile Personal Communication by Satellite (GMPCS). Recently one of the most notable mergers was that between Birla-Tata-AT&T and BPL Communications to form the country's largest mobile phone company (BPL-Batata) (Figure 3.3) which is now known as "IDEA-Cellular."

3.5.2.2. PCOs

One of the unique innovations of Indian telecommunications is the public call offices spread all over the country for urban population and Village Public Telephones (VPTs) for rural population so that people can call any place in India or abroad. As against the NTP 1994 target of provision of one PCO for 500 urban populations, an achievement of urban PCO penetration of one PCO per 522 was achieved. As regards the provision of total telephone lines in the country DoT has provided, the statistics indicate that recently 8.73 million telephone lines were provided against the Eighth Plan target of 7.5 million lines. During the year 2004-05, a total of 2.35 lakh PCOs had been added. Up to November 2004, a total number of 17.55 lakh PCOs had been provided so that the general public who could afford to have a telephone of their own could have access to telephone facility. Up to December 2004, 3,138 Village Public Telephones were provided. As on December 31, 2004, the total number of villages having VPT are 5,12,820. The telecom density that was hardly one at the time of the introduction of the reforms in 1994 has nearly gone up to three, which is not that remarkable.

3.5.2.3. Internet

The explosive growth of the Internet is another important development during this decade. Government recognized the significance of Internet, and in 1998 came up with the Internet Service Providers' Policy that threw open the opportunity of providing the backbone services to not only the Department of Telecom but also other organizations. Total internet connection as on December 2004 is 23,68,709 and dial up connections increased from 7,54,220 to 9,13,163. CLI based Accountless Internet Service too increased from 3,63,827 to 7,50,869. Number of cities where CLI made operational too increased from 31 to 100.

3.5.2.3.1. Net Telephony

Today Voice over IP networks is leading the communications revolution worldwide. As per the recommendations of TRAI recently Internet telephony has been legalized in India. As a result "Net telephony has opened new business opportunities for India's ISPs and cyber cafes. India's telecom consumers now simply enter a cyber cafe and can talk over the Net, paying Rs. 5 per minute, depending upon the destination. For example, a call to the United States, that used to cost about Rs. 40 per minute, now costs Rs. 5 through the Internet. This offers stiff competition to international long distance service providers but at the same time also helps lower charges for long distance communication both for STD and ISD."[16] ·

According to forecast estimation, India's IP telephony market is expected to grow at a rate of 119% to reach Rs. 13,000 crore. But to maintain its competitiveness globally, India must invest in building its telecom infrastructure and increase PC and Internet penetration. Number of Internet subscribers is likely to exceed 7.7 million. The first batch of internet telephony products hit the retail market with three Internet service providers namely Caltiger, Net4India and IceNet. More and more cyber cafes are mushrooming across the country that has resulted in net access rates falling to Rs. 10 per hour.[17]

3.5.2.3.2. Internet and PC

India is perceived to have a special comparative advantage in IT and in IT enabled services. However, sustaining this advantage depends critically on high quality telecommunication. Like the per capita income, today number of PCs and Internet users are considered as indicators of development. Therefore, substantial growth of broadband is necessary to meet the needs and development of IT related sectors. Two important indicators of IT penetration in Indian market are Internet use and availability of Personal Computers (PCs). There has been significant expansion in both during the last decade.

Table 3.4. Growth in Personal Computers and Number of Internet Users

Year	Estimated Number of Internet Users	Availability of Personal Computers
1992	1,000	410,000
1993	2,000	560,000
1994	10,000	800,000
1995	250,000	1,200,000
1996	450,000	1,500,000
1997	700,000	2,000,000
1998	1,400,000	2,700,000
1999	2,800,000	3,300,000
2000	5,000,000	4,600,000

Source: Yearbook of statistics, 1991-2000, ITU, As given by Manas Bhattacharya, "Telecom Sector in India: Vision 2020", India: Vision 2020, Planning Commission, Government of India, New Delhi, p. 656.

Despite impressive growth in the number of Internet users and availability of PCs, number of users of Internet (Table 3.4) is still a negligible fraction in comparison to India's total population. Per capita availability of PC is also comparatively low in relation to many developed nations. As in December 2001, number of personal computers available per 100 persons in USA was 62.25. At the same period world average on number of personal computer available per 100 persons was 8.42 (Table 3.5). However, in India the situation is not encouraging because only 0.58 personal computers are available per 100 persons.

Internet booths and cyber cafes have played an important role in expanding and popularizing IT among the masses and promoting domestic market for personal computers. However, their expansion crucially hinges on the growth of telecommunications infrastructure. In India, a spectrum of technologies has been utilized to connect remote villages, which includes Wireless in Local Loop (WLL), wireless cum wired technology developed by C-DOT[18], radio systems, switching systems of different capacities integrated with underground cables, CorDect and medium capacity satellite systems. It is visualized that with the growth of telecom infrastructure, creation of information at the fingertips of society is not so distant a future.

Table 3.5. PC and Internet – International Comparison (As in Dec. 2001)

Country	No. of PCs per 100 persons	Internet Users per 10,000 persons
USA	62.25	4995.10
UK	36.62	3995.01
Australia	51.71	3723.05
Brazil	6.29	465.58
Mexico	6.87	362.23
South Africa	6.85	700.58
Egypt	1.55	92.95
Japan	34.87	4547.10
Malaysia	12.61	2394.96
China	1.93	260.00
Pakistan	0.41	34.49

Contd...

Country	No. of PCs per 100 persons	Internet Users per 10,000 persons
India	0.58	68.16
Asia	3.31	437.49
World	8.42	823.24

Source: World Telecom Development Report 2002, as given in Tenth Five-Year Plan (2002-2007), Infrastructure, Vol. II, p.1052.

3.5.2.3.3. Call Centers

Call Center business in India is experiencing a very favourable atmosphere presently, because the leased line prices have fallen dramatically due to competition. The local loop has improved significantly. Over and above high bandwidth links are also being built. This new environment has created an opportunity for foreign companies to either outsource their call center operations to India-based companies or set up their own call center/integrated back-office hub in India. This has allowed foreign companies to capitalize on the availability of cheaper labour and better telecommunications.

India has become a favourite destination for outsourcing of back-office operations. This has opened the doors for India's highly skilled and educated resource pool. Today graduates as well as undergraduates from all disciplines are acquiring comprehensive training in soft skills, English language and accent neutralization. It is estimated that nearly 1.1 million jobs will be created in the IT-enabled services sector in India by 2008. Analysts in India say that the demands for personnels to manage these call centers are explosive. Greater development of call centers, and highly skilled educated resource pool became a reality mainly due to the quantity and quality enhancement that has taken place in the telecom sector.

3.5.2.3.4. Cyber cafes and Internet Use

In the initial stage cyber cafes and Internet usage was considered an urban phenomenon in India. According to Steward, the cyber cafes appeared on the Indian scene in the mid-1990s, mainly in metropolitan cities like Mumbai, Delhi, Bangalore and Chennai. However, cyber cafes over the years have mushroomed throughout India and today can even be found in small towns and some of the bigger villages mainly due to home use of the Internet which earlier remained out of reach for substantial proportions of the society in India. Cyber cafes seem to serve a crucial portion of Indian society as access points for the use of computers and the Internet. In general, the cyber-cafe users are young, the average age being 26 years. More than 70 per cent of the users are below 30. The biggest group of users are employees (44.9 per cent), followed by students (36.8 per cent), housewives (6 per cent), and the self-employed (5.5 per cent) with others (unemployed, retired, etc.) being 6.8 per cent.[19]

This does not mean that cyber cafes and Internet usage is limited to educated population only rather illiterate people are also using cyber cafes and Internet for various reasons. The General Secretary of the Internet cafe and DTP Owners Association of Kerala, Mujeeb Poolakal, says, "Nowadays, compared to the last two years, also illiterate people are coming for their needs. They come to collect information and mostly they want to send e-mails to other places or other countries. So now illiterate people are starting to come and they ask do you have this or that facility here, do I get this or that information here and so on."[20] This statement shows that illiterate people are recognizing the utility of cyber cafes and Internet. But we have to accept the fact that the use of cyber cafes and Internet by illiterate people at present are only to a minimum extent.

Since there is a lack of regulation for registration, and authoritative measurement, the exact number of cyber cafes in India can be estimated only roughly. In 2001, the Indian Market Research Bureau (IMRB) estimated around 12,000 cyber cafes in India. Caslon Analytics estimates the number of cyber cafes for all of India as approximately 50,000 in 2004.[21] These estimates show that cyber cafes are slowly becoming as access points to the Internet to a large proportion of the Indian population. That is why Amitabh Kumar, Chairman and Managing Director of Videsh Sanchar Nigam Limited visualizes greater growth of internet usage in India and says, "India has an advantage that the size of the market which can potentially go online is extremely large. Our middle class segment can exceed

200 million and take advantage of discounted airfares, online publications, online education as well as business-to-business transactions."[22]

3.5.2.4. Audio, Video and Digital Technologies

Convergence of audio, video and digital technologies is another important development in the global telecom scene today. The NTP 1999 declared, "Access to telecommunication is of utmost importance for achievement of the country's social and economic goals and availability of affordable and effective communication for the citizen is the core of the vision and goal of telecom policy." The policy promised that a balance between the provision of universal service to rural areas and the provision of high level services capable of meeting the needs of the country's economy would be provided, aiming to create a modern and efficient telecommunication infrastructure. Convergence of IT, media, telecom, and consumer electronics is planned to propel India into becoming an IT superpower. Another objective of the policy was to convert PCOs wherever justified into public tele-info centers having multimedia capability of ISDN services, remote database access, Government and community information system, etc.

3.5.2.5. Software Exports

India has seen remarkable growth of software exports from the country. This was possible because of the high-speed data connectivity of at least 64 kbps. The Software Technology Parks (STPs), introduced in the 1990s have boosted software exports of India from 100 million dollars in 1990 to more than four billion dollars recently. The heart of STPs is the earth station with connectivity to satellites for speedy communication overseas. Today, nearly 75% of the software exports are taking place from the STPs. The policy initiatives taken by the Government has created an environment where Indian telecommunication can take a great leap forward.

The Indian IT Industry recorded a compound annual growth rate of more than 42.4 per cent between 1995 and 2000. Software continues to contribute a major portion of the Indian IT industry's revenues. India's exports of computer software beat global recession in 2001-2002 (April-March) to grow by a healthy 31.4 per cent. In absolute terms, software and services exports went up to $7.8 billion in 2001-02 as against $5.9 billion in 2000-01. This represents 13.3 per cent of India's manufacturing exports.

The steady growth in exports of software is due to effects of software giants setting up bases in India to meet their global software requirements. India's exports of electronics hardware grew by 13.6 per cent in 2001-02 to $1.183 million from $1.041 million in 2000-01. The IT manufacturing industry has over 150 major hardware players supported by over 800 ancillary units and small time vendors engaged in sub-assemblies and equipment manufacturing. The combined export of software and services, and electronics hardware registered a growth of 28.7 per cent in 2001-02. In absolute terms, India's overall IT exports grew to $9.04 billion in 2001-02 from $7.0 billion in 2000-01. In 1999-2000, more than 185 of the Fortune 500 companies outsourced their software requirements to Indian software houses.

Nirupam Bajpai therefore strongly feels that the Government could do more for this industry by allowing new entry of major international players in telecom. These companies could lay down a tremendous fibre optic network in India and increase the bandwidth available for Indian business and put India even closer to the international scene[23], so that India's world-class engineers and scientists could keep India in the very forefront of this new technology.

3.5.3. Trend in Supply and Demand of DELs

The number of DELs in operation (i.e., main line in operation) has been taken as supply whereas demand has been computed by adding the number of subscribers in the waiting list to the number of DELs in operation. However, it is required that we keep in mind that the number in the waiting list, in certain cases, is unlikely to reflect potential demand for telecom services in the economy. The actual demand may be much more than what is revealed through waiting list. In the areas where telecom infrastructure is not adequate, demand may not get registered at all and remain suppressed.

Table 3.6. DEL: Supply and Demand (millions)

Year ending March 31	Direct Exchange Lines (DELs)	Waiting List	Demand
1981	2.15	0.45	2.6
1983	2.47	0.66	3.13
1985	2.90	0.84	3.74
1987	3.49	1.12	4.61
1989	4.17	1.42	5.59
1991	5.07	1.96	7.03
1993	6.80	2.85	9.65
1995	9.80	2.15	11.95
1997	14.54	2.89	17.43
1999	21.59	1.98	23.57
2001	32.44	2.92	35.36

Source: Indian Telecommunication Statistics 2002, Ministry of Communications, Government of India, as given in Infrastructure, February 2003, CMIE, Mumbai, p. 254.

Table 3.6 shows an interesting phenomenon. Total demand tends to exceed supply by a margin which does not get narrowed down as supply expands. Despite the increase in the number of mainlines for every hundred inhabitants, the waiting list for a connection is higher now than at the beginning of the 1990s. More than 2.92 million people are waiting for about 20 per cent of the current number of lines. Expressing its view on the unmet effective demand in telecommunication, the 1994 World Development Report on infrastructure for development said that, "Excess demand for infrastructure, coupled with very low rates of compensation to infrastructure staff, breeds corruption in both service and investment decisions. Where connections are rare and service is poor, employees often demand side payments from users to install or repair connections especially in telecommunications...."[24] It shows that market for fixed line is supply constrained and demand tends to increase as supply expands. Figure 3.2 also reveals that there is significant growth in supply of DEL in the 90s, the eventful decade of sectoral reforms. The growth momentum is sustained in the current decade with a positive supply gap.

3.5.4. Trends in Telecom Tariff

The globalization policies of the Government in telecommunication sector have resulted in substantial decline in tariffs for both basic and cellular services. This was done with the objective that rates should move in line with costs in a manner that growth of tele density and affordability are not affected. During the reform period, tariffs for all telecom services have shown a significant downward trend. It is evident from Table 3.7.

Table 3.7. Decrease in Tariffs for Local Calls

Distance	2000	2001	2002	2003	2004
Up to 50 kms	1.20	1.20	1.20	1.20	1.20
Above 50 kms. and up to 200 kms	6.00	4.80	4.80	2.40	2.40
Above 200 kms and up to 500 kms	15.60	12.00	4.80	4.80	2.40
Above 500 kms and up to 1000 kms	21.60	18.00	9.60	4.80	2.40
Above 1000 kms	30.00	24.00	9.60	4.80	2.40

Source: Annual Report 2004-2005, Department of Telecommunications, Ministry of Communications and Information Technology, Government of India, New Delhi, p. vi.

Table 3.8. Trends in Tariffs (Rs. per minute)

	1998-99	1999-2000	2001	2002	2003
NLD (Beyond 1000 km.)	30.0	30.0	24.0	9.6	4.8
ISD (United States)	61.2	61.2	49.2	40.8	24.0
Mobile	14.5	6.1	2.4	1.9	1.6

Source: Economic Survey 2003-2004, Government of India, Ministry of Finance, p. 182.

Consistent with the worldwide trend and keeping in view the market reality, Indian telecom sector has rebalanced the tariff structure. The chief features of the tariff order of TRAI were substantial reductions in long distance and international call charges, increases in rental and local charges, and steep cuts in the cost of leased lines. The first phase of rebalancing was done on May 1, 1999 when long distance STD and ISD tariff were reduced by about 23 per cent. The second tariff rationalization was done on October 1, 2000 and it further reduced long distance STD rates by an average of 13 per cent and ISD rates by 17 per cent. The third rationalization of tariffs came to effect from 14th March, 2002. This has resulted in reduction of STD tariffs by up to 56 per cent and of ISD tariffs by up to 47 per cent. It is clear from Table 3.8 that the STD charges for various distance slabs have declined during this period.

Besides International Long Distance charges have also come down during this period. Globalization period definitely brought greater benefits to the consumers in the form of decrease in tariffs. Though the rationalization of tariffs brought about revenue stress on the operators but it also brought about greater efficiency in the telecom sector. So we can say that various policy measures incited by the Government have resulted in significant reduction in long distance tariffs due to competitive pressures introduced in the telecom sector. Liberalization also caused some operators to promote a more rapid reduction in rates than planned. For example, mobile cellular tariffs were forced to reduce their monthly rental rates to Rs. 160 and maximum call charge to Rs. 1.90 per minute.

3.5.5. Growth in Tele-Density

The telecom network in India is not small in absolute terms. With over 12 million lines, it is the 14th largest in the world. Yet it suffers from an abysmally low penetration of 8.59 per 100 populations as in December 2004 when the world average was over 17.2 as in 2001.[25] Several steps were taken to improve the tele density in the country during globalization period. For this purpose additional Direct Exchange Lines were added to the existing ones. Over and above intensive efforts were made to cover more villages through Village Public Telephones. Also private sectors were encouraged to provide telecom facilities at a faster pace. As a result the total tele-density[26] in the country has increased from 1.28 as in March 1996 to 8.59 as in December 2004. The urban tele-density was 3.95 as on March 1996, but it increased to 25.90 as in December 2004. The rural tele density was only 0.29 as on March 1996, but it increased to 1.69 as in December 2004.[27] Within nine years the total tele-density has grown by 6.71 fold and the urban tele-density has grown by 6.55 fold and the rural tele-density has grown by 5.82 fold (Figure 3.4). This is a positive indication to prove that the globalization and liberalization policies introduced by the Government in telecommunication sector have resulted in positive growth.

When compared, India with other developed countries in terms of total tele-density, India's tele-density is very low. Despite greater achievement in terms of network expansion and mobile technology, India's tele-density is low. For this many hold the size of the population responsible. It is also true that countries with smaller network sizes than India are having much higher tele densities. This is evident from Table 3.9.

Table 3.9. Number of Main Telephone Lines per 100 Inhabitants

Country	1995	2001	2003
USA	60.73	66.45	116.43
UK	50.18	57.78	143.13
Brazil	8.51	21.69	42.38
China	3.30	13.81	42.32
India	1.29	3.38	6.60
Pakistan	1.70	2.4	4.42
World	12.3	17.2	—

Source: World Telecommunication Development Report 2003, ITU, as given in Economic Survey 2003-04, and 2002-03, Government of India, pp. 180 and 188.

However, in terms of total tele density[28], i.e., the sum of fixed lines and mobile subscribers per 100 inhabitants, India's comparative ranking in the world improved from 160 in 1990 to 145 in 2000, an improvement by 15 positions.[29] But Table 3.9 shows that countries like China and Brazil have gone much ahead of India in terms of tele-density. China started out with a higher tele density than India as of 1995, and obtained a higher growth rate over the following years. However, there is a consensus that the country needs a much higher volume of voice telephony, and tele-density needs to go up from existing levels of 8.2 per cent eventually to developed country levels of over 100 per cent.

3.5.6. Trends in Manufacture and Export of Telecom Equipments

India is a major manufacturer and exporter of a wide range of telecom equipments and services. The total production of telecom equipments and cables in terms of value has increased from Rs. 3,985 crore in 1992-93 to Rs. 8,300 crore in 1996-97 which further increased to Rs. 10,760 crore during 1999-2000. It further increased to Rs. 15,437 crore during 2001-02. The growth in telecom equipment production is illustrated in Table 3.10.

Table 3.10. Manufacture of Telecom Equipments

Year	Production (Rs. in Crore)	Year (Rs. in Crore)	Production
1992-93	3,985	1998-99	10,000
1993-94	5,500	1999-00	10,760
1994-95	7,000	2000-01	12,271
1995-96	7,750	2001-02	15,437
1996-97	8,300	2002-03	14,400
1997-98	9,960	2003-04	14,000

Source: Annual Report 2000-01 and 2004-05, Department of Telecommunication, Ministry of Communications and Information Technology, Government of India, New Delhi, pp. 4 and 11.

Table 3.10 reveals that manufacture of telecom equipments reached a total production of Rs. 15,437 crore during the year 2001-02. This is the highest production of telecom equipments that the telecom sector has ever achieved. From the year 2002-03 telecommunication manufacturing sector has experienced decline in its total production and its production has reduced to Rs. 14,000 crore for the year 2003-04.

India has been recognized as a key supplier of products and technologies for rural Telecom. Significant efforts are undertaken by the Government to increase the exports of telecom equipment services. Growth in exports of telecom equipment and services is seen in Table 3.11.

Table 3.11. Export of Telecom Equipments

Year	Service (Rs. in Crore)	Consultancy (Rs. in Crore)	Hardware (Rs. in Crore)
1993-94	456	118	58
1994-95	598	207	131
1995-96	1,108	235	310
1996-97	1,458	270	240
1997-98	2,232	313	296
1998-99	2,376	383	250
1999-2000	3,230	337	180
2000-01	2,882	368	450
2001-02	4,149	378	150
2002-03	3,050	327	402
2003-04	****	388	570

Source: Annual Report 2000-01 and 2004-05, Department of Telecommunication, Ministry of Communications and Information Technology, Government of India, New Delhi, pp. 4 and 11.

From Table 3.11 it is noted that there was a burst in the exports of services, consultancy and hardware in 1995-96 and the growth has been maintained both in the case of services and consultancy. Export of hardware has displayed a declining trend up to the year 1999-2000. But for the year 2000-01, the export of hardware achieved significant growth and the export of hardware sector obtained Rs. 570 crore for the year 2003-04.

3.5.7. Developments in Foreign Direct Investment

Foreign Direct Investment up to 100 per cent has been allowed in the telecom manufacturing sector and services like e-mail, voice-mail and internet, etc. For infrastructure providers up to 74 per cent DDI is allowed in case of radio paging service and end-to-end bandwidth providers. In case of Basic, Cellular, National and International Long Distance Service and Value Added Services, FDI is limited to 49 per cent. FDI up to 49 per cent is also permitted in an investment company, set up for making investment in the telecom companies' license to operate telecom services. During the period August, 1991 to September, 2004, 930 proposals of foreign direct investment of Rs. 41,369.11 crore were approved. The actual inflow of FDI up to August, 2004 was Rs. 10,273.05 crore.

Table 3.12. Inflow of FDI in Telecom Sector (Rs. in crore)

Year	FDI Inflow	Year	FDI Inflow
Till 1993	2.06	1999	212.67
1994	14.02	2000	288.58
1995	206.74	2001	3,970.90
1996	764.83	2002	1,081.50
1997	1,245.19	2003	301.40
1998	1,775.64	2004 (August)	409.52
Total			10,273.05

Source: Annual Report, 2004-2005, Department of Telecommunication, Ministry of Communication and Information Technology, Government of India, New Delhi, p. 13.

Table 3.12 and Figure 3.5 reveal that there has been greater inflow of foreign direct investment since the year 1993. In 1993 only Rs. 2.06 crore had come into India in the form of foreign direct investment. But actual inflow of FDI has increased to Rs. 3,970.90 crore during the year 2001. Out of this Rs. 10,273.05 was received through foreign direct investment from August 1991 to August 2004, manufacturing and other services received Rs. 6,822.55 crore as foreign direct investment and cellular, basic and telephone services received Rs. 3,359.50 as foreign direct investment. Globalization process incited in India thus created greater confidence and security in the minds of investors towards telecom sector which in turn attracted greater foreign direct investment in the telecom sector. That is why in terms of foreign direct investment telecom sector stood second.

3.5.8. Financial Performance

Table 3.13 indicates the financial performance of the department of telecommunication, which indicates a positive growth when we compare post-globalization data with the year 1980-81. The net receipts was only Rs. 157 crore in the year 1980-81 but it increased to Rs. 7,898 crore during the year 1998-99, which shows a considerable growth of 50.30 fold within 20 years of development. Comparative study between the year 1980-81 to 2002-03 shows that the net receipts has grown by 16.17 fold. Surplus over its expenditure was Rs. 125 crore in the year 1980-81, but for the year 2000-01 surplus recorded was Rs. 5,265 crore which is a growth of 42.12 fold. The positive growth in its financial performance is due to the spread of wireless access technology. The adoption in this technology has resulted in substantial reduction in the jelly filled cable and other associated wireless infrastructure.

Table 3.13. Financial Performance of the Department of Telecommunication

(Rs. Crore)

Year	1980-1981	1990-1991	1996-1997	1998-1999	1999-2000	2000-2001	2001-2002	2002-2003
Gross Receipts	632	3405	12266	17744	18257	10175	4274	5911
Networking Expenses	475	1857	6089	9846	10763	4798	2427	3371
Net Receipts	157	1548	6177	7898	7494	5377	1847	2540
Dividend to General Revenue	32	220	292	252	172	112	—	—
Surplus/Deficit	125	1328	5885	7646	7322	5265	—	—

Source: Economic Survey 2004-05, p. s-48.

Though the telecom sector is performing well with regard to performance for finance, yet the internal resources generated by the telephone companies are quite inadequate to meet the needs of the sector. The finance ministry has therefore claimed that unless FDI limits are lifted, large investments of Rs. 1,60,000 crore cannot be made. Table 3.14 shows the current annual surplus and reserves of six telecom companies—BSNL, MTNL, Bharati Televentures, Tata Telecom, Reliance Infocom and VSNL are in the excess of Rs. 57,000 crore in the financial year 2003, Rs. 65,834 crore in 2004 and Rs. 39,637 crore in 2005 (Reliance Infocom information not available). It shows that Indian telecom sector is not having sufficient reserves and surplus to carry out the entire expansion work that is necessary in urban and rural areas of India.

Table 3.14. Reserve and Surplus of Indian Telephone Companies

(Rs. in Crore)

Company	2003	2004	2005
BSNL	8400	9500	10500
MTNL	8867	9861	10906
Bharati Televentures	1803	2400	3350
VSNL	5265	7004	9860
Tata Teleservices	3701	4013	5021
Reliance Infocom	28978	33056	N.A
Total	**57014**	**65834**	**39637**

Source: Web sites of all Companies and as given by D. Chennappa, "FDI in Telecom in India: A Study", *Southern Economist*, Vol. 44, No. 10, September 15, 2005, p. 31.

3.5.9. Work Efficiency

Work efficiency of an organization is measured in terms of modernization and total number of staff employed to maintain and operate various capital equipments. Number of staff employed to operate and maintain 1000 DELs shows the ratio between the staff and DELs and the working efficiency of the staff undertaken. Table 3.15 and Figure 3.6 indicate that there is increasing decline in the total staff employed per 1000 DELs.

Figure 3.6 indicates that the manpower of the telecom sector has been employed in an efficient manner. In the year 1990-91 total number of staff employed per 1000 DELs was 74 and the ratio was 1:13.51, i.e. for 14. DELs 1 person has been employed to look after the working and maintenance of the same. Within 10 years of reforms, the work efficiency has improved considerably because during the year 2000-01 only 12 persons were employed for 1000 DELs, which means the ratio between per DELs and the staff employed was 1:83.33, i.e. for 83 DELs 1 staff was employed. For the year 2003-04, the ratio between the Staff employed and per DELs has further declined to 1:200. This indicates that the telecommunication sector has been employing its staff in an efficient manner to bring about greater cost-effectiveness in telecom sector. However, well-run phone companies worldwide use only 5 to 10 employees per 1000 phones.[30] A reduction from 74 (1990-91) to 5 (2003-04) employees per 1000 phones has taken nearly fifteen years. Taking nearly 15 years objectively cannot be considered as a satisfactory state of cost minimization and work efficiency.

Table 3.15. Staff per 1000 DELs

Year	Staff per 1000 DELs	Year	Staff per 1000 DELs
1990-91	74	1997-98	24
1991-92	64	1998-99	20
1992-93	57	1999-2000	15
1993-94	49	2000-01	12
1994-95	43	2001-02	9
1995-96	35	2002-03	8
1996-97	29	2003-04	5

Source: Annual Report 2004-05, as given by Ajay Shah, "Telecommunication – Monopoly vs Competition", India Development Report 1997, p. 243.

Work efficiency can also be measured in terms of quality service provided by telecommunication sector. Quality service can be interpreted to mean an ideal situation where minimum phone faults, breakdown free services and punctual in attending to the demands and complaints of the consumers. Worldover it is recognized today that quality service would influence indirectly the financial performance of the organization. The lower the breakdowns and phone faults the better would be the image of the telecommunication sector and customers patronage is likely to improve yielding more revenue. Table 3.16 and Figure 3.7 show that service of telecom sector has improved in terms of phone faults. For the year 1990-91 per 100 stations 18.5 phone faults were being registered per month. This has been reduced to 9.4 phone faults per month for 100 stations in the year 2003-04. Table 3.16 shows the quality service provided during last fifteen years. This also shows that there is every possibility to decrease the rate of phone faults over the years and to minimize it to the lowest level possible.

3.5.10. Rural Telephony

The Rural Sector plays a very important role for the balanced growth of our country and as found out by a survey every single effect in the telecom sector has a sixfold effect on

Table 3.16. Phone Faults

Year	Per 100 Stations per month	Year	Per 100 Stations per month
1990-91	18.5	1997-98	17.4
1991-92	19.0	1998-99	16.4
1992-93	18.2	1999-2000	15.5
1993-94	18.3	2000-01	13.8
1994-95	17.6	2001-02	12.5
1995-96	15.8	2002-03	10.5
1996-97	17.2	2003-04	09.4

Source: Annual Report 2004-2005, Department of Telecommunication, Ministry of Communication and Information Technology, Government of India, New Delhi.

the economy of India. To achieve sustainable development it is essential that people away from the capital city, representing the bulk of society, are given the opportunity to participate in and benefit from the global information revolution, even if in only the most basic ways. As Hudson rightly said, Information is critical to the social and economic activities that comprise the development process. Telecommunications, as a means of sharing information, is not simply a connection between people, but a link in the chain of the development process itself.

Table 3.17 reveals that there is constant growth in providing Village Public Telephones. Out of the 6,07,491 villages in the country, 5,24,606 villages have been provided with VTPs as on December 31, 2004. Of this, 5,11,941 VPTs have been provided by BSNL. The number of rural DELs in the country has increased from 122.72 lakh as on March 31, 2004 to 130.37 lakh as on December 31, 2004. But the share of rural areas DELs to the total DELs is comparatively very low to the urban areas share to the total DELs. As in December 2004 only 14 per cent of DELs are installed in the rural areas wherein the urban areas share in the total DELs is 86 per cent (Figure 3.8). The annual report of 2004-2005 of Department of Telecommunications is hopeful of greater development in the rural areas with the implementation of non-lapsable Universal Service Obligation Fund and broadband networking in the rural and remote areas.

Table 3.17. Details of Village Public Telephones

Status as on	Total VPTs
April 1995	1,72,511
April 1996	2,04,008
April 1997	2,60,727
April 1998	3,03,582
April 1999	3,40,640
April 2000	3,74,605
April 2001	4,08,922
April 2002	4,28,214
April 2003	5,13,127
April 2004	5,22,263
December 2004	5,24,606

Source: Various Annual Reports of Department of Telecommunication, Government of India.

Today in rural areas the growth and development is much slow in comparison with urban areas of India. The telephone traffic is mainly confined to villages that are close by or to villages within the same telecom center itself. It is obvious therefore that unless and until telephone service is made available in all the villages, it is difficult to expect higher calling rates and better traffic loading. Long distance calls revenues are less and hence phones are far less to justify the provision of rural telephone service and consequently the service has to be subsidized. This is a heavy burden on the exchequer.

3.6. TELECOM AND IT SECTOR

3.6.1. Employment Opportunities and ICT

Employment benefit of ICT (Information Centered Technology) occurs across wide range of skill spectrum. Apart from growth of employment and income in industries due to ICT, a whole range of ICT enabled activities and services have started booming. According to Noronha Frederic estimate nearly 6,00,000 jobs would be created in cyber kiosks in India in addition to possible employment due to spillover effects.[31] Some such examples include operations like data entry, preparation and maintenance of database, revenue accounting, preparation of payroll, processing of insurance claims, human resource services, call center operations, running of customer support centers, medical transcription, content development and animation, website services, software development, hardware repair and maintenance, systems engineering, systems design and integration, etc.

The process of job creation and productivity growth is expected to bring about market expansion supporting growth of domestic hardware and software industries broadening the base of ICT development. This, in turn, will induce R&D spontaneity enabling India to transit from the status of an importer of sub-assemblies of IT and telecom hardware to a higher state of development endowed with strong domestic manufacturing base of sophisticated hardware and software products booming from indigenous ideas, innovation and comparative advantage.

The Government on its own has taken major initiative to computerize work of various ministries and departments. Many State Governments have already computerized records, certificates, registration of deeds, issue of licences, various payments systems etc. Computerization is also spreading very fast in the field offices of the Government, financial and educational institutions. According to one estimate, 12,000 out of 45,000 bank branches have implemented major computerization.[32] Growing legitimacy of IT based transactions in Government has allowed successful implementation of e-business and e-commerce in the private sector. As a result India has succeeded in reducing transaction costs and increasing productivity. According to Manas Bhattacharya "in time to come, the battle against digital divide will be won and ICT will be leveraged to benefit the poor. Apart from higher earnings associated with productivity gains and job creation, benefits for the poor will also result from risk mitigation and reduction in vulnerability.... There will be general improvement in the quality of life of the poor.... E-education and e-medicine will surmount all the access barriers to reach the remote and isolated locations."[33]

3.6.2. Telecommunication Education in India

As India ventures into the telecommunications boom, it is necessary for its people to be part of the latest technological know-how. This transition can be brought about by means of skill oriented quality education in telecommunication. Since a number of major players in the country are investing in the upcoming telecommunications industry, it is necessary to prepare and train people in technological know-how.

Students at large could develop broad knowledge in business, technical, and communication disciplines as well as a depth of knowledge in specific elective areas chosen to best fit their career aspirations. This program in telecommunication is specifically designed to provide future telecommunication leaders who can manage telecommunication projects efficiently. These leaders are supposed to be equipped with management tools apart from technological understanding. India also has an excellent R&D and training standards. India needs to reform its rules, create more global awareness, change its policies in favour of more opportunities and encourage its major players to invest in the economy.

3.6.3. Trend in Technology

Technologies of mobile telecommunications and Internet are going to set the outline of further technological progress in the current decade and the next. The most recent initiative aims at convergence of voice and data received from multiple sources, both web based and real time video streams, in mobile hand held devices. Global satellite systems, mobile handsets and calling cards have made virtual presence possible almost everywhere and anywhere overcoming the barriers of distance, topography and remoteness.

3.7. CONTRIBUTION OF GLOBALIZATION TO TELECOM SECTOR

Economic liberalization has been very fruitful for Indian telecommunications industry. It has brought about significant progress. One of the important features of the liberalization process was that the entire spectrum of telecom services and the operation of market dynamics were open to the private sector. Starting from basic telephone with manual exchange to formation of Mahanagar Telephone Nigam Limited (MTNL) in 1986, India has seen a lot of changes in this effect.

3.7.1. Globalization and Opportunities

Globalization process introduced in telecom sector has brought about following opportunities:

- We have technically educated, motivated an intelligent workforce, who if given proper incentives like quality living and benefits, can be retained in India.
- India possesses cheap labor to attract foreign investments.
- Telecom software, telecom professionals, telecom infrastructure and telecom services are the key players in shaping today's economy.
- Revenue sharing strategies are leading to mergers and acquisitions, helping companies to enter new business opportunities, and generate employment, boosting the country's economy.
- Privatization of VSNL, along with its partnership with Tata has benefited not only the two companies but also the country at large.
- Information technology growth can push India into an IT superpower.
- India has huge project plans with foreign countries, which can attract further mergers, investments.
- Foreign companies that are facing problems in home market have already identified India as a potential market for business and therefore they are heavily investing in India.
- Software exports from Software Technology Parks are a huge potential business.
- Though global telecom picture looks gloomy but India possesses the competitive advantage in terms of its huge market size. Lot of new entrants in the telecom business are bringing investment opportunities.

- Telecom educational institutes are coming up to keep the professionals at par with the changing technology.
- New opportunities are generating more employment and creating a knowledge-based economy.
- Privatization of services in telecom sector has led to keen competition, as a result of which prices are reduced and more business opportunities are created.
- Increased availability of bandwidth has opened doors to new schemes making efficient usage, providing value added services and generating profits.
- For cellular operators providing long distance is a lucrative business opportunity and they can also concentrate on providing many value added services.
- Provision of not only basic services, but also, Internet, cellular, medical transcription, call center, prepaid services along with telecom software projects are potential opportunities for generating employment in the country.

Over and above, the globalization process has brought about certain benefits to the economy as a whole and consumers in particular. Following are the few achievements of globalization process introduced in telecommunication sector.

3.7.1.1. Emergence of Competition

Indian telecommunications sector has always been like a "Natural Monopoly". But this monopoly could not sustain itself with the technological changes taking place in the telecom sector. Dismantling of monopolies lead to emergence of keen competition and lowering of tariffs, leading to consumer satisfaction, better services, technological upgradation and sound infrastructure.

All telecom services like basic, national long distance, cellular, VSAT, etc., were opened to the private sector with free competition except those limited by Spectrum (cellular). The Indian telecom sector is the eighth largest network, with annual growth rate of more than 22% for basic services and almost 100% for Internet and cellular services. The lines added to basic services in last 5 years are one-and-a-half times more than that added in the last 5 decades.

3.7.1.2. Greater Benefits to Consumers

Before liberalization VSNL had a monopoly over international long distance calls. The end of Government monopoly has made a tremendous impact on the telecom sector as far as customers are concerned. While on the one hand VSNL will begin to face the challenge posed by private companies such as Bharti Telesonic, on the other hand consumers have already started enjoying a decline in ISD tariffs and improved services in international telephony. In fact, prominent Internet service providers have announced tariff slash of up to about Rs. 5 from Rs. 55 per minute (It is between Delhi and New York). India has a huge ISD market which accounts for transactions of about Rs. 7,500 crore.

India is proud today because various telecom reforms committed under NTP-99 are almost complete, some ahead of schedule. The impact of these reforms has been overwhelming because national long distance charges dropped by more than 60%, cellular air time charges are down by 8 times with even cheaper handsets. There is also an increased availability of bandwidth with efficient usage.

3.7.2. Limitations

The period of intensified globalization process has contributed many changes in the telecom sector. In certain areas the changes have been more profound. Despite these transformations, the pace of progress continues to be slow in the telecom sector in India. In a number of areas the reform process undertaken is yet to be touched. Apart from this, reform process in telecom sector is faced with several problems which are to be addressed to achieve the ideal type of development. The following are the limitations that are foreseen within the development of telecom sector in India:

- Slow reform process and slow liberalization affect the changes and makes the progress slow.
- Foreign companies wanting to invest in India are put-off due to continuously changing rules and tax policies.

- Since 1994 reform process, telecom density has only gone up to 3 as compared to the global average of 14.
- Though cellular is the most attractive business today, but still the overall number of cellular subscribers is very low and this market really needs to be tapped.
- China's early liberalization and the fast growing economy may prove to be a hindrance for India.
- Price regulations based on pre-set rate of return hinder the growth.
- Young, hardworking and intelligent workforce want to leave the country due to poor economic conditions and exploitation.

3.7.2.1. Ignorance in Scientific Research

Despite the fact that the number of cyber cafes in the urban areas of India has increased significantly, cyber cafes are mostly ignored in scientific research and political programs, which seem to prefer to concentrate on other public access services in libraries, community access centers, village information centers, schools or universities. Little attention has been paid so far to this obviously successful market-driven access model and there is a lack of empirical data, as well as a lack of user surveys measuring the usage patterns of these enterprises. Therefore, the users, the usage patterns and the relevance of cyber cafes for particular social groups in India remain almost unknown.

3.7.2.2. Privatization Failed to Touch Rural Areas

In early 90s, the Government recognized that private investment and association of the private sector would be absolutely necessary to bridge the resource gap. Reforms and investments are possible by placing primary responsibility for investment and service provision with the private sector and by placing sector planning and regulation responsibility with the Government. As a result the basic telecom services are to be privatized. The private sector in telecom sector is seen to be concentrating on 200 million middle class population of India, residing in about 300 cities and about 4,500 towns. The rural sector consisting of about 0.6 million villages does not seem to be their cup of coffee.

The bid held in 1994 had no companies bid for the telecom circle in Assam, North Eastern States, Andaman and Nicobar, Jammu & Kashmir and Himachal Pradesh. It seems that the Naxalite affected areas and terrorism affected area carry no commercial value for these companies. All the sectors whether in difficult terrorist affected areas, rural, or urban should get an equal opportunity for development. So far, the public sector incumbents have spearheaded expansion of rural telephony with very little contribution by the private sector. By the end of December 31, 2001, out of 0.4 million villages, the private operators covered only 718 villages and the rest was by the public sector. Private sector presence is prolific in Public Call Offices (PCOs) and Internet Kiosks in the cities and towns. However, there are certain pilot projects in the rural sector working to evolve cost-effective wireless technological solutions in partnership with local service providers.

3.7.2.3. Affordability

Affordability is the key to success in India. Till about few years ago, telephone infrastructure in India cost about Rs. 30,000 per line. Hence, the yearly revenue had to be 35 per cent of the investment (15 per cent finance charges, 10 per cent depreciation and 10 per cent operation) to break even which was next to impossible as it implied revenues of Rs. 11,000 per year per line, or a bill of Rs. 1,000 per month for a subscriber. Only 2 to 3 per cent of India's population can afford this. The scenario, however, is changing. The cost of telephone and Internet connection can easily be brought down to Rs. 10,000 per line. When the cost comes down to Rs. 10,000 per line, 50 per cent of the Indian population will be able to afford a telephone connection. India is a potential market size of 150-200 million telecom and Internet connections.[34]

3.7.2.4. Regulation of Government Sector

Regulation assumes the objective of profit-maximization on the part of those being regulated. It is in this context that incentive regulation makes sense. However, public sector undertakings controlled by Government do not necessarily follow a profit-maximization objective, nor do profits typically form an important element in performance. Government public sector undertakings are governed and controlled by vote bank norms rather than profit-maximization and financial performance. It is in this context that private operators also fear irrational competition from the Government owned telecommunication companies. Globalization process has not made any significant change in the philosophy on the basis of which various decisions are made within the Government owned public sectors like BSNL and MTNL.

3.7.2.5. Failed in Universal Service Obligation

The traditional strategy in India has consisted of using cross-subsidies, charging urban consumers more and rural consumers less. "The Universal Service Obligation Fund (USOF) in India's telecom sector is a unique institutional innovation which ensures provision of services at minimum cost in rural areas through a system of open bidding. At present, USOF is funded by imposing a levy of 5 per cent of adjusted gross revenue of telecom companies."[35]

It is said that many of the distortions in the Indian telecommunication system have their origin in the universal service objective. There is a basic conflict between achieving universal service objectives through prices and service conditions, and allowing competitive market forces to operate unfettered. At times, the universal service objective has been utilized to serve other interests. The Universal Service Fund was set up in order to resolve this basic conflict and achieve the universal service objective in a competitively neutral manner. The universal service argument must, therefore, be used most sparingly for justifying constraints on competitive market forces through license conditions, tariffs or access charges.

One of the prime concerns of the Government has always been to ensure accessibility and availability of telecommunication services, which may not be viable on pure commercial considerations. Universal Service Obligation thus arises from the requirements imposed as a result of Government policy, legislation, or regulation for providing telecommunication services, to certain customers, which can only be met at a loss or under cost conditions.

So far, Rs. 1700 crore have been made available to the operators for rural telephony. For the year 2005-06, a provision of Rs. 1200 crore was made for USOF support. As per the claims of Ministry of Communications and Information Technology 76,000 Public Tele-Info Centers and 5,000 High Speed PTCs will be set up to provide broadband connectivity in the rural areas. Further, the support is being used for the replacement of 1.84 lakh Multi Access Radio Relay based VPTs. 50 per cent of such VPTs have already been replaced and the remaining shall be replaced as early as possible. In spite of these claims we have not succeeded in providing telecom facilities to entire villages in India. Nearly 15-20 per cent of our villages in India are not yet connected with telecommunication facilities, and have not yet seen telephones in these areas. However, even if it is connected it does not function for many months and no one is there to repair the already established telecom installations in the rural areas. One of the objectives of National Telecom Policy 1994 was to achieve Universal Service covering all villages as early as possible. The Universal Service Obligation was built into the license of Basic Service providers itself in the form of DELs & VPTs targets that a private basic service provider was obliged to meet. Due to various reasons, the goal set out in NTP 94 for VPTs as well as USO was not achieved.

3.7.2.6. Socio and Political Considerations

Each stage of the liberalization process in India has been marked by awarding of contracts and licenses to those with most access to the state's decision-making processes along with many court battles and scandals. Liberalization concept has not emerged strongly at the ground level due to more democratic and pluralistic society. Many things going on simultaneously in the Indian telecommunications landscape reveal the many influences at work on the Indian State. The most powerful liberalization coalition includes international and domestic businesses supported by foreign Governments and international organizations. The opposing group also includes trade unions and politicians. As a result, the Indian states are juggling between these interest groups in producing one of the most complex liberalization programs ever undertaken.

India offers an interesting case of a state facing pluralistic pressures which has liberalized its marketplace, but safeguards and checks against unrestrained authority are few. Political institutions have long succumbed to the party in power, usually driven by special interests, and only recently have opposition parties started playing a significant role.

3.8. CONCLUSION

Telecommunications have played a critical role in shaping India's march towards progress and the importance they hold for the future of India cannot be overstated. "A new framework for infrastructure policy, consisting of competition between multiple players, under a regulatory framework defined by the state has made much headway in the area of telecom. The successful implementation of reforms since 1991 has resulted in unprecedented growth of the sector. It has enabled the adoption of latest available technologies. The perception about telecom services, until recently considered an elitist luxury, has changed to a preferred good of mass consumption with increasing usage of telecom and IT services. The benefits from increased market access for the masses, improved productivity and market efficiency, and unprecedented innovation in business models and organizational structures are now widely recognized."[36]

Therefore, we can conclude by saying that, "the liberal argument is in favor of making the best possible use of the forces of competition as a means of coordinating human efforts, not an argument for leaving things just as they are. It is based on the conviction that, where effective competition can be created, it is a better way of guiding individual efforts than any other. It does not deny, but even emphasizes, that, in order that competition should work beneficially, a carefully thought out legal framework is required and neither the existing nor the past legal rules are free from grave defects."[37]

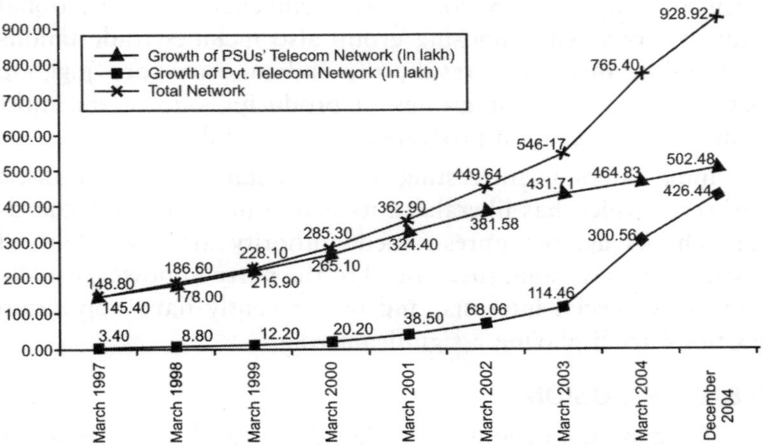

Figure 3.1. Growth of Telecom Network (PSUs & Private) (In lakh)

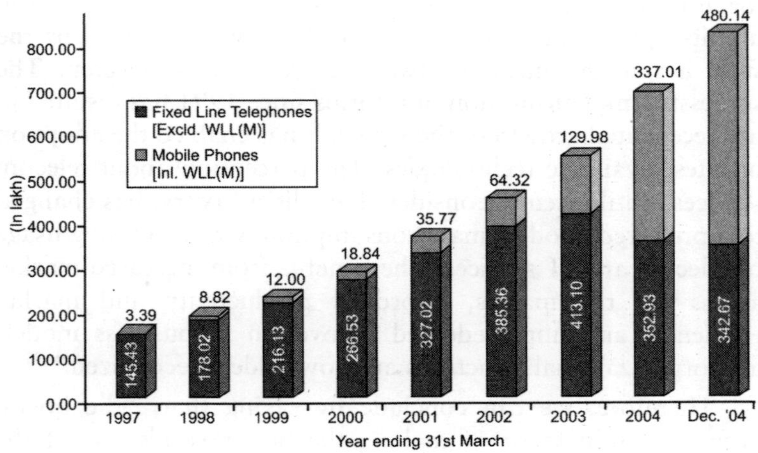

Figure 3.2. Fixed Line Telephones and Celullar Mobile Phones

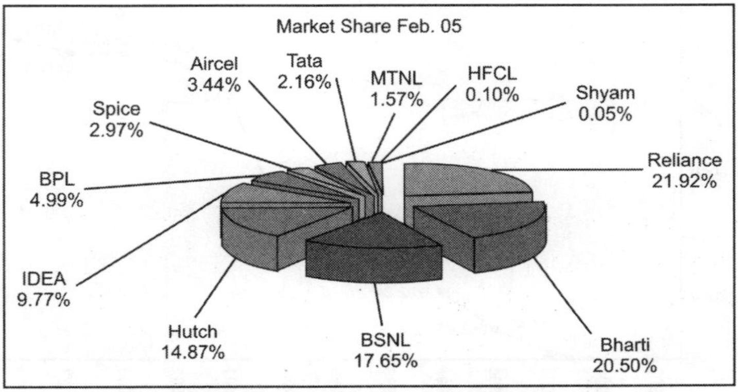

Figure 3.3. Market Share of Mobile Subscribers

Source: COAI, AUTSPI, Statistics Ex. MTNL (WLL), IndianInfoline.com, India infoline feature, "Telecom Sector Update, Feb. 2005", March 11, 2005.

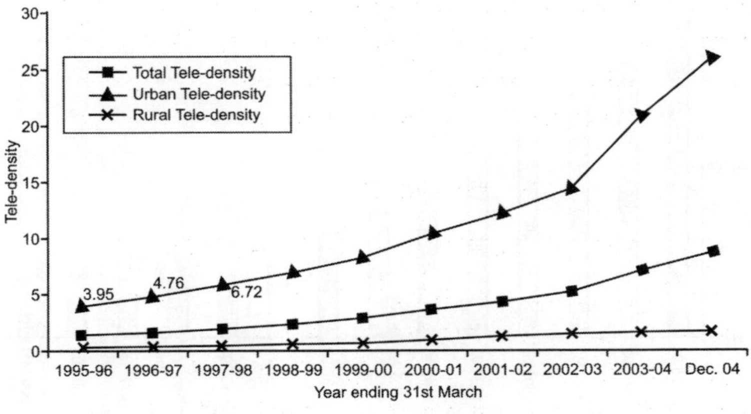

Figure 3.4. Tele-density (Number of Telephones per 100 Population) Since 1995-96

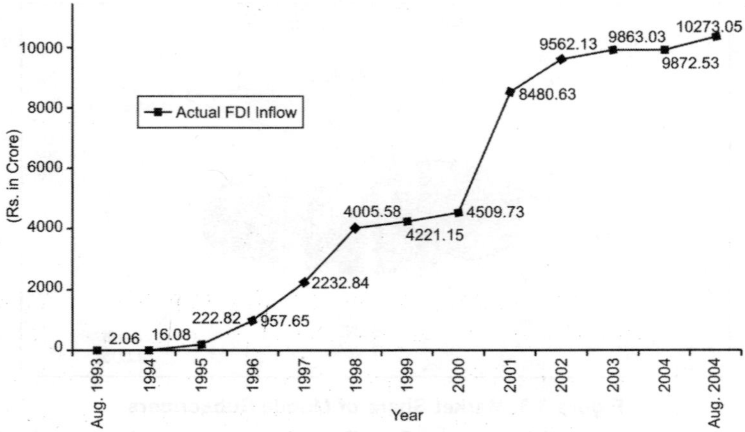

Figure 3.5. FDI Inflow year-wise (August 1991 to January 2004)

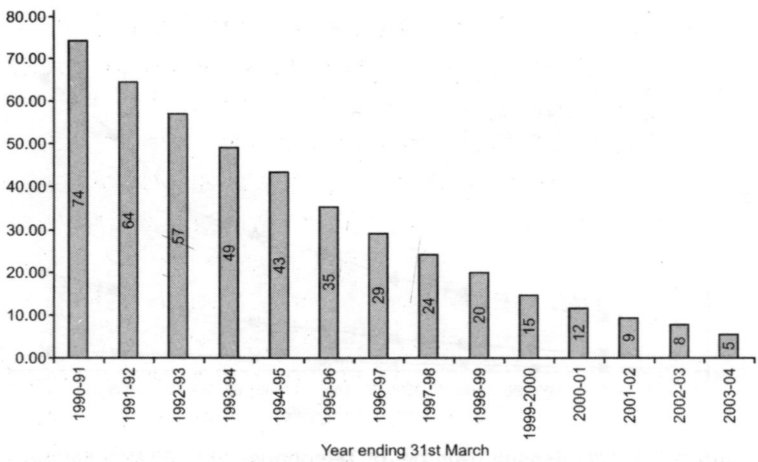

Figure 3.6. Staff per 1000 DELs

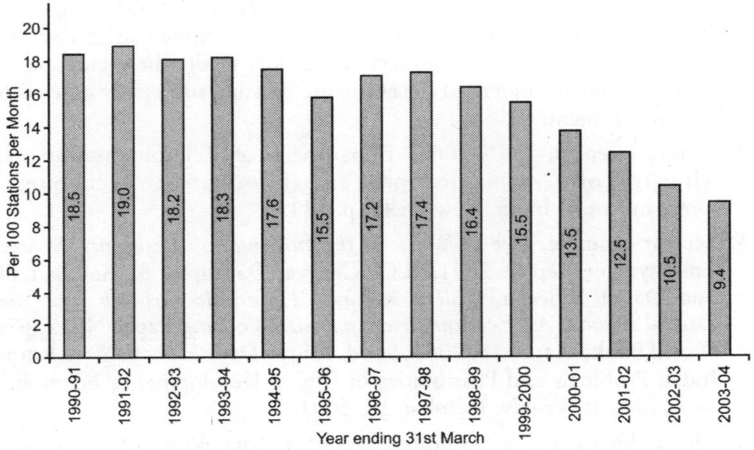

Figure 3.7. Phone Faults (BSNL & MTNL)

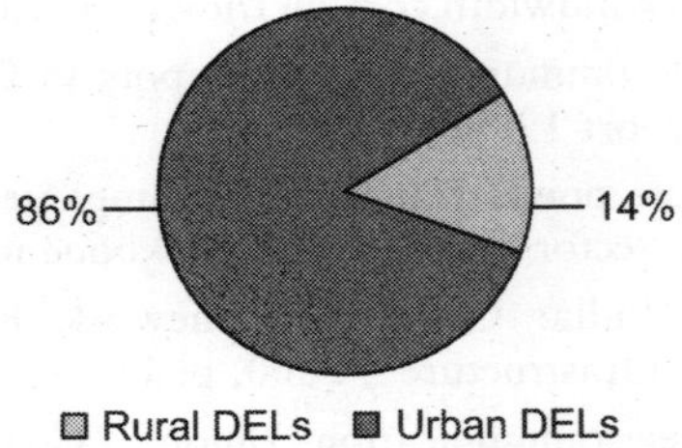

Figure 3.8. Share of Rural and Urban Areas in the Total DELs as on December 2004

END NOTES

1. Quoted from the website http://www.indiainfoline.com/nevi/vsmt.html
2. Government divested 25 per cent strategic stake of Videsh Sanchar Nigam Limited (VSNL), a public sector monopoly incumbent in ILD telephony to Tata Group in the private sector out of 52.97 per cent equity held by the Government. This was followed by opening up of ILD business to private players from April 1, 2002, terminating VSNL monopoly two years ahead of schedule, VSNL, 16th *Annual Report, 2001-2002*, p. 5.
3. Till 1986 telecommunication was a public utility owned by the Government of India. Mahanagar Telephone Nigam Limited (MTNL) was created in 1986 as a PSE to take out telecommunication services from the Government entirely in the cities of Delhi and Mumbai. It

was in the same year that VSNL was created in the ILD segment. Bharat Sanchar Nigam Limited (BSNL) was formed as a PSE on October 1, 2000 as a telecom service provider in all other places. Both these incumbents inherited the entire pre-existing subscriber base with the Government.

4. *Annual Report, 2004-2005*, Department of Telecommunications, Ministry of Communications and Information Technology, Government of India, New Delhi, p. 111.
5. See for example, *Life at Work in the Information Economy*, World Employment Report 2001, ILO, Geneva; Dasgupta, S., Somik Lall and David Wheeler, *Policy Reform, Economic Growth and the Digital Divide: An Econometric Analysis*, Working Paper No. 2567, World Bank, March 28, 2001; Sood, Aditya Dev, 'How to Wire Rural India, Problems and Possibilities of Digital Development', *Economic and Political Weekly*, October 27, 2001.
6. Manas Bhattacharya, "Telecom Sector in India: Vision 2020", India Vision 2020, Planning Commission, Government of India, New Delhi, p. 665.
7. http://www.indiabandwidth.com/dir1/longdist21.html
8. Ajay Shah, "Telecommunication: Monopoly vs Competition", India Development Report 1997, p. 239.
9. Public and private power transmission companies, Indian Railways, and other public sector agencies with backbone networks.
10. World Bank, "India: Country Framework Report for Private Participation in Infrastructure", 2000, p. 11.
11. International Telecommunication Union, "Competition Policy in Telecommunication: The Case of India", November 2002, p. 10.
12. *Economic Survey 2002-2003*, p. 191.
13. ITU, World Telecommunication Development Report 2002, Geneva, 2002, p. 13.
14. http://www.india-cellular.com/News-July-2002.html
15. IndianInfoline.com, India infoline feature, "Telecom Sector Update, Feb. 2005", March 11, 2005.
16. http://www.indiabandwidth.com/dir1/longdist32.html
17. http://www.indiabandwidth.com/dir1/longdist32.html
18. Noronha Frederic, Internet for All: Indian Villagers to Get Access at Prices they can Afford, www.tenet.res.in.
19. Businessworld, *The Marketing Whitebook 2005*, New Delhi, India, 2005, p. 72.

20. Anikar M. Haseloff, "Cybercafes and their Potential as Community Development Tools in India", *The Journal of Community Informatics*, Vol. 1, No. 3 (2005), p. 14.
21. As referred by Anikar M. Haseloff, "Cybercafes and their Potential as Community Development Tools in India", *The Journal of Community Informatics*, Vol. 1, No. 3 (2005), p. 2.
22. Uday Lal Pai, *India Tops Internet Reliability In Asia*, http://asia.internet.com/cyberatlas/0913-india.html
23. Nirupam Bajpai, *Ten Years of Indian Reforms: The Unfinished Agenda, Infrastructure*, CMIE, Mumbai.
24. *World Development Report*, 1994, p. 31.
25. *Indian Infrastructure Report, 2004*, 3i Network.
26. The tele-density means telephone per 100 population.
27. *Annual Report 2004-2005*, Department of Telecommunications, Ministry of Communications and Information Technology, Government of India, New Delhi, p. 98.
28. India's tele-density as on December 31, 2004 was 8.59.
29. ITU, *World Telecommunication Development Report, 2002*, Geneva, 2002, p. 56.
30. Ajay Shah, "Telecommunication: Monopoly vs Competition", *India Development Report, 1997*, p. 243.
31. *Ibid.*, p. 318.
32. www.nasscom.org.
33. Manas Bhattacharya, "Telecom Sector in India: Vision 2020", *India Vision 2020*, Planning Commission, Government of India, New Delhi, p. 673.
34. Shoba Warrior, Telecom Sector Offers Big Growth Opportunity, *Rediff Report*, May 18, 2002.
35. *Economic Survey, 2004-2005.*
36. *Economic Survey, 2003-04*, p. 180.
37. Source is unknown.

Transport Sector and Globalization in India

4

4.1. INTRODUCTION

It is universally recognized that an effective transport system is crucial for sustained economic growth and modernization. It is also considered that transport plays a significant role in the overall development of a nation's economy. Inadequacy in this infrastructure is an important deterrent for the success of a nation's effort in diversifying its production and trade. It is not only the key infrastructural input for the developmental process but also plays a significant role in promoting national integration.

The twenty-first century made us to realize that transport innovations and developments influence the pace and growth of economic development. Obstacles in movement restrict the market, increase production cost and raise prices beyond competitive reach of the consumers. Therefore, a higher rate of growth will mean higher transport demand. Many say that transport sector runs parallel to the growth of GDP. Transport is also necessary for connecting villages with towns, market centres and in bringing together remote and developing regions closer to one another. Transport being a key input for production processes, adequate provision of transport infrastructure and services helps in increasing productivity and lowering production costs.

India's resolution to move to greater heights in transport sector is certainly going to cause greater demand for transport which in turn will lead us to experience a high growth rate. The Ninth Plan therefore rightly emphasized "the need for improving the capacity and quality of the transportation system through technological upgradation and removing distortions in the inter-modal mix by evolving a national tariff and investment policy.... It also laid stress on...the need for ensuring an improved transport system to provide speedy, efficient, safe and economical carriage of goods and people."[1] Today, other modes have developed providing transport more effectively and efficiently. Pipelines for the movement of liquids, aircraft for higher speed long distance travel and trucks offering speed, flexibility and door to door service for short and medium levels provide better alternatives.

Road transport has close linkages with the economic development and social integration of the country. It is the dominant mode of transport for movement of passengers and freight in India. It is ideally suited for short, medium and long distance traffic. The long distance traffic is served by National Highways and State Highways, inter-district and intra-district traffic by major district roads, feeder traffic connecting rural centres of production to market outlets by other district roads and local traffic by village roads and urban roads. It has extra advantage in terms of easy availability, flexibility of operation, adaptability to individual need, door-to-door service and reliability. It is the main means of transport in hilly and remote areas. As a result road transport earned an increasingly higher share of passengers and traffic freight in comparison to other modes of transport. It is one of the basic infrastructures for economic development of backward areas. It also provides feeder services to rail traffic, airways, ports and harbours.

Road transport also has a unique role in the movement of people and goods and offers a cheaper and more viable means of transport. It is used to meet the needs of local movement of goods and passengers. In recent times the multiplication of road transport has been necessitated due to the enormous increase in population. The history of motor transport in India began in the year 1898. Since then there has been a gradual development of mechanical mode of transport in the country. In the beginning of 19th centaury though motor vehicles were seen in all the motorable roads in the country, but the importance of mechanical mode of transport was realized during the period of First World War.[2] After the First World War a number of disposed vehicles were used as the means of transportation of civilians. As a result the popularity of transport increased and the number of more vehicles in India went on increasing continually.

With Independence of India, passenger road transport industry has been growing fast with a huge growth potential. The various State Transport Undertakings came into existence gradually after the enactment of the RTC Act of 1950. The development of road transport further developed as a result of inclusion of road transport activity in the list of industries to progressively nationalized under Industrial Policy Resolution Act of 1956. To fulfill the social responsibility of the Government in the transport device several State Transport Undertakings have come into existence over the years. The progress made by the State Transport Undertakings in all its operational aspects during the early four decades of Independence of India is indeed commendable.

4.2. ROAD SECTOR PRIOR TO 1991

To promote socio-economic development of a country it is essential to have adequate infrastructure facilities. Roads establish rural-rural, urban-urban and rural-urban connectivity by encouraging the flow of goods and services and mobility of people between regions. "There has been a steady growth in the road network between 1950-51 and 1989-90. The total length of national highways has increased by about 70 per cent between 1950-51 and 1989-90 while the increase in the case of all other roads is of the order of 544 per cent."[3] Thus quantitatively India's road length is highly impressive and comparable with any other large country in the world.

In 1950-51 only 39 per cent of total length was surface. This rose to 43.3 per cent in 1970-71 and 46.7 per cent in 1984-85. This leaves over 50 per cent of the road length in the country unsurfaced. Therefore, in qualitative terms and carrying capacity India's road network is not internally comparable. The road traffic in terms of all types of motor vehicles and goods carriage has increased rapidly since Independence. "In comparison with the growth of vehicular population as well as freight and passenger traffic, the road network has registered an annual growth rate of over 4 per cent i.e., from 0.4 million kms in 1951 to 3 million kms in 1995. Further, the network has a large proportion of village roads which are generally of limited value from the point of view of heavy vehicular traffic. The main arterial network comprising the National Highways and the State Highways is just over 5.0 per cent of the total road system, while it carries more than 75 per cent of the road based traffic. This trunk route system has grown even more sluggishly than the road system as a whole. ... Most of the growth has occurred in the rural road sector, while the National and State Highways have expanded at the rate of 1.24 and 1.82 per cent per annum respectively."[4]

The Ninth Five-Year Plan states that "the capacity of the highways system in terms of carpet width is not adequate. In spite of heavy congestion on most of the National Highways and State Highways only 3.41 per cent of the National Highways and 0.57 per cent of the State Highways are standard multilane. In the case of the National Highways about 74 per cent of the network is double lane, while about 78 per cent of State Highways is either single standard lane or below in spite of the fact that the volume of traffic on some of the State Highways is comparable to that plying on the National Highways."[5]

The differential growth rates in capacity augmentation on the arterial network and traffic demand therefore "has led to the present situation in which large section of the National Highways and some sections of the State Highways are used well over 100 per cent of their intended economic capacity. The result of this mismatch between traffic growth and capacity is slow speeds, high vehicle operating costs, environmental pollution and high incidence of accidents. Further the road assets deteriorate fast because of increased traffic and heavier loads. Poor maintenance of assets also results in a much larger proportion of the network becoming unserviceable."[6]

4.3. LIBERALIZATION ERA AND POLICY INITIATIVES

Within the given situation the planners thought that a well defined plan taking a perspective of 15-20 years can alone help us to address the important issue of capacity constraint experienced in this sector. It was felt that "an integrated policy ...would inform the road development programme with accent on gradual modification of the modal mix through a suitable inter-modal coordination mechanism."[7] Various policy initiatives, decisions and programmes such as setting up of the National Highway Authority of India was set up under the NHAI Act, 1988, adaptation of modern road construction technology, construction of modern high density corridors, establishment of central road fund revamped, development of State Highways and major district roads, incentives to attract private and foreign direct invest in the transport sector, regular maintenance of roads, and Land Traffic Act, 2002 were undertaken to enhance the performance of transport sector during this period.

So the primary objective of this chapter is to find out a comparative performance of transport sector prior to liberalization and post-liberalization period. Is it that the transport sector has improved in its qualitative and quantitative performance due to various policy initiatives implemented during post-liberalization period? Is the transport sector in general better than what it was prior to liberalization? Which are the areas in which the performance of transport sector has improved? This chapter tries to answer these questions and examines the performance of transport sector.

4.4. PERFORMANCE OF TRANSPORT SECTOR

4.4.1. Growth of Transport Sector

The aggregate length of roads in India has increased from 0.4 million km in 1950-51 to 3.3 million km in 2000-01. For many years, railways were the dominant mode of transport in India. However, there has been a gradual shift from rail to road. In 1960, it was estimated that railways carried 85 per cent of goods traffic (in ton km) and 51 per cent of passenger traffic (in passenger km). By 2001, it was reported that this had declined to 32 per cent of goods traffic and 13 per cent of passenger traffic. Inland water transport (IWT) has remained a minor player in the nation's transport systems, with a traffic share of less than one per cent (0.15 per cent).

During the 1990s, India's economy has grown by 6 to 7 per cent a year, and its total transport demand has grown by about 10 per cent a year. The road sector, which already enjoys an 80 per cent share of land transport demand, has witnessed a 12 per cent annual growth in freight demand and 8 per cent in passenger demand. Meanwhile, both air and ocean transports have enjoyed healthy growth. But the demand for rail transport has grown at a slower pace, at just 1.4 per cent a year for freight and 3.6 per cent a year for passenger.

The demand for transport will, in all likelihood, grow by at least 10 per cent a year because of 7-8 per cent GDP growth per year. India's total road network now approaches 3 million kilometers. It is the second largest road system in the world. But the existing road network suffers from problems such as inadequate pavement thickness, distressed bridges, a large number of railway crossings, absence of urban bypasses, and poor riding quality. Of the total 34,000 kilometer National Highway network, 5 per cent is four lanes, 80 per cent is two lanes, and 15 per cent is one lane. The aggregate length of roads has increased eightfold, but traffic has increased almost twenty-fold. The length of national highways has increased only 1 per cent a year, and the length of State Highways has increased 1.8 per cent a year. These results in lower speeds and higher fuel consumption and emissions.

As a result nearly half of the total consumption of petroleum products in India is attributed to the transport sector. This sector also accounts for a substantial and growing proportion of air pollution in cities. There is a significant variation in construction quality and road conditions nationwide. India's highways carry approximately 60 per cent of the country's total freight, measured in billions of tons per kilometer. This demand is expected to double every 12 years. The demand for passenger transport is expected to double every 8 years.

4.4.2. Growth in National and State Highways Length

National and State Highways length have increased over the years. The growth of National Highways length had been much more than what was expected during liberalization era when it is compared with the period prior to liberalization. During 1980-81 to 1990-91 net increase in National Highways has been 1,873 kms; whereas between the year 1990-91 to 2004 September the net increase in the total length of National Highways has been 31,919 kms. It is important to note that there has been 94.85 per cent growth in National Highways length in terms of kms during post-liberalization period whereas this growth was just 5.89 per cent during 1980-81 to 1990-91.

Table 4.1. National and State Highways Length

(km)

Year	National Highways	State Highways	% change in National Highways	% change in State Highways
1981-82	31777	95654	00.33	1.37
1982-83	31767	96969	-0.03	2.01
1983-84	31817	97041	0.16	1.96
1984-85	31852	99262	0.11	2.29
1985-86	32088	100461	0.74	1.21
1986-87	32305	100970	0.68	0.51
1987-88	32446	115989	0.44	14.87
1988-89	32886	123131	1.36	6.16
1989-90	33479	124266	1.80	0.92
1990-91	33650	127311	0.51	2.45
1991-92	33666	128622	0.05	1.03
1992-93	33916	129876	0.74	0.97
1993-94	34249	132401	0.98	1.94
1994-95	34262	134085	0.04	1.27
1995-96	34508	135187	0.72	0.82
1996-97	34849	137119	0.99	1.43
1997-98	38517	136489	10.53	-0.46
1998-99	49585	137950	28.74	1.07
2004 September	65569	131899	32.23	-4.4

Source: Infrastructure, Centre for Monitoring Indian Economy, p. 92, and Buddhadeb Ghosh & Prabir De, *Indian Infrastructure Database 2005*, Bookwell, New Delhi, Vol. II, p. 741.

But in terms of State Highways prior to liberalization its growth had been much greater in comparison to post-liberalization period. Between the years 1980-81 to 1990-91 net addition to State Highways length has been 31,654 kms, whereas during 1990-91 to September 2004 net addition to State Highways length has been only 4,588 kms which is very marginal in nature. The Government along with National Highways should also give proper attention and consideration to state highways so that simultaneous development of roads is possible for better transportation.

4.4.3. National Highways and Its Achievements

There has been considerable growth in the National Highways in terms of quantitative growth. The achievements relating to four-laning, two-laning, strengthening of roads during post-globalization period has been satisfactory keeping in view of the quantitative growth achieved since Independence. Table 4.2 provides a clear picture of the different achievements during post-globalization period.

Table 4.2. Achievements on National Highways

Period	Total Length* (km)	Widening to Two Lanes (km)	Widening to Four Lanes (km)	Strengthening of Pavement (Nos)	Major Bridges
1947-1960	24000	14000**	Nil	Nil	169
1960-1990	33612	16000	267	9000	302
1990-2001	58112	3457	1276	7000	87
2001-2004$	65569				
Total		33457	1543	16000	558

Notes: * Length at the end of the period.

** Includes a length of 6000 km which were already two lane at the time of declaration as National Highways.

$ Up to September only.

Source: Tenth Plan, Planning Commission, Government of India.

From the year 1960 to 1990, i.e. for 30 long years the total road length added is just 9,612 kms. But between the years 1990-2001, i.e. within a period of 10 years India has succeeded in constructing net road length of 24,000 kms. Nearly 7,457 kms of road length has been added during 2001 to 2004. This is a great achievement within given context of the Indian economy. With regard to widening of four lanes nearly 1,276 kms work was undertaken and completed during this period. Nearly 7000 kms strengthening of pavements has been completed. This indicates that India has achieved greater growth in terms of national highways during post-globalization period.

4.4.3.1. Projects Undertaken

In recent times, there has been a realization that infrastructural constraints, particularly in the transport sector, hinder economic growth. The major impetus in the modernization of the roads sector, however, came only after the announcement by the Former Prime Minister Atal Bihari Vajpayee in October 1998 of undertaking the building of Rs. 54,000 crore cross country expressways. The Golden Quadrilateral links—Delhi, Mumbai, Chennai and Kolkata—the major metropolitan cities in the country. It involves a total length of 5,846 km of road, costing over Rs. 25,050 crore.[8]

The second part of the project involved connecting Srinagar with Kanyakumari and joining Silchar with Porbandar with four/six lane highways. North-South and East-West Corridors of NHDP covers a distance of 7300 km and it costs over Rs. 30,000 crore. As on 30 November 2004, four/six laning of 675 km has already been completed and work on 388 km is under progress. The remaining will be awarded in a phased manner.[9] Other works include connecting of major ports[10] to NHDP highways by about 400 km of roads. Over and above this more than 75 Railway overbridges are being constructed on NHDP crossing.

The Ministry of Road Transport and Highways has already identified seven National Highways stretches under this new initiative that will be taken up for 4-laning. These seven stretches extend over a length of 622 km in five States and would be 4-laned at an approximate cost of Rs. 2500 crore. The stretches are: (i) 100 km long Vadape-Gonde Section on NH-3 in Maharashtra, (ii) 118 km long Pimpalgaon-Dhule Section on NH-3 in Maharashtra, (iii) 45 km long Raipur-Aurang Section on NH-6 in Chhattisgarh, (iv) 57 km long Bharatpur-Jaipur Section on NH-11 in Rajasthan, (v) 115 km long Barhi-Ranchi Section on NH-33 in Jharkhand and (vi) 79 km long Meerut-Muzaffarnagar Section on NH-58 in Uttar Pradesh. The thrust to road development can be gauged from the fact that in

50 years (1947-1997) only 556 km of National Highways were 4-laned, but in a span of less than seven years, over 24,000 km would be 4-laned.

Four/six laning of 20 sections of the corridors, totaling about 265 km has been taken up for immediate implementation. Implementation of the balance 6,700 km will be taken up in stages to be completed by 2008-09. Apart from NHDP, there are about 41,290 km of NH which will be maintained with the funds available from the budget. Many development works[11] have been undertaken on the NH. During 2004-05, 264 proposals costing Rs. 615.322 crore have been sanctioned. A total of 221 km of single lane has been widened to two-lane.

The implementation of the project is entrusted to the National Highway Authority of India (NHAI). While implementing this project the primary focus of NHAI will be on developing international standard roads with enhanced features like (i) better riding surface, better road geometry, better traffic management and adequate signages, markings and safety barriers, (ii) divided carriage ways and service roads, (iii) grade separators, over bridges and underpasses for uninterrupted traffic flow, (iv) bypasses and (v) wayside amenities along with ambulances and cranes.

4.4.3.2. Capital Expenditure through NHAI

Capital expenditure through the National Highways Authority of India also increased sharply over the years. Total capital expenditure through NHAI for the year 1999-2000 accounted for Rs. 746 crore and it further rose to Rs. 1,261 crore, and Rs. 9,525 crore for the years 2000-01 and 2003-04 respectively.

Table 4.3. Capital Expenditure through NHAI

Year	Capital Expenditure (Rs. crore)	Per cent to GDP
1999-2000	746	0.04
2000-01	1,261	0.06
2001-02	3,997	0.18
2002-03	6,584	0.21
2003-04	9,525	0.33
2004-05 (Projected)	9,000	0.29

Source: Economic Survey 2004-05, p. 207.

In terms of GDP percentage total capital expenditure through NHAI accounted for 0.04 per cent for the year 1999-2000 and it increased to 0.33 per cent GDP for the year 2003-04. It is remarkable to notice that within five years total capital expenditure through NHAI has increased 8.2 fold. Indian economy could achieve increased capital expenditure mainly due to determined efforts undertaken by the Governments to build national highways throughout the Ninth Five-Year Plan period.

4.4.4. Rural Roads

Road connectivity and access to important social and economic centers is considered to be a key component of rural development. "Rural roads and different modes of transportation act as ambassadors between the villages and the towns. They play an important role in the marketing of agricultural produces, purchase of agricultural and consumable articles, attending schools, colleges, hospitals and the offices, etc., by the rural people and thereby assist in the development of the country. ... They play a stupendous role in the supply of input factors, enlarging the size of the market, fetching better price, promoting labour mobility, providing a fillip to the establishment and development of industrial enterprises, etc. So much is the role of rural roads in the overall development of the economy."[12] That is why over the years rural roads were given importance in the planning process. As a result several schemes[13] have been implemented at different times towards the development of rural roads. The main objective of these schemes is to provide earth tracks within the village and to provide connectivity to State Highways and National Highways. But connectivity through all weather roads has still a long way to go. Status of accessibility of villages by all weather roads is given in Table 4.4.

States like U.P., M.P., Bihar, Orissa and Rajasthan and many hill states have low levels of village connectivity, which indicates that there still exist regional imbalances in the connectivity of villages. Under the Pradhan Mantri Gram Sadak Yojana (PMGSY) the Government has given greater importance to rural road development and village connectivity by allocating 50 per cent of the additional duty of Re. 1.00 per litre on diesel.

Out of 8,25,647 habitations requiring road connection under the PMGSY, those still unconnected are only 1,62,576.[14] The current value of the existing rural road network is estimated at about Rs. 2,400 billion. The maintenance of the existing rural road network requires about Rs. 50 billion per year, out of which only 20-30 per cent is available. The solution to this problem has traditionally been sought in more budgetary allocations rather than in improving the efficient use of existing funds. The need is to develop a national policy framework that emphasizes the sustainable management of rural road assets.

Table 4.4. Connectivity of Villages with Roads

Population Category	Total No. of villages	Number of Villages Connected				
		1980	1985	1990	1995	2000
1500 and above	71623	37950 (53%)	49495 (69%)	59722 (83%)	65704 (92%)	71000 (99%)
1000-1500	58229	21970 (38%)	28732 (49%)	35362 (61%)	44120 (76%)	52000 (89%)
Less than 1000	459465	107324 (23%)	142020 (31%)	166311 (36%)	173837 (38%)	200000 (43%)
Total	589317	167244 (28%)	220247 (37%)	261395 (44%)	283661 (48%)	323000 (55%)

Note: Figures withinin percentage is percentage of villages in each population category to the total number of villages in that category. The basis for population is 1981 census.
Last column gives quick estimates.

Source: Planning Commission.

The policy must emphasize sustainable financing, and community participation in maintenance. Community participation offers great help for mobilizing the support of local communities in resource generation, land acquisition, and tailoring the rural road programs. In this situation the Government's role is to build up the capacity of local communities for managing their road network. Local Government functions, Panchayat Raj bodies at district, block and village levels are expected to play an increasingly positive role in the construction and management of rural roads. The need for establishing close coordination between various rural organizations, local Governments, institutional arrangements and funds is necessary. Thus a suitable framework needs to be developed to encourage local communities to assume responsibility for their roads through limited financial support from the Government.

4.4.5. Growth of Motor Vehicles

Road transport is normally divided into traditional and modern categories. Bullock carts, camel carts, rickshaws, bicycles, hand carts, *thelas*, tongas, etc., fall under the traditional category while scooters, cars, trucks, buses, etc., fall under the modern or mechanized category. Very little data is available on the travel characteristics of the non-motorized modes of transport. It is said that in terms of tonne kms and passenger kms the share of non-motorized modes in total traffic is only five per cent and eleven per cent respectively. But the non-motorized modes are relatively inexpensive, environment-friendly, involve simple technology, have large employment potential and sustain the rural economy.

Table 4.5. Road Transport: Non-transport Motor Vehicles

Year	Two wheelers registered	Car registered	Jeeps registered	Tractors registered	Trailors registered	Other vehicles registered
1981-82	3065000	946763	141278			718382
1982-83	3511868	1060742	136003	577324	158650	58483
1983-84	4233872	1103090	178795	640727	172626	59814
1986-87	7658269	1442175	266980	603595	204257	334711
1988-89	10617219	1874003	394845	1081202	299684	124552
1989-90	12393548	2104985	438274	1152138	351200	133715
1990-91	14199858	2266506	443734	1269071	344561	145393
1991-92	15660801	2461519	480922	1419119	380801	170481
1992-93	17060105	2553990	505591	1517200	403092	173722
1993-94	18338480	2714639	555293	1672063	464398	167850
1994-95	20831428	2875651	614567	1737264	480790	145437
1995-96	23252287	3150951	671682	2091598	535489	210215
1996-97	25693206	3520660	725524	2156871	590178	215993
1997-98	28514522	3850892	828484	2326520	691037	200632
1999-00	33912954	4574013	896270	2641223	761799	300506

Note: Tractors and trailors are included in other vehicles for the year 1981-82.

Source: Infrastructure, Centre for Monitoring Indian Economy, February 2003, p. 118.

The development of mechanized transport has taken place at a rapid pace in the country. For instance, the number of vehicles registered in India has increased by over nine times during the period 1981-2000. In 1981, the total number of motor vehicles stood at 51.81 lakh which shot up to 483.93 lakh in 2000. Increase in mechanized transport is mainly due to industrialization and modernization that has been initiated through the liberalization process.

Table 4.6. Road Transport: Transport Motor Vehicles

Year	All Vehicles registered	Passenger three wheelers registered	Goods LCVs registered	Taxis registered	Buses registered	Trucks registered
1980-81	5181394	142073		100845	153909	554000
1981-82	6055000	161740		119297	173000	613000
1982-83	6718539	181955	48126	154459	177748	647633
1983-84	7759351	238979	55710	142426	195807	719269
1984-85	9170000	276006		160355	223000	822000
1985-86	10489835	338225		172837	227000	863000
1986-87	12346545	385924	51294	185946	246848	966546
1987-88	14732341	425545		201651	265804	1114000
1988-89	16693087	490562	108714	211881	293751	1196674
1989-90	19332206	538358	130325	253672	312301	1324196
1990-91	21374216	617365	156931	243748	331096	1355953
1991-92	23507413	669538	130183	262338	358165	1513546
1992-93	25346462	727996	148006	284405	380229	1592126
1993-94	27227173	756797	141585	347118	418845	1650105
1994-95	30294656	897383	144848	350331	423383	1793574
1995-96	33782720	1010344	349419	381011	448415	1681309
1996-97	37231533	1165140	454857	415740	488169	1805195
1997-98	41118302	1359035	540185	474785	506375	1877481
1998-99	44875000					
1999-00	48392925	1577463	803451	571410	476355	1877481

Note: Goods LCVs are included in other vehicles for the year 1981-82 to 1989-90.

Source: Infrastructure, Centre for Monitoring Indian Economy, February 2003, p. 117.

4.4.6. Physical Performance of SRTUs

There has been overall improvement in the performance indicators of SRTUs over the years. Vehicles productivity has increased from Rs. 257 revenue earning km per bus held per day in 1989-90 to Rs. 305 revenue earning km per bus held per day in 2001-02. Staff productivity has increased from 35.3 revenue kilometer per worker per day in 1989-90 to 47.8 revenue km per worker per day in 2001-02. Fuel efficiency improved from 4.35 kilometers per litre to 4.69 km per litre during the same period. Bus staff ratio to fleet operated has also improved from 1:7.63 in 1976-77 to 1:7.16 km in 2001-02. However, the performance of the undertakings, their performance, efficiency and productivity have varied from State to State. The undertakings in Andhra Pradesh, Karnataka, Haryana, Himachal Pradesh, Maharashtra and Tamil Nadu performed very well in physical terms while those in the northeast, Bihar and Orissa lagged behind. The State which has been performing considerably well has continued to perform well and those States which have not been performing have not improved in their performance in any way. This goes to prove that the liberalization era has in no way improved the performance of SRTUs.

4.4.6.1. Financial Performance

Financial performance of an enterprise does not refer to the rate of profits, it has been earning. Above all it denotes the trends of its expenditure and income and consequent surplus or deficit. As far as the financial performance of the State Road Transport undertaking is concerned, it has been reporting losses on a continual basis year after year. Economic reforms in no way could improve its financial performance. In spite of increase in the gross receipts of State Road Transport Undertakings over the years the SRTUs have not succeeded in reducing their operating expenditure as well as total expenditure over the years. As a result the reported losses have been on an increase. For example, for the year 1991-92, the reported net loss was of Rs. 650.89 crore (Table 4.7). It increased to Rs. 1055 crore for the year 1998-99 and further increased to Rs. 1886 for the year 1997-98. According to the Tenth Five-Year Plan, the total loss by the undertakings had increased to Rs. 8,843 crore in the

Ninth Plan as compared to Rs. 2,679.71 crore in the Eighth Plan. So we can say that STUs have been inefficient, uneconomical and incapable in dealing with finance despite an improvement in the physical parameters.

Table 4.7. Financial Performance of State Road Transport Undertakings

Items	1992-93	1995-96	1996-97	1997-98	1998-99	1999-2000
1. *Gross Receipts*	6643	9006	9494	11125	11984	13685
(i) Operating Revenue	6202	8478	8909	10490	11351	12953
(ii) Misc. Receipts	446	527	585	635	633	732
2. *Total Expend.*	7008	9607	10511	12495	13577	15571
(i) Operating Expend.	4943	6967	7680	9278	10075	11809
(ii) Dep. Res. Fund	756	699	705	821	877	871
(iii) Taxes	916	1220	1308	1433	1558	1705
(iv) Int.	308	313	365	441	479	567
(v) Misc. Expend.	265	402	485	522	588	618
3. Net Profit/Loss (1-2)	-344	-594	-1055	-1593	-1886	N.A
4. Internal Resorces (3+2ii)	232	105	-342	-549	-716	-1015
5. Term loan re-payments/ adjustments	302	403	315	526	317	473
6. Contribution to the Plan (4 -5)	-70	-299	-665	-1075	-1033	-1488

Source: Planning Commission.

If we take individual SRTUs into consideration most of the SRTUs incurred losses and are faced with serious financial constraints. As per Table 4.8 other than Maharashtra and Tamil Nadu all other SRTUs are faced with heavy losses over the years. Maharashtra S.R.T.C made a profit of Rs. 15.95 for the year 1995-96 and it increased to Rs. 117.72 crore for the year 2000-01. In the same way the S.T. of Tamil Nadu made a profit of Rs. 122.17 crore for the year 1995-96 and it rose to Rs. 244.27 crore for the year 1998-99. Unfortunately, the total profit earned decreased to Rs. 163.51 crore for year 2000-01.

Table 4.8. State Road transport Companies: Profit/Loss

(Rs. Crore)

Year	1995-96	1996-97	1997-98	1998-99	1999-2000	2000-2001
A.P.S.R.T.C.	45.07	6.32	-49.73	-98.64	-151.85	-209.95
Bihar S.R.T.C.	-38.37	-35.77	—	-48.35	-50.48	—
Calcutta S.T.C.$	-58.59	-67.94	-74.87	-72.93	68.47	-77.23

Contd...

Year	1995-96	1996-97	1997-98	1998-99	1999-2000	2000-2001
Delhi T.C.	-400.36	-302.59	-209.06	-195.52	-238.70	-217.05
Gujart S.R.T.C.*	-37.52	-87.95	-226.39	-182.43	-401.97	-370.07
Himachal Road .T.C.	-12.85	-21.16	-7.13	-16.18	-48.54	-34.76
Karnataka S.R.T.C.	-48.00	-94.05	37.61	-9.25	-21.06	-16.05
Kerala S.R.T.C.	-16.66	-28.03	-51.00	72.35	-123.43	-116.20
M.P.S.R.T.C.	-51.59	-62.99	-66.37	-80.82	-63.51	—
Maharashtra S.R.T.C.#	15.95	146.79	104.87	164.21	151.51	117.72
Manipur S.R.T.C.	-2.58	—	0.33	—	—	—
Meghalaya T.C.	—	-2.69	-3.34	-2.19	-2.76	-1.84
Mizoram S.T.	-6.49	-6.59	-4.67	-3.81	-5.46	-8.68
Nagaland S.T.	-8.02	-8.30	-7.00	-7.09	-9.56	-9.05
Orissa S.R.T.C.	-11.49	-10.51	—	-15.18	-18.75	-11.68
Rajasthan S.R.T.C.	7.85	4.02	3.96	-37.48	-71.87	-83.39
Sikkim N.T.	-7.01	-4.02	-4.05	-10.15	-8.64	-6.79
S.T. of Tamil Nadu@	122.17	191.13	111.31	244.27	193.17	163.51
S.T. Haryana	-27.16	-26.06	-41.71	-90.69	-100.40	-72.21
S.T. Punjab	-23.51	-39.27	-53.30	-69.80	-77.73	-96.52
Tripura Road T.C.	-4.25	-4.19	-5.33	-8.19	-6.08	-8.25
U.P.S.R.T.C.	-41.87	-48.14	-44.14	-20.97	-82.32	-97.85

Notes: * In Gujarat S.R.T.C. profit/loss of Ahmedabad Municipal T.S. is also included.

$ In Delhi T.C. profit/loss of Pepsu Road T.C. and Pimpri-Chinchwad Municipal T.C. are included.

In Maharashtra S.R.T.C profit/loss of Kolhapur Municipal T.U., Pune Municipal T.U. Solapur Municipal T.U., and Thane Municipal T.U. are included.

@ In S.T. of Tamil Nadu profit/loss of Metropolitan T.C. (Chennai), Metropolitan T.C. (Chennai Divn. II), T.N.S.T.C. (Coimbatore Divn. I) T.N.S.T.C. (Coimbatore Divn. II), T.N.S.T.C. (Kombakonam Divn. II), T.N.S.T.C. (Madurai Divn. I), T.N.S.T.C. (Madurai Divn. II), T.N.S.T.C. (Salem Divn. I), T.N.S.T.C. (Salem Divn. II), T.N.S.T.C. (Villupuram Divn. I) and T.N.S.T.C. (Villupuram Divn. II) are included.

Source: Infrastructure, Centre for Monitoring Indian Economy, February 2003, p. 141.

The financial performance of the SRTUs, therefore, in general has been dismal and making losses because of the fact that the fares are not commensurate with the costs. These losses developed financial weakness and ultimately hampered the performance of SRTUs as well as the various quality services rendered to the traveling general public in India. Uneconomic fares, heavy interest burdens and uneconomic routes are considered to be the main causes for the poor financial performance of the SRTUs. The Ninth Five-Year Plan too holds the same reasons for the poor financial performance of SRTUs. According to the Ninth Five-Year Plan "uneconomic fares, delay in revision of fares, loss on account of concessional travel and operations on uneconomic routes"[15] are the main reasons for the losses incurred by SRTUs.

Accepting courageously the poor financial performance by the SRTUs Tenth Five-Year Plan says "the poor financial performance by the SRTUs, despite an improvement in the physical parameters, is a matter of concern. High rate of taxation, low fare structure, concessions to meet social responsibility, over-staffing, increasing interest burden and unhealthy competition among private operators"[16] are the major causes for making SRTUs operations uneconomic. Over and above there are wide differences in the fares charged by various State Governments. "The fare charged in the plains in Haryana is 35.76 paise per passenger km against 18.22 paise in Tamil Nadu. In the hills, Himachal Pradesh charges 45.75 paise per passenger km"[17] while Jammu and Kashmir charges 21.25 paise per passenger km.

Unless the public transport is developed in the real sense by higher productivity and better service to the traveling public, the mobility as well as economic development cannot be possible, because transport is an infrastructure for development. The future policies should be guided by efficiency of operations of existing undertakings, and to which they can provide consumer satisfaction and find necessary resources through internal generation. This implies that profit and service motives are balanced in the years to come. For this the SRTUs should take necessary measures to run it on commercially feasible lines.

4.4.7. Performance of Private Sector

A number of incentives are given to the private sector for the development of road projects. These include, the Government bearing the costs for project feasibility studies, shifting of utilities/services, environmental clearance, cutting of trees, and land for the right of way and way side amenities. Over and above this the land required for wayside amenities was treated as land required for the project and a 10-year corporate tax holiday was availed of within 20 years after commissioning of the project. In the external sector, external commercial borrowing of up to 35 per cent of the project cost was also permitted and import duties on modern and high-capacity road construction equipment were removed and foreign direct investment up to 100 per cent too was allowed. Under the foreign equity, the total foreign equity up to 15 billion rupees was allowed and investment in NHAI bonds was exempted from the capital gains tax.

Comprehensive guidelines for private sector participation have been issued. Necessary legislative measures to facilitate private investment have been taken by amending the National Highways Act, 1956. Various tax and fiscal incentives have been provided for promoters to attract investments in the highways sector. Model Concession Agreements for projects costing more than Rs. 100 crore and also for smaller projects costing less than Rs. 100 crore have been finalized. Model Concession Agreement for annuity based projects is also in progress. This is expected to bring uniformity in the various agreements for projects to be undertaken on BOT basis. Till now, 34 projects have been taken up by the private sector with a committed investment of about Rs. 6,000 crore and 18 such projects have already been completed.

The private sector has been involved in implementing a large number of National Highway projects. The Private sector involvement was mainly related to bypasses and bridges. It was implemented by the private sector on a build-operate-transfer basis. In all, 29 such projects involving a sum of 15,000 million rupees were taken up by the private sector. But the success with regard to the private sector has not produced the desired level of result. The National Highway Authority of India has so far awarded 21 projects to the private sector through three models namely build-operate-transfer, annuity and special purpose vehicle. These projects aggregate to a total length of 1,109 km of highways. The total cost of these projects is 68,670 million rupees. The details are shown in Table 4.9.

Table 4.9. Models of NHAI Projects, Road Mileage and Cost

	Model Length (km)	Estimated Cost	(Millions of Rupees)
BOT – Toll basis	435	33	140
Annuity basis	476	23	540
Special purpose vehicle	198	11	990
Total	109	68	670

It is evident from Table 4.9 that the response of the private sector in developing National Highways has not been very encouraging. In order to encourage greater participation of the private sector, it was decided to follow the annuity approach. In this model the concessionaire does not need to bear the commercial risks involved in road operation rather the concessionaire provides road services in accordance with the project requirements as stipulated by NHAI. The concessionaire is compensated with fixed semi-annual payments for his investments in the project.

The project is awarded to a concessionaire on the basis of the lowest annuity payment demanded. The payment made to the concessionaire takes into consideration the cost of construction and maintenance during the concession period, the cost of raising funds for financing the project and a return on equity. Normally, the period of concession is 17.5 years, which includes a construction period of 2.5 years. The system of payment is based on incentives, which ensures that the roads are maintained in good condition and equity of service provided in accordance with the predetermined standards.

This model is being increasingly used for the development of highways linking major ports. Although the private sector is now playing a role in the development of National Highways, the contribution of the private sector has been about 20 per cent of the costs of National Highway Development Projects. Therefore, there is need to increase the share of the private sector in the future. It is possible only when the private sector gains more confidence in undertaking road projects, the investment environment becomes more investor friendly and conducive to private participation.

In spite of these initiatives the performance of private sector in road sector has been poor. Realizing this fact the Tenth Five-Year Plan recognizes the need to re-examine the reasons for poor investor response and states that "Private sector response, however, has been poor particularly in the BOT mechanism, which was expected to be the mainstay of private sector participation. This happened despite the fact that the legal formalities have long been completed and Model Agreements are available for BOT operations. Under BOT, the investor is expected to build the road, maintain it for a fixed term and thereafter transfer it to the Government. The return to investor is in the form of toll charges. However, uncertainty about revenue from tolls has discouraged investors from coming forward with BOT proposals. Other mechanisms of private sector participation like the annuity-based BOT, where the Government commits a fixed annual payment to the investors in return for construction and maintenance for a pre-defined term, has received more encouraging response."[18] Therefore, Tenth Five-Year Plan suggests for re-assessment of investor risks in BOT projects and measures to make earning from tolls more predictable, so that the user-charges through levying tolls on roads remain an effective means of supplementing fund.

However, involvement of the private sector in providing passenger transports services has eased the pressure on the State Road Transport Units. Therefore, restrictive Government policies according to Tenth Five-Year Plan, the role of the Government should only be to ensure better transport services for the public. Nevertheless, the private sector should also be encouraged to operate services on unprofitable routes through tax incentives. In the long-run the private sector will play a vital role in providing all passenger transport services.[19]

4.4.8. Change in Public and Private Sector Participation

Passenger transport services through road transport are provided both by SRTUs and private operators. Following liberalization, and globalization the share of SRTUs in the total fleet of buses has declined with the entry of private operators to meet the incremental passenger traffic demand. In the year 1980-81, the public sector held 43 per cent of the total number of buses in the country. But its share came down to 23.79 in the year 1997-98. As a result the share of the private sector in the total number of buses increased from 57.36 per cent in 1980-81 to 76.21 per cent in 1997-98. But if we take the traffic carried by other commercial and personalized vehicles, the share of the private sector will account for about 90 per cent of the total passenger traffic.

It is interesting to note from Table 4.10 that the public sectors decline in the share of percentage held to total buses is 12.60 per cent prior to liberalization, i.e. between 1980-81 to 1990-91 and it is only 8.25 per cent in the globalization era, i.e. between 1990-91 to 1997-98. It means that the very purpose of liberalization has not been achieved because prior to liberalization change of passengers transport services from public sector to private sector was much higher in comparison to post-liberalization period.

Table 4.10. Buses in the Public and Private Sector

Year	Buses held by Public Sector	Buses held by Private Sector	Total Buses held	% share of Buses held in Public Sector to Total Buses held (Per cent)	% share of Buses held by Private Sector to Total Buses held (Per cent)
1981-82	73900	99400	173300	42.64	57.36
1982-83	75700	109500	185200	40.87	59.13
1983-84	76600	122600	199200	38.45	61.55
1984-85	80200	143000	223200	35.93	64.07
1985-86	84000	143300	227300	36.96	63.04
1986-87	88800	156400	245200	36.22	63.78
1987-88	94800	174400	269200	35.22	64.78
1988-89	99200	178700	277900	35.70	64.30
1989-90	102300	195700	298000	34.33	65.67
1990-91	106100	225000	331100	32.04	67.96
1991-92	106900	251300	358200	29.84	70.16
1992-93	109500	271500	381000	28.74	71.26
1993-94	109700	282400	392100	27.98	72.02
1994-95	110300	314600	424900	25.96	74.04
1995-96	111084	316588	427672	25.97	74.03
1996-97	111042	377127	488169	22.75	77.25
1997-98	113826	364650	478476	23.79	76.21

Source: Infrastructure, Centre for Monitoring Indian Economy, February, 2003, p. 113.

4.4.9. Accidents

Despite the increasing number of high performance motor vehicles coming on public roads over the years, the road conditions more or less remained the same. There is also a direct relationship between the average speed of vehicles and the rate of accidents. Poor driving conditions, mixed traffic and encroachment activities also contribute to the growing number of road accidents. As a result in India number of persons killed in road accidents has been increasing. Accident is defined as a mishappening during the period in which vehicle is in use, resulting in injury to or death of a person and/or animal and damage of any property. Rates of accident are the measure of incidence of accidents.

Table 4.11. Road Accidents

Year	Number of road Accidents	Persons Killed	Persons Injured	Accidents/ 1000 Vehicles	Accidents/ 100 km of Road	Vehicle Density per 100 km of Road Length
1981-82	166200	30700	126000	27.45	10.75	391.68
1982-83	177000	32800	134100	26.35	11.21	425.46
1983-84	195000	35100	156200	25.13	12.03	478.82
1984-85	207000	39200	163400	22.57	12.27	543.59
1985-86	215500	40000	176400	20.54	12.48	607.72
1986-87	234000	44400	189000	18.95	13.14	693.40
1987-88	246700	46600	214800	16.75	13.38	799.19
1988-89	270000	50700	229700	16.17	14.06	869.48
1989-90	282600	54100	244100	14.62	14.24	974.47
1990-91	294000	56600	257200	13.75	14.69	1067.67
1991-92	276400	59700	277600	11.76	13.67	1162.90
1992-93	279325	60860	289726	11.02	13.62	1236.28
1993-94	315657	64002	312080	11.59	15.19	1309.94
1994-95	349043	71140	323162	11.52	16.55	1436.47
1995-96*	355103	71943	329938	10.51	15.42	1467.21
1996-97#	290415	61000	290773	07.80	12.11	1552.10
1997-98^	298052	62821	296820	07.25	12.13	1673.04

Notes: * Excludes data for West Bengal.

Excludes data for Karnataka, Madhya Pradesh and West Bengal.

^ Excludes data for Haryana, Karnataka, Madhya Pradesh and West Bengal. Including these states total persons killed are 81000.

Source: Infrastructure, Centre for Monitoring Indian Economy, February, 2003, p. 113.

In 1999, 81,000 persons died in road accidents. It represents a 13 fold increase in 30 years. In the same way the number of fatalities remains high. The number of fatalities has increased to over 70,000 per annum. "The fatalities per 10,000 vehicles in India are 21 as against one to two in high-income countries and four to six in some lower income countries."[20] The death rate on India's roads per 10,000 vehicles is around 10 times higher than the levels seen in the European Union. India's share in the world vehicle population is only 4.3 per cent whereas its share in fatality is 13 per cent. The severity of accidents in India is evident from the fact that on an average one person gets killed in five accidents. About 65 per cent of the casualties occur on the National and State Highways.

The total estimated social cost on account of accidents in the country is estimated at Rs. 55,000 crore per year. The annual road safety toll is estimated at roughly 75,000 deaths, 1.7 million serious injuries and 6.4 million minor injuries, with economic losses of about Rs. 550 billion.[21] But the number of accidents however has come down from about 10 accidents per 1,000 vehicles in the year 1997 to about 7 in the year 2002.

With improvement of highways the rate of accidents may go up unless some remedial measures are taken. It is said that about 83 per cent of road accidents occur because of the fault of the drivers. Most of the drivers in India are less educated, economically poor and not able to cope up with the adverse consequences of accidents as a result they are not able to avert accidents and protect themselves and others from accidents. Therefore, it is necessary to introduce adequate measures to minimize road accidents by introducing road safety devices, training of drivers and instructors, awareness programmes for the public and transport users, computerization of the licensing system, creation of pedestrian and cycle paths, exclusive bus lanes and automated parking lots in major cities. Over and above this, a multi-disciplinary and dynamic approach covering engineering, education and enforcement of traffic rules is necessary to reduce the number of accidents taking place in India.

4.5. NEED FOR LARGE INVESTMENT

Road infrastructure in the country requires significant augmentation. The growth transport and the demand for transport services in the last 50 years have been significant. At present about 800 billion tonne kms of freight and 2,300 billion passenger kms is handled by the transport system. The total transport demand is also growing at 10 per cent a year in the last decade. The Rakesh Mohan Committee therefore had reported a requirement of 66,000 km of National Highway network and 1,45,000 km of State Highway network by 2001. An ADB study estimates that 10,000 km of expressway network would be required by 2020. The government's estimates in this regard were 4,885 km of expressway by 2005 on a priority basis, and 15,766 km by the year 2020. This can be compared with the current length of 49,585 km of National Highway network reported in the MOST annual report (1998-99) and that of State Highways at 1,35,200 as on 31st March 1998.

"Corresponding to the highway requirements listed above, the Rakesh Mohan Committee estimates that Rs. 320 million would be required by 2000-01 and Rs. 630 billion between 2000-01 and 2005-06. An additional Rs. 90 billion would be required for maintenance of the highway network by 2000-01. Between 2000-01 and 2005-06, this figure goes up to Rs. 115 billion. The Governments own estimates are relatively modest at Rs. 270 billion by 2000-01 and Rs. 610 billion between 2000-01 and 2005-06. Furthermore, for the Ninth Five-Year Plan (1997-2002) has estimated that a sum of Rs. 745 billion (at 1996 prices) will be required to address the deficiencies of the existing national highway network."[22]

In the last decade when the economic reforms were introduced, the economy experienced an unprecedented growth of Gross Domestic Product by 6 to 6.5 per cent. The coming years may have even higher growth rates of 8 to 10 per cent and it is going to cause increase in transport demand.[23] However, the existing unresolved issues and concerns such as the congestions, constraints in movement and high cost transport are going to cause still greater pressure on the transport sector. The unsolved problems of the existing deficiencies coupled with increased demand for transport is going to demand greater investment to transport sector.

Substantial investments thus will be required in this sector. The road sector in India has relied almost exclusively on funds provided through the budgetary process. However, the share of the road sector in the plan outlay has been constantly declining and the realization is dawning that budgetary support may not be adequate to requirements of the road infrastructure in the country. This trend is exemplified by the discontinuation of capital contribution to the State Road Transport Undertakings from 1993-94 onwards. Therefore, encouraging private sector investment is imperative.

4.6. CONCLUSION

In the globalized and liberalized era of Indian economy transport system needs to be looked at as integrated structure in which various modes of transport complement each other. There is need of a structure in which each mode of transport sector is able to operate on a "level playing field" so that comparative advantages and economic efficiencies are properly reflected in the costs for users. Over the years large investments have been made for the development of the transport sector in India. This has resulted in the expansion of transport infrastructure and facilities. In spite of these impressive achievements, the transport infrastructure has not been developed to the extent that it can effectively address the problems of accessibility and mobility needs for the movement of people and goods. About 40 per cent of villages are yet to be linked with all-weather roads.

Today, therefore, along with increase in quantity, there is a need for "appreciable developments of qualitative nature such as emergence of a multi-modal system in the form of container transport, reduction in areas of obsolete assets, improvement in the self-financing capacity of the sector and the establishment of new centres of excellence for manpower development."[24] This requires large amounts of financial resources. It is estimated that it would be necessary to increase the level of investment by up to three-four times its present level in real terms in order to meet the existing capacity shortages and deficiencies and to accommodate the future growth of transport demand in India. As a result the Indian transport system is far from adequate both in terms of expansion and capacity.

END NOTES

1. *Tenth Five-Year Plan*, Government of India, Vol. 2, Chapter 8.3, "Infrastructure, Transport", p. 931.
2. D.K. Kulshrestha, *Transport Management in India*, Mittal Publications, New Delhi, pp. 13-17.
3. *Eighth Five-Year Plan*, Planning Commission, Government of India, New Delhi.
4. *Ninth Five-Year Plan*, Planning Commission, Government of India, New Delhi, p. 791.
5. *Ibid.*, p. 792.
6. *Ibid.*
7. *Ibid.*, p. 794.
8. Out of the total GQ length of 5,846 km as on November 2004, 4,203 km length work had been completed and it is already four laned and the remaining length of work is under implementation.
9. According to the Annual Report 2004-05 of Department of Road Transport and Highways, the work on remaining length of NSEW corridor is scheduled to be awarded by June 2005 and it is targeted for completion by December 2007.
10. Major ports include Haldia, Paradip, Vishakhapatnam, Chennai, Tuticorin, Cochin, Mangalore, Mormugoa, Jawahar Lal Nehru Port and Kandla. The NHAI has also implemented four laning of about 356 km of highways to provide connectivity to 12 major ports and 777 km on other National Highways. As on 30 November, four laning of about 69 km roads of port connectivity and 194 of other National Highways has been completed.
11. Development works include riding quality, widening to four or two lanes, strengthening construction of bypasses and rehabilitation and construction of bridges. As on 30 October 2004, 264 km length of road is strengthened and works on rehabilitation and construction of 29 bridges was completed.
12. J. Made Gowad, "Road net-work—A Critical Look", *Infrastructure Development for Economic Growth* Edited by M.V. Srinivasa Gowda and Susheela Subrahmanya, Deep & Deep Publications, New Delhi, 1997, p. 279.

13. Following are the rural schemes implemented for the development of rural areas. They are namely, the Minimum Needs Programme, National Rural Employment Programme, Command Area Agency, Employment Assurance Scheme etc. Few other programmes have been merged into the Jawahar Rozgar Yojana.
14. Source: Ministry of Rural Development.
15. *Ninth Five-Year Plan, op. cit.*, p. 807.
16. *Tenth Five-Year Plan, op. cit.*, p. 961.
17. *Ninth Five-Year Plan, op. cit.*, p. 808.
18. *Tenth Five-Year Plan, op. cit.*, p. 959.
19. *Ibid.*, p. 962.
20. *Ibid.*, p. 963.
21. G. Tiwari, *Transportation Safety Issues: Institutional Restructuring Proposed for India*, IIT, Delhi, 2001.
22. *Road Transport in India*, Kaushik Deb, TERI, p. 6.
23. Mahesh Kapoor, "*Transport: Vision 2020*", *India Vision 2020*, Planning Commission, Government of India, pp. 707-708.
24. R.S. Mishra, "Globalistion and Development of Indian Transport Sector", *The Indian Economic Association 85th Conference Volume*, Thiruvananthapuram, 2002, p. 414.

Impact of Economic Reforms and Indian Railways

5

5.1. INDIAN RAILWAYS IN GENERAL

The present policies of economic reforms and liberalization have led to a scenario of increasing integration of domestic economy with global markets calling for modern and efficient means of infrastructural support. This has created enormous pressure on the Railway sector for better facilities. However, Railways always had an advantage of being less energy intensive and more environment friendly.

Indian Railways is one of the largest railway systems in the world. Also the Indian Railways holds a prominent position in the public sector. It carries about 11 million passengers and over 1.20 million tonnes of freight per day. The rail system occupies a unique position in the socio-economic map of the country and is considered a means and a barometer of growth. The Railway provides inter city freight and passenger services as well as suburban commuter rail services in major cities.

In addition, it owns and operates almost all other rail transport support services, including design and manufacturing of rolling stock, rail catering, schools, technical institutes, housing, hospitals, and hotels. Its revenues account for about one per cent of GDP, and the Railways is also the Indian organization with the maximum number of employees, numbering 1.6 million. It is managed by the Railway Board and is divided into nine Zonal Railways. The rail network is extensive. Of the network's 63,000 km of track, about 44,000 km is broad gauge and the rest are mainly meter gauge. But only 15,000 km are of multi-track. It has the electrified networks with 13,490 km and account for 24 per cent of the total route kilometer.

However, there has been a continuous decline in the share of railways in total traffic. Its share of the freight traffic came down from 89 per cent in 1951 to less than 40 per cent in 2000. Over the same period, the share of passenger traffic came down from 68 per cent to less than 20 per cent. This decline in the share of railways has caused serious distortions and leading to various adverse consequences. In order to reverse the trend, it is necessary that the capacity of Indian Railways be augmented. Equally important is the need to improve the quality of rail services through technological upgrading and modernization.

5.2. DEVELOPMENT OF INDIAN RAILWAYS

In the mid-nineteenth century Railways came to India at the initiative of the Government and as per requirement of the public. In the early stages Railways networks in India was not for the mobility of people at large rather it was "meant to facilitate military movement for the defence of the sub-continent and for the export of raw-materials from India to England to help British Industry and earn profit. Along with political and military aims, the other motive was to serve the interest of the British investors and the British Industries."[1] At the end of the Second World War, due to the existence of surplus staff, recoupment of rolling stock Indian Railways faced great problems. Besides this the partition of Indian and thereafter Independence further aggravated the difficulties and problems of Indian Railways. As a result all management activities of the Railways were disrupted. Thus various Five-Year Plans were undertaken to overcome management difficulties and to meet the requirement of the anticipated traffic of men and materials.

5.3. POLICIES TOWARDS PRIVATE PARTICIPATION IN RAILWAY

5.3.1. Build-Own-Lease-Transfer Scheme (BOLT)

In order to raise the funds for the projects having long gestation period and to attract private sector for investment in railways and to bridge the gap between the requirement and availability of funds, Indian Railways initiated a BOLT scheme. This scheme aimed at the participation of private sector financiers in the development of rail infrastructure which included electrification, gauge conversion, doubling of existing railway line projects, etc. The BOLT scheme, however, did not succeed in attracting the private sector. One of the reasons was that the financiers faced certain risks mainly on account of time and cost overruns. Considering the progress made so far, it can be concluded that private sector participation in the Railway sector has not met expectations. Indian Railways therefore need to identify the major obstacles to private sector participation and take steps to remove those obstacles.

5.3.2. Special Purpose Vehicle

Under SPV Indian Railway prepares a project report indicating the cost of the various components of the project as well their viability. If the Railways decide to participate in the project, the responsibility of land acquisition lies with the Indian Railways. The land required for a project is to be made available on lease to SPV. Commercial utilization of the Railway land may also be allowed. The SPV scheme also envisages the participation of the private sector and other beneficiaries and national-level infrastructure funding institutions for the development of Railway infrastructure through appropriate concessions. Revenue from commercial operations would accrue to SPV through revenue sharing with Indian Railways or through payment of access charges by the Railways. In case of green field projects, SPV is free to decide the process relating to project development, construction and maintenance. The concession period allowed for a SPV project is for 33 years.

5.3.3. Build-Own-Transfer

This is an improved version of the earlier BOLT scheme described above. The BOT model envisages private sector participation through the formation of a consortium of construction contractors and financers. Under the scheme, the concessionaire will design, build and own the facility. After the concession period is over, the facility will be transferred to the Railways. In order to give sufficient comfort to the lenders, the access charges will go in an escrow account through a tripartite agreement between the Railways, project sponsors and the lenders. Finally, the facility created will be maintained and operated by Indian Railways.

5.3.4. Rakesh Mohan Committee Recommendations

Rakesh Mohan in his report on infrastructure has suggested following recommendations to Indian Railway for immediate implementation and to face several challenges within the new economic environment:

- Institutional separation of policy, regulation and business functions. (Policy-makers would set policy and pay for what they ask for).
- Indian Railway to be corporatized as a business entity with a clear commitment from the Government that it will have freedom to manage and to operate on commercial lines.
- A clear differentiation between social obligations and performance imperatives should be implemented.
- Commercialization of Indian Railway that includes spin-off non-core businesses, and adopting lines of business structure and commercial accounting format.
- New management that provides leadership teams committed to changing the status quo.
- Reviewing and making changes in legislation as needed.

5.3.5. Major Recommendations of Expert Group

The Expert Group of Indian Railways made recommendations. They are:

- The root cause of financial problem confronting the Indian Railways is found in lack of adequate productivity increases that are commensurate with real wages over time.
- Indian Railways has to modernize and expand its capacity to serve the emerging needs of the growing economy.
- Indian Railways has to adopt a "strategic perspective" to achieve high growth in both the passenger and freight segments.

- Along with achievement of higher growth the Indian Railway will have to explore every avenue of reduction in costs.
- The Export Group has made detailed projections for the potential of passenger traffic and revenue growth. Among the investment strategies the panel has favoured a "High Growth Startegy" which will require focused remunerative investment and corresponding organizational restructuring of Indian Railway internally and in relationship with Government, including corporatisation.
- Higher profitability in freight segment through a long-term strategy of improved speed of freight trains, up-gradation of rolling stock, specific commodity related investment, improved signaling and communication, setting up additional container depots, rationalization of the freight rates structure to remove distortions.
- Unremunerative investments must be stopped.
- The key challenge for Indian Railway in the passenger traffic segments is to maintain its obligations on low price services while at the same time increasing both capacity and utilization in upper classes, through a strategy for growth in traffic as well as appropriate tariff rebalancing.
- The Government of India should be in charge of setting policy direction. Indian Rail Regulatory Authority (IRRA) should be set up to regulate tariffs. Indian Railways must eventually be corporatised into Indian Railways Corporation (IRC).
- Indian Railways Corporation (IRC) would be governed by reconstituted Indian Railways Executive Board (IREB).
- The restructuring of Indian Railways will require massive investment.

5.4. GUIDING PRINCIPLES FOR INDIAN RAILWAY

Indian Railway faces several challenges in adapting to the new economic environment. But if economic reforms are based on several accepted principles Indian Railway will find it easy to function. Following are the principles suggested:

- Railway enterprise functions should be separated from the government's policy, regulatory, and social support functions.
- Enterprise functions should become lines of business, including social services performed under contract with Government.
- The organization of the Railways should reflect a mix of factors and objectives, including geography, market location and dispersion, balance of passenger and freight traffic, competition within and between modes, and the desired roles of the public and private sectors in providing rail assets and services.
- Non-core activities should be managed separately, so that management can focus on core activities.
- There are a number of general options for rail restructuring. These include infrastructure separation and zonal based rail enterprises

5.5. PERFORMANCE OF RAILWAY

5.5.1. Freight

Indian Railway has been playing a shrinking role in freight. This is due to a shift toward trucks as highways and the railways have been unable to meet shipper capacity or quality requirements at an acceptable price. There is constant increase in the freight loading performance of railways from the year 1980-81 to 2003-04. But trends in the total revenue earning freight traffic for the period 1990-91 to 2000-01 reflect a slowing down as compared with the period 1980-81 to 1990-91. In the years 1980-81, the total revenue earning freight traffic is 195.9 million tonnes and it increased to 318 million tonnes for the year 1990-91. So the total revenue earning freight traffic during this period has increased by 1.6 fold. It works out to be 62.32 per cent increase over 1980-81.

During the year 2000-01, the total revenue earning freight traffic is 473.5 million tonnes and its performance is only 1.4 fold as compared with the year 1990-91. It works out to be 48.89 per cent growth over 1990-91 (Table 5.1). Over and above this the total revenue earning freight traffic is 557.4 million tonnes for the year 2003-04. Its performance is just 1.2 fold as compared with the year 2000-01 and it works to be 17.71 per cent increase over the year 2000-01. Before globalization period Railways had 62.32 per cent increase in the total revenue earning fright traffic and it declined to 48.89 within ten years of globalization period and it further declined to 17.71 per cent increase in the total revenue earning fright traffic.

Rail freight must play a larger role in the coming decades, but the Railways cannot fulfill that role unless it is allowed to create and respond to market incentives, and unless its social obligations are funded directly rather than by taxing freight shippers. If these social burdens were paid directly such a reduction would bolster the railways' competitiveness, possibly requiring it to invest in considerable new capacity. Indian Railway should license private operators to handle the different streams of freight traffic. By focusing on more than one commodity and customers, the private companies would be in the best position to capture the targeted traffic.

Ninth Five-Year Plan realized the fact that "the Railways cannot afford to continue the historical rate of growth of three to four per cent in freight traffic movement and it needs to pursue a high growth rate."[2] Therefore, the Plan suggested in improving the quality of its services by introducing "door to door service through the process of containerization with necessary road links as a part of service"[3] and the delivery goods through introduction of faster freight trains to reduce the time taken in delivery of goods. It also suggests making freight service to be 'user friendly' and "introduction of high speed rolling stock, elimination of differential speed between passenger and freight trains, introduction of higher axle load at selected routes, improvement in connectivity to ports and assets reliability, improvement in terminal operations, etc."[4]

Table 5.1. Total Revenue Earning Freight Traffic (Million Tonnes)

	1980-81	1985-86	1990-91	1994-95	1998-99	2000-01	2002-03	2003-04#
Total Revenue Earning	195.9	258.55	318	365	420	473.5	518.7	557.4
Coal	64.1	101.64	135.06	172.4	197.6	223.7	235.9	251.7
Raw materials for Steel plants	20.2	22.99	15.90	36.6	35.9	38.6	41.0	44.0
Pig iron & finished steel from steel plants	—	8.85	10.01	12.0	11.0	11.9	13.6	14.3
Iron ore for exports	—	12.54	13.14	9.8	11.5	14.6	15.7	26.7
Cement	9.6	17.96	28.74	31.5	36.8	42.9	46.2	49.5
Foodgrains	18.3	24.10	25.29	20.7	27.6	26.7	45.6	45.4
Fertilizers	—	13.62	18.31	21.5	27.8	27.0	26.5	25.8
Mineral oils (P.O.L.)	15.0	18.63	25.05	27.7	33.0	36.2	34.0	32.0
Other Goods	68.7*	38.22	36.50	32.8	39.9	52.0	59.2	68.0

Notes: * This includes Pig iron & finished steel from steel plants, Iron ore for exports, and Fertilizers, etc.
Provisional.

Source: Ministry of Railways and Economic Survey of various years.

5.5.2. Productivity

During the period from 1950-51 to 2003-04 the freight transport output measured in terms of net tonne kilometer has increased by 8.3 times and the passenger output of non-suburban passenger kilometers by 7.4 times, while the network has grown by only 1.17 times in terms of route kilometers and 1.36 times in terms of track kilometers. Other inputs, such as number of passenger coaches, wagons and tractive efforts of locomotives, have grown by 2.0 to 2.6 times only. The increase in transport output has been brought about by more intensive utilization of the available assets, improvement in productivity and technological upgradation. Table 5.2 gives a detailed picture of Railway productivity.

Over the years Railways has sustained improvement in the utilization of assets. Table 5.2 shows that wagon utilization has registered a continuous improvement. It increased from 1,449 net tonne km per wagon per day in the year 1987-88 to 2,554 net tonne km per wagon per day in 2003-04. It is an increase of about 76.25 per cent. During post-liberalization period net tonne km per wagon per day growth is greater than pre-liberalization period. Passenger traffic originating too increased from 3,792 million in the year 1987-88 to 5,112 in the year 2003-04. There is an increase of 34.8 per cent over 1987-88. Transport services which is the product of the number of passengers carried and the average distance traversed were 533 billion during 2003-04. It is an increase of 97.4 per cent from the level of 269.4 billion in 1987-88. The wagon turn-round also improved from 12.8 days in 1984-85 to 7.7 days in 1999-2000. Track utilization improved from 6.30 NTKM to 6.85 NTKM. It is 7.2 per cent growth. The manpower productivity in passenger km improved by more than 17 per cent and in terms of net tonne km by almost 6 per cent over this period.

Though the Railways have recorded a gradual improvement in assets utilization but there is ample scope for improvements in productivity when comparisons are made with the achievements of Railway systems elsewhere. The wagon utilization in terms of NTKMs per wagon per day, has recorded considerable improvement but even higher levels of performance are possible if the average running speed and the efficiency of

Table 5.2. Productivity Performance of Railway Sector

	1980-81	1987-88	1990-91	1994-95	2000-01	2003-04*	2004-05#
NTKMs per Wagon Per day (BG)		1449	1455	1590	2042	2554	2670
NTKs (billion)		222.53	235.14	249.6	312.4	381.2	301.2
Passenger traffic Originating (million)	3613	3792	3744	3914.9	4833	5112	4125
Passenger Kilometre (billion)	208.6	269.4	280.8	319.4	457	533	423

Notes: * Provisional.
Up to December 2004.

Source: Eighth, Ninth, Tenth Five-Year Plans and Economic Survey.

terminal handling are improved. Although some steps have been taken to improve the reliability of the rolling stock, there is a long way to go in controlling the adverse impact of the various types of failures. Measures will have to be taken to reduce the operational costs by a change in the practices and systems which would result in improving the overall mobility of the rolling stock, less detention at terminals and better output in the workshops. Over and above proper inventory management is necessary to improve the operating results.

5.5.3. Resource Mobilization

It is interesting to note from Table 5.3 that over the years the Railways has shown a greater reliance and emphasizes on the gross budgetary support and market borrowing rather than emphasizing the need for financing the railway plan through internally created resources. Over the years the actual internal resource mobilization has been dropping. It has dropped from Rs. 3,452 crore in 1997-98 to Rs. 2,463 crore in 2001-02. At the initial stage one may tend to believe that internal resource mobilization has increased over the years from Rs. 1,064 crore in the year 1985-86 to Rs. 2,463 in the year 2001-02. But if we compare the percentage contributed through internal resource it is less in comparison to the year 1985-86 to 2001-02. In the year 1985-86, internal resource contributed 54.8 per cent towards total resources invested, but it is only 23.0 per cent for the year 2001-02.

Table 5.3. Resource Mobilization

Year	Internal Resource		Gross Budgetary Support		Gross Borrowing	
	Crore	% age	Crore	% age	Crore	% age
1985-86	1064	54.8	878	45.2	—	—
1986-87	1317	48.8	1379	51.7	—	—
1989-90	1789	39.2	1774	38.9	1000	22.0
1990-91	2091	42.7	1631.8	33.3	1170	24.0
1991-92	2131	40.0	1694	31.8	1500	28.2
1997-98	3452	42.0	1992	34.0	2795	34.0
1999-00	3550	39.0	2588	29.0	2919	32.0
2000-01	2901	31.0	3597	38.0	2887	31:0
2001-02	2463	23.0	5641	52.0	2753	25.0

Source: Eighth, Ninth and Tenth Five-Year Plans.

.When Indian Railway was strapped for funds for its annual plans it was decided to go to the market for borrowing. Up to the year 1998-99, there has been continuous increase in the market borrowing. But from the year 1999-00, there has been gradual decline in market borrowing of funds. At present market borrowing is done through three sources that is leasing of rolling stock through the Indian Railway Finance Corporation, leasing of wagons under the Own Your Wagon Scheme and Private participation in execution of projects through Build Operate Lease Transfer or Build Operate Transfer.

Table 5.3 also indicates that in the initial stages of globalization period there has been a decline in the sum total of budgetary support provided in the various annual plans. From the year 1999-2000, there has been an increase in the total budgetary support provided to the Railways. For the year 2001-02 the total budgetary support has reached more than 50 per cent of total money invested in the Railways. It indicates that the Railways has gone back once again to pre-economic liberalization period. This is not a good sign because the Government objective of "the role of the Government as 'owner' and 'sole provider' to that of a 'facilitator' and of safeguarding the interests of the vulnerable sections of the community by legal and institutional framework"[5] may not be achieved in the near future. Therefore, it is necessary to rationalize the tariff policy so that the recovery of the full distributed cost from all categories of freight are done for the generation of internal resource generation. Moreover, the passenger fares need to be aligned more with cost. Regular periodic increases of fares are necessary to absorb cost escalation based on predetermined productivity norms.

5.5.4. Financial Performance

The financial performance of Indian Railways mostly has been surplus. In 1950-51, the surplus was only Rs. 15.05 crores but it increased to Rs. 31.01 crores by the year 1960-61. In 1980-81, 1983-84 and 1985-86, the Railways indicted the deficit to the extent of Rs. 198 crores, Rs. 44.9 crores and Rs. 195.6 crores respectively. However, in 1990-91, the trend has changed and it recorded Rs. 175 crores as surplus. From then on the railway is recording surplus with regard to its financial performance. For the years 2000-01, the Railways recorded Rs. 763 crores as surplus and Rs. 1,115 crores as surplus in the year 2002-03. But surplus began to decline from the year 2003-04 and 2004-05 as Rs. 1,091 crores and Rs. 993 crores respectively. So on the whole, it can be said that Railways has shown surplus trend in its revenue gross receipts during post-liberalization period.

In spite of shocks such as hike in diesel prices, higher dearness allowance rates, decontrol of the prices, increase in electricity tariff and procurement of foreign exchange at higher rates, Railways improved in its financial performance by showing higher surplus for many years mainly on account of cost reduction and economy measures coupled with the implementation of a detailed action plan to enhance earnings through market strategies and plug leakages of revenue through extensive checks.[6] Over and above main factor responsible for increase in surplus is due to increase in traffic and increase in rates and fares. The passenger traffic has been rapidly increasing over the years.

The gross receipts consist of total annual income obtained by Railways from all kinds of traffic. This include casual labour, various ancillary enterprises like telegraph earnings, rent from railway quarter and bungalows, tools, catering sales, proceeds of unclaimed goods, coal, cinder trees on the line, advertisement fee, etc. The gross traffic receipts increased from Rs. 2,624 crores to Rs. 12,096 crores during 1980-81 to 1990-91. That is to say that the gross traffic receipts increased to 360.97 per cent in the year 1990-91 as compared to the year 1980-81. The gross traffic receipts increased from Rs. 12,096 crores to Rs. 34,880 crores during 1990-91 to 2000-01. That is to say that the gross traffic receipts increased to 188.35 per cent in the year 2000-01 as compared to the year 1990-91. The gross traffic receipts increased from Rs. 34,880 crores to Rs. 44,902 crores during 2000-01 to 2004-05. That is to say that the gross traffic receipts increased to just 28.73 per cent in the year 2004-05 as compared to the year 2000-01. On the whole, it can be said that

Table 5.4. Financial Performance of Indian Railways

(Rs. Crore)

	1980-81	1990-91	2000-01	2002-03	2003-04	2004-05*
1. Gross Traffic receipt	2624	12096	34880	41068	42905	44902
2. Working expenses	2537	11154	34667	38026	39482	41417
3. Net miscellaneous receipts	40	171	858	788	1055	993
4. Net revenues	127	1113	1071	3830	4478	4478
5. Payment to general revenues	325	938	2131	2665	3087	3305
6. Surplus (+) or deficit (–)	–198	175	763	1115	1091	873
7. (i) Capital at charge	6096	16126	32662	37757	45672	50161
(ii) Investment from capital fund	0	0	10390	10390	10390	10390
(iii) Total	6096	16126	43052	51099	56062	60551
8. Item 4 as % of item	8 2.1	6.9	2.5	7.5	8.0	7.4

Note: * BE.
Source: Ministry of Railways.

percentage of growth in the gross traffic receipts during post-globalization is considerably lower as compared to pre-globalization period.

5.5.5. Goods Handled

There has been constant increase in various commodities and goods carried by Indian Railways from 1980-81 to 2003-04. Number of commodities namely coal, raw materials for steel plants, pig iron and finished steel from steel plants, iron ore for exports, cement, food grains, fertilizers, mineral oils and other goods have been carried by Indian Railways. As on 1980-81, Indian Railway handled total traffic of 147.65 billion tonnes of goods and it increased to 235.79 billion tonnes of goods (Table 5.5). Percentage of change in goods carried as on 1990-91 over 1980-81 was of 59.70 per cent. As on 1995-96, the total goods carried by Indian Railways increased to 270.49 billion tones and it further increased to 312.37 billion tonnes for the year 2000-01. However, percentage of change in goods carried as on 2000-01 over 1990-91 was 32.44 per cent which is 27.26 per cent less than the percentage of change in goods carried during 1980-81 to 1990-91.

In terms of goods carried by Indian Railways was concerned, ten years of growth achieved during pre-reforms period was much greater than the growth achieved during ten years of post-reforms period. Goods carried by Indian Railways further increased to 381.24 billion tonnes as on 2003-04 and percentage of change in goods carried as on 2003-04 over 1990-91 was 61.69 per cent. Similar trend is also seen in earnings from goods carried by Indian Railways. Total earnings from goods carried as on 1980-81 was Rs. 1,550.9 crore and it increased to Rs. 8,247 crore for the year 1990-91. Percentage of change in total earnings from goods carried as on 1990-91 over 1980-81 was 431.76 per cent. Though the total earnings from goods carried by Railways increased to Rs. 23,045.4 crore as on 2000-01, yet percentage of change in total earning from goods carried during this period over 1990-91 was 179.43 per cent and this percentage is much less than the increased percentage achieved during 1980-81 to 1990-91. So the various policy

Table 5.5. Goods Carried

(Billion tonne-km.)

Commodity	1980-81	1990-91	1995-96	1999-2000	2000-01	2001-02	2002-03	2003-04*
1. Coal	36.37	85.90	111.98	126.77	133.44	141.09	141.72	147.85
2. Raw materials for steel plants (excl. coal)	4.25	7.51	14.16	13.05	13.53	14.67	13.37	15.43
3. Pig iron and finished steel from steel plants	8.56	11.56	12.45	12.42	12.05	12.43	13.25	13.93
4. Iron ore for exports	7.29	7.54	5.94	6.88	7.93	8.29	8.59	13.23
5. Cement	7.19	18.94	18.64	24.77	24.91	24.78	24.82	27.62
6. Food grains	24.31	35.59	34.57	38.18	33.10	42.03	63.91	67.93
7. Fertilizers	8.92	17.27	21.19	25.58	23.00	22.84	22.61	22.09
8. Mineral oils	11.66	15.12	19.28	18.65	19.87	19.78	19.22	18.69
9. Other goods	39.10	36.36	32.28	38.90	44.54	47.32	45.70	54.47
10. Total revenue-earning-traffic	147.65	235.79	270.49	305.20	312.37	333.23	353.19	381.24
11. % of change over previous	—	59.70			32.44			61.69
12. Earnings from goods carried (Rs. crore)	1550.9	8247.0	14972.8	—	23045.4	24586.8	26231.5	—
13. % of change over previous		431.76			179.43		218.07	

Note: * Provisional

Source: Economic Survey 2005-06, Government of India, New Delhi, p. S. 27.

directions undertaken during post-liberalization period did not succeed in stimulating the needed increase in total earnings from goods carried by Railways.

5.5.6. Railways Market Share

For many years, Railway is the dominant mode of transport in India. However, there has been a gradual shift from rail to road. Railways had a market share of 88 per cent of freight and 68 per cent of the passenger business in land transport in 1950-51. In 1960, it was estimated that railways carried 85% of goods traffic (in ton km) and 51% of passenger traffic (in passenger km). But it has "come down to about 40 per cent of freight and about 20 per cent of passenger market share in 1999-2000 while road transport has moved from 12 per cent to 60 per cent."[7] It was reported further that it had declined to 32% of goods traffic and 13% of passenger traffic. Mahesh Kapoor while stating the reason for the loss of market share by railways says, "In a situation of less supply of transport and a high priority to the bulk traffic, the more cumbersome 'smalls' and wagon load traffic was gradually discouraged and the railway's unit of movement became a train load. This improved productivity and wagon fleet reduced substantially despite and increase in traffic.[8] Bulk traffic also started moving on high capacity trucks while pipelines siphoned off the high tariff traffic petroleum products."[9]

5.5.7. Railway Accidents

Insufficient maintenance of rail tracks and rolling stock is leading to more accidents and train de-railings, higher operating costs, and lost revenue from suspended operations on the affected lines. The major train accidents are mostly due to human failure and the impacts of such accidents are more severe in the super fast trains. The other cause of accidents include failure of equipment such as rolling stock, tracks, etc., and sabotage.

There is constant decline in the number of accidents taking place (Table 5.6). In the year 1980-81, 1,013 accidents took place and it declined to 532 for the year 1990-91 and it further declined to 464 for the year 2000-01. Total number of accidents trend for the period 1990-91 to 2000-01 reflects a slow down decline as compared with the period 1980-81 to 1990-91. In the year 1980-81, the total number of accidents amount to 1,013 and it declined to 532 for the year 1990-91. So total number of accidents decline is 1.90 fold and it works out to be 47.48 per cent decline over 1980-81. During the year 2000-01, total numbers of accidents is 464 and its decline is only 0.87 fold as compared with the year 1990-91. It works out to be only 12.78 per cent decline in the total number of accidents over 1990-91. So, before globalization period the total number of accidents decline is 47.48 per cent whereas during globalization period its decline is only 12.78 per cent. Accident per million train kilometer declined from 0.55 in 2001-02 to 0.41 in 2003-04 and further to 0.31 in 2004-05.[10]

Table 5.6. Railway Accidents

(Numbers)

	1980-81	1985-86	1990-91	1995-96	2000-01
Total Accidents	1013	707	532	398	464*
Collisions	69	46	41	29	20
Derailments	825	588	446	296	344
Level Crossing	90	62	36	68	83
Fire in Trains	29	21	09	05	15

Note: * Includes 2 Miscellaneous Accidents.
Source: Infrastructure, Centre for Monitoring Indian Economy, p. 80.

It is interesting to note that damages caused on account of railway accidents are on increase over the years. Detailed damage caused as a result of railway accidents are given in Table 5.7. Though there has been greater decline in the number of railway accidents yet the damage caused due to accidents has been on increase. In the year 1980-81, cost of damage to rolling stock is only Rs. 705 lakh. But it increased to Rs. 3,873 lakh for the year 1990-91 and it further increased to Rs. 4,421 lakh for the year 1995-96. However, cost of damage to rolling stock declined to Rs 3,571 lakh in the year 2000-01.

With regard to cost of damage in permanent way is concerned there is a constant increase. In the year 1980-81, cost of damage in permanent way accounted for Rs. 394 lakh, but it increased to Rs. 745 lakh in the year 1990-91 and further increased to Rs. 2,813 lakh in the year 1995-96. However, cost of damage in permanent way declined to Rs. 1,819 lakh for the year 2000-01. What is interesting to note is over the years Railway has improved in reducing the number of hours of interruption to through communication. In the year 1985-86 interruption to through communication hours accounted for 17,218, but it declined to 10,041 hours in the year 1990-91. It further declined to 6,661 hours in the year 1995-96 and finally it declined to 5,031 hours for the year 2000-01. This goes to prove that over the years Railways has learned to handle accidents and crisis in an effective way. As a result it has succeeded in reducing hours of interruption to a considerable extent.

Table 5.7. Damages of Railway Accidents

	1980-81	1985-86	1990-91	1995-96	2000-01
Number of passengers killed (Numbers)	117	66	220	406	55
Number of passengers injured (Numbers)	496	269	595	681	281
Compensation paid (Rs. lakh)	45	221	229	536	886
Cost of damage to rolling stock (Rs. lakh)	705	864	3873	4421	3571
Cost of damage in permanent way (Rs. lakh)	394	329	745	2813	1819
Interruption to through communication (Hours)	8919	17218	10041	6661	5031

Source: Infrastructure, Centre for Monitoring Indian Economy, February 2003, p. 82.

Tenth Five-Year Plan too recognizes importance of Railway safety and suggests proper training and motivation of its labour force so that the staff is disciplined and dedicated.[11] There is also need for upgrading the safety infrastructure through induction of technical aids to support the human element, enhancing the asset reliability, improving the work culture, ethos and strengthening the technical and human based safety systems. Efforts should also be made to modernize the Railway protection force by providing them modern equipment, weaponry, better training facilities, simulators for locomotive drivers, development of computer based training modules and upgrading the information system so that proper security of railway property and the passengers could be ensured. The probability of human failure should be reduced considerably by enhancing the accountability of the operational staff. Another area of concern is the unmanned level crossing. It is necessary to generate awareness especially in rural areas on the precautionary measures in using such unmanned level crossings.

5.5.8. Passengers Operations

Passenger satisfaction and their growth constitute major component for evaluation of performance of any transport sector and this is true of Indian Railways too. The passengers originating, passenger earnings, and average rate per passenger are indicators of effective performance and operations of Indian Railways over the years. In the year 1980-81, passengers originating was 3,613 million and it increased to 3,858 million for the year 1990-91 (Table 5.8). The growth as in 1990-91 over 1980-81 was of 6.78 per cent. It further increased to 4,833 million for the year 2000-01 and its growth as on 2000-01 over 1990-91 was 25.27 per cent. It is indicative of the fact that passengers originating percentage growth during post-reforms period has been much higher than the period during pre-reforms period.

Table 5.8. Passengers Operations of Indian Railways

	1980-81	1990-91	1995-96	2000-01	2001-02	2002-03*
1. Passengers originating (million)	3613.0	3858.0	4018.0	4833.0	5093.0	4971.0
2. Passenger kilometers (billion)	208.6	295.6	342.0	457.0	490.9**	515.0
3. Passenger earnings (Rs. crore)	827.5	3144.7	6124.5	10515.1#	11196.4#	12575.4
4. Average lead: passenger traffic (km.)	57.7	76.6	85.1	94.6	96.4	103.6**
5. Average rate per passenger – kilometer (paise)	4.0	10.6	17.9	22.9	22.7	24.3**

Notes: * Provisional.
** Revised
# Includes Metro Railway/Kolkata's earnings.

Source: Ministry of Railways.

However, this is not true of passengers earning and average rate per passenger kilometer. In the year 1980-81, passenger earnings was of Rs. 827.5 crore and it increased to Rs. 3,144.7 crore for the year 1990-91 and percentage of change as on 1990-91 over 1980-81 is 280.02 per cent. Though the passenger earnings increased to Rs. 10,515.1 crore for the year 2000-01, yet the percentage of change for the year 2000-01 over 1990-91 was 234.37 per cent which is less in comparison to the percentage of change achieved during pre-liberalization period. Average rate of per passenger kilometer was 4.0 paise during 1980-81. However, it increased to 10.6 paise in the year 1990-91 and the percentage of change as on 1990-91 over 1980-81 was of 165 per cent. The average rate per passenger kilometer further increased to 22.9 paise in the year 2000-01 and the percentage of change as on 2000-01 over 1990-91 was 116 per cent. It means that the percentage of growth taken place in terms of average rate per passenger kilometer during pre-liberalization was much larger than the growth that has taken place during post-liberalization period. Other than originating, performance of operations of Indian Railways in passengers earning and average rate per passenger kilometer was not satisfactory during post-liberalization period.

5.6. MEASURES TO STRENGTHEN RAILWAY SAFETY INFRASTRUCTURE

During 2000-01, Government of India took the following measures to strengthen the railway safety infrastructure. Special Railway Safety Fund—a non-lapsable fund with Rs. 17,000 crore set up to wipe out the arrears in the renewal of vital safety equipment within a fixed time frame of 5-7 years, for replacing old assets including tracks, bridges, rolling stock, signaling equipment and other safety enhancement items, as per recommendations of the Railway Safety Review Committee.

A non-lapsable Special Railway Safety Fund (SRSF) of Rs. 17,000 crore was set up in 2001-02 to wipe out the arrears in renewal and replacement of over-aged assets of track, bridges, rolling stock, signaling gear and some safety enhancement works within a fixed time frame of six years. The expenditure under SRSF in the first three and half years was Rs. 10,182 crore. For the year 2005-06 (BE), allocation (net) for the SRSF is Rs. 3,522 crore, with Rs. 2,699 crore from the General Exchequer and Rs. 823 crore from the Ministry of Railways.

Over and above this, following initiatives were introduced to strengthen railway safety infrastructure:

- Funds allocated from the diesel cess being used for safety-related works pertaining to level crossing and for road over and under bridges.
- Sanction of manning 165 unmanned level crossings given during 2001 as against 53 during 1999-2000.
- Track circuiting of run-through lines on all stations with permitted speed of more than 75 kmph completed.
- Provision of 25 Watt VHF sets roadside stations for communication between drivers, guards and staffs were made.
- Bogie mounted brake system being introduced on wagons in place of the conventional pull/push road type air brake system.
- Development and indigenous manufacture of Centre Buffer Couplers.
- A cohesive strategy for enhanced security of rail users under formulation as per recommendations of the High-level Committee on Enhanced Security on Railways.

5.7. POLICY DIRECTION

To reemerge as the dominant transport sector in India it requires to undertake some more efforts and these include:

5.7.1. Encourage More Private Parties

In the long run, it is necessary to encourage private parties to provide door-to-door services and end the monopoly of CONNOR. Private parties can own wagons in which they can transport containers and carry them through trucks to the warehouses of their customers.

5.7.2. Avoid Delays and Make Projects Attractive

In spite of the flexibilities offered it has been reported that the Own-Your-Wagon scheme has not attracted many private parties. Similarly many of the projects proposed under the BOLT scheme have not received enthusiastic response from private entrepreneurs. Unnecessary delays due to procedural formalities and uncertain return on income are the reasons. Delays add to the cost, thus reducing the profitability of the projects. It may be necessary for the Railway authorities to make the projects more profitable by offering the development of auxiliary facilities to private parties. If the profitability of the projects are still in doubt, then Government-private partnerships may be created to instill confidence in the private parties. Once projects become sufficiently profitable Government may divest and reinvest the money on other risky projects.

5.7.3. Frame Agreements Properly

Encouragement of private parties to partially take part in Railway functioning is an important feature of the new strategy of Indian Railways. Agreements with private parties should be framed without ambiguity to avoid difficulties later. For example, allocation of risks should be clearly specified. It may require framing of additional rules in due course depending upon the then emerging scenario.

5.7.4. Run Reliable, Punctual Container Trains

To capture growing road freight traffic, it is necessary to run train services punctually and according to pre-specified schedules. The marketing strategy proposes such special parcel services. These should be operated on a scheduled guaranteed time delivery basis. If the services are convenient, time guaranteed and profitable to private truck operators, they will prefer these trains to running the energy inefficient trucks for long distances. Using trains they can then provide door-to-door freight services with guaranteed time delivery. This will capture a lot of long distance road freight traffic. There will also be phenomenal savings in diesel as train consumers only one-ninth as much diesel as a truck per TKM. In the long run, competition should be encouraged by allowing private entry to operate such container trains.

5.7.5. Rationalize Railway Passenger Fares

The excess of Railway earnings over expenses is much smaller compared to the investment needs. Earnings of Indian Railways have to be improved. A major portion of the losses in earnings occur in the subsidized second class and season ticket passenger fares. Hence a more rationalized cost based fare structure, especially in the suburban train operations, should be attempted.

5.7.6. Provide More Differential Services at Differential Prices

At present, only two services are offered in suburban train services. It may be worthwhile to attempt to provide further differentiated services to cater to different sections of commuters. This will help Railways to best utilize the consumers surplus. These differential services can also be used to provide cross-subsidization in passenger fare structures. Similar attempts may also be made in non-suburban services.

5.7.7. Create a Long Term Fund for Capacity Additions

A nominal percentage may be charged in fares which may form part of a long term fund for railway capacity additions. Charging an additional 20-25 per cent increase in fares and ear-marking can meet the investment requirements of railways, particularly when these are supplemented by borrowing from the capital market.

5.7.8. Avoid Encroachments of Railways by Long Term Lease

Encroachment of railway land near the railway lines by slum dwellers affects the profitability of railways. Railways will not be able to exploit the commercial value of these encroached lands. Augmentation of railway lines becomes difficult. To avoid these difficulties the land should be leased for commercial purposes or given on a long term lease for the development of telephone or electric lines or roads, if feasible.

5.7.9. Joint Implementation for Attracting Foreign Funds

In addition, we wish to highlight one important policy direction for financing capacity augmentation in Indian Railways.

This involves identifying the opportunities for joint implementation in the context of global climate change for attracting investments from developed countries in Indian Railways.

5.8. CONCLUSION

Rail reforms must be based on proved principles derived from international experiences, and adjusted to fit the Indian environment because the challenges facing Indian Railways have much in common with the situations driving rail reforms elsewhere. The question as far as Indian Railways is concerned is not just the need for change rather, the question is how to define reform options, fit them to Indian conditions and objectives, and implement the decided reforms. Indian Railways is still vital to the economy, so implementation must be carefully planned. That is why Rakesh Mohan Committee emphasizes that the evidence for rapid, deep-seated change is clear, compelling and overwhelming. Therefore "an effective restructuring strategy should focus not only on developing a well thought out restructuring plan, but also on strategies for generating a momentum for change, and creating champions for change in the process."[12]

Indian Railways has performed well in several directions. However, in order to exploit its potential much more investment is required from private as well as from the Government. Some efforts in this direction of doubling of track on busy routes, lying of new lines, withdrawal of needless concessions and benefits to certain categories of rail users, etc., should be done. In addition to these, stabilization of passenger and freight rates is essential. Above all good planning and timely implementation of proposed projects is the need of the hour.

END NOTES

1. S.M. Imamul Haque, *Management of Indian Railways*, Mittal Publications, New Delhi, 1989, p. 2.
2. *Tenth Five-Year Plan*, Planning Commission, Infrastructure, Transport, Chapter 8.3, Vol. 2, p. 939.
3. *Ibid.*

4. *Ibid.*, p. 943.
5. *Economic Survey 2000-2001*, p. 172.
6. L. Krishnaveni, "Performance of Railways", *Infrastructure Development for Economic Growth*, M.V. Srinivasa Gowda and Susheela Subrahmanya (eds.), Deep & Deep Publications, New Delhi, 1997, p. 274.
7. Mahesh Kapoor, "Transport: Vision 2020", *India Vision 2020*, Planning Commission, Government of India, p. 698.
8. Wagon fleet came down from 400946 in 1980-81 to 222147 in 2000-01, while the freight went up from 196 mt to 474 mt in the same period.
9. Mahesh Kapoor, "Transport: Vision 2020", *India Vision 2020*, Planning Commission, Government of India, p. 698.
10. *Economic Survey 2005-06*, Government of India, New Delhi.
11. It is said that more than 65 per cent of railway accidents are attributed to failure of the railway staff, which lacks in adequate training, proper discipline and dedication.
12. Rakesh Mohan, *India Infrastructure Report*, Rakesh Mohan Committee, 1994.

Impact of Economic Reforms and Indian Ports

6

6.1. INTRODUCTION

The importance of maritime infrastructure in facilitating international trade has been recognized all over the world. Ports are the gateways for India's international trade by sea and about 95 per cent by volume and 70 per cent by value of the country's foreign trade is carried on through maritime transport.[1] However, India's share in global merchandise trade was at around 0.75 per cent. Therefore, it is necessary to strengthen the maritime infrastructure to have a favorable impact on the country's internal and international trade as well as on its economic growth. There are 12 major ports and 139 operable minor and intermediate ports along the 7,517 kilometers coastline of the country which are mainly serving foreign trade. Of these, 11 have special status as major ports under the Central Government's purview. State Governments oversee the remaining ports. The major ports are currently operated as Port Trusts, which exercise both statutory and commercial functions. When the Major Port Trusts Act was enacted, six ports were named.[2] After which five more[3] ports and then one more[4] have been added. All the major ports are administered by the Port Trust except for the newly constructed Ennore Port which is run by a company named Ennore Port Limited registered under Companies Act, 1956.

Although there has been significant improvement in port performance due to a series of reform actions, performance is still far below in comparison to ports in Asia. The problem seems to be that real berth capacities have not been used efficiently. Equipment use on berths is extremely low and resulting in high turnaround times for vessels. In addition, low productivity of equipment and labor increases handling costs for cargo and containers. These factors inhibit major shipping lines from bringing mother container ships for handling at Indian ports, adding to the transport costs of exports and imports. Beside this many ports also suffer from draft limitations, resulting in slow turnaround times for vessels. All this has resulted in higher transport costs, undermining India's exports.

With infusion of new technology and capacity building, the congestion at Indian Ports in the 1990s has witnessed reduction in most places and operational efficiency has also improved leading to capacities being marginally ahead of demand. However, with the projected growth of traffic and growing containerization, there is need to expand the capacities in the sector through investment from both public and private sector.

Port capacity can be increased quickly through better management, operations and through private concessions.[5] With minor ports becoming more and more similar to major ports, the regulatory power of Tariff Authority of Major Ports (TAMP) should be extended to cover minor ports so that distortions arising between major and minor ports can be effectively resolved. Reforms may be initiated in such a way that the regulatory mechanism is kept at distance from the political structure and pressures. Integration of economy with other countries will ensure that existing port and transport facilities are used more effectively and this in turn will cause development of new ports which are economically sound and financially attractive.

The economic crisis of 1990s was precipitated mainly by the growth of public expenditure in the 1980s. An attempt was made to resolve this crisis through the introduction of stabilization and structural adjustment programmes in the year 1991. One of the important planks of the stabilization measures was the compression of public expenditure and to promote private investment in infrastructural sector from internal and external sources. This chapter attempts to analyze Indian ports and shipping in the pre-reform and post-reform period and assess the impact these had on the infrastructural development in India.

6.2. MAJOR PROBLEMS

Very often Indian port could not utilize the outlays allocated under various Five-Year Plans and the some part of the outlay remains unutilized. According to Indian Ports Association this gap is due to poor resource mobilization, uncertainty over return on investments and inordinate delay in project execution. Easy flow of foreign funds for port development often leads to sub-optimal utilization of existing facilities. Very often new facilities are created without considering the social cost benefits or sustainability of such expansions. In the absence of proper evaluation of social cost benefit there will be overestimation of port traffic projections. At some ports, round-the-clock cargo pilferage goes on because of the lukewarm attitude of the port authorities.

"The operational efficiency of our ports is low. Even a small country like Sri Lanka could plan and construct a port at Colombo which is four times bigger than Bombay port and operate 20 times more efficiently at a cost of approximately 20 per cent of that of Bombay port or about 50 per cent of that of Madras. The Colombo port's termınal was built specially for transshipping cargo and specifically capitalizing on the weakness of the Indian ports which do not have adequate facilities to handle line haul vessels."[6] Thus it is rightly said that Indian ports are inadequate for servicing fully containerized ships or very large crude carriers carrying well over a million tons.[7]

Indian ports are not equipped with the modern computerized operations which enable the authorities to know the complete details of the cargo on the cargo on board through satellites even while the ship is on the high seas. This knowledge saves the turnaround time. Our ports still depend on traditional manual unloading methods. As a result the additional cost burden borne by the Indian exporters and importers is estimated at $250 million a year according to the World Bank. Owing to lack of infrastructure and poor productivity, the major ports are not able to attract mainline vessels.

Indian ports also suffer from lack of space. The price of land adjacent to ports has gone up abnormally. The port managements are not in a position to acquire them. As a result expansion plan could not be undertaken in any of the ports in a big way. Exporters are greatly handicapped because of huge congestion at major Indian ports. Losses suffered by exporters are largely in the shape of missed orders and huge demurrage charges payable in foreign exchange. Therefore, the style of management of ports needs to be improved.

6.3. OPERATIONAL PERFORMANCE

India's total port throughput was 287 million tonnes in 2000-01 of which 251 million tonnes (88 per cent) went through the 12 major ports. The Government estimates that the current capacity of the major ports is overstretched by 217 million tonnes, substantially below throughput levels. India's ports have struggled to keep up with the increase in demand. Average ship turnaround time increased between 1990 and 1996, reflecting a 30 per cent increase in the number of vessels sailing from the major ports and only a 10 per cent increase in capacity.

6.3.1. Performance Indicator of Indian Shipping

As shown in Table 6.1, the major performance indicators for the ports have improved over the years. The average turnaround time has declined from 7.5 days during 1996-97 to 3.5 days during 2003-04 and the improvement within seven years of reforms was of 53.33 per cent, which is a marvelous achievement indeed. Similarly, the average pre-berthing detention too has come down from 3.1 days in 1996-97 to 1.4 days in 2001-02 and the percentage of decline is of 54.84 per cent.

The average output per ship berth day for all major ports taken together has improved from 4,497 tonnes to 9,080 tonnes and the percentage of change during last seven years of reform period was of 101.91 per cent. In the same way the total number of vessels sailed as on 1996-97 was 13,119 and it further increased to 15,402 as on 2001-02 and the percentage of change as on 2001-02 over 1996-97 was 17.40 per cent. The performance indicators such as total cargo vessels sailed, average turnaround time, average pre-berthing detention and output per ship berth day reveal that the performance of Indian ports and ships during post-globalization period has been good.

Table 6.1. Performance Indicators

Item	1996-97	1997-98	1998-99	1999-2000	2000-01	2001-02	2002-03	2003-04
Total Cargo Vessels Sailed (No.)	13119	14077	14540	15067	14885	15402	—	—
Av. Turn Round time (Days)	7.5	6.3	5.7	5.1	4.2	4.4	3.7	3.5
Av. Pre-berthing Detention (Days)	3.1	2.3	2.0	1.7	1.2	1.4	—	—
Output per ship berth day (Tonnes)	4497	4912	5167	5871	6961	7024	8455	9080

Source: Buddhadeb Ghosh & Prabir De, *Indian Infrastructure Database 2005*, Bookwell, New Delhi, 2005, p. 841, and Economic Survey 2003-04 & 2004-05 and Annual Report 2004-05, Ministry of Shipping, Government of India.

6.3.2. Cargo Handling

As far as cargo handling is concerned there has been considerable improvement from the year 1981-82 to 2000-01. In the year 1980-81 total cargo handled by major ports registered 87.98 million tonnes. It increased to 287.59 million tonnes for the year 2001-02 and 344.5 million tonnes for the year 2003-04. A comparative study between 1980-81 and 1990-91 reveals that for the year 1980-81 total cargo handled at major ports was 87.98 million tonnes and it increased to 151.67 million tonnes for the year 1990-91. It means 63.69 million net growth only and 72.39 per cent growth has been achieved by all major ports in India in total cargo handling in the year 1990-91 over 1980-81.

Table 6.2. Commodity-wise Traffic at all Major Ports

'000 tonnes

Year	POL	Fertilizers finished	Fertilizer raw material	Food grains	Iron ore	Coal	Other cargo	Total
1981-82	34154	2951	2142	2376	22836	3148	18099	087984
1982-83	45340	3780	243	2347	25114	4875	14894	093697
1983-84	47943	1893	2342	3417	22218	4164	14666	096377
1984-85	49004	4226	2915	1313	21952	4422	17902	105823
1985-86	54890	4106	2700	1133	26041	7538	20435	119613
1986-87	53070	2387	4075	1402	28811	8551	24272	124366
1987-88	58917	1417	4165	1672	30609	12723	26960	134602
1988-89	63166	1648	4738	3388	28748	15406	25977	147061
1989-90	61968	2921	5193	1533	32738	17692	25084	147577
1990-91	64004	2879	6064	1528	33186	19659	25627	151665
1991-92	69303	3148	3962	1246	31904	22209	25630	157598
1992-93	73610	3582	3797	2321	32100	23910	29525	166575
1993-94	76922	4256	3187	1440	29830	26427	32900	179260
1994-95	82151	4388	4107	0877	34128	30309	40513	197262
1995-96	91065	5779	3836	2862	34917	31326	45953	215338
1996-97	98080	3346	3833	3256	34517	34872	50823	227257
1997-98	104004	4850	7963	3021	33047	41831	49258	251659
1998-99	107444	4664	8105	3571	40732	42762	50886	251720
1999-2000	116704	5541	6408	2719	34288	42492	61969	271923
2000-01	108347	3028	9076	1989	36090	53361	64844	281105

Contd...

Year	POL	Fertilizers finished	Fertilizer raw material	Food grains	Iron ore	Coal	Other cargo	Total
2001-02	103313	3522	9869	3853	40460	50198	71116	287588
2002-03	109600	*	8600	8500	50600	48400	87300	313500
2003-04	122300	*	7500	6800	59400	48900	99600	344500
2004-05	126601	3823	5812	3787	76193	52826	114583	383625

Note: * Included with fertilizer and raw material.
Figures for 2004-05 are provisional.

Source: Annual Report 2004-05 and 2003-04, Ministry of Shipping, Government of India, New Delhi.

But for the year 2003-04, the total cargo handled by all major ports increased to 344.5 million tonnes. It means that there has been a net increase of 172.53 million tonnes and 113.75 per cent growth in total cargo handling has been registered over the year 1990-91. This means that with regard to net total cargo handling and percentage of growth achieved in total cargo handling, the growth in post-globalization period has been much greater in comparison to the period prior to globalization process because net increase in total cargo handling as well as the percentage of growth is much higher during post-globalization period in comparison to pre-globalization period.

But in total cargo handling in comparison to other countries, India has to travel a long way. As a result India is not in a position to achieve significant transaction in international trade. Significant productivity gains could be achieved at major Indian ports only by moving closer to average world standards on cargo-handling operations. The total costs of moving a container through a terminal are on average 70-80 per cent greater in India than in Japan and the United States, where labor costs are much higher. Low handling productivity rates mean that ships spend a long time at berth. The Shipping Corporation of India reports that its ships spend 52 per cent of their time in ports. Consequently, ship turnaround time in Indian ports is commonly between five and six days, compared to one day or less in other ports in the region.

With regard to container traffic India has achieved considerable amount of growth in this aspect. But when it is compared with the largest international ports, India still lags behind in terms of container traffic. In the year 2002, Hong Kong processed 19.1 million Twenty-foot-equivalent units (TEUs). The 10th largest port, Antwerp, processed 4.8 million TEUs. In contrast, JNPT handled roughly 2 million TEUs in 2002-03.

6.4. GROWTH OF INDIAN TONNAGE AND NUMBER OF VESSELS

6.4.1. Total GRT and Ships

Indian shipping tonnage which was only 1.92 lakhs Gross Registered Tonnage (GRT) on the eve of Independence now stands at 7.70 million GRT as on 31.12.2004. The total Indian shipping tonnage was only 5.74 million GRT as on 1981 and it increased to 6.04 million GRT as on 1991. So the net addition of total GRT between the years 1981 to 1991 was 0.3 million GRT and the percentage of change in the year 1991 over 1981 was 5.22. Total Indian shipping tonnage increased to 6.81 million GRT as in 2001 and the net addition to total GRT between the year 1991 and 2001 was 0.77 million GRT. The percentage of change over the year 1991 is 12.75 per cent.

It is interesting to note that total GRT percentage growth between the year 1981 to 1991 was just 5.22 per cent but between the year 1991 to 2001 it increased to 12.75 per cent which is more than 100 per cent growth over 1981-1991. The total Indian shipping tonnage further increased to 7.70 million GRT and the percentage of change as in 2004 over 1991 was 27.48 per cent which was 5.26 fold greater in comparison to the growth achieved in the pre-liberalization period. The growth rate of Indian shipping tonnage achieved during post-globalization was much greater in comparison to the growth rate of Indian shipping tonnage achieved during pre-globalization period.

Table 6.3. Indian Shipping Tonnage

Year	Coastal		Overseas		Total	
	Ships	G.R.T.	Ships	G.R.T	Ships	G.R.T
01.04.1981	59	2,49,633	331	54,94,887	390	57,40,520
01.04.1982	64	2,87,412	339	56,53,422	403	59,40,834
01.04.1983	69	3,40,904	333	56,64,004	402	60,40,908
01.04.1984	72	3,37,264	335	057,90,29	407	06,27,563
01.04.1985	99	3,42,336	329	59,76,193	428	63,18,529
01.04.1986	100	3,01,896	262	54,54,491	362	57,56,337
01.04.1987	120	4,13,632	254	53,46,961	374	57,60,593
01.04.1988	129	4,43,331	237	50,99,875	366	55,43,206
01.04.1989	146	4,55,244	243	52,47,461	389	57,02,705
01.04.1990	152	5,12,467	256	54,65,991	408	59,78,258
01.04.1991	163	5,23,733	255	55,15,587	418	60,39,320
01.04.1992	169	5,61,316	243	53,45,663	412	59,06,979
01.04.1993	187	6,40,115	250	56,33,142	440	62,76,618
01.04.1994	204	6,44,140	238	56,35,246	442	62,79,386
01.04.1995	214	6,93,267	237	58,61,882	451	65,55,419
01.04.1996	226	7,08,362	254	63,91,891	480	71,00,253
01.04.1997	233	6,93,331	248	62,21,749	481	69,15,080
01.04.1998	234	6,42,838	244	62,00,318	478	68,43,156
01.04.1999	250	6,56,174	240	62,12,021	490	68,68,195
01.04.2000	273	6,81,605	240	62,31,361	513	69,12,966
01.04.2001	316	6,97,242	230	61,19,357	546	68,16,599
01.04.2002	336	7,33,658	224	60,87,279	560	68,20,937
01.04.2003	425	8,05,262	191	53,72,297	616	61,77,559
01.04.2004	436	8,07,808	203	61,36,398	639	69,44,256
31.12.2004	454	8,08,392	215	68,92,568	669	77,00,960

Source: Annual Report 2004-05, Ministry of Shipping, Government of India, New Delhi, pp. 21 & 124.

Net number of vessels added between years 1981 to 1991 was 28 and its growth rate was 7.8 per cent during the same period. However, during 1991 to 2001 net number of vessels added accounted for 128. Its growth rate during this period was 30.62 per cent which is 3.92 fold greater growth rates in comparison to the period 1980-1991. This proves that the growth rate achieved in terms of number of vessels during post-globalization period is much greater in comparison to the growth rate achieved in terms of number of vessels during pre-globalization period.

6.4.2. Overseas GRT and Ships

Indian overseas shipping tonnage which was only 0.73 lakhs Gross Registered Tonnage (GRT) on the eve of Independence now stands at 6.14 million GRT as on 31.12.2004. The total Indian overseas shipping tonnage was only 5.49 million GRT as on 1981 and it increased to 5.52 million GRT as on 1991. So the net addition of total GRT between the years 1981 to 1991 was 0.03 million GRT and the percentage of change in the year 1991 over 1981 was 0.54. Total Indian overseas shipping tonnage increased to 6.12 million GRT as on 2001 and the net addition to total GRT between the year 1991 and 2001 was 0.6 million GRT. The percentage of change over the year 1991 is 10.86.

It is interesting to note that total overseas GRT percentage growth between the year 1981 to 1991 was just 0.03 per cent but between the year 1991 to 2001 it increased to 10.86 which is more than 362 fold growth over 1981-1991. The total Indian overseas shipping tonnage further increased to 6.14 million GRT and the percentage of change as on 2004 over 1991 was 11.23 which was 374 fold greater in comparison to the growth achieved at the pre-liberalization period. The growth rate of Indian overseas shipping tonnage achieved during post-globalization was much greater in comparison to the growth rate of Indian overseas shipping tonnage achieved during pre-globalization period.

Net number of overseas vessels as on 1981 was 331 but it reduced to 255 overseas ships as on 1991, which means that during this period 76 overseas ships were reduced and its growth rate was -22.96 per cent during the same period. However, in the year 1991 to 2001 net number of overseas vessels reduced to 25. Its growth rate during this period was -9.80 which means that its negative growth rate has been brought down considerably from -22.96 to -9.80 in comparison to the period 1980-1991. This indicates that the negative growth rate experienced in terms of number of overseas vessels during post-globalization period is much less in comparison to the negative growth rate experienced in terms of number of overseas vessels during pre-globalization period.

6.4.3. Coastal GRT and Ships

With regard to Indian coastal shipping tonnage it was only 1.19 lakhs Gross Registered Tonnage (GRT) on the eve of Independence, but now it stands at 8.84 million GRT as on 31.12.2004. The total Indian coastal shipping tonnage was only 3.14 million GRT as in 1981 and it increased to 5.23 million GRT as in 1991. So the net addition of total GRT between the years 1981 to 1991 was 2.09 million GRT and the percentage of change in the year 1991 over 1981 was 66.56. Total Indian coastal shipping tonnage increased to 6.97 million GRT an in 2001 and the net addition to total GRT between the year 1991 and 2001 was 1.74 million GRT. The percentage of change over the year 1991 is 33.26. It is interesting to note that total overseas GRT percentage growth between the year 1981 to 1991 was 66.56 per cent but between the year 1991 to 2001 it reduced to 33.27 and the drop in growth was 2 fold over 1981-1991.

Though the total Indian coastal shipping tonnage increased to 8.08 million GRT and the percentage of change as in 2004 over 1991 was 54.49, it was still less in percentage in comparison to the growth achieved at the pre-liberalization period. The growth rate of Indian coastal shipping tonnage achieved during post-globalization was much less in comparison to the growth rate of Indian coastal shipping tonnage achieved during pre-globalization period. So globalization process incited has not improved the performance of total Indian coastal shipping tonnage.

The net number of coastal vessels added between years 1981 to 1991 was 104 and its growth rate was 176.27 per cent during the same period. However, 1991 to 2001 net number of coastal vessels added accounted for 153. Its growth rate during this period was 93.86 per cent which is 82.40 per cent less growth rate in comparison to percentage of growth achieved during 1980-1991. This indicates that the growth rate achieved in terms of number of coastal vessels during post-globalization period is comparatively small to the growth rate achieved in terms of number of coastal vessels during pre-globalization period.

6.5. GROWTH OF TRAFFIC MAJOR AND MINOR PORTS

6.5.1. Growth of Cargo Traffic

As regards the growth of traffic at major and minor ports is concerned there has been considerable improvement from the year 1981-82 to 2000-01. Since traffic handled at minor ports was not available for 1981-82 to 1984-85, the comparative study is limited to 1985-86 to 2004-05. In the year 1985-86, traffic handled by all ports registered 120.91 million tonnes. It increased to 368.50 million tonnes for the year 2000-01 and 518.28 million tonnes for the year 2004-05. A comparative study between 1985-86 and 1990-91 that is pre-liberalization period reveals that for the year 1985-86 total traffic handled at all ports was 120.91 million tonnes and it increased to 164.45 million tonnes for the year 1990-91. It means that net growth of traffic handled in all ports increased to 43.54 million tonnes and change of percentage of traffic handled as in 1990-91 over 1985-86 was 36.01. The average growth rate achieved during pre-liberalization period was 8.15 per cent.

For the year 2004-05 the total traffic handled by all ports increased to 518.28 million tonnes. It means there has been a net increase of 353.83 million tonnes and 215.16 per cent change in total traffic handling has been registered over the year 1990-91. This is 179.15 per cent increase of change in terms of growth in traffic handled by all ports during post-globalization period. It means that the net total traffic handling and the percentage of growth achieved in total traffic handling during post-globalization period has been much greater in comparison to the period prior to the globalization process.

However, it is interesting to note that the average growth achieved in growth of traffic handled by all the ports during post-reforms was 8.72 per cent. This was just 0.57 per cent more than the growth achieved during pre-reforms. Hence various policies adopted during post-reforms period did not contribute sufficiently for the growth of traffic handled at all ports in India.

The percentage of change that has taken place in terms of traffic handled by major ports during 2004-05 over 1985-86 is of 220.70. But the comparative study of major and minor ports in terms of traffic handled during post-globalization period and prior to globalization period reveals different picture altogether. In 1990-91 total traffic handled by major ports registered a 26.79 per cent increase as compared to 1985-86. But in 2004-05 total traffic handled by all major ports registered 144.91 per cent increase from 26.79 per cent in 1990-91 and the difference between these two periods was 118.12 per cent with regards to total traffic handled by major ports. But in 1990-91 total traffic handled by minor ports registered an 890.70 per cent as compared to 1985-86.

Table 6.4. Growth of Traffic Handled at Minor and Major Ports

(Million Tonnes)

Year	Major Ports	Non-Major Ports	All Ports	Percentage of change over previous years in all ports
1985-86	119.62	01.29	120.91	*
1987-88	134.60	05.92	140.52	16.21
1988-89	147.06	09.08	156.14	11.11
1989-90	147.57	10.86	158.43	1.47
1990-91	151.67	12.78	164.45	3.80
Pre-reforms period average growth				**8.15**
1991-92	156.64	13.26	169.90	3.31
1992-93	166.50	15.40	181.90	7.06
1993-94	179.02	19.47	198.49	9.12
1994-95	195.89	22.28	218.17	9.91
1995-96	215.21	25.71	240.92	10.43
1996-97	227.26	27.83	255.09	5.88
1997-98	251.66	38.61	290.27	13.79
1998-99	251.74	36.31	288.05	-0.76
1999-2000	271.97	63.38	335.35	16.42
2000-01	281.13	87.37	368.50	9.89

Post-reforms period average growth for 10 years				**8.50**
2001-02	287.58	95.52	383.10	3.96
2002-03	313.55	108.30	421.85	10.11
2003-04	344.80	118.86(P)	463.66(P)	9.91
2004-05 (P)	383.63	134.65	518.28	11.78
Post-reforms period average growth for 5 years				**8.94**
Total average growth during post-reforms period				**8.72**

Notes: (P) Provisional.
* Information not available.

Source: Annual Report 2004-05, Ministry of Shipping, Government of India, as given by Buddhadeb Ghosh and De, *India Infrastructure Database 2002*, Vol. II, Bookwell, New Delhi, p. 861.

However, in 2004-05 total traffic handled by all minor ports registered 953.59 per cent increase from 890.70 per cent in 1990-91 and the difference between these two periods was 62.89 per cent with regard to total traffic handled by minor ports. It means that the performance of minor ports in terms of total traffic handled during pre-globalization period is greater in comparison to major ports. But the performance of major ports during post-globalization period is better in comparison to minor ports. So globalization has given the much needed boost to major ports in terms of total traffic handled in comparison to minor ports.

6.5.2. Passenger Traffic

In 1980-81, all major ports handled 388.20 hundred passengers and it increased to 413.70 hundred passengers during 1987-88. But after 1987-88, there was a decline in the number of passengers handled by all major ports and in 1990-91 the ports handled 156.40 hundred passengers only. Table 6.5 shows that the trend of decline in the number of passengers traveling through Indian ports began during pre-liberalization period itself.

However, one can see a certain revival in terms of passengers during post-liberalization period. In 1991-92, numbers of passengers increased to 162.40 hundred and it further increased to 252.00 hundred as in 2001-02. The same trend was also seen in all minor ports. The number of passenger traffic at minor ports was 15,152 hundred as in 1996-97 and it increased to

16,010 hundred as in 2000-01. This achievement could be considered as a remarkable one because Indian ports have achieved an increase in number of passengers in spite of people's preference to travel by air.

Table 6.5. Passenger Traffic at Ports in India

Year	(In '000) All Major Ports	(In '000) All Minor Ports	Total
1980-81	388.20		
1985-86	399.90		
1986-87	406.00		
1987-88	413.70		
1988-89	193.30		
1989-90	159.80		
1990-91	156.40		
1991-92	162.40		
1992-93	202.70		
1993-94	215.60		
1994-95	266.20		
1995-96	295.90		
1996-97	277.20	15152	15152
1997-98	266.00	17043	17309
1998-99	256.00	15321	15577
1999-2000	234.00	15994	16228
2000-01	275.00	16010	16285
2001-02	252.00	—	—

Source: Buddhadeb Ghosh & Prabir De, *Indian Infrastructure Database 2005*, Bookwell, New Delhi, 2005, pp. 874 & 875.

6.5.3. Performance of Indian Ships in Overseas Trade

There has been a continuous growth in the participation of Indian ships in India's overseas trade. As in 1984-85 total cargo handled by Indian lines in India's overseas trade amount to 29,020 hundred tonnes and it increased to 38,860 hundred tonnes as in 1991-91. Change of percentage as in 1990-91 over 1984-85 was 25.32 per cent. Similarly as in 1991-92 the total cargo handled by Indian lines in India's overseas trade amount to 41,010 hundred tonnes and it further increased to 60,970 hundred tonnes as in 1998-99 and the percentage of change as on 1998-99 over 1991-92 was 20.02 per cent. So the percentage of change that has taken place during post-liberalization period is less than the percentage of change that has taken place during pre-liberalization period. The average percentage of share of Indian lines in total cargo handling of India's overseas trade was 36.41 per cent during pre-reform period and during post-reform the average share of Indian lines in the total cargo handling of Indian overseas was 31.65 per cent. It means that the average share of Indian lines in total cargo handling in India's overseas trade has reduced to 4.76 per cent during post-reform period in comparison to pre-reform period.

Table 6.6. Participation of Indian Ships in India's Overseas Trade

('000 tonnes)

Year	Indian Lines	Foreign Lines	Total Cargo	% Share of Indian Lines in Total Cargo	% Share of Foreign Lines in Total Cargo
1984-85	29020	51760	80780	35.92	64.08
1985-86	30150	56270	86420	34.89	65.11
1986-87	32950	54180	87130	37.82	62.18
1987-88	36620	53350	89970	40.70	59.70
1988-89	34880	67050	101930	34.22	65.78
1989-90	38210	68550	106760	35.79	64.21
1990-91	38860	70490	109350	35.54	64.46
Change over					
1984-85	25.32%	36.17%			
Average share				*36.41*	*63.59*
1991-92	41010	70790	111800	36.68	63.32
1992-93	42660	79640	122300	34.88	65.12
1993-94	46070	90900	136970	33.64	66.36
1994-95	42020	104530	146550	28.67	71.33
1995-96	46000	120100	166100	27.69	72.31
1996-97	51280	120900	172180	29.78	70.22
1997-98	63530	138910	202440	31.38	68.62
1998-99	60970	139040	200010	30.48	69.52
Change over					
1991-92	20.02%	70.78%			
Average share				*31.65*	*68.35*

Source: Infrastructure, Centre for Monitoring Indian Economy, February 2003, p. 233.

There has been a continuous growth in the participation of Indian ships in India's overseas trade. As in 1984-85 total cargo handled by Indian ships in foreign lines in India's overseas trade amount to 51,760 hundred tonnes and it increased to 70,490 hundred tonnes as in 1990-91. Change of percentage as in 1990-91 over 1984-85 was 36.17 per cent. Similarly as in 1991-92 the total cargo handled in foreign lines in India's overseas trade amount to 70,790 hundred tonnes and it further increased to 1,39,040 hundred tonnes as in 1998-99 and the percentage of change as in 1998-99 over 1991-92 was 70.78 per cent. So percentage of change that has taken place during post-liberalization period was much greater than the percentage of change that has taken place during pre-liberalization period in the performance of Indian ships in foreign lines in India's overseas trade.

The average percentage of share of foreign lines in total cargo handling of India's overseas trade was 63.59 per cent during pre-reform period and during post-reform period the average share of foreign lines in the total cargo handling of Indian overseas trade was 68.35 per cent. It means that the average share of foreign lines in total cargo handling in India's overseas trade has remarkably increased to 5.93 per cent during post-reform period in comparison to pre-reform period. It is interesting to note that as regards the performance of Indian ships in Indian overseas trade, the performance of foreign line has been much better during post-reform in comparison to the performance of Indian line.

6.6. FINANCIAL PERFORMANCE OF INDIAN PORTS

6.6.1. Operating Financial Performance of Indian Ports

Table 6.7 shows the total financial performance of Indian ports in terms of operating income, operating expenditure, operating surplus, total income, total expenditure and net surplus obtained during pre-reforms (1986-87 to 1990-91) period and the post-reforms period (1991-92 to 2003-04). Table 6.7 shows the increasing trends in operating income, operating expenditure, operating surplus, total income and total expenditure can be noticed during pre-reform and post-reform period. But it is disturbing to note that from 1997-98 to 2001-02 a declining trend in the net surplus is observed. It means that the economy has failed to maintain the increasing momentum achieved in financial performance in terms of net surplus during post-reform period.

For the year 2003-04 the operating income received by Indian ports accounted for 4201.41 crore and the percentage of growth over 1987-88 was of 182.84 per cent. But for the years 1997-98 the operating income registered by Indian ports was 3051.33 crore and the percentage of change over 1986-87 was of 105.44 per cent. The operating income obtained by Indian ports as on 1990-91 was 1091.59 crore and the percentage of change over the year 1987-88 was 55.60 per cent.

Table 6.7. Operating Financial Performance of Indian Ports

Year	Operating Income	Operating Expenditure	Operating Surplus	Percentage of Change over Previous Years in Operating Surplus
1987-88	701.50	533.73	167.77	
1988-89	886.52	589.20	297.32	77.22
1989-90	0990.91	667.96	322.95	9.94
1990-91	1091.59	738.82	352.77	9.23
Average growth during pre-reforms				**32.13**
1991-92	1198.37	849.31	349.06	-1.05
1992-93	1485.40	973.95	511.45	46.52
1993-94	1738.68	1069.86	668.82	30.77
1994-95	1989.22	1229.09	760.13	13.65
1995-96	2360.32	1364.47	995.85	31.01
1996-97	2654.44	1604.96	1049.48	5.39
1997-98	3051.33	1849.80	1201.53	14.49
2002-03	3862.60	2583.34	1279.27	6.47
2003-04	4201.41	2641.42	1560.00	21.94
Average growth during post-reforms				**18.80**

Source: Infrastructure, Centre for Monitoring Indian Economy, February 2003, pp. 196-206 and Buddhadeb Ghosh and Prabir De, *India Infrastructure Database 2002*, Vol. II, Bookwell, New Delhi, pp. 892 & 902.

However, the average growth rate of operating surplus of financial performance during pre-liberalization period was

32.13 per cent, but it is disturbing to know that the average operating surplus of financial performance has declined to 18.80 per cent during post-reforms. This means that the percentage of growth achieved in terms of operating surplus in financial performance during pre-reforms period was much greater than the growth achieved during post-reforms period. It is mainly due to increasing operating expenditure without considerable increase in the operating income of Indian ports during post-liberalization period.

6.6.2. Financial Performance of Indian Ports

As regards the total income of Indian ports there has been a constant increase. In the year 1986-87, total income of Indian ports was Rs. 777.71 crore and it increased to Rs. 1258.18 crore for the year 1990-91 and percentage of change during 1990-91 over 1986-87 is of 61.78 per cent. The total income further increased to Rs. 4805.70 crore for the year 2001-02 and percentage of change over 1991-92 was 232.05 per cent.

Table 6.8. Financial Performance of Indian Ports

(Rs. Crore)

Year	Income	Expenditure	Net Surplus	Percentage of Change over Previous Years in Net Surplus
1986-87	777.71	616.65	161.06	
1987-88	821.38	694.03	127.35	-20.93
1988-89	1052.77	757.29	295.48	132.02
1989-90	1141.63	851.97	289.66	-1.97
1990-91	1258.18	930.42	327.76	13.15
Average growth rate during pre-reforms				**30.57**
1991-92	1447.36	1100.22	347.14	5.91
1992-93	1786.46	1276.18	510.28	47.00
1995-96	2758.64	1877.19	881.45	37.67
1996-97	3171.63	2123.90	1047.73	18.86
1997-98	3607.31	2390.72	1216.59	16.11
1999-2000	4050.39	3235.50	814.89	-23.66
2000-01	4261.80	4166.20	95.60	-88.27
2001-02	4805.70	4223.30	582.40	509.20
Average growth rate during post-reforms				**48.67**

Source: Buddhadeb Ghosh & Prabir De, *Indian Infrastructure Database 2005*, Bookwell, New Delhi, 2005, pp. 874, 875, 888, 890, 891.

But at the same time there is also increase in total expenditure of Indian ports. The total expenditure was Rs. 616.65 crore as on 1986-87 and it increased to Rs. 930.42 crore for the year 1991-92. It further increased to Rs. 4223.30 crore for the year 2001-02. The percentage of change in total expenditure as on 1990-91 over 1986-87 was 50.88 per cent and the percentage of change in total expenditure as on 2001-02 over 1990-91 was 283.94 per cent. This proves that the percentage of change experienced in expenditure of Indian ports during post-reforms was much higher than the percentage of change seen in the income of Indian ports.

However, it is noteworthy to observe that the trend is not the same with regard to income of Indian ports. During pre-reform period the percentage of change seen in the income of Indian ports was much greater than the percentage of change that has taken place in the expenditure of Indian ports. However, the average growth of net surplus of financial performance during pre-reform period was 30.57 per cent but it was 48.67 per cent during post-reforms period. This means the average growth of net surplus achieved during post-reforms period was much greater in comparison to the average growth of net surplus achieved during pre-reforms period, because average growth achieved during pre-reform period accounted for 30.57 per cent and the average growth achieved during post-reform period accounted for 48.67 and difference between these two periods was of 10.10 per cent.

6.7. EMPLOYMENT OPPORTUNITIES AND LABOUR EFFICIENCY

Number of persons employed at all major ports in India is declining over the years. In the year 1987 total number of persons employed in Indian ports was 1,02,244 and it declined to 98,760 for the year 1990. The trend of decline in employment opportunities available in Indian ports was in no way reversed even after various reform measures were undertaken during liberalization period. As a result the total number of persons employed further reduced to 73,314 as on 2001.

Table 6.9. Employment at Indian Ports

Year	All Listed Major Ports	Dock Workers with DLB's all ports	Dock registered Traffic (In Numbers)	Passenger Traffic (In '000)	Cargo (In Million Tonnes)
1986-87	—	2091	23221	406.00	120.91
1987-88	102244	2060	22496	413.70	140.42
1988-89	101719	3035	21200	193.30	156.14
1989-90	100583	2995	20490	159.80	158.43
1990-91	98760	2947	18014	156.40	164.45
1991-92	97955	2863	17755	162.40	169.90
1992-93	93112	1772	15314	202.70	181.90
1993-94	89662	1281	15976	215.60	198.49
1994-95	99038	1579	7202	266.20	218.17
1995-96	94016	1411	7240	295.90	240.92
1996-97	92574	1764	6521	277.20	255.09
1997-98	91147	1494	6014	266.00	290.27
1998-99	90168	1057	4955	256.00	288.05
1999-2000	88694	877	4968	234.00	335.35
2000-01	84917	723	4469	275.00	368.50
2001-02	73314	450	4274	252.00	383.10

Source: Buddhadeb Ghosh & Prabir De, *Indian Infrastructure Database 2005*, Bookwell, New Delhi, 2005, pp. 874, 875, 888, 890, 891.

It is pertinent to point out that the total employment provided by Indian ports registered a decline during pre-reforms period as well as post-reforms period. But this decline is much greater during post-reform period because during this period the total employment provided by Indian ports registered 21.26 per cent, whereas during pre-reform period it registered only 4.19 per cent and the difference in decline in the employment opportunities in Indian Ports is of 17.07 per cent between pre-reforms and post-reforms period. The decline in the employment opportunities provided by the Indian ports has in no way affected the growth in cargo traffic handled by all ports as well as the growth in the passengers handled by the ports. Despite decline in the number of persons employed there has been an increase in the total cargo traffic handled. Less number of persons handling larger amount of cargo and passengers means that the manpower of the Indian ports has been employed in an efficient manner.

In the year 1987-88, 1,02,244 staff was employed to handle 140.42 million tonnes cargo, which means that one staff was handling just 0.0014 million tonnes of cargo in a year. However in the 1990-91, 98760 staff members were employed to handle 164.45 million tonnes of cargo and the average handling of cargo per staff member accounts to 0.0017 million tonnes in a year. It means that during pre-reforms period the work efficiency has improved to 17.64 per cent. In the year 2001-02, total number of employees was 73,314 which is less than the number of staff employed as in 1990-91. 73,314 staff members have handled 383.10 million tonnes and the average handling of cargo per staff amounts to 0.0052 million tonnes. It means that the work efficiency of staff working in Indian ports has increased to 205.88 per cent in comparison to the year 1990-91. This indicates that over the years the Indian ports and shipping sector has been employing its staff in an efficient manner to bring about greater cost-effectiveness in its transportation sector.

6.8. MEETING THE DEMAND FOR PORT SERVICES

Increases in demand are likely to require an increase in capacity of more than 70 per cent during the period covered by the Ninth Five-Year Plan. Port capacity, based on current operating practices, is around 217 million tonnes for the 11 major ports. In 1997 total traffic was 251 million tonnes—an apparent use rate of 115 per cent. However, this figure accounts for wide differences in traffic segments. For containers, current capacity is assessed at about 15 million tonnes, while total traffic in 1997 was more than 20 million tonnes, showing an apparent use rate of 133 per cent.

Previous analysis agrees that implementing rational management and working practices should increase the overall capacity of Indian ports by about 35 per cent.[8] For container operations, the figures suggest that at least a 40 per cent improvement in handling and processing capacity is not beyond reach. If these changes were implemented today, they would allow Indian ports to provide world-class service without having to expand infrastructure. However, the traffic growth trend—around 6 per cent, and close to 18 per cent for containers—means that significant capacity expansion will still be needed even if a 40 per cent improvement is achieved in coming years.

The Government envisions demand growth for port services of around 200 million tonnes, with estimated around 415 million tonnes in 2001-02. It is therefore planning to add 122 million tonnes of port capacity over the Ninth Five-Year Plan period. Approximately, 45 million tonnes, or around one-third of capacity, is expected from the private sector, in addition to 31 million tonnes from captive schemes. The Government also anticipates productivity increases of around 11 million tonnes.

In the long-term, minor ports are expected to play an increasingly important role in meeting India's transport needs. The Planning Commission estimates total capacity of the major ports at about 550 million tonnes a year; by 2020 MOST projects that demand is likely to be about 1,200 million tonnes, indicating the important role that minor ports will play.

6.9. PORTS AND SHIPPING OUTLAY AND EXPENDITURE UNDER THE FIVE-YEAR PLANS

The figures in Table 6.10 bring out the disturbing trends from plan outlay on ports and shipping during the Sixth and Seventh Plan period (coinciding with pre-reform period) and the Eighth and Ninth Plan periods (coinciding with post-reform period). With regard to ports the actual expenditure has been much more than the total plan outlay during pre-reforms period. But as regards shipping the actual expenditure was much higher than the plan outlay during pre-reforms period. However, the average share plan outlay for ports, shipping and light house in the transport sector has been 5.6 per cent and the average share of expenditure in the transport sector for ports, shipping and light house has been just 3.6 per cent during pre-reforms period. Nearly 2 per cent of total outlay allocated to ports and shipping was not being spent by this transport sector during pre-reforms period revealing a certain amount of complacency prevailing in this sector.

Table 6.10. Ports and Shipping Outlay and Expenditure under the Five-Year Plans

(Rs. Crore)

	Ports	Shipping	I.W.T.	LH & LS	Total	Share of Ports & LH & LS in the Transport Sector (%)
Sixth Plan (1980-85)						
Outlay	647	755	72	12	1513	5.5
Expenditure	725	468	63	*	1256	5.1
Seventh Plan (1985-90)						
Outlay	1230	827	226	30	2313	5.6
Expenditure	1513	720	188	*	2421	2.1
Average Share Pre-reform Period						
Outlay						5.6
Expenditure						3.6
Eighth Plan (1992-97)						
Outlay	3557	3669	331	57	7614	6.4
Expenditure	2302	3033	152	25	5512	3.6
Ninth Plan (1997-2002)						
Outlay	9813	5912	408	*	16133	12

Contd...

	Ports	Shipping	I.W.T.	LH & LS	Total	Share of Ports & LH & LS in the Transport Sector (%)
Expenditure	5092	2425	202	*	7719	6.6
Average Share of Post-reform Period						
Outlays						9.2
Expenditure						5.1
Tenth Plan (2002-2007)						
Outlay	1224	7121	903	*	9248	4.2

Note: * Included in Ports.
Source: Buddhadeb Ghosh & Prabir De, *Indian Infrastructure Database 2005*, Bookwell, New Delhi, 2005, p. 895.

The complacent attitude of Indian ports and shipping has not changed much during post-reforms period either. During the Eighth Five-Year Plan total outlay allocated to ports was Rs. 3,557 crore of which only Rs. 2,302 crore was spent. Even during the Ninth Plan Period the total outlay to ports was Rs. 9,813 crore of which only Rs. 5,092 crore was spent. The same trend is seen regarding shipping, I.W.T, Light House, and Light ships. The total share of outlay for ports, shipping, light house, and light ships in the transport sector during the Ninth Five-Year Plan was 12 per cent of which only 6.6 per cent was expenditure. Also the average share of total outlay for ports and shipping, etc., in the transport sector during post-reform period was 9.2 per cent but its expenditure during the same period was 5.1 per cent.

It means that the ports and shipping sector failed to invest on capital goods and creation of better facilities which is nearly 4.2 per cent of its total outlay during post-reforms period. So with regard to utilization of plan outlay ports and shipping sector has not shown sufficient progress during post-reform period. Globalization process has not shown the way to the port and shipping sector of its shortfall in approved plan outlays from actual plan expenditure during different plan periods.

6.10. PRIVATE INVESTMENT

The major ports of the country handled 281 million tonnes of cargo in 2000-01. By the end of 2007, Indian ports are expected to handle 415 million tonnes of cargo. This will require huge investments for the creation of additional facilities. There is also an urgent need for the modernization of existing ports to improve their operational efficiency. Above all the capacity of the major ports was not adequate to meet the traffic demand. However, efforts were made to create additional capacities and new port facilities. But even today a number of major ports suffer capacity constraints.

In this situation public sector alone will not be in a position to modernize the ports sector through its investment. Therefore, there is a need for the private sector to play an important role in this sector. The Major Ports Act of 1963 allows private provision of services at the major ports. The legislation already permits private sector intervention in port operations in the form of leasing of port assets, construction and operation of facilities, leasing of equipment for cargo handling, pilot age, and captive facilities for port-based industries.

In order to improve efficiency, productivity and quality of services as well as to bring in competitiveness in port services, the port sector has been thrown open to private sector participation. This is in consonance with the general policy of liberalization of economy of the Government. Various areas of port functioning such as leasing out existing assets of the port, construction and creation of additional assets, leasing of equipment for port handling and leasing of floating crafts from the private sector, pilotage and captive facilities for port based industries have been identified for participation and investment by the private sector. Joint venture formations between major port and foreign port, between major port and minor ports without tender as well as between major port and companies following tender route are permitted by the Government. These measures are aimed at facilitating port trusts to attract new technology, introduce better managerial process, expedite implementation of schemes, promote strategic alliance with minor ports for creation of optimal port infrastructure and enhance confidence of private sector in funding ports.

"Broadly, the following areas have been identified for the private sector participation in port sector:

- Operation and setting up of container terminals.
- Setting up of warehousing and storage facilities.
- Operation and maintenance of various cargo handling terminals.
- Operation and maintenance of floating crafts.
- Provision of pilotage, dredging and carnage services.
- Maintenance of other miscellaneous services."[9]

The Central Government has adopted policy measures aimed at opening the port sector to private investors and operators. Based on the Major Ports Act of 1963, this policy was strengthened at the federal level by the 1996 "Guidelines on Privatization", which provides a more precise framework for private participation in the major ports. At the state level maritime states have issued policy statements in the form of infrastructure policy or port policy papers. Gujarat was the first state to publish a port policy statement in 1995; Karnataka is the most recent. Private sector participation in development and operations of port infrastructure is the most prominent feature in each document.

As far as major ports are concerned, two container terminals are now operational, one being P&O Australia's container terminal at the Jawaharlal Nehru Port Trust and second the recently opened PSA-Sical terminal at Tuticorin. Construction of one 150-meter container berth was completed. Four largely captive ports, all based in Gujarat, are being developed with private financing. In addition to the projects mentioned, several other projects at the State and Central Government levels have been offered to the private sector, largely for the development of new facilities.

"Over the years the private sector participation in the development of ports has been very encouraging. So far 13 private sector projects have been operationalized having an investment of Rs. 2,597.20 crore and capacity addition of 47.40 MTPA. There are 24 other projects having investment of

Rs. 7158.40 crore and capacity addition of around 89.29 MTPA under various stages of evaluation and implementation."[10] Private sector participation in the development of ports in India is encouraged through Build, Operate and Transfer (BOT) or through joint venture projects. Some of the measures introduced for encouraging private sector participation in ports are the following:

- Relaxation of Cabotage law.
- Enactment of the Multimodal Transportation of Goods Act, 1993.
- Ports having berth reservation facilities.
- Leasing of berths to private entrepreneurs.
- Leasing of land and water front for setting up ship repair facilities.
- Creation of storage facilities.
- Privatization of try docks and liberalization of licensing procedures.

6.11. SECTOR REGULATION

The Tariff Authority for Major Ports (TAMP) was established in 1997 as a distinct body under the umbrella of MOST to regulate port tariffs independently from the Port Trusts. TAMP was created in response to protests by private partners in the port system that they could not expect fair treatment on tariff matters from the Port Trust. TAMP has responsibility for setting the tariffs of the major ports. It can also set tariffs for private licensers operating at a major port. TAMP is supposed to promote rationalization of the tariff system, applying uniform principles at ports to develop cost-based prices. TAMP's overall objective is to move towards competitive pricing.

TAMP allowes the operator to have a tariff ceiling based on container handling charges currently levied at Jawaharlal Nehru. Cargo-related charges will be specified in rupees. In this ruling TAMP held that port operators should not be allowed to charge or calculate tariffs in foreign currency for cargo handling services.

6.12. POLICY RECOMMENDATIONS FOR THE PORTS SECTOR

Although there has been progress in bringing the private sector into port development and operation, reforms are needed to provide greater commercial autonomy to all the port trusts. It is also necessary to enhance competition among ports, and provide the necessary institutional structure for a modernized ports sector. Indian ports have the potential for emerging as world hubs. This requires an immediate upgradation of their handling technology, an modernization of their equipment and management. These demand commercialization. For this there could be a three-tiered structure policy for the interests of the Central, State and local agencies involved in ports sector.

6.12.1. Restructuring the Ports Sector

It is necessary to restructure the existing ports sector. There could be statutory authorities independent of political interests to deal with the policy of regulatory and commercial aspect. This in turn will help to reduce conflicts of interest of various organizations involved in the Ports Sector. Statutory authorities could be created at each major port and TAMP could continue to play the role of higher reference to other statutory organizations.

6.12.2. Improving Inter-Ministerial Coordination

MOST and the Ministry of Railways have a shared interest in finding a common approach to create inter-modal platforms that would reduce transport costs and increase trade competitiveness. In normal situations the cargo transfer between Indian Railways and the local port railways results in delays. Therefore, a common approach is necessary to enhance the impact of such developments and integrate them into the inland transport network as a whole. Even at the port level, systematic cooperation between Indian Railways, Container Corporation of India, and the Central Warehousing Corporation would definitely improve the investment in the ports system.

6.12.3. Addressing Labour Problems

Rearrangement of the workforce consistent with modern traffic and cargo handling requirements cannot be avoided in the ports sector. Before bringing the private sector into Ports sector it is necessary to introduce management skills and resolve problems related to workforce so that the existing social protection could ensure that the staff adjustment process is acceptable. These provisions could also include retraining, voluntary retirement, indemnity payments for voluntary departure, and creation of a temporary workers' pool.

6.12.4. Autonomous Port Authorities

Autonomous port authorities should be made to operate on commercial lines so that they can raise resources from the primary market by way of equity and debt and from financial institutions. They should also be allowed to fix tariffs so as to cover their debt obligations and earn a reasonable return on equity. Port authorities should be delegated powers to create new technical ports required for modernization.

6.12.5. Training Institutes

Training institutes should be set up to improve the technical skills of the existing labour in line with modernization of ports. Enhanced technical skills will help to minimize the unionized labour problems, because they are capable of functioning in a new environment and privatization.

6.13. CONCLUSION

The development of the port and shipping is a prerequisite for sustained growth of the economy. Availability of adequate ports and shipping services is also considered a key to encourage foreign direct investment. India for long suffered from transport bottlenecks, mainly because of budgetary constraints and managerial inefficiencies. To overcome this handicap, conscious efforts need to be made to improve work efficiency and availability of modern equipment facilities within Indian ports and ships. In this regard the importance of private sector participation in bridging the resource gap and improving the operational and managerial efficiency has also been greatly recognized. For this it is necessary to apply "market principles" for the development of ports and shipping infrastructure and services. In this regard some success has been achieved in associating the private sector in ports projects. Efforts are also being made to make private participation models such as BOT more investor-friendly in the ports sector by focusing on downside risks of low traffic volumes. However, there is still a long way to go in this sector. Therefore, a revised strategy is necessary to pursue and further liberalization in the future. Drawing lessons from experiences in the past, it is necessary to formulate new policies, offering more attractive incentive packages and developing mechanisms to ensure greater participation of the private sector. With the involvement of the private sector in the shipping and ports, the private sector definitely will gain more confidence in undertaking transport projects through partnership arrangements with the public sector so that the overall environment becomes more conducive to the consumers with better infrastructure facilities in the port and shipping sector.

END NOTES

1. *Annual Report, 2004-05*, Ministry of Shipping, Government of India, New Delhi, p. 95.
2. These ports are namely, Kolkata (including Haldia), Mumbai, Chennai, Cochin, Kandla, and Vishakhapatnam.
3. These include Paradip, Tuticorin, New Mangalore, Mormugao, and Jawaharlal Nehru.
4. This includes Ennore.
5. It is evident from the fact that the recently completed private container terminal at Nhava Sheva handled about 733 TEUs a day in its first year of operation, compared with 330 TEUs a day at the adjacent public container terminal.
6. Satya Sundaram, "Ports-Policy Imperatives", M.V. Srinivasa Gowda and Susheela Subrahmanya, *Infrastructure Development for Economic Growth*, Deep & Deep Publications, New Delhi, 1997, p. 307.
7. The Colombo port can handle fourth generation container vessels doing 50 to 60 moves per hour with ease, India is served almost exclusively by small feeder vessels which in turn go on to Colombo where the containers are transshipped from the feeder vessels to the large mother vessels for onward transshipment. India is made to pay a high price if we consider the cost of operating the feeder vessel, loading cost at Indian ports and the costs at Colombo. Indian ports

are totally inadequate for servicing fully containerized ships or very large crude carriers carrying well over a million tonnes.

8. Raghuvansi 1996; Shashikumar 1998; Fairplay 1996a, 1996b.
9. R. Ramanathan, "Transport a Crucial Infrastructure", *India Development Report, 1997*, p. 235.
10. *India 2006: A Reference Annual*, Publication Division, Ministry of Information and Broadcasting Government of India, New Delhi, 2006, p. 824.

Civil Aviation and Economic Reforms in India

7

7.1. INTRODUCTION

As India modernizes rapidly, the Civil Aviation sector has acquired a vital role in the economic growth and development of the country. The role of Civil Aviation sector in linking various parts of the country and enabling speedy movement of men and material hardly need be emphasized. In India air transport plays an important role in places where industrial and commercial centers are located. The full potential of the Civil Aviation sector in India, however, has yet to be realized. This means an improvement in the quality of services, competitive pricing, better airport infrastructure, etc. In the past, steps were taken to improve the quality of air transport services. The emphasis was on liberalization of the air transport sector in order to encourage private sector participation. Over the years, the Government has disengaged itself considerably from commercial airline operations. Private sector participation in domestic air services has been aimed at bridging the resource gap in investments to meet the growing demand and improve the managerial and operational efficiency of air services. The process of disinvestment of public sector airlines namely, Air India and Indian Airlines is under active consideration. In order to make the major airports world class, a decision has been taken to restructure the existing airports at Delhi, Mumbai, Chennai and Kolkata through long-term leases. While the process of disinvestment of Indian Airlines and Air India has received some setbacks, progress with regard to private sector participation in the development of the four metropolitan airports at Delhi, Mumbai, Chennai and Kolkata has been satisfactory.

7.2. BRIEF HISTORY

In India civil aviation started in 1920 with the construction of some aerodromes by the Government. In 1927 Civil Aviation department was set up. After Second World War considerable importance was attached for the development of private airliners with Government help. Before the year 1953, there were nine private airlines in operation along with many war surplus aircraft. However, all airlines were considered sick financially and beyond recovery.

In order to overcome financial difficulties and to achieve recovery in 1950, Air Transport Enquiry Committee was set up and this Committee recommended the nationalization of all private airline companies. Accordingly in 1953, Air Transport Corporation Act was passed. This Act paved the way for the establishment of Indian Airlines Corporation for internal services and Air India International for providing external services. Vayudoot service was introduced for running internal services to different under-developed and inaccessible areas. As a result of nationalization of air transport the scheduled services was reserved for corporations and it provided monopoly to national carriers and associates for scheduled services.

In September 1990 air taxi operations commenced but its extensive expansion began only in February 1992. However, the air taxi operation was confined to highly profitable routes and was only for non-scheduled operations. Air taxi operations, however, grew like scheduled services and then it was decided to repeal Air Corporations Act with effect from 1.3.1994. This was undertaken to remove monopoly of air corporations on scheduled services so that private airlines could operate in scheduled service. The repeal of Corporations Act made possible for the private sectors to participate in the national carriers. The Government as a result has ended the monopoly of Indian Airlines and Air India on the scheduled operations. Also in May 1993, the Vayudoot was merged with Indian Airlines in order to contain its mounting losses.

With a view to achieve better regulation of air transport services and taking into account the need for air transport services of different regions of the country, the Government issued Route Dispersal Guidelines on 1.3.1994. In accordance with Route Dispersal Guidelines, all routes were divided into Category I, II, IIA and III. There are three main functional divisions—regulatory, infrastructural and operational—in civil aviation sectors. Operational function deals with airline capacities while infrastructural pertains to airport and allied facility development. The third segment is the regulatory and developmental functions which are carried out by the Ministry of Civil Aviation and the offices of the Directorate General of Civil Aviation. Indian and private operators provide domestic air services in India, and Indian and selected private operators also provide international air services. Pawan Hans Limited provides helicopter support services. Infrastructural facilities are provided by Airports Authority of India.

At present there are ten scheduled airlines operating on the domestic network rendering the passengers a wide choice of flights. Apart from this, at present 41 companies are holding non-scheduled operators permit. The policy on domestic air transport service was approved in April 1997 according to which barriers to enter and exit from this sector have been removed. Over and above this, the choice of aircraft type and size has been left to the operator. But equity from foreign airlines, directly or indirectly in this sector has been prohibited.

As on 31 May 2005, India has bilateral Air Services Agreement with 100 countries. A revised liberalized Agreement has been concluded with USA recently. Liberalized agreements have also been concluded with some important traffic markets like UK, China, Australia, Germany and France. With a view to optimally utilize our bilateral entitlements, Indian scheduled carriers with at least five years continuous operations in domestic sector and fleet size of 20 aircrafts have also been permitted to operate to all overseas destinations except Gulf Countries of UAE, Qatar, Oman, Bahrain and Kuwait as well as Saudi Arabia.

7.3. ADMINISTRATION OF CIVIL AVIATION

The Ministry of Civil Aviation is responsible for the formulation of national policies and programmes for development and regulation of Civil Aviation and for devising and implementing schemes for orderly growth and expansion of civil air transport. Its functions also extend to overseeing the provision of airport facilities, air traffic services and carriage of passengers and goods by air. The Ministry oversees the development and regulation of civil aviation in the country including, *inter alia*, establishment of new aerodromes, maintenance and upgradation of the existing aerodromes, regulation of carriage of traffic by air and ensuring civil aviation safety and security. The Ministry is also administratively responsible for the Commissioner of Railway Safety, a statutory body set up under the Railway Act. Attached or Subordinate Organizations include, Director General of Civil Aviation, Bureau of Civil Aviation Security and Commission of Railway Safety which are under the administrative purview of the Ministry of Civil Aviation.

The Directorate General of Civil Aviation is the principal regulatory body in the field of civil aviation. It is responsible for regulation of air transport services within India and for formulation and enforcement of civil air regulations, air safety and airworthiness standards. All regulatory functions of International Civil Aviation Organization are also co-ordinated by them. The Bureau of Civil Aviation Security is responsible for laying down the standards of pre-embarkation security and anti-sabotage measures in respect of civil flights in India. The Commissioner of Railway Safety deals with matters pertaining to railway safety in rail travel and operation and for this purpose performs certain statutory functions laid down in the Railway Act. In addition to framing policies, the Ministry provides guidance to these organizations in the implementation of policy guidelines and monitors and evaluates their interface with Parliament. It also supervises implementation by the organization of the special programmes of Government, particularly those intended for weaker sections.

7.4. AIR TRANSPORT UNDER VARIOUS FIVE-YEAR PLANS

A sum of Rs. 15.34 crore was actually spent on the development of Air Transport under the First Five-Year Plan. During the plan, Airports of Bangalore, Khewal, Kampalpur, Pasigha, Chandigarh, Kandla and Udaipur, etc. were built. The outlay for the Second Five-Year Plan was Rs. 30.53 crore, out of which Rs. 16 crore were to be spent on the Indian Airline Corporation and Rs. 14.53 crore on Air India International Services. By the end of the Second Five-Year Plan, about 9.7 lakh passengers took advantage of the scheduled services of the Civil Aviation and 7.4 lakh kgs of goods were transported.

The Third Five-Year Plan envisaged Rs. 55 crore for the development of Air Transport but only a sum of Rs. 47 crores could be actually spent. In the year 1966, Indian Aircraft completed the flight of 557.8 lakh kms. The Fourth Five-Year Plan envisaged spending Rs. 202 crore for the development of Air Transport. During this plan, the facility of Delhi, Bombay, Culcutta and Madras Airports were increased.

Under the Fifth Five-Year Plan, Rs. 334.9 crore was allocated for the purpose of development of Air Transport. The Sixth Five-Year Plan envisaged Rs. 850 crore for the development of air transport. Out of this amount, Rs. 227 crore was to be spent by Air India and Rs. 272 crore by Indian Airlines. This Plan had the objectives of (i) to provide additional capacity at the international airport to relieve heavy congestion at peak hours; (ii) to provide additional workshop and maintenance facilities in order to get self-reliance; and (iii) to provide additional safety oriented equipment at airports. Seventh Plan has provided Rs. 730.21 crore for civil aviation which would suffice to meet the expenditure on ongoing schemes and a few new schemes to be started during plan period.

The competitive environment on domestic services has been, in effect, existent since April, 1993. By November 1996, 34 aircraft in the 120 plus category, belonging to private air taxis, were in operation and they catered to 41.1 per cent of the market. The number of passengers carried by air taxi operators has increased from 15,000 in 1990 to 4.1 lakh in 1992, 29.2

lakh in 1993 and 42.6 lakh during 1997. Thus the Indian Airlines has been facing stiff competition from these private operators. In order to face such competition, several measures have been taken to adopt a marketing approach in decision making and also to improve quality of its service. It has improved its passenger facilities both on board and on the ground, on time performance flight safety measures and has also increased employee participation to provide better services.

During Eighth Plan, Air India achieved a traffic growth at a rate of 14.4 per cent. In terms of targets, the capacity available ending 1997 was 3061.6 million kms and anticipated capacity utilization was 1983.3 million revenue tonne kms. Rs. 3998 crores were approved for the plan period of 1992-97.

At present, six scheduled private airlines provide regular domestic air services along with Indian Airlines. There are 40 non-scheduled operators providing air taxi/non-scheduled air transport services. The number of passengers availing of private sector air services has increased from 15,000 in 1990-91 to 6.7 million in 2001-02. Moreover, Airport Authority of India (AAI) earned profit after tax deduction of Rs. 276 crore in 2001-02 against Rs. 214.1 crore in 2000-01. Government of India has approved restructuring of four metro Airports viz. Chennai, Kolkata, Mumbai and Delhi.

7.5. CARGO TRAFFIC PERFORMANCE

India's air traffic is highly concentrated at a few airports. Therefore, in order to help the Indian exporters and make their exports more competitive, the Government introduced in April 1992 an 'open sky policy' for cargo. Under this policy foreign airlines or association of exporters can bring any freighters to the country to carry cargo. It has also permitted market forces to determine cargo traffic with IATA rates as the floor rates.

Table 7.1 illustrates the growth of cargo traffic and operational performance in civil aviation. In 1980-81, the total cargo handled at AAI Airports was about 178.70 thousand tonnes and in 1990-91 the total cargo handled increased to 377.3 thousand tonnes. The growth of cargo handled at AAI Airports as in 1990-91 over 1980-81 was 111.14 per cent.

Whereas in 2000-01, the total cargo handled at AAI Airports was about 842.15 tonnes and its percentage of change as on 2000-01 over 1990-91 was 123.18 per cent. It is just 12 per cent more than the growth achieved during 1980-81 to 1990-91. It means that the open sky policy for cargo adopted by the Government did not help in increase of total cargo handled at AAI Airports.

With regard to revenue tonne kilometers, Indian Airlines and Air India had not performed well during post-reforms period. Total revenue tonne kilometers by Air India and Indian Airlines was 138.04 crore as on 1980-81 and it increased to 208.02 crore for the year 1990-91 and percentage of growth as on 1990-91 over 1980-81 is of 50.69 per cent. But in the year 2000-01 total revenue tonne kilometers by Air India and Indian Airlines increased to 227.87 crore and the percentage of change as on 2000-01 over 1990-91 was 9.54 per cent, which is 41.15 per cent less than what was achieved during pre-reforms period. Entry of large number of private aircrafts into handling cargo traffic is the main reason attributed towards decline in the total revenue tonne kilometers in Indian Airlines and Air India during post-reforms period.

For Indian Airlines and Air India total available tonnes kilometers was 2286 millions in 1980-81 and it increased to 3187 millions in 1990-91. For Indian Airlines and Air India additional air cargo in terms of total available tonnes kilometers as on 1990-91 over 1980-81 is of 39.41 per cent. It further increased to 3573 millions in the year 2000-01 and additional air cargo in terms of total available tonnes kilometers increased to 12.11 per cent as on 2000-01 over 1990-91. In the same manner total revenue tones kilometers for Indian Airlines and Air India in 1980-81 was 1400 million and it further increased to 2080 million and 2279 million in 1990-91 and 2000-01 respectively. Percentage of total revenue tonnes kilometers change as on 1990-91 over 1980-81 was 48.57 per cent and 9.57 per cent change in 2000-01 over 1990-91. So in terms of capacity available and capacity utilized performance during pre-reforms was much greater in comparison to post-reforms period.

Table 7.1. Growth of Cargo Traffic in Civil Aviation

	1980-81	1990-91	1995-96	2000-01	2001-02	2002-03	2003-04
1. Revenue tonne kilometers (Rs. crore)							
(i) Air India	98.01	138.10	161.90	150.14	139.90	156.10	177.30
(ii) Indian Airlines	40.03	69.92	72.27	77.73	75.55	84.51	87.75
Total	138.04	208.02	234.17	227.87	215.45	240.61	265.05
2. Cargo handled at (Thousand tonnes)							
AAI Airports	178.70	377.33	561.58	842.15	854.28	979.36	1068.20
3. Indian Airlines							
(i) Available tonne kilometers (Million)	663	927	1046	1154	1200	1308	1334
(ii) Revenue tonne kilometers (Million)	420	699	723	777	756	845	878
(iii) Load Factor %		75.2	69.1	67.4	62.9	64.6	65.8
4. Air India							
(i) Available tonne kilometers (Million)	1623	2260	2610	2419	2393	2496	2984
(ii) Revenue tonne kilometers (Million)	980	1381	1619	1502	1619	NA	NA
(iii) Load Factor %		61.1	62.0	67.4	60.8	64.6	61.2
5. Total of 3 and 4							
(i) Available tonne kilometers (Million)	2286	3187	3656	3573	3593	3804	4318
(ii) Revenue tonne kilometers (Million)	1400	2080	2342	2279	2375	—	—

Source: Annual Report of Ministry of Civil Aviation and various Five-Year Plans.

7.5.1. International Freight Traffic

The total freight carried internationally has been growing over the years. Other than year 2001-02, the percentage of change over previous years has been positive and only in the year 2001-02 its growth over previous year has been negative. In 1998-99, total international freight traffic to India and from India has been 413215 tonnes of which 83861 tonnes have been by Indian operators and 329353 tonnes have been by foreign operators (Table 7.2). In 1999-2000, total international freight traffic increased to 454271 tonnes and the percentage of change over previous years has been 9.9 per cent which can be considered as a remarkable growth in the field of international freight traffic. 87401 tonnes and 366870 tonnes have been by Indian operators and foreign operators respectively during 1999-2000 and the percentage of change over the previous years with regard to Indian operators and foreign operators has been 4.2 per cent and 11.4 per cent respectively. In the international freight traffics sector performance and growth of foreign operators has been greater in comparison to the growth achieved by Indian operators during 1999-2000.

It is interesting to note that within the foreign operators the percentage of change that has taken place in international freight traffic as on 2000-01 over previous year has been 14.5 per cent but with regard to Indian operators it is just 2.2 per cent. Greater growth registered by the foreign operators in international freight traffic brought about greater growth in the total growth of international freight traffic. In 2002-03 too foreign operators once again registered greater growth and the percentage of change over previous year has been 12.3 per cent by the foreign operators and the percentage of change over previous year by Indian operators has been 7.9 per cent which is greater than the growth achieved during 2000-01 by Indian operators.

Table 7.2. International Freight Traffic To and From India

Year	Operator	Freight (Tonne)			% Change over
		To	From	Total	Previous Year
1998-99	Indian	28046	55816	83861	
	Foreign	110012	219341	329353	
	Total	138058	275157	413215	
1999-2000	Indian	27039	60362	87401	4.2
	Foreign	125477	241393	366870	11.4
	Total	152516	301755	454271	9.9
2000-01	Indian	28753	60568	89321	2.2
	Foreign	145423	274677	420100	14.5
	Total	174176	335245	509421	12.1
2001-02	Indian	26564	59506	86070	-3.6
	Foreign	147792	263869	411661	-2.0
	Total	174356	323375	497731	-2.3
2002-03	Indian	27884	64982	92866	7.9
	Foreign	162495	299646	462141	12.3
	Total	190379	364628	555007	11.5
Average	Indian				2.68
	Foreign				9.05
	Total				7.8

Source: Ghosh, Buddhadeeb & Prabir De (2005), *Indian Infrastructure Database 2005*, Bookwell, New Delhi, Vol. II.

Total average growth of international freight traffic of last five years has been 7.8 per cent and the average growth of international freight traffic achieved by foreign operators has been 9.05 per cent. Whereas the average growth achieved by Indian operators during this period has been 2.68 per cent. It means that Indian operators have not benefited much in a tangible way from the policies implemented during post-reforms period. Foreign operators on the other hand benefited the most in terms of free sky policy followed during post-reforms period.

7.6. PASSENGERS TRAFFIC

7.6.1. Domestic Passengers Traffic

In 1980-81, AAI Airports handled about 107.38 lakh passengers and it increased to 177.23 and 420.27 lakh passengers as in 1990-91 and 2000-21 respectively. The additional percentage of growth in terms of passengers handled by AAI

Airports as in 1990-91 over 1980-81 and as in 2000-01 over 1990-91 is 65.05 per cent and 137.13 per cent respectively with the top five international airports—Mumbai, Delhi, Chennai, Kolkata, and Trivandrum service representing about 71 per cent of total air traffic activity. So in terms of percentage of growth achieved in passengers handled by AAI Airports during post-reforms period is greater in comparison to the growth achieved during pre-reforms period because during post-reforms period AAI Airports achieved 137.13 per cent growth while it achieved only 65.05 per cent during pre-reforms period which is 70.08 per cent less in reference to the growth achieved during post-reforms period.

Table 7.3. Growth of Passengers Traffic in Civil Aviation

	1980-81	1990-91	1995-96	2000-01	2001-02	2002-03	2003-04
1. Total fleet strength:							
(i) Air India	17	24	26	26	29	30	35@@
(ii) Indian Airlines	49	56	59	52	53	53	56**
Total:	66	80	85	78	82	83	91
2. Number of passengers carried (Lakh)							
(i) Air India	14.18	21.61	28.53	33.00	31.30	34.56	38.35
(ii) Indian Airlines	54.29	78.66	77.40	59.90	55.25	56.54	59.00
Total:	68.47	100.27	105.93	92.90	86.55	91.10	97.35
3. Passengers handled at (Lakh)							
AAI Airports	107.38	177.23	256.40	420.27	399.83	437.23	487.01

Note: ** Includes eleven airbuses A-300 acquired on dry lease.
@@ Includes 15 aircraft taken on dry lease.
Source: Ministry of Civil Aviation.

But the fact is quite different with regard to number of passengers carried by Air India and Indian Airlines. In 1980-81, total number of passengers carried by Air India and Indian Airlines accounted for 68.47 lakh and further increased to 100.27 lakh in 1990-91 (Table 7.3). Percentage of growth achieved during pre-reforms period in terms of number of passengers carried by Air India and Indian Airlines as on 1990-91 over 1980-81 is 46.44 per cent. Although number of passengers carried by Air India and Indian Airlines increased to 105.93 lakh in 1995-96, yet it decreased to 92.90 lakh in 2000-01 and further decreased to 91.10 lakh in 2002-03 and its growth as on 2000-01 over 1990-91 is of -7.35 per cent. So the growth achieved during post-reforms period in terms of number of passengers carried by Indian Airlines and Air India is a negative one. Free entry of large number of private operators in civil aviation is the main reason attributed towards fall in the number of passengers irrespective of the increase in total number of fleet strength from 66 to 78. It is evident from Table 7.4 and Figure 7.1.

Table 7.4. Domestic Passenger Traffic

Year	Passenger Traffic Carried by Scheduled Indian Carriers (Lakhs)
1981-82	48.50
1982-83	55.60
1985-86	86.17
1986-87	91.96
1990-91	74.71
1991-92	86.21
1992-93	76.61
1995-96	121.88
1996-97	117.00
2000-01	137.12
2001-02	128.56
2002-03	139.51

Source: Ghosh, Buddhadeb & Prabir De (2005), *Indian Infrastructure Database 2005*, Bookwell, New Delhi, Vol. II.

In 1991, total passengers carried by all airlines was 8.06 million and it further increased to 11.98 million passengers in 1995. However, domestic passenger traffic was 13.22 million in 2000 and it registered 18.17 million passengers for the year 2004. So percentage of change that has taken place as on 2004 over 1991 is 125.43 per cent and passenger growth as on 2000 over 1991 is 64 per cent and the average growth of domestic passenger traffic achieved during post-reforms period is 8.33 per cent. During initial stages of post-reforms period growth in the domestic passenger traffic was not seen much. But greater increase in the domestic passenger traffic has been witnessed only from the year 1994-95. However, 8.33 per cent average growth achieved in domestic passenger traffic did not result in the growth of passenger traffic in Air India and Indian Airlines. Reason for it is clear from Figure 7.2.

In 1991, percentage share of private operators in carriage of domestic passengers was only 0.4 per cent. But it increased to 52.8 per cent in the year 2000. The growth rate of private operators in carriage of domestic passengers as in 2000 over 1991 was 209.6 per cent and the average growth rate during post-liberalization period has been 20.96 per cent. The share of private operators in carriage of domestic passengers in civil aviation further increased to 65.5 per cent. This means that the Government sector no longer plays a leading role in the domestic civil aviation operations rather it is the private sector which plays a dominant role in carriage of domestic passengers. Liberalization of Indian sky is considered to be the dominant reason for the success of private sector in civil aviation operation in India. Open sky policy followed by the Government has attracted a number of private players in this sector which created an atmosphere of competition among domestic carrier players in civil aviation sector. In this competition private sector performed comparatively better in terms of low fare and facilities. As a result large numbers of passengers were attracted towards private air operators which caused increase in the share of number of passengers carried by the private operators.

7.6.2. International Passengers Traffic

The total passengers carried internationally have been growing over the years. Other than year 2001-02, the percentage of change over previous years have been positive and only in the year 2001-02 its growth over previous year has been negative due to the Afghanistan war which occurred during this year. In 1998-99, total international passengers traffic to India and from India has been 11,01,6376 of which 33,12,222 have been carried by Indian operators and 77,04,154 have been carried by foreign operators (Table 7.5).

In 1999-2000 total international passengers traffic increased to 1,14,53,041 and the percentage of change over previous years has been 4.0 per cent. Number of international passengers carried by Indian operators and foreign operators has been 34,59,153 and 79,93,888 respectively during 1999-2000 and the percentage of change over the previous years with regard to

Table 7.5. International Passengers Traffic To and From India

Year	Operator	Passengers (No.)			% Change over
		To	From	Tot al	Previous Year
1998-99	Indian	1631526	1680696	3312222	
	Foreign	3765699	3938455	7704154	
	Total	5397225	5619151	11016376	
1999-2000	Indian	1706326	1752827	3459153	4.4
	Foreign	3950719	4043169	7993888	3.8
	Total	5657045	5795996	11453041	4.0
2000-01	Indian	1751437	1842132	3593569	3.9
	Foreign	4267154	4417205	8684359	8.6
	Total	6018591	6259337	12277928	7.2
2001-02	Indian	1683962	1772973	3456935	-3.8
	Foreign	4146327	4304511	8450838	-2.7
	Total	5830289	6077484	11907773	-3.8
2002-03	Indian	1909443	2047591	3957034	14.5
	Foreign	4464419	4738749	9203168	8.9
	Total	6373862	6786340	13160202	10.5
Average	Indian				4.75
	Foreign				4.65
	Total				4.46

Source: Ghosh, Buddhadeb & Prabir De (2005), *Indian Infrastructure Database 2005*, Bookwell, New Delhi, Vol. II.

Indian operators and foreign operators has been 4.4 per cent and 3.8 per cent respectively. In the international passenger traffic, performance and growth of Indian operators has been greater in comparison to the growth and performance attained by foreign operators during 1999-2000.

It is interesting to note that within the Indian operators the percentage of change that had taken place in international passenger traffic as in 2000-01 over previous year had been 8.6 per cent but with regard to Indian operators it was 3.9 per cent. During this period greater growth registered by the foreign operators brought about greater growth in the total growth of international passenger traffic. But in 2002-03 too it was Indian operators who registered greater growth in international passenger traffic and the percentage of change over previous year has been 14.5 per cent by the Indian operators and the percentage of change over previous year by foreign operators have been 8.9 per cent which is greater than the growth achieved during 2000-01 by foreign operators.

Total average growth of international passengers traffic of last five years has been 4.6 per cent and the average growth of international passenger traffic achieved by foreign operators has been 4.65. Whereas the average growth achieved by Indian operators during this period has been 4.75 per cent. It means that Indian operators performed better during post-reforms period and benefited from the policies implemented during post-reforms period.

7.7. FINANCIAL PERFORMANCE

7.7.1. Air India

Air India earned a profit from the year 1984 to 1994-95 that is during pre-reforms period and initial stages of post-reforms. The strategy however could not be sustained for long because of hike in ATF prices, increase in landing and navigational charges, increase in insurance premium rates. As a result Air India experienced losses for the year 1995-96 and 2000-01.

Table 7.6. Air India: Financial Performance

	1979-80	1990-91	1995-96	2000-01	2001-02	2002-03	2003-04
Revenue							
Operating	397.37	1626.88	3426.55	4927.45	4751.36	5275.91	5987.98
Expenses							
Operating	401.47	1428.65	3647.56	4924.35	4805.89	5465.63	6104.24
Profit/Loss	-4.10	198.23	-221.01	3.10	-54.53	-189.72	-116.26
Total Revenue	402.06	1747.96	3562.70	5278.84	5032.94	5689.88	6322.07
Total Expenses	417.04	1666.73	3834.54	5323.24	5017.50	5556.02	6229.74
Net Profit/Loss	-15.09	81.23	-271.84	-44.40	15.44	133.86	92.33

Source: Various Five-Year Plans and Annual Report, Ministry of Civil Aviation.

However, during other years Air India has earned a profit in spite of competition received from private airline operators by resorting to aggressive marketing initiatives, cost control measures and increased utilization of aircraft. One cannot visualize a tangible effect of liberalization on financial performance as far as Air India is concerned. Profit earned by Air India during post-reforms period is not stable and constant rather there was so much of fluctuation within financial performance of Air India.

7.7.2. Indian Airlines

Profitable character is a necessary component for survival of any organization. During pre-liberalization period profitable character was lacking in financial performance of Indian Airlines. It was running at loss rather than at profit. Disinvestment of Indian Airlines and market strategy has been adopted during post-reforms period with assumption that these steps undertaken will enhance the performance of Indian Airlines and this in turn will alter the existing situation of loss into profit.

But the Indian Airlines financial performance clearly (Table 7.7) indicates that the ever-increasing trend of loss has in no way changed during post-reforms period rather the increasing trend is also visible during post-reforms period. The loss was Rs. 2.34 crore in the year 1979-80 and it increased to Rs. 64.59 crore in 1990-91. The net loss incurred in 1995-96 is Rs. 109.98 crore and it further increased to Rs. 250.12 crore and Rs. 328.28 crore in 2000-01 and 2001-02 respectively. One of the reasons for poor financial performance is the burden assumed by the airlines after the merger of Vayudoot and the absorption of high increase in the inputs cost.

During pre-reforms period Indian Airlines was able to cross-subsidize non-commercial routes from surplus profit earned from the commercial profitable routes. With the introduction of private airlines and consequent decline in the market share and profitability on trunk routes the capacity of Indian Airlines to cross-subsidize these routes has been severely eroded. As a result Indian Airlines is suffering from ever increase in net losses even during post-reforms period. Policies initiated during post-reforms period did not create positive impact on the financial performance of Indian Airlines.

Table 7.7. Indian Airlines: Financial Performance

(Rs. Crores)

	1979-80	1990-91	1995-96	2000-01	2001-02	2002-03	2003-04	2004-05
Revenue Operating	205.04	1124.00	2466.81	4292.95	4665.63	4101.50	4649.80	5041.00
Expenses Operating	191.40	1073.00	2310.30	4390.57	4874.91	4236.23	4524.70	5024.50
Profit/Loss	13.64	51.00	135.31	-97.62	209.28	134.73	125.10	16.50
Total Revenue	207.68	1169.00	2489.84	4300.45	4672.13	NA	NA	5047.50
Total Expenses	210.02	1234.00	2599.82	4550.57	5000.41	NA	NA	5072.25
Net Profit/Loss	-2.34	-64.59	-109.98	-250.12	-328.28	NA	NA	-24.75

Source: Various Five-Year Plans and Annual Report, Ministry of Civil Aviation.

It is therefore necessary to create a conducive policy framework to overcome the problem of ever increase in net losses incurred. For this it is also essential to take suitable financial and organizational measures to make the airlines a viable and a vibrant enterprise. The Ninth Five-Year Plan rightly "calls for the restructuring of Indian Airlines in which all stakeholders will be involved."[1] Along with it should also aim at a sound capital base and 'organizational restructuring will' so that it can function as a company managed by a Board constituted of professionals. There is a need to evolve fleet planning strategy which takes into account the route structure of the Indian Airlines so as to ensure optimum utilization of resources, particularly aircrafts.[2]

7.7.3. Airport Authority of India

The net profit of the Airport Authority of India increased from Rs. 57.39 crore in 1990-91 to Rs. 241.08 crore in 2000-01 and the growth as on 2000-01 over 1990-91 is of 273.02 per cent and the average growth in the net profit of the Airport Authority of India during post-reforms period was 27.30 per cent annually. The net profit growth as on 2001-02 over 2000-01 is 24.71 per cent. The Airport Authority of India therefore has significantly improved its financial performance during post-reforms period. This growth is mainly due to increase in the number of private operators as well as due to growth in traffic in civil aviation sector.

Table 7.8. Airport Authority of India: Financial Performance

	1989-90	1990-91	1995-96	2000-01	2001-02	2002-03	2003-04	2004-05
Revenue	227.83	230.89	1003.33	1873.44	2244.84	2384.49	2630.59	2769.65
Expenses	83.38	96.12	727.28	1514.36	1767.86	1887.44	2086.63	2169.32
Profit/Loss before tax	64.67	57.39	N.A	214.08	266.98	282.05	314.96	348.32

Source: Various Five-Year Plans and Annual Report, Ministry of Civil Aviation.

As a result Airport Authority of India was able to achieve the goal of upgradation of infrastructure and modernization of communication facilities and maintenance of existing infrastructure during post-reforms period. Over and above to keep pace with the growth of international trade and for the promotion of exports, the airport infrastructure was upgraded in terms of storage pace, better handling capacity and development of cargo complexes at Delhi and Mumbai Airports. Investments were also made in respect of hinterland airports having potential for exports and tourism. Investments were made for the development of air strips and upgradation of communication facilities and other infrastructure in the northeast and Nicobar Islands as private investments were unlikely in these areas.

7.8. STAFF STRENGTH IN CIVIL AVIATION

Post-reforms period has resulted in reduction in the total number of staff strength maintained by Indian Airlines, Air India and Alliance Air. In 1993-94, staff strength of Indian Airlines, Air India and Alliance Air were 40,090 of which 837 were pilots and co-pilots, 3,411 were other flight personnel, 14,208 were maintenance and overhaul personnel, 9,810 were ticketing sales personnel and 11,824 were others.

Over the years there has been a growth in number of flights, passengers carried and freights. Increase in number of flights, passengers carried and freights did not result in increase of staff strength in Indian Airlines, Air India and Alliance Air. In 1994-95, 1995-96, 1997-98 and 1998-99 there is minor increase in staff strength of Indian Airlines, Air India and Alliance Air. But in other years there was considerable reduction in the staff strength of these airlines.

In 2002-03 staff strength of Indian Airlines, Air India and Alliance Air were 36,204 of which 903 were pilots and co-pilots, 2,882 were other flight personnel, 8,022 were maintenance and overhaul personnel, 8,598 were ticketing sales personnel and 15,799 were others. In comparison with 1993-94 total staff strength of Indian Airlines, Air India and Alliance Air was reduced to 3,886 and the change as on 2002-03 over 1993-94 has been 9.7 per cent. This means that less staff is employed to accomplish greater volume of work, leading to greater improvement in the work efficiency of the staff employed. So post-reforms period has been an effective instrument to bring

Table 7.9. Staff Strength of Indian Airlines, Air India and Alliance Air

Year	Pilots Co-pilots	Other Flight Personnel	Maintenance and Overhaul Personnel	Ticketing Sales Personnel	Others	Grand Total	% of Change over Previous Years
1993-94	837	3411	14208	9810	11824	40090	
1994-95	791	3351	14244	9767	11985	40138	0.12
1995-96	764	3251	11043	9736	15401	40195	0.14
1996-97	847	3342	9403	9619	16596	39803	-0.96
1997-98	854	3296	9608	9626	16964	40348	1.37
1998-99	933	3189	9439	9823	17849	41233	2.19
1999-2000	887	3149	8701	9168	16678	38585	-6.42
2000-01	861	3093	8931	9000	15958	37844	-1.92
2001-02	893	2985	8320	8675	16299	37172	-1.78
2002-03	903	2882	8022	8598	15799	36204	-2.60
Average percentage of change							-1.10

Source: Ghosh, Buddhadeb & Prabir De (2005), *Indian Infrastructure Database 2005*, Bookwell, New Delhi, Vol. II.

about greater work efficiency in the staff employed by Indian Airlines, Air India and Alliance Air.

7.9. PRIVATE SECTOR PARTICIPATION

Developing airport infrastructure must be placed within the broader context of growth in air travel and development of the aviation sector. Key issues to address include the future deregulation of the Indian aviation industry and its effect on market size, the role of the public sector in providing airline services[3] and bilateral arrangements and alternative mechanisms to increase traffic for scheduled and non-scheduled carriers. The plans for airport expansion must be viewed in the light of traffic levels, which include modest growth in traffic at some international airports.

As construction of airports is highly capital intensive, Government alone will not be able to meet the investment requirement. Private sector therefore will have to be encouraged to participate in the construction of airports at Greenfield level. Also there is a need for the participation of private sector in the development of airports both for reasons of bridging the gap in resources as also to bring in greater efficiency in management of airports.

The Policy on Airport Infrastructure thus, approved by the Cabinet in December 1997, endorsed the Government's focus on increasing private sector participation. Following are the private sector initiatives undertaken. As a first undertaking the partially privately financed Cochin airport has recently been commissioned on a Build-Own-Operate (BOO) basis. It will operate both domestic and international flights catering to passenger and cargo traffic. The State of Kerala has offered guarantees for the entire amount of the term loan, while the Housing and Urban Development Corporation has provided financing up to Rs. 98 crores. The Government of Kerala also has provided 26 per cent of the equity. The Airports Authority of India will provide air traffic control services.

Tata Industries Ltd. (India), Raytheon Engineering and Constructors (United States), and Information Technology Park Investments (Singapore) proposed constructing an international airport on a BOO basis at Bangalore, but the project was abandoned. Several key issues had to be resolved for the project to proceed. These included future traffic allocations, terms for the transfer of ownership titles to make land available, and strengthening of related infrastructure activities.

The Government of Karnataka has recently taken initiatives to restart the project. The AAI and a State Government agency signed a memorandum of understanding for further action. Under the memorandum, the two parties have invited offers from firms to act as partners in the development and operation of the airport. It is proposed that the airport be developed as a joint venture in which the public sector[4] holds at least 26 per cent of the equity. The joint venture agreement will also detail responsibilities concerning provision of basic infrastructure for the airport.

Two new Greenfield airports with private sector participation are proposed to be set up at Bangalore and Hyderabad. These airports are to be set up as joint ventures where the private partners will hold 74 per cent equity and State Governments and AAI will together hold the balance 26 per cent. The State Government of Andhra Pradesh and Karnataka have selected the private sector partners. The project of the new Greenfield airport at Devanahalli near Bangalore is to be implemented on a Build-Own-Operate basis. Construction work at Greenfield airports of international standards at Hyderabad and Bangalore have commenced. The two airports are likely to be operational by the middle of the year 2008.

"The international airport in Delhi and Mumbai are being modernized and upgraded through private sector participation. In the Joint Venture (JV), AAI and other Government PSUs will be holding 26 per cent equity. The balance 74 per cent will be held by the strategic partner. FDI in this transaction has been capped at 49 per cent. Expressions of Interest (EOI) were invited and bidders were shortlisted. On the basis of the evaluation of Technical and Financial Bids, the private partners for modernization and development of Delhi and Mumbai airports have been selected. The two separate JV companies for Delhi and Mumbai airports would be handed over to the JVCs. It has been estimated on preliminary basis that the capital investment to the extent of Rs. 7,961 crore and Rs. 6,131 crore will be required for Delhi and Mumbai airports respectively over a period of 20 years in 4 stages of 5 years each."[5]

'In-principle' decision has been taken to modernize Chennai airport through JV route. Over and above approval has already been granted to set up a Greenfield airport in Goa. Approval has been obtained to build new international terminals at Ahmedabad and Trivandrum airports. State Governments are encouraged to set up Greenfield airports with private sector participation. Proposals to set up Greenfield airports in Navi Mumbai, Kannur in Kerala, Ladhowal near Ludhiana and Pakyong near Gangtok in Sikkim are in the pipeline.

7.9.1. Performance of All Private Sectors in Domestic Airlines

Traffic and operating statistics of all private domestic airlines reveal greater volume of growth obtained in terms of aircraft departure, aircraft flown kms, passengers carried, available seat, cargo carried, and available cargo. In 1995-96, aircraft departure of all private domestic airlines was 42,122 in number and total aircraft flown kms was 30,145 thousand (Table 7.10). Aircraft departure and aircraft flown kilometers increased to 1,07,211 and 90,867 thousand respectively for the year 2002-03.

Total passengers carried by all private domestic airlines account to 2,891 thousand and total seats available during 1995-96 were 3,162 million. In 2002-03, number of passengers carried by all private domestic airlines increased to 7,704 thousand and number of seats available with private airlines too increased to 11,306 million. With regard to cargo carried by all private domestic airlines, it was 222.3 million tonnes in 1995-96 and it increased to 651.0 million tonnes in 2002-03.

A comparative study between 1995-96 and 2002-03 reveals that the percentage of change that was achieved as in 2002-03 over 1995-96 in aircraft departure of private domestic airlines was 154.52 per cent and in aircraft flown is of 201.43 per cent. Within the context of private domestic airlines percentage of change achieved as in 2002-03 over 1995-96 in passengers carried and available seats was of 166.48 and 257.56 respectively. Even in cargo handled and carried, the private domestic airlines

Table 7.10. Traffic and Operating Statistics of All Private Domestic Airlines

	1995-96	1996-97	1997-98	1998-99	1999-2000	2000-01	2001-02	2002-03
Aircraft Departure	42122	53724	47528	56431	68715	83012	93662	107211
Aircraft Flown Kms (000)	30145	39381	40531	48077	57706	68006	76435	90867
Passengers Carried (000)	2891	3474	3670	4489	5422	6613	6433	7704
Available Seat (Million)	3162	7677	5107	6292	7541	8700	9647	11306
Cargo Carried Tonne Kms (Million)	222.3	296.7	324.5	371.0	443.0	541.9	526.7	651.0
Available Tonne Kms	301.3	451.4	499.8	623.0	784.0	910.2	999.8	1165.8

Source: Ghosh, Buddhadeb & Prabir De (2005), *Indian Infrastructure Database 2005*, Bookwell, New Delhi, Vol. II.

Percentage of Change as on 2002-03 over 1995-96

Aircraft Departure	154.52
Aircraft Flown Kms (000)	20143
Passengers Carried (000)	166.48
Available Seat (Million)	257.56
Cargo Carried Tonne Kms (Million)	192.85
Available Tonne Kms	278.60

attained change of percentage as in 2002-03 over 1995-96 was 192.85. This is indicative of the fact that all private domestic airlines have benefited the most from the bold economic open sky policies implemented during post-reforms period. As a result private domestic airlines to a larger extent have succeeded in increasing their market share.

7.10. NEED FOR ECONOMIC REGULATION

The principal focus of air travel regulations are technology and safety. Economic and environmental considerations receive little attention. The Directorate General of Civil Aviation should continue to play the vital role of technical and safety regulator. Economic regulation should be handled by a separate independent authority, which may require legislation. As with all infrastructure regulatory agencies, the authority's powers should be clearly defined to ensure that it concentrates on areas where competition is restricted.

Economic regulation would encompass pricing for air and land activities, performance and service standards for concessionaires, market access and the impact of horizontal and vertical integration, and asset valuation and land use. The regulator would be expected to regulate leases according to contract terms. Experience in India suggests that entrusting these activities to regulators rather than to Government departments can provide greater transparency. Environmental issues such as noise, emissions, water, sewage, fuel storage, and waste disposal would have to be addressed, as would squatters and dwellers on airport properties. Due to the monopoly nature of the airports and their economic importance, efforts are taken by the Government to set up an independent Airport Economic Regulator for tariff setting and monitoring of performance standards.

7.11. FUTURE OF AIR AVIATION

7.11.1. Future Demand for Airport Capacity

Policy initiatives have had a marked impact upon airline traffic. The entry of low cost carriers (LCCs), offering no-frills flights which are 30 to 35 per cent cheaper than the regular flights, has changed the profile of the air passengers. Domestic and international traffic grew by 24.2 per cent and 18 per cent, respectively, in April-December, 2005. Private airlines now account for 68.9 per cent of domestic traffic. During April-December 2005, international and domestic cargo recorded a growth of 11.7 per cent and 6.6 per cent, respectively. This growth is the second highest in the world, next to China, for the second consecutive year.[6]

The Foundation for Aviation and Sustainable Tourism forecasts that growth in domestic air traffic will be 8.5 per cent and growth in international air traffic will be 6 per cent annually through 2005. Based on these projections, passenger traffic should reach about 63 million people by the same date. The potential for growth in both passenger and cargo traffic could be significantly higher.

In China air travel growth has averaged about 20 per cent annually over the past five years. The need for additional airport infrastructure is strongly linked to developing competitive markets for air passenger and cargo traffic. To meet future growth in demand for air traffic, overcome airport congestion, and upgrade facilities to world-class standards, the AAI has developed an investment plan of about $800 million, or a yearly investment of about $160 million. The investment gap of Rs. 1,100 crores is expected to be financed by increasing private participation, borrowing funds in the domestic capital markets, and raising airport fees.

7.11.2. Future Proposed Undertakings

It is proposed to restructure and modernize the Mumbai and Delhi airports through the joint venture route. To assist in the restructuring process, M/s ABN-AMRO Asia Corporate Finance (I) Pvt. Limited and Air Plan Australia have been appointed as financial Consultant and Global Technical Advisor, respectively. An Empowered Group of Ministers has been constituted to oversee the process of restructuring.

Two new Greenfield airports with private sector participation are proposed at Bangalore and Hyderabad. In these Greenfield airports, private partners will hold 74 per cent equity in the joint venture and State Governments and Airports Authority of India (AAI) will together hold the balance 26 per cent.

Airports Authority of India is also considering development of non-metro airports. Indian Financial Consultants (IFC) and Global Technical Advisors (GTA) have been appointed for ten airports, namely Ahmedabad, Amritsar, Goa, Guwahati, Lucknow, Madurai, Jaipur, Mangalore, Trivandrum and Udaipur to assist AAI in identifying commercial activities to enhance non-aeronautical revenue including world class design for the terminal buildings.[7] These consultants will carry out a detailed techno-economic feasibility study and prepare business and financial plans and model specific to each airport for adoption by AAI. Besides these 10 airports, AAI proposes to carry out similar studies for 15 more airports for which Notice Inviting Tenders (NIT) have been issued.

Airport Authority of India (AAI) is also considering development of non-metro airports. Indian Financial Consultants (IFC) and Global Technical Advisers have been appointed for ten airports, namely Ahmedabad, Amritsar, Goa, Guwahati, Lucknow, Madurai, Jaipur, Mangalore, Trivandrum and Udaipur. The techno-economic feasibility study (TEFS) have been received for all the 10 non-metro airports from GTA and IFC. The works pertaining to these 10 non-metro airports are being taken up by AAI in a phased manner. The terminal building and associated infrastructure like car park/roads and air side work, with an estimated cost of Rs. 1,437 crore for Phase-I (2006-08), will be taken up by AAI. The land use plans recommended by GTA/IFC for enhancement of non-aeronautical revenue will be restricted to passenger-related services or related to Aircraft Services[8] or Air Traffic Services as per provisions of the AAI Act and State Government/Local body bye-laws.

In addition to these 10 non-metro airports, AAI has identified 15 more non-metro airports, namely, Agatti, Aurangabad, Bhopal, Bhubaneswar, Coimbatore, Indore, Khajuraho, Nagpur, Patna, Port Blair, Rajkot, Trichy, Vadodra, Varanasi and Vizag, for development. For carrying out TEFS for each of these 15 airports, the process for appointment of

GTA and IFC is nearing completion. Five more airports, namely Agartala, Dehradun, Imphal, Ranchi, and Raipur, have been identified for carrying out the TEFS, for which process for appointment of GTA is being initiated. The consultants will identify the viable development works, specific to each airport. The approximate cost of development of these non-metro airports is estimated to be of the order of Rs. 5,000 crore.[9]

7.11.3. Suggested Path for Future

The primary orientation should be to enlarge and upgrade airports and allied infrastructural facilities. To achieve the required capacity of airports private investment should be encouraged for which it is necessary to minimize procedural formalities and removal of unnecessary confusions. The Tenth Five-Year Plan and other Five-Year Plans have suggested the following path for the future enhancement of infrastructure facilities in civil aviation sector and to provide quality air services to the consumers:

- Accelerate the process of disinvestment of Government equity in Indian Airlines and Air India.
- Consider increasing the share of foreign equity on both domestic and international carriers with a view to attracting new technology and management expertise.
- Reconsider bar on equity participation by foreign airlines in a company formed for domestic air transportation.
- Speed up the process of long-term lease of the four metro airports in order to make them world class airports.
- Replace the route dispersal guideline system that provides air services to northeast and other isolated areas with a more transparent and efficient system.
- Increase private sector participation in the provision of infrastructure facilities as well as air services.
- Ensure adequate security arrangements at various airports in view of the increased threat perception.
- The civil aviation sector should aim at being financially self-sustaining. Efforts to generate larger internal

resources could be made. For this it is necessary to encourage private sector to cater to the growing demand for air services on short haul routes.

- Priority should be given to upgrading infrastructure and modernizing communication facilities to permit full utilization of aircraft capacity. Maintenance of infrastructure already created should receive immediate attention.
- Among the different modes of transport, civil aviation is closely linked with the development of tourism, as the vast majority of tourists coming to India, arrive and depart by air. Capacity constraints are often felt on air travel to and from India particularly during the peak tourist season. Tourist charters would be encouraged.
- Airborne trade has been increasing in importance and now accounts for more than a quarter of total foreign trade in value terms. Stress will be given on upgrading airport infrastructure in terms of increased storage space, better handling capacities and augmentation of upliftment capacity for carriage of more cargo.

Over and above this the following recommendations could be considered to increase wide-range of world class facilities within the context of civil aviation sector:

- It is necessary to undertake a wide-ranging privatization of operations at existing airports.
- Review the very functioning of the Airport Authority of India and shift the functions of the Airport Authority of India away from operations and focus on its policy, planning and statutory functions.
- It is essential also to create a separate independent authority to handle economic regulation for the sector and define the authority's powers clearly to ensure that this independent authority concentrates on the areas where competition is restricted.
- Any restriction on the import of specific type of aircrafts should be reduced considerably and any real location of aircrafts from one domestic operator to another should

also be freely allowed. An operator should be free to choose his aircraft which increases his profitability.

- Restrictions on the entry of private players in the industry should be made open to all operators so that there could be healthy competitive environment in the long run, which would improve the efficiencies of air operation and the overall quality of service.
- The existing training school should be made to cater to the needs of both public and private operators equally. If needed the private sector should be free to build more training schools.
- To minimize the problems due to labour unrest in Indian Airlines, several strategies of employee participation should be experimented. These strategies could be making employees joint equity owners of the airlines and introducing an incentive scheme tied directly to the financial performance of the airlines, etc.
- To enable distribution of excess workforce from Indian Airlines to private operators, a voluntary Retirement scheme in Indian Airlines should be initiated.

7.12. CONCLUSION

It is recognized all over that civil aviation is as critical as other infrastructure in the development of economic resources of any country. Given the importance of the civil aviation sector in India's context, it is relevant to examine the impact of globalization on civil aviation sector. Private sector participation has registered remarkable growth in terms of growth in number of passengers carried, growth in total percentage of passengers handled and increase in volume of freights carried. Increase in private sector participation in the civil aviation sector has been a remarkable achievement during globalization period.

In fact it is worth to analysis the performance of international traffic in civil aviation during globalization period. Total average growth of international passengers traffic of last five years have been 4.6 per cent and the average growth of international passenger traffic achieved by foreign operators has been 4.65 per cent. Whereas the average growth achieved by Indian operators during this period has been 4.75 per cent. It means that Indian operators performed better during post-reforms period and benefited from the policies implemented during post-reforms period. The Airport Authority of India too has significantly improved its financial performance during post-reforms period. This growth is mainly due to increase in the number of private operators as well as due to growth in traffic in civil aviation sector.

However, Indian Airlines and Air India have not changed in their basic performance of loss incurred. Number of policies implemented during globalization period has not succeeded in changing Indian Airlines and Air India into a profit-making undertaking. But in terms of staff performance Indian Airlines, Air India and Alliance Air have performed remarkably well during post-reforms period. In comparison with 1993-94, total staff strength of Indian Airlines, Air India and Alliance Air were reduced to 3,886 on 2002-03 and the change as on 2002-03 over 1993-94 has been 9.7 per cent. This means that less staff is employed to accomplish greater volume of work and leading to greater improvement in the work efficiency of the staff employed. So post-reforms period has been an effective instrument to bring about greater work efficiency in the staff of Indian Airlines, Air India and Alliance Air. From the above discussion it is clear that India has made noticeable improvement in civil aviation sector in terms of private sectors performance, financial performance, and staff efficiency since 1991-02 mainly as a result of various Government programmes and open policies implemented. However, the rising financial loss during the reform period poses a serious challenge which calls for an immediate sustained response from the Ministry of Civil Aviation and the Government of India.

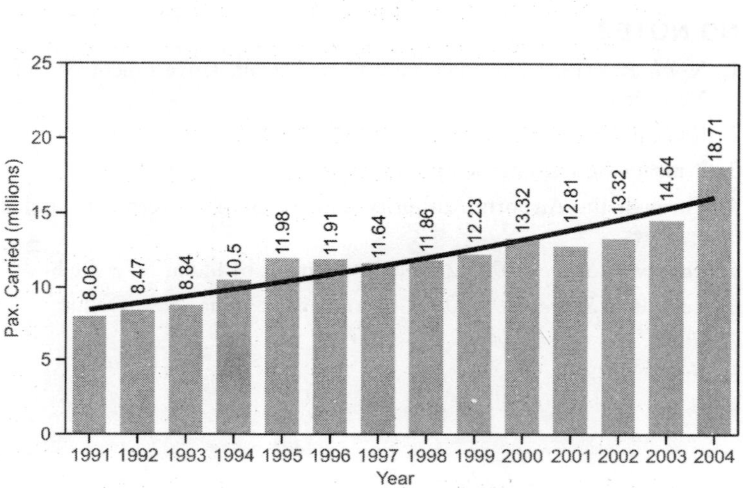

Figure 7.1: Growth of Domestic Passenger Traffic

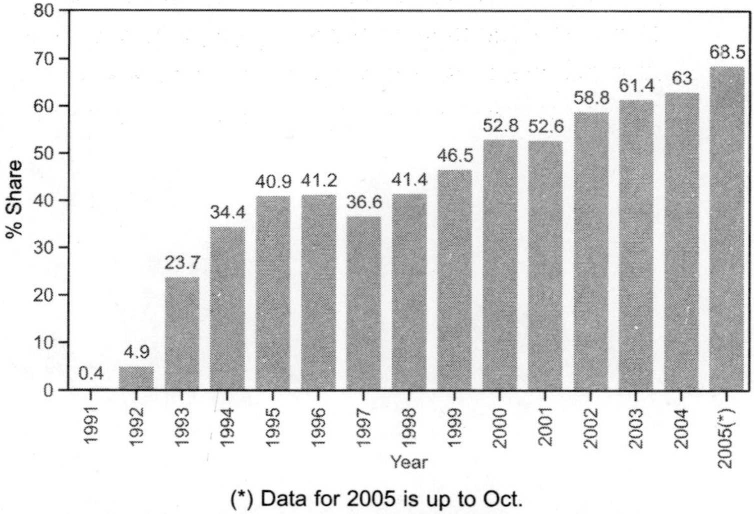

(*) Data for 2005 is up to Oct.

Figure 7.2: Share of Private Operators in Carriage of Domestic Passengers

END NOTES

1. *Ninth Five-Year Plan*, Planning Commission, Government of India, New Delhi, p. 836.
2. *Ibid.*, p. 837.
3. It means both domestic and international.
4. Through the Airports Authority and the State Government and its agencies.
5. *Economic Survey 2005-2006*, Government of India, New Delhi.
6. *Economic Survey 2005-06*, Government of India, New Delhi.
7. *Ibid.*
8. *Ibid.*
9. *Ibid.*

Globalization and its Effect on Financial Sector in India

8

8.1. INTRODUCTION

As the economy grows and becomes more sophisticated, the banking sector has to develop in a way that it supports growth and does not dampen growth. A sound financial sector is thus considered to be a prerequisite for efficient macroeconomic management. It is well-known that the financial sector plays a crucial role in the development process of a country. The process of financial intermediation enhances capital accumulation through the institutionalization of savings and investment. The gains to the real sector of the economy, therefore, depend on how efficiently the financial sector performs this basic function of financial intermediation. Banks form the core of the financial system in most countries and our country is no exception to this rule. Thus, how efficient a country's financial system is, depends to a large degree, on how efficient the banking system is. This chapter will present a detailed account of the broad lines on which reforms in financial sector have progressed and will then narrate the distinguishing features of the reforms in India. Further, a broad assessment of the impact of reforms will precede a description of the work in progress.

8.2. A BRIEF HISTORY OF INDIAN BANKING

8.2.1. Before Reforms

The formal commercial banking history in India can be traced back to the 18th century. The first commercial bank in India was the Hindustan Bank, which was set up by an English agency house in Calcutta in 1770. However, the origin of modern commercial banking in India can be associated with the setting up of the first Presidency bank, viz. the Bank of Bengal, in Calcutta in 1806. Two other Presidency banks were set up in Bombay and Madras in 1840 and 1843 respectively. Most of the equity of these banks was held by the East India Company. These banks acted as bankers to the government. Later on, all the Presidency banks were merged to form the Imperial Bank of India in 1921.

In 1935, the Reserve Bank of India (RBI) was set up as the central bank of the country. At the time of independence, there were 640 banks out of which only 96 were scheduled banks and the rest were non-scheduled banks. Banking was concentrated in metros, cities and port towns, with a large proportion of total advances going to trade. The Imperial Bank of India was nationalized in 1947 and renamed State Bank of India (SBI) and SBI and its associates were entrusted with the task of serving the developmental needs of the economy. Prior to 1967, it was felt that commercial bank credit was flowing mainly to the large and well-established business houses, and not so much to sectors such as agriculture and small-scale industries. As a result, in 1969, 14 private banks were nationalized under the Nationalization Act of 1969.

In the second phase six more private banks were nationalized in 1980. However, private banks and foreign banks were allowed to coexist with the public sector banks (PSBs), their activities were closely monitored and highly restricted through regulated entry and strict branch licensing. "With the nationalization of banks, a large number of regulatory measures were adopted by the RBI to achieve a desired sectoral allocation of credit, e.g., subsidized lending rates to priority sectors, provision of refinance facilities, set up credit guarantee schemes, rural and semi-urban branching, ceiling on deposit rates and differential lending rates depending on borrower's level of income and type of loan. These measures led to a phenomenal growth of the banking system, especially that of the public sector banks. In fact, during the early 1990s, public sector banks owned nearly 90 per cent of total business in the banking industry."[1]

Describing the state of the financial sector in India until the beginning of the 1990s, Rakesh Mohan writes that before 1991 the Indian financial sector was "characterized by administered interest rates, large pre-emption of resources by the authorities and extensive micro regulations directing the major portion of the flow of funds to and from financial intermediaries. While the true health of financial intermediaries, most of them public sector entities, was marked by relatively opaque accounting norms and limited disclosure, there were general concerns about their viability. ... There was very little transparency and depth in the secondary market trading of such securities. Interest rates on government securities, the predominant segment of fixed-income securities, were decided through administered fiat. The market for such securities was a captive one where the players were mainly financial intermediaries, who had to invest in government securities to fulfill high statutory reserve requirements. There was little depth in the foreign exchange market as most such transactions were governed by inflexible and low limits and also prior approval requirements. ... The end result was low levels of competition, efficiency and productivity in the financial sector, on the one hand, and severe credit constraints for the productive entities, on the other, especially for those in the private sector. ...The lack of commercial considerations in credit planning and weak recovery culture resulted in large accumulation of non-performing loans. This had no impact on the confidence of depositors."[2]

During this period there was hardly any secondary market for government securities, and such transactions were highly opaque and operated through over-the-telephone deals. The provision of fiscal accommodation through ad hoc treasury bills led to high levels of monetization of fiscal deficit during the major part of the 1980s. However, the process of nationalization of commercial banks and 'social control' of financial institutions did have considerable positive implications. "The sharp increase in rural branches of banks increased deposit and savings growth considerably. There was a marked rise in credit flow towards economically important but hitherto neglected activities, most notably agriculture and small-scale industries. The urban-bias and marked preference of banks to lend to the industrial sector, especially large industrial houses, was contained."[3] The implicit guarantee by the government and the public ownership created an impression of infallibility of these institutions. Thus a need to go for financial reforms in the banking sector was experienced. Expressing the need for reforms in the financial sector Y.V. Reddy says, "by the end of the eighties, the financial system was considerably stretched. The directed and concessional availability of bank credit with respect to certain sectors resulted not only in distorting the interest rate mechanism, but also adversely affected the viability and profitability of banks. The lack of recognition of the importance of transparency, accountability and prudential norms in the operations of the banking system led also to a rising burden of non-performing assets."[4]

8.2.2. Reforms

The rapid growth, owing to excessive focus on quantitative achievements, made many banks inefficient, unprofitable and under-capitalized. Recognizing these problems, the RBI launched the banking sector reforms in 1992 on the recommendations of the first Narasimham Committee on financial sector reforms (1991). The areas of reform were entry deregulation, branch de-licensing, deregulation of interest rates, and allowing Public Sector Banks (PSBs) to raise up to 49 per cent of equity in the capital market. Other areas of change, regarding statutory norms, were a gradual reduction of the Cash Reserve Ratio (CRR) and the Statutory Liquidity Ratio (SLR), setting capital adequacy norms of a minimum 8 per cent Capital to Risk-weighted Assets Ratio (CRAR), and imposition of stringent income recognition and provisioning norms.

While these reforms were underway, there were some important developments taking place in the world economy, especially the movement towards global integration of financial services. With increasing global focus on the need for adequate regulation and supervision of banks, in view of the South-East Asian Crisis and the Basel Committee recommendations, the report of the second Narasimham Committee (April 1998) paved the way for the 'second generation reforms' in the Indian banking industry. The Committee laid stress on prudential measures like higher CRAR, allowing for market risk on government securities, stricter Non-Performing Assets (NPAs) norms, introduction of assets-liabilities management and risk management guidelines. Around the same time (May 1998), the working group for harmonising the role and operations of Development Finance Institutions (DFIs) and banks (the Khan Committee) recommended a consolidation of the banking system through a move towards universal banking, mergers between banks and DFIs, and harmonising the role, operations and regulatory frameworks of the two. Thus in terms of process "the first has been its gradualism, wherein reforms were undertaken only after a process of close and continuous consultation with all stakeholders.... The second has been a constant rebalancing of reform priorities predicated upon the domestic and global business environment, institution of prudential practices, upgradation of the regulatory and supervisory framework, institution of appropriate institutional and legal reforms and the state of openness of the economy. The third important feature of the reforms has been its harmonisation with other policies dictated, among others, by the state of preparedness of the financial sector and above all, the underlying macroeconomic environment. Fourth, the reforms have progressed with emphasis on the common person with the aim of developing a system that is responsive to the needs of all sections of society."[5]

Thus "the last decade has witnessed major changes in the financial sector – new banks, new financial institutions, new instruments, new windows, and new opportunities – and, along with all this, new challenges. While deregulation has opened up new vistas for banks to augment revenues, it has entailed greater competition and consequently greater risks. Demand for new products, particularly derivatives, has required banks to diversify their product mix and also effect rapid changes in their processes and operations in order to remain competitive in the globalized environment."[6] India embarked economic reforms in the wake of a balance-of-payments crisis in 1991. One of the main aims of the reforms was reforms in the financial sector, and the banking sector. As a result reforms were undertaken in various segments of financial markets, so that the banking sector can perform its role in an efficient manner. In the last two decades, financial sector reforms have aimed at promoting a diversified, efficient and competitive financial sector. The ultimate objective is to improve the efficiency of available resources and promoting accelerated growth of the economy.

The thrust of these reforms was to promote a diversified, efficient and competitive financial system, with the ultimate objective of improving the allocative efficiency of resources, through operational flexibility, improved financial viability and institutional strengthening. More specifically, according to Dr. Manmohan Singh, financial reforms tried to achieve the following programmes such as: "(i) Modifications in the policy framework within which various components of the financial system operate; (ii) Improvement in the financial health and competitive capabilities by means of prescribing prudential norms which include, among others, capital adequacy as a major requirement; and (iii) Improving the regulatory framework and financial infrastructure."[7]

However, regarding the three broad major objectives and the need for financial reforms, C.P. Chandrasekhar and Parthapratim Pal writes that "there are three broad objectives that the process of financial liberalisation serves: (i) it opens the country to new forms and larger volumes of international financial flows, in order to attract a part of the substantially increased flows of capital to the so-called "emerging markets" since the late 1970s; (ii) to facilitate these inflows it liberalises to differing degree the terms governing outflows of foreign exchange in the form of current account investment income payments and in the form of capital account transfers for permitted transactions; and (iii) it transforms the structure of the financial sector and the nature and operations of financial firms in a manner that makes the financial system resemble that in countries like the US and the UK."[8]

Besides this, the purpose of reforms was to infuse technological efficiency and productivity in the banking sector and also to serve as a demonstration effect on existing banks. As a result a "set of micro-prudential measures were instituted, to impart greater strength to the banking system and also to ensure their safety and soundness with the objective of benchmarking against international best practices (risk-based capital standards, income recognition, asset classification and provisioning requirements for non-performing loans as well as provisioning for 'standard' loans, exposure limits for single and group borrowers, accounting rules, investment valuation norms)."[9]

Dr. Y.V. Reddy, while stating the reform measures undertaken in the financial sector says that "the reforms have focused on adopting appropriate processes in order to ensure development of various segments of the markets. In the banking sector, the Indian Banks' Association (IBA) has emerged as an important self-regulatory body working for the growth of a healthy and forward-looking banking and financial services industry. In the debt market segment, the RBI interacts closely with Fixed Income Money Market Dealers Association of India (FIMMDA) and the Primary Dealers Association of India (PDAI) for overall improvement of government debt markets and promoting sound market practices. With regard to the payments system infrastructure, the introduction of the Real Time Gross Settlement (RTGS) system since 2004 has made it possible for large value payments to be transacted in a faster, efficient and secure manner. In order to enhance transparency of secondary market trades in government securities, a screen based anonymous order matching system has been operationalised."[10]

India has had more than a decade of financial sector reforms during which there has been substantial transformation and liberalization of the financial system. It is, therefore, appropriate to take stock and assess the efficacy of our liberalization and globalization approach incited over the years. It is useful to evaluate how the financial system has performed in an objective quantitative manner. It is important to weigh the gains against losses incurred by the industry over a sufficiently long time horizon encompassing the period of reforms. This chapter intends to study the performance and efficiency of banks during pre-reforms and post-reforms period of the financial sector, in particular the banking sector in India.

8.2.3. Reforms and Growth

The financial reforms initiated during early 90s have resulted in rapid growth and development. Emphasising greater growth achieved in the financial sector Dr. Y.V. Reddy states that the financial reforms brought about "a range of instruments in domestic and foreign currency are traded in financial markets. In addition, the market in corporate bonds has been spurred with increased use of external credit ratings. Further, derivative products covering forwards, swaps and options as also structured products are transacted enabling corporates and banks to manage their risk exposures. The market in securitised paper both mortgage backed and asset backed securities has also grown significantly supported by a well-developed credit rating industry.... Moreover, the access to credit has improved, through newly established domestic banks, foreign banks and bank-like intermediaries.... There have also been significant improvements in the information infrastructure."[11]

The accounting and auditing of intermediaries has strengthened. Availability of information on borrowers has improved which will help reduce information asymmetry among financial entities. The technological infrastructure has developed in tandem with modern-day requirements in information technology and communications networking. Moreover, the concept of finance has permeated across various institutions and a 'finance view' of all market transactions has emerged. Finally, the quality of human capital involved in the financial sector has typically been of the highest genre, facilitating non-disruptive progress of the reforms process.

8.2.4. Improvement in Capital Adequacy

Capital adequacy of the banking sector recorded a marked improvement and stood at 12.8 per cent at the end of March 2005, comparable to 13.0 per cent for the US during the same period. Typically, the capital adequacy position of developed countries has remained range-bound within 10-14 per cent and judged from that standpoint, our capital position compares favourably with those numbers.

8.2.5. Progress of Commercial Banks

8.2.5.1. Expansion of Branch Network

The expansion of branch network peaked during the 1970s, 1980s and 1990s. But there has been slowdown in branch expansion since the 1990s. In June 1980, number of commercial banks was 34,594 and it further increased to 60,570 in the year 1990. It means that during pre-reforms period the expansion of branch network has been 75.09 per cent as on 1990 over the year 1980. But as on March 2003, the number of commercial branches was only 68,561. It means the net increase as on 2003 over 1990 is just 7,991 and expansion of branches during post-reforms was just 13.19 per cent (Table 8.1). However, the population per bank branch has not changed much since the 1980s, and has remained at around 15,000. It is often asserted that the Indian banking sector is saddled with too many branches, adding to its high intermediation costs. Therefore, according to Rakesh Mohan, "the reform process has maintained the gains in terms of the outreach of bank branches achieved in the phase of social banking."[12]

Table 8.1. Progress of Commercial Banking in India

Indicators	June 1969	June 1980	March 1991	March 1995	March 2000	March 2003
1. No of commercial banks	73	154	272	284	298	292
2. No of bank offices	8,262	34,594	60,570	64,234	67,868	68,561
Of which Rural and semi-urban bank offices	5,172	23,227	46,550	46,602	47,693	47,496
3. Population per office ('000s)	64	16	14	15	15	16
4. Per capita deposit (Rs)	88	738	2,368	4,242	8,542	12,253
5. Per capita credit (Rs)	68	457	1,434	2,320	4,555	7,275
6. Priority sector advances@ (per cent)	15.0	37.0	39.2	33.7	35.4	33.7*
7. Deposits (per cent of national income)	15.5	36.0	48.1	48.0	53.5	51.8

Notes: @ Share of priority sector advances in total non-food credit of scheduled commercial bank.

* As at end-March 2002.

Source: Reserve Bank of India.[13]

8.2.5.2. Proportion of Bank Deposits to National Income

The proportion of bank deposits to the national income has improved considerably during post-reforms period in comparison with the improvement in terms of bank deposits to the national income during pre-reforms period. In 1980, the proportion of bank deposits to the national income was 36 per cent and it improved to 48.1 per cent for the year 1991. The percentage of change that has taken place as on March 1991 over 1980 is 33.61 per cent. But for the year 2000, the proportion of bank deposit to the national income increased to 53.5 per cent and the percentage of change in the proportion of bank deposit to the national income as on March 2000 over March 1991 was 11.22 per cent (Table 8.1). However, according to Rakesh Mohan, "the discernible increase in the proportion of bank deposits to national income is reflective of the enhanced deepening of the Indian financial system during the period.... This also implies an increase in the average business per bank branch, which is likely to have improved the viability of individual bank branches including those in the rural and semi-urban centres. In the post-reform period, banks have consistently maintained high rates of growth in their assets and liabilities. This is particularly credible given the low inflationary situation that prevailed in this period compared to the earlier periods, most notably in the 1980s. On the liability side, there has not been much compositional change since the initiation of reforms whereby deposits continue to account for about 80 per cent of the total liabilities. On the asset side, however, there is a definite increase in the share of investments. While the share of loans and advances did decline in the 1990s, it has recovered in recent years."[14]

8.2.5.3. Progress of Per Capita Deposits and Credits

A comparative study of per capita deposits reveals that there have been considerable increases in per capita deposits and credit during post-reforms period. In June 1980, per capita deposit was Rs. 738 and it further increased to Rs. 2368 in March 1991 and the percentage per capita deposit increase as on March 1991 over June 1980 is 220 per cent. But in March

2000, per capita deposit increased to Rs. 8,542 (Table 8.1) and percentage per capita increase as on March 2000 over March 1991 is 260.73 per cent which is a higher growth than the growth achieved during pre-reforms period.

There has been substantial increase in per capita credit over the years. In June 1980, per capita credit was Rs. 457 and it further increased to Rs. 1,434 and the percentage of per capita credit increase as on March 1991 over June 1980 was 213.78 per cent. The per capita credit further increased to Rs. 4,555 in March 2000 and the percentage of change that has taken place as on March 2000 over March 1991 was 217.64 per cent. This is higher than the percentage of change that has taken place during pre-reforms period.

8.2.5.4. Banks Operations in Terms of Investment

Despite the large decline in SLR in the 1990s, the sharp increase in investments by banks according to Rakesh Mohan "is reflective of their attempt to evolve treasury operations into profit centres."[15] Stating significant reasons for the increase in investments he says that the reduction in cash reserve ratio freed substantial amounts of bank resources, and enabled banks to concentrate on investment operations with greater vigour (Table 8.2).

Table 8.2. Select Balance Sheet Indicators of Commercial Banks Operating in India (Per cent)

	As a Ratio of Total Assets/Liabilities			
	Deposits	Total Investments	Non-SLR Investment	Loans and Advances
1991-92	77.7 (17.1)	28.9 (28.4)	.. ..	46.8 (13.7)
1992-93	78.4 (13.9)	30.5 (19.0)	.. ..	45.0 (8.6)
1993-94	80.3 (15.5)	35.4 (31.1)	5.0 ..	38.7 -(3.0)
1994-95	78.9 (16.3)	33.6 (12.2)	4.6 (9.4)	40.5 (24.0)
1995-96	76.4 (12.7)	31.0 (7.4)	3.5 -(11.7)	42.1 (20.9)

Contd...

	As a Ratio of Total Assets/Liabilities			
	Deposits	Total Investments	Non-SLR Investment	Loans and Advances
1996-97	79.9 (17.5)	33.3 (20.6)	5.0 (60.2)	41.0 (9.2)
1997-98	81.0 (19.8)	34.2 (21.5)	7.1 (69.3)	40.8 (17.6)
1998-99	81.1 (19.7)	35.7 (24.9)	8.6 (45.3)	38.8 (13.9)
1999-2000	81.1 (16.3)	37.3 (21.3)	9.1 (22.4)	40.2 (20.3)
2000-01	81.5 (17.7)	38.0 (19.3)	8.9 (14.2)	40.6 (18.5)
2001-02	78.5 (14.3)	38.2 (19.4)	8.7 (16.5)	42.0 (22.7)
2002-03	79.8 (12.4)	40.8 (18.1)	8.1 (3.3)	43.6 (14.7)
2003-04*	80.5 (17.5)	41.7 (19.7)	7.2 (2.9)	45.0 (15.3)

Notes: * Based on supervisory returns.
.. not available, SLR: statutory liquidity ratio.
Figures in brackets are annual growth rates.
Source: Reserve Bank of India.[16]

The major increase in investment by Indian banks since 1990s is also on account of their investment in government securities. The "subdued industrial growth since 1997 also led to lower credit demand, providing banks further incentive to place their resources in risk-free government securities.... In the 1990s, greater orientation towards investment activities and aversion to credit risk exposure may have deterred banks from undertaking their 'core function' of providing loans and advances, banks seem to have struck a greater balance between investment and loans and advances in recent years."[17]

Greater balance between investment and credit were maintained during post-reforms period in the financial sector because financial measures undertaken in the post-reforms period sought to restructure and reorient the entire banking system. Such a banking system "improved the functioning of the banking system and forced the banks aloof from directly undertaking investment for fear of loss of income and growing volume of non-performing assets."[18] However, this is not achieved without stress and strain. It is said that the public sector banks are found to be working more under stress in the post-reform period. The reform process generated a sense of fear psychosis in the financial sector as they are to be more cautious about Non-Performing Assets and low generation of income.

8.3. OPERATIONAL EFFICIENCY

8.3.1. Public Sector Banks in Comparison to Private Sector Banks

One of the major objectives of banking sector reforms has been to enhance efficiency in total earnings, interest earnings and net interest earnings (Table 8.3). The position of public sector banks continues to play a predominant role as these banks account for nearly three-fourths of assets and income. It is important to note that public sector banks have responded positively to the new challenges and competitions that came into play due to reforms introduced in the banking sector.

The predominance of public sector banks in India's financial sector according to Rakesh Mohan "is reflected in the increase in share of these banks in the overall profit of the banking sector. From the position of net loss in the mid-1990s, in recent years the share of public sector banks in the profit of the commercial banking system has become broadly commensurate with their share of assets, indicating a broad convergence of profitability across various bank groups.... [Even in terms of] operational flexibility, public sector banks are competing effectively with private sector and foreign banks. The market discipline imposed by the listing of most public sector banks has also probably contributed to this improved performance. Public sector bank managements are now probably more attuned to the market consequences of their activities."[19]

Table 8.3. Bank Group-Wise Shares: Select Indicators (Per cent)

	1995-96	2000-01	2002-03
Public sector banks			
Income	82.5	78.4	74.5
Expenditure	84.2	78.9	74.8
Total assets	84.4	79.5	75.7
Net profit	-39.1	67.4	64.8
Gross profit	74.3	69.9	76.6
Private sector banks			
Income	8.2	12.6	18.5
Expenditure	7.4	12.3	18.6
Total assets	7.7	12.6	17.5
Net profit	59.3	17.8	15.6
Gross profit	10.1	14.4	18.7
Foreign banks			
Income	9.4	9.1	7.0
Expenditure	8.3	8.8	6.6
Total assets	7.9	7.9	6.9
Net profit	79.8	14.8	19.6
Gross profit	15.6	15.7	4.7

Source: Reserve Bank of India.[20]

Table 8.4. Earnings and Expenses of Scheduled Commercial Banks (Rs billion)

Year	Total Assets	Total Earnings	Interest Earnings	Total Ex-penses	Interest Ex-penses	Establish-ment Ex-penses	Net Interest Earning
1951	12	1	0	0	0	0	0
		(3.8)	(3.1)	(2.6)	(0.9)	(1.3)	(2.2)
1969	68	4	4	4	2	1	2
		(6.2)	(5.3)	(5.5)	(2.8)	(2.1)	(2.5)
1980	582	42	38	42	27	10	10
		(7.3)	(6.4)	(7.2)	(4.7)	(1.7)	(1.8)
1991	3,275	304	275	297	190	76	86
		(9.3)	(8.4)	(9.1)	(5.8)	(2.3)	(2.6)
2000	11,055	1,149	992	1,077	690	276	301
		(10.4)	(9.0)	(9.7)	(6.2)	(2.5)	(2.7)
2002	15,355	1,510	1,270	1,395	875	337	395
		(9.8)	(8.3)	(9.1)	(5.7)	(2.2)	(2.6)
2003	16,989	1,724	1,407	1,553	936	3,809	471
		(10.2)	(8.3)	(9.1)	(5.5)	(2.2)	(2.8)

Note: Figures in brackets are ratios to total assets.
Source: Reserve Bank of India.[21]

Over and above this there has been a general reduction in the operating expenditure as a proportion of total assets due to the greater emphasis given to income and expenditure management. This is noteworthy of Indian banks because this has been achieved in spite of large expenditures incurred by Indian banks (Table 8.4) in installation and upgradation of information technology in the banking sector.

Moreover, in order to address manpower redundancies, public sector banks also incurred large expenditures under voluntary premature retirement of nearly 12 per cent of their total staff strength. The process, however, resulted in reduced operating expenditure in the medium-term. The Indian experience thus according to Dr. Y.V. Reddy "has shown that a strong regulatory framework which is non-discriminatory, market discipline through listing on stock exchanges and operational autonomy has had positive impact on the functioning of the public sector banks."[22]

8.3.2. Cost Efficiency

Table 8.6 reveals that the cost inefficiency underwent a decline over the years. In general, public banks appear to have performed better than the private, new private and foreign banks with respect to cost-efficiency (Table 8.5). However, when we estimate the group-effects frontier, new private banks turn out to be the least cost-efficient group. The temporal behaviour of public and private banks seems to be quite stable and there does not appear to be any appreciable change in their mean cost-efficiency over time. Compared to them, foreign banks appear to have achieved a rapid improvement in cost-efficiency even though they started from a very low level. New private banks too exhibited a rapid rise in cost-efficiency till the year 2000. However, this performance could not be sustained due to poor practices of some banks and their cost efficiency suffered from 2001 onwards.

Deregulation does not seem to have had any significant impact on cost-inefficiency. The coefficient of size is positive and significant suggesting that cost-inefficiency is positively related to size. In terms of group dummies, the signs convey that the public banks are more cost efficient than the private banks. This is followed by new private and foreign banks.

Table 8.5. Cost Efficiency Estimates

	Industry Frontier				Group Effects Frontier			
Year	PUB	PVT	FOR	NPVT	PUB	PVT	FOR	NPVT
1986	89.32	90.16	25.34	93.04	92.05	18.94		
1987	91.00	91.17	27.54	93.62	92.54	18.17		
1988	91.03	91.38	21.38	93.63	92.69	16.50		
1989	92.69	91.89	30.40	94.69	93.02	21.21		
1990	93.59	92.74	31.84	95.14	93.65	24.06		
1991	93.43	92.74	32.01	95.09	93.60	24.77		
1992	92.18	93.76	42.92	94.35	94.22	32.82		
1993	91.84	93.23	33.56	94.46	94.33	26.69		
1994	90.63	92.52	40.05	93.56	94.12	33.29		
1995	91.15	92.41	40.41	93.89	94.17	38.69		
1996	90.82	91.34	43.65	39.33	93.91	93.41	37.29	6.82
1997	91.49	88.43	43.90	48.57	94.09	91.95	39.46	8.66
1998	91.87	90.13	45.95	58.98	94.26	93.28	40.10	9.54
1999	91.68	90.56	43.39	56.71	94.20	93.21	39.52	10.28
2000	92.28	89.84	46.39	73.80	94.39	94.09	41.68	15.56
2001	93.20	89.25	49.79	60.77	95.67	93.93	46.57	7.99
2002	94.24	92.77	57.23	61.31	95.67	94.28	48.65	8.24
2003	93.78	88.58	56.66	9.47	95.32	93.71	50.38	7.16

Source: Rudra Sensarma, "Cost and Profit Efficiency of Indian Banks during 1986-2003: A Stochastic Frontier Analysis", *Economic and Political Weekly*, March 19, 2005, p. 1204.

Table 8.6. Determinants of Cost Inefficiency

	Industry Frontier		Group Effects Frontier	
Coefficient	Estimate	P-value (Per Cent)	Estimate (Per Cent)	P-value
CONST	2.8667	0	0.5498	0
TIME	-0.0606	0	-0.0811	0
DEREG	-0.1096	22	0.092	30
SIZE	0.2043	0	0.2477	0
PUB	-5.9495	0	-5.0865	0
PVT	-5.0592	0	-4.0442	0
FOR	-1.4335	0	0.2994	0

Source: Rudra Sensarma, "Cost and Profit Efficiency of Indian Banks during 1986-2003, A Stochastic Frontier Analysis", *Economic and Political Weekly*, March 19, 2005, p. 1204.

According to Rudra Sensarma, public banks appear to be more cost efficient than the private banks. This is because private banks took the lead in investing in new revenue generating practices such as computerization of branches, computer training of employees, upgradation of technology etc., which led to additional costs. Foreign and new private banks appear to be poor performers in terms of cost efficiency because "these banks pay high salaries to employees and maintain costly real estate in metros and urban areas, thus incurring huge expenditure on both counts. Moreover, the public and private banks have a historical advantage of having well entrenched business structures and knowledge of the local markets in India which most of the new foreign and private banks do not. Further, foreign banks make intensive use of technology which may lead to their huge costs."[23] Thus, it can be inferred that public banks have shown higher cost efficiency than private banks during post-reforms period, which was not so during pre-reforms.

However, a study undertaken by Abhiman Das, Ashok Nag and Subhash C. Ray reveals that Indian banks are still not much differentiated in terms of input oriented or output oriented technical efficiency and cost efficiency. According to them, "it is not unexpected because input and output prices are yet to be determined by the free play of market forces of demand and supply. Most interestingly, Indian banks are becoming sharply differentiated in terms of revenue efficiency and profit efficiency. This would imply that even within the existing environment, a bank can still improve its profitability significantly, by adopting the best practices observed within the sector. The results clearly underscore the need for choosing a proper product-mix in shaping the revenue and profitability of Indian banks."[24] They have also observed that "the median efficiency scores of Indian banks, in general, and of bigger banks in particular, have improved considerably during the course of our study period. This sends out a very positive signal about the effect of the reform process on the performance of the Indian banking sector."[25]

8.3.3. Profitability

Since the mid-1990s, profitability levels of commercial banks have ranged between 0.7-0.8 per cent, with certain exceptions during few years. Interest earning was Rs. 38 billion in 1980 and it increased to Rs. 275 billion in 1990. So the percentage of increase as on 1990 over 1980 was 623.68 per cent (Table 8.7). Though the interest earning further increased to Rs. 992 billion in the year 2000 but the percentage of increase as on 2000 over 1990 was just 260.72 per cent which is much lower in comparison to the growth achieved during pre-reforms period. However, there is clearly an improvement over the interest earning because the interest earning which was just Rs. 38 billion increased to Rs. 1,407 billion, which could be considered a remarkable achievement during post-reforms period. Even in terms of net interest earning, commercial banks have achieved constant growth during post-reforms period. In 1980, the net interest earning was Rs. 10 billion, which increased to Rs. 86 billion in 1991 and it further increased to Rs. 471 billion in 2003. This is mainly due to faster decline in interest expenditure in comparison to interest income.

Table 8.7. Profit Efficiency Estimates

	Industry Frontier				Group Effects Frontier			
Year	PUB	PVT	FOR	NPVT	PUB	PVT	FOR	NPVT
1985	89.32	90.16	25.34	93.04	92.05	18.94		
1986	92.55	93.83	76.35	91.10	91.55	40.40		
1987	91.71	94.04	69.63	89.59	92.20	35.32		
1988	92.84	92.83	75.44	91.19	91.43	41.59		
1989	79.11	86.00	56.81	74.28	79.30	30.80		
1990	88.35	92.21	65.76	85.07	88.60	38.76		
1991	89.83	92.94	65.53	87.53	89.84	37.86		
1992	91.86	93.76	68.72	90.69	91.62	41.77		
1993	85.31	93.52	71.40	84.74	91.91	47.82		
1994	85.18	94.67	70.99	84.36	94.46	51.78		
1995	90.58	93.94	66.68	90.16	92.93	45.70		
1996	84.62	89.27	62.21	86.02	84.39	86.22	42.46	75.80
1997	90.21	93.01	67.05	78.08	90.71	91.09	50.10	64.95
1998	91.70	91.50	61.75	76.12	92.67	88.98	45.15	62.58

1999	89.05	91.98	57.29	74.06	89.61	89.67	42.51	59.38
2000	88.71	90.65	54.22	80.32	89.09	87.61	41.12	64.83
2001	73.32	92.33	48.20	76.51	72.43	90.40	36.46	69.96
2002	84.30	90.47	49.58	76.45	84.29	87.64	41.13	66.18
2003	85.05	89.57	50.65	74.38	85.28	87.43	41.91	59.13

Source: Rudra Sensarma, "Cost and Profit Efficiency of Indian Banks during 1986-2003: A Stochastic Frontier Analysis", *Economic and Political Weekly*, March 19, 2005, p. 1205.

Private banks appear to have performed better than the public, new private and foreign banks in terms of profit efficiency of Indian banks during post-reforms period (Table 8.7) according to the study undertaken by Rudra Sensarma. In the words of Rudra Sensarma, "although, prior to deregulation, public banks had been doing almost as well as the private banks, but subsequent to deregulation, private banks took the lead in improving the quality of their services[26] thereby generating higher revenues and thus outperformed public banks. However, public sector banks succeeded to maintain much higher profit efficiency than foreign banks"[27] throughout the reforms period.

The operating expenses of banks in India are also much more aligned to those prevailing internationally. The operating expenses of Indian banks were around 2.21 per cent during 2003-04 and 2.16 per cent during 2004-05. However in developed countries, in 2004, banks' operating expenses were 3.5 per cent in the US and 2.8 per cent in Canada and Italy and 2.6 per cent in Australia. In other developed countries such as Japan, Switzerland, Germany and the UK, the operating expenses of banks were in the range of 1.1 to 2.0 per cent.[28] Bank profitability level in India has also shown an upward trend for most banks during financial reforms. This is achieved because "bank employees ... have adopted a cautious line of approach which compelled them to purse a loan policy that assured regular returns from borrowers engaged in profitable lines of economic activities."[29]

8.3.4. Commercial Banks Credits and Financial Reforms

Provision of credit is one of the fundamental functions of banks. The effective discharge of this function is part of the intermediation process. The sectoral deployment of credit must keep pace with the changes in the structure of the economy. The banking industry in India needs to keep these in mind and equip itself to be able to assess and meet the credit needs of the emerging segment of the economy.

Banking sector reforms have changed the trends and patterns of banking credits over the past few years. Reforms introduced over the years have brought about serious regional and sectoral inequalities in the deployment of commercial credit in this country. The nationalization of the major banks in 1969 was based on economic reasoning of removal of imperfection in the allocation of credit and credit in favour of rural, poor and agricultural sector. With the nationalization of banks there was a rapid expansion of the banking network into rural and semi-urban areas. There was an increase in the share of agriculture and small industry and transport and trade in the total credit deployed.

Dr. Y.V. Reddy says that "the reforms have accorded greater flexibility to banks to determine both the volume and terms of lending. The RBI has moved away from micro regulation of credit to macro management. External constraints to the banking system in terms of the statutory premptions have been lowered. All this has meant greater lendable resources at the disposal of banks... As a result of reforms, borrowers are able to get credit at lower interest rates... The lending rate between 1991-92 and 2001-02 has declined from about 19.0 per cent to current levels of 10.5-11.0 per cent."[30] However, these low rate loans are available to more highly rated borrowers than to small and medium enterprises. It is noticed that there is also inadequate flow of resources to rural areas, and particularly to agriculture. Banking reforms have thus also adversely affected the pattern of credit delivery. Since 1991, there has been a reversal of the trends in the ratio of directed credit to total bank credit and the proportion thereof going to the agricultural sector. This is mainly due to change in trend in favour of industries and large business houses.

"The number of loan accounts has fallen by 60 lakhs in six years, and the fall is largely confined to agriculture, transport operators and trade. The new private banks and foreign banks are increasing their presence in the emerging business of loans for personal and professional services. New growth areas for lending have emerged in retail lending, particularly in home and automobile finance. There is a striking regional dimension to the developments of the last few years. The emerging banks and the existing ones are competing to expand in South, and North-West India attracted by the growing credit business in a milieu with strong banking habits. This has resulted in a drastic reallocation of total commercial credit from the poorer agricultural states to Delhi, Maharashtra and Tamil Nadu. The situation is one where private banks are left to 'skim the cream' without investing in the long-term development of banking habits."[31] As a result the non-performing loans to total loans of commercial banks were at a high of 15.7 per cent at the end of March 1997. It further declined to 5.2 per cent at the end of March 2005. However, during the same period in several leading European economies[32], the non-performing loans ranged within 4-7 per cent of total loans and this is lower than those in most Asian economies.[33] Net non-performing loans also witnessed a significant decline and stood at 2.0 per cent of net advances at the end of March 2005.

During the period 2001-04, the total outstanding credit to the agricultural sector extended even by public sector banks which was within the range of 15-16 per cent of net bank credit as against the target of 18.0 per cent. The ratio of agricultural credit to net bank credit offered by private sector banks increased from 7.1 per cent to 11.8 per cent. However, it was still below target according to Reserve Bank of India.[34] According to a study undertaken by the EPW Research Foundation[35] relating to the period 1972 to 2003, the share of agriculture in total bank credit had steadily increased under impulse of bank nationalization and reached 18 per cent towards the end of the 1980s. But, thereafter, the trend has been reversed and the share of the agricultural sector in credit has dipped to less than 10 per cent in the late 1990s. Even the number of farm loan accounts with scheduled commercial banks has declined in absolute terms from 27.74 million in March 1992 to 20.84 million in March 2003. Similarly, the share of small-scale industry accounts and their loan amounts in total bank loans has fallen equally drastically. The number of accounts has dropped from 2.18 million in March 1992 to 1.43 million in March 2003, and the amount of credit as a percentage of the total has slumped from 12 per cent to 5 per cent, that is, less than one-half of what it was three decades ago, in the early 1970s.[36]

It is necessary therefore to emphasize the need for expanding credit to agriculture, and Provision of credit for high-tech agriculture should not be considered as different from providing credit to industry. The agricultural sector, being the backbone of Indian economy, commercial banks should have no hesitation in providing adequate credit to this sector. It is also required to extend the provision of credit to small and marginal farmers for which special attention is required. Apart from providing credit, the banks could extend a helping hand in terms of advice on various matters related to agriculture.

Developing a truly long-term capital market must be a key objective for government, which through greater fiscal restraint and creative financial engineering needs to reduce its own crowding out effect in India's financial and banking systems. India's insurance and pension industries hold out important hopes for mobilizing long-term capital from India's abundant savings base. Lifting the ceiling on foreign direct investment in insurance would clearly help India's emerging pension industry. This in turn would reduce government's dominance in the banking industry and encourage greater freedom for the growth of private domestic banks and foreign banks.[37] In this transition however, effective use of capital should be ensured so that the return on equity and a consequent enhancement of shareholder value could be guaranteed. For which banks could adopt a more dynamic approach to use of capital, in which capital will flow quickly to its most efficient use.

8.3.4.1. Agricultural Credit and Financial Reforms

Financial sector reforms initiated in 1991 included various measures in the area of agricultural credit such as deregulation of interest rates of co-operatives, and Regional Rural Banks; deregulation of lending rates of commercial banks for loans above Rs. 2 lakh; recapitalization of select Regional Rural Banks; introduction of prudential accounting norms and provisioning requirements for all rural credit agencies; increased refinance support from Reserve Bank of India and capital contribution to NABARD; constitution of the Rural Infrastructure Development Fund (RIDF) in NABARD for infrastructure projects; introduction of the Kisan Credit Card (KCC) and stipulation of interest rate not exceeding 9 per cent for crop loans up to Rs. 50,000 extended by the public sector banks. These measures were taken with the view to enhance agricultural credit availability as well to increase the vital role played by agricultural sector within the Indian economy.

As a result agricultural credit started to grow after bank nationalization and it has been growing continuously since then. This is evident from Table 8.8. Over the years there has been a significant increase in the access of rural cultivators to institutional credit. The total credit was Rs. 3,292 crore in the 1980-81 and it further increased to Rs. 9,830 crore (Table 8.8). Therefore, the percentage of increase as on 1990-91 over 1980-81 was 1.97 per cent. The total credit further increased to Rs. 41,386 crore and the percentage of increase as on 2001-02 was 3.21 per cent. This means that the total institutional credit provided to agricultural sector has increased during reforms period. But the cooperatives share of institutional credit to agriculture sector over the years has declined. In the year 1970-71, institutional credit to agriculture sector was of 100 per cent and it further declined and touched 61.6 per cent. In the year 1990-91, cooperatives share of institutional credit to agricultural sector further declined to 49 per cent and it reached 44.0 per cent in the year 2001-02.

Table 8.8. Institutional Credit to Agriculture

Year	Share in Total (Per Cent)			Total
	Cooperatives	Scheduled Commercial Banks	Regional Rural Banks	(Rs Crore)
1970-71	100.0	–	–	744
1980-81	61.6	38.4	–	3,292
1990-91	49.0	47.6	3.4	9,830
2001-02P	44.0	45.0	11.0	41,386
2002-03	34.0	57.2	8.7	69,480
2003-04	30.9	60.3	8.7	86,897

Source: Handbook of Statistics on the Indian Economy, RBI; Annual Report, NABARD.[38]

Commercial banks' share of institutional credit to agriculture sector has however increased over the years. The commercial banks' institutional credit to agricultural sector was just 38.4 per cent in the year 1980-81 and it increased to 60.3 per cent in the year 2003-04. The main story in the expansion of rural credit in the 1980s and 1990s has been the ascendancy of commercial banks, along with Regional Rural Banks, with a corresponding fall in the share of co-operatives. Number of financial reforms and 58 years of independence in India have not succeeded in substituting informal moneylending channels for institutional credit. However, the nationalization of banks in 1969 and the subsequent spread of rural bank branches have made a difference in reducing the share of moneylenders in agricultural credit.

This is evident from Table 8.9. This is mainly due to the remarkable feature of the widespread network of rural financial institutions. At the time of nationalization in June 1969, the total number of rural offices of scheduled commercial banks was 1,833, which then increased significantly to 32,115 by March 2005. The number of co-operative institutions catering to agriculture went up from 95,871 in June end 1980 to over 1,10,000 in 2003. The share of the rural branches of scheduled commercial banks in the total increased sharply from 22 per cent in June 1969 to 46 per cent by March 2005.[39]

Table 8.9. Relative Share of Borrowing[#] of Cultivator Households from Different Sources (in per cent)

Sources of Credit	1951	1961	1971	1981	1991	2002[$]
Non-Institutional	92.7	81.3	68.3	36.8	30.6	38.9
of which:						
Moneylenders	69.7	49.2	36.1	16.1	17.5	26.8
Institutional	7.3	18.7	31.7	63.2	66.3	61.1
of which:						
Co-op Soc/Banks, etc.	3.3	2.6	22.0	29.8	30.0	30.2
Commercial Banks	0.9	0.6	2.4	28.8	35.2	26.3
Unspecified	—	—	—	—	3.1	—
Total	100.0	100.0	100.0	100.0	100.0	100.0

Notes: $ AIDIS, NSSO, 59th Round, 2003.
Borrowing refers to outstanding cash dues.
Source: All India Debt and Investment Surveys.[40]

It is interesting to note that there appears to be an increase in demands of credit from moneylenders during the year 2002. According to Rakesh Mohan, "this is reflected in the increasing concern in recent years over the effectiveness, governance and financial health of rural co-operative banks and the attention being given to rural lending by commercial banks."[41] This also reveals that there are several gaps in the system like inadequate provision of credit to small and marginal farmers, paucity of medium and long-term lending and limited deposit mobilization and heavy dependence on borrowed funds by major agricultural credit purveyors. Therefore, efforts are required to address and rectify these issues. Hence, strong and viable agricultural financial institutions are needed to cater to the requirements of finance for building the necessary institutional and marketing infrastructure.

8.3.4.2. Bank Credit to Small Scale Industries

The Small Scale Industries (SSIs) in India play a vital role in the growth and development of Indian economy. It is evident from the substantial contribution made by the small scale industries. The share of small scale industries output (gross) to total GDP in 2001-02 stood roughly at 14 per cent. As per the latest census information, the SSI sector generated employment of as many as 249 lakh people. In terms of the total workforce[42] SSI employment constitutes a share of 6.2 per cent. During 2001-02, the export of SSIs stood at US $14,199 million. SSI units during 1987-88 to 2001-02, recorded an annual average growth (compound) of 12 per cent in production at current prices. During the same period, employment in the registered sector increased by a compound growth rate of 3.8 per cent.[43] On the other hand, the nominal bank credit to the sector increased only by 11.7 per cent annually.

The credit available to SSI however is not in proportion to the contribution made by the SSI towards the development of Indian economy. Table 8.10 presents the growth in bank credit to small scale industry. The average annual growth in credit to SSI sector was 11.4 per cent during 1991-92 to 2003-04, and growth in credit to total industry was high at 14.4 per cent. However, the total credit growth was at 16.3 per cent during the same period. Thus, credit to SSI witnessed a low growth rate during the post-reforms period. It is also observed from Table 8.10 that "the annual growth rates in credit to the SSI sector fluctuated widely between -3.6 per cent to 21.7 per cent compared with the range of 7.3 per cent to 27.1 per cent for total industry. Further, the share of credit to total industry in total bank credit increased in the first half of 1990s, declining after 1996-97, with fluctuations, from 49.3 per cent to 38 per cent in 2004. The share of SSI declined continuously from 13.9 per cent in 1992 to 8.1 per cent in 2004. Thus, the decline in the share of SSI is rather steep than that of total industry."[44]

Table 8.10. Growth in Total Bank Credit to Industry (Manufacturing) and SSI Sector (Per cent)

Year (end March)	Growth Rate in Bank Credit			Per Cent Share in Total Bank Credit		Total Industry
	Total	Total Industry	SSI Sector	Total Industry	SSI Sector	SSI Sector
1992	10.1	10.4	5.6	47.7	13.9	29.0
1993	18.8	21.1	10.8	48.6	12.9	26.6
1994	8.3	7.3	14.3	48.2	13.6	28.3
1995	19.9	13.6	21.7	45.6	13.8	30.3

1996	20.7	27.1	17.4	48.0	13.5	28.0
1997	11.7	14.8	11.5	49.3	13.4	27.2
1998	16.0	14.8	19.8	48.8	13.8	28.4
1999	15.9	16.7	12.9	49.2	13.5	27.5
2000	20.3	13.7	10.4	46.5	12.4	26.7
2001	17.0	10.6	5.5	43.9	11.2	25.4
2002	21.8	14.8	11.6	41.1	10.2	24.7
2003	15.2	14.1	-3.6	41.0	8.6	20.9
2004	16.5	8.1	10.7	38.0	8.1	21.4
Annual average growth rate	16.3	14.4	11.4			

Note: Data for 2002 are not adjusted for merger of ICICI.
Source: Basic Statistical Returns of Scheduled Commercial Banks (various issues) and Handbook of Statistics, 2003-04, RBI.[45]

Examining the credit disbursement of scheduled commercial banks to the SSI sector, it was observed that the share of SSI sector in total bank credit and in credit to the total industry varied between 12.9 to 13.9 per cent and 24.7 to 30.3 per cent, respectively, during the period 1991-92 to 2001-02, which decreased thereafter to 8.1 per cent and 21.4 per cent in 2003-04, respectively. The growth in credit to the SSI sector fluctuated between 5.5 per cent and 19.8 per cent, except in 1994-95 (21.7 per cent growth) and 2002-03 (-3.6 per cent). According to K.S. Rama Chandra Rao and others, the growth rates in credit to the SSI sector recorded low or negative rates during 2001 to 2003, as against high growth rates in the earlier period for small sized banks when we view banks according to their size and total assets. They feel that the decline in the share of SSI loans of the commercial banks is mainly due to the high incidence of bad loans arising out of SSI advances.[46] In this given situation commercial banks will definitely try to play safe by diverting funds to other sectors that yield higher returns. Thus there is a need felt to impose specific quantitative restrictions within the priority sector so that commercial banks could increase the share of SSI loans provided to small scale industries.

8.3.5. Risk Management

In the initial stages of globalization Indian banks were managing each risk in isolation. Now it is argued that it is no longer safe to manage each risk independently. Enterprises worldwide are now replacing isolated risk management with an integrated framework of risk management which is proactive, systematic and spans across the entire organization. Banks in India are also moving from the individual risk management system to an integrated enterprising wide risk management system because a number of effective risk management systems determine the health of the financial system and its ability to survive economic shocks.[47] Banks would, therefore, be required to allocate significant resources towards this endeavour.

Besides this, for effective financial stability in the banking sector proper corporate governance is necessary at every level. Very often a number of risk management failures reflect a breakdown in corporate governance which arise due to poor management of conflicts of interest, inadequate understanding of key banking risks and poor broad oversight of the mechanisms for risk management and internal audit. Corporate governance is, therefore, the foundation for effective risk managements in banks and thus the foundation for a sound financial system. Indian banks after reforms must cultivate good governance principles and appropriate checks and balances in their operations. Dr. V. Leeladhar has given four forms of oversight that should be included in the "organisational structure of any bank in order to ensure appropriate checks and balances: (1) oversight by the board of directors or supervisory board; (2) oversight by individuals not involved in the day-to-day running of the various business areas; (3) direct line supervision of different business areas; and (4) independent risk management, compliance and audit functions. In addition, it is important that key personnel are fit and proper for their jobs."[48] In this direction there is also an urgent need to upgrade the accounting framework and accounting system of Indian banks.

Post-reforms in the banking sector allowed banks to use outsourcing for achieving strategic aims. This is undertaken for the purpose of rationalization of operational costs and for tapping specialist expertise. Outsourcing in the banking sector has however given rise to several risks like, strategic risk, reputation risk, compliance risk, operational risk, exit strategy risk, counterparty risk, country risk, access risk, concentration risk and systemic risk. This can lead to financial losses and reputational risk for the bank and could also lead to systemic risks for the entire banking system in a country.[49] Therefore, outsourcing banks should take steps to ensure that the service provider employs the same high standard of care in performing the services as would be employed by the banks if the activities were conducted within the banks and not outsourced.

8.3.6. Growth in FII Investment in India

Reforms initiated in the financial sector caused a significant increase in the inflows of portfolio capital. The flows through Foreign Institutional Investors (FIIs) was relatively stable during the period 1992-2002, but has recorded an extraordinary flow since April 2003. The average flow of FII investments has been $1,776 million a year during 1993-94 to 1996-97. However, net FII investment dipped to an average of $295 million during 1997-99, due to the South-East Asian crisis. The average FII investment again rose to $1,829 million during 1999-2000 to 2001-02, only to fall to $377 million in 2002-03. Inflows averaged $9,800 million a year during 2003-05 and are estimated at $8,280 million during the first 11 months of 2005-06. Going by data from the Securities and Exchange Board of India (SEBI), while cumulative net FII flows into India since the liberalization of rules governing such flows in the early 1990s till the end of March 2003 amounted to $15,804 million, the increment in cumulative value between that date and the end of December 2005 was $25,267 million.

Liberalization has thus drawn the attention of foreign investors resulting in a rise in portfolio investment in the Indian capital market. During the first half of the 1990s, India accounted for a larger volume of international equity issues than any other emerging market.[50] Over recent years, India has emerged as a major recipient of portfolio investment among the emerging market economies. This is also reflecting the confidence of cross-border investors on the prospects of Indian securities market.

Ever growing FII investment can however have certain negative effects on the economy because FII investments constitute a large share of the equity capital of a financial entity and any FII pull-out can have significant implications for the financial health of India. Similarly, if any set of developments encourages an unusually high outflow of FII capital from the market, it can impact adversely the value of the rupee and set off speculation in the currency that can in special circumstances result in a currency crisis. Growing FII presence is disconcerting according to C.P. Chandrasekhar and Parthapratim Pal "because the effort to attract such flows and manage any surge in such flows that may occur has a number of macroeconomic implications. Most importantly, inasmuch as financial liberalisation leads to financial growth and deepening and increases the presence and role of financial agents in the economy, it forces the state to adopt a deflationary stance to appease financial interests."[51]

8.3.7. Changes in Banking Practices

Financial reforms have also resulted in a disturbing decline in credit provision.[52] Following the reforms, the credit deposit ratio of commercial banks as a whole declined substantially from 65.2 per cent in 1990-91 to 49.9 per cent in 2003-04 (Table 8.11) despite a substantial increase in the loanable funds base of banks through periodic reductions in the CRR and SLR by the Reserve Bank of India starting in 1992.

It could be the result of a decline in demand for credit from creditworthy borrowers in the system. However, C.P. Chandrasekhar and Parthapratim Pal argue that "the decrease in the credit deposit ratio has been accompanied by a corresponding increase in the proportion of risk-free government securities in the banks major earning assets, i.e. loans and advances, and investments." Table 8.11 reveals that the investment in government securities as a percentage of total earning assets for the commercial banking system as a whole was 26.13 per cent in 1990-91. But it increased to 32.4 per cent in 2003-04.[53] This points to the fact that lending function of the commercial sector may have been gradually shifting towards investments in government securities. It may be due to the fact that government securities may be offering relatively high, near risk-free returns. Above all banks are allowed to have greater choice in terms of investments including corporate commercial paper and equity. Most of the banks thus are in search of higher profitability investments rather than lending.[54] This clearly indicates the change that has occurred in terms of banking practices due to globalization process initiated within the financial sector.

Table 8.11. Credit Deposit Ratio and Investment in Government Securities (As percentage of total earning assets during 1990-91 to 2003-04, for scheduled commercial banks)

Year	Credit Deposit	Ratio Investment in Govt Securities (as Percentage to Total Earning Assets)
1990-91	65.2	26.13
1991-92	60.6	29.06
1992-93	58.9	29.47
1993-94	55.5	34.08
1994-95	61.6	32.61
1995-96	58.2	31.57
1996-97	55.1	33.88
1997-98	53.5	34.4
1998-99	51.7	33.8
1999-2000	53.6	33.4
2000-01	53.1	33.2
2001-02	53.4	28.1
2002-03	78.6	31.6
2003-04	49.9	32.4

Source: Estimated from various issues of Indian Banks' *Association, Performance Highlights of Banks in India, and Reserve Bank of India, Report on Trend and Progress of Banking in India.*[55]

8.4. CRITICAL EVALUATION

The financial reforms initiated in 1991-92 have made significant progress. In overall terms, banks are much healthier, customers are better served through improved technology and development needs more responsively met. The regulatory architecture has been strengthened by the creation of SEBI for securities markets and mutual funds, and the Insurance Regulatory Development Authority for the insurance sector. There is a growing realization within domestic banks about the ability to conduct business across national borders. Indian banks have realized that the ability to cope with the possible downside risks would depend on the soundness of the financial system and the strength of the individual participants. It is also realized that the adoption of appropriate prudential, regulatory, supervisory, and technological framework on par with international best practices would enable strengthening of the domestic banking system. This in reality would help in fortifying against the risks that might arise out of globalization.[56] But in reality this is not true as regards the functioning of commercial banks. Following are the points which the banking sector should seriously consider itself for its significant growth and development:

- In order to improve the autonomy and efficiency of public sector banks, it is essential to minimize government interference and to strengthen the quality of bank boards. With the exception of the Reserve Bank and the State Bank, the quality of autonomy enjoyed by other bank boards remains suspect.
- High quality talent with domain knowledge cannot be attracted by the present salary structure; the dilemma of market-oriented emoluments in a 'public sector bank' needs resolution.
- It is necessary to strengthen accounting procedures, so as to fully reflect market values of all assets in publicly disclosed statements, and ensure that losses are fully revealed to shareholders, depositors and supervisors, regardless of whether they stem from NPAs or higher interest rates. A bank that does not honestly report bad news will never get around to solving problems.

- The uniformity of practice relating to asset classification and adequacy of provisioning based on more truthful classification of assets is not easy. Indeed, while NPAs have significantly declined, some of the numbers remain suspect depending on how truthfully assets have been classified. The entire area of asset allocation, asset quality and capital adequacy needs to be looked into. Methodologies for risk assessment of asset quality and provisioning in the light of the perceived risk are critical for meeting norms.
- The high fiscal deficit is cited as a reason for all types of conservative policies in the financial sector and monetary economics. But it does not, in any way, constrain reforms in banking that are aimed at increasing competition. If government equity in public sector banks cannot be reduced and there is no consensus, then the absence of competition will perpetuate inefficiency. Efforts towards consolidation, mergers and acquisition also remain stymied. It is in this context that the enhanced presence of foreign banks in India, and greater ease of entry for domestic banks, can greatly help in improving the productivity and efficiency of Indian banking.
- The performances of public sector banks in terms of profitability have been much lower than the private banks. However, there has been divergent performance in terms of profit among public sector banks. Some of the public sector banks have performed at par with private and foreign banks. Dr. Y.V. Reddy feels that it reflects performance management. In his words, "As a group, however, the performance of PSBs in terms of profitability, spreads, non-performing assets and standard assets position seems to have been lower than that of the new private sector and foreign banks. There have been significant divergences in performance among the public sector banks—some have performed on par with private and foreign banks, whereas the performance of others has been relatively unsatisfactory."[57]

- "The accepted roadmap for presence of foreign banks in India is in two phases: the first phase comprises of three components namely, foreign banks with first time presence choosing to operate through a branch licence or set up a 100% Wholly Owned Subsidiary (WOS); existing foreign banks expanding branches through a liberal branch licensing procedure; converting existing branches to Wholly Owned Subsidiaries or be allowed to have an equity up to 74% in private Indian banks identified by the Reserve Bank for restructuring. Over the years of reforms nothing has been heard or done on the implementation of this roadmap; either no foreign banks are eligible or they remain uninterested."[58]
- "An important issue, specifically relating to the banking sector, is consolidation. Despite the liberalization process, the structure of the Indian banking system has continued without much change though development of finance institutions were merged with banks. The consolidation process within the banking system in recent years has primarily been confined to a few mergers in the private sector segment induced by financial position of the banks. Some mergers may take place in future for compliance with minimum net worth requirement or norms on diversified ownership."[59]
- The problems with regard to rural banks and cooperative banks have been the experience of constraints on timely credit availability, its high cost, neglect of small farmers and continued presence of informal lenders. Most part of the cooperative credit structure is multilayered, under-capitalised, over-staffed and under-skilled, often with high level of delinquent loans.[60] Therefore, it is necessary to revitalise rural banks and cooperative banks and urban cooperative banks in a medium-term framework so that they are able to sustain themselves in their financial transactions that are underway.
- It has been argued that liberalisation involving controls on inflows and outflows of capital have resulted in an increase in financial fragility in developing countries

and making them prone to periodic financial and currency crises. Analyses of individual instances of crises have tended to conclude that the nature and timing of these crises had much to do with the shift to a more liberal and open financial regime.

- As financial reforms are in progress various resource limitations will be experienced by low-income households and this will continue to constrain their access and use of financial products. Therefore, the challenge facing the financial sector in India is to develop appropriate policies, procedures and products that can overcome these difficulties.[61] For this significant growth and development of micro-finance activities could be undertaken during financial reforms. Self-help groups formed by non-government organizations could play an important constituent of this development process in India. Over and above a "Technical Group has also been proposed to renew the existing legislative framework governing moneylending and its enforcement machinery so as to provide for greater credit penetration by the financial sector in the rural areas at reasonable rates of interest."[62]

8.5. SUGGESTIONS

8.5.1. Provide Long-term Finance

There is a need for banks to provide adequate long-term finance, particularly to small and medium industries. The gradual disappearance of development banks created a situation whereby adequate long-term finance is not available to medium and more particularly small industries. To provide adequate long-term finance to industry, two important changes are called for:

(i) need to develop an active debt market in the country which will satisfy the long-term capital requirements of large and medium industries; and,

(ii) banks should expand their credit portfolio to include increased provision of long-term finance to small scale industries.

8.5.2. Organizational Restructure

One of the weaknesses of the Indian banks and financial institutions is that they suffer from inadequate operational flexibility. Financial institutions are subject to so many regulations and controls. The degree of direction in operational matters has interfered seriously with the functioning and the autonomy of credit decision making. The fulfilment of the targets of credit sanctions and disbursements without adequate regard to qualitative aspects of lending, the repayment and recovery of dues, has led to the growth of overdues. Administrative intervention and politicisation of loan created the phenomenon of loan melas. Loan melas represented a virtual repudiation of the professional approach to bank credit operations.[63] As a result the credit system in India became the subject of competitive populism and a hostage to electoral politics. In the name of social banking cannons of sound banking were forgotten. Therefore "corporate planning combined with organizational restructuring are a necessary prerequisite to achieve desired results in terms of productivity and profitability. A properly designed management system that improves productivity and drives the behaviour of employees in delivering quality service must be clearly spelt out. There must be a vision to which employees can relate."[64] For this public sector banks need to be given greater autonomy in terms of the management of staff, recruitment and promotion of personnel and in determining the organizational structure.[65] Greater accountability must necessarily go hand in hand with greater autonomy. Emphasis should be placed on qualitative improvement of portfolio in the financial sector rather than its quantitative expansion. This means that those who can afford to pay commercial rates and qualify on normal banking considerations, credit should be disbursed to them without any deviation from the principles of commercial viability.[66] In this process the special requirements of the really needy should not be forgotten, rather it should find recognition.

8.5.3. Innovation in Customers Service

Innovation and customer service are going to be key drivers of success in the future. In an increasingly open and integrated world economy, commercial banks will need to develop an ability to respond to a wide range of expectations from customers, seeking different kinds of products and services. Depositors demand high levels of transaction efficiency; borrowers look for prompt, adequate and innovative responses; and finally, regulators expect banks to manage growth and diversification in a prudent manner.[67] Certainly, India cannot achieve growth on a sustainable basis without a strong, stable and efficient financial system.

8.5.4. Need for Advanced Technology

Innovation in technology and revolution in information and communication technology have emerged as dynamic sources of productivity growth. Technology is therefore a key driver in the banking industry, which creates new business models and processes, and also creates revolution in distribution channels. In the banking sector, IT can reduce costs, increase volumes, and facilitate customized products. In the dynamics of payment system of the banking IT sector gets manifested to a greater extent. Strengthening of information technology in banks could improve the effectiveness of asset-liability management in banks. Above all, building up of a related database on a real time basis would enhance the forecasting of liquidity greatly at the branch level. This could enhance the quality of risk management systems in banks. While doing so they derive maximum advantage from their investments in technology and avoid wasteful expenditure which might arise on account of uncoordinated and inadequate adoption of technology.

In order to derive greater utility from the IT sector and to maximize greater benefit as a result of interaction between IT and banking sector, Bimal Jalan (former Governor, RBI) suggests that "banks have to take pro-active measures to:

- further strengthen their infrastructure in respect of standardization, high levels of security and communication and networking;
- achieve inter-branch connectivity early;
- popularize the usage of the scheme of electronic funds transfer (EFT); and

- institute arrangements for an RTGS environment online with a view to integrating into a secure and consolidated payment system."[68]

8.5.5. Need for Non-banking Finance Companies

Until recently, the money market in India was narrow and circumscribed by tight regulations over interest rates and participants. The secondary market was underdeveloped and lacked liquidity. Several measures have been initiated and include new money market instruments, strengthening of existing instruments and setting up of the Discount and Finance House of India (DFHI).

8.5.6. The Capital Market

There has been a dramatic improvement in the country's stock market trading infrastructure during the last few years. Significant institutional changes have taken place in the securities markets with the emergence of electronic trading, a clearing corporation and a depository. Expectations are that India will be an attractive emerging market with tremendous potential. However, in our over-enthusiasm to develop the capital market one should not harm and destroy the other instruments of saving. The number of shareholders in India is estimated at 25 million. However, only an estimated two lakh persons actively trade in stocks. Unfortunately, during recent times the stock markets have been constrained by some unsavoury developments, which have led to retail investors deserting the stock markets.

8.5.7. Need for Legislative Measures

Several legislative measures need to be undertaken to enable further progress in the financial sector. These could be related to ownership, regulatory focus, development of financial markets, and bankruptcy procedures. Over and above this credit delivery needs changes in legal and incentive systems. "There is need to focus on reduction of transaction costs in economic activity, and enhancing economic incentives. Severe penalties in law, including criminal proceedings, may not be substitutes for increasing enforceability."[69] While emphasizing the need for new legislative measures for the new environment Montek S. Ahluwalia writes, "The legal system must be one in which the laws are clear and transparent, procedures are speedy, the judiciary is independent of politics and outcomes are perceived to be fair"[70] so that the ordinary citizens and small businesses are not hurt and large corporations are much less vulnerable. For this drastic change is needed in the legal system of India.

The financial sector in India is faced with the problems of 'overhang' problems such as non-performing assets of banks and financial institutions. It is necessary to solve these issues upfront. It is necessary "to distinguish between what the financial sector can contribute and what fiscal action can contribute to matters relating to poverty alleviation. In the interest of efficiency and stability of financial sector, intermediation may have to be progressively multi-institutional rather than wholly bank-centred. Social obligations may have to be distributed equitably among banks and other intermediaries...Mechanisms have to be found to reconcile these dilemmas."[71]

8.5.8. Universal Banking

Faced with pressures of globalization and international financial liberalization, many feel that the concept of universal banking structure would help in improving the competitive strength of Indian banking. The general trend has been towards downstream universal banking where banks have undertaken traditionally non-banking activities such as investment banking, insurance, mortgage financing, securitization and particularly, insurance. Upstream linkages, where non-banks undertake banking business are also on the increase.

A.K. Khandelwal feels that "Acquisition of a 'universal banking' structure could be perceived as a strategic reaction of certain players to these changed circumstances. As revealed by the experience (including that of India for last few years) universal banking model enables financial players to offer different products and services—more or less interrelated, depending on the internal resources available and the competitive dynamics in each financial market. A universal banking character would offer them more options for penetrating more quickly, new segments within the financial service sector, as guided by the customer demands and for generating revenue synergies through the provision of multiple services. Moreover, a universal banking model is quite effective in promoting social welfare by reducing the corporate financing costs for ultimate borrowers."[72] Reserve Bank of India too while expressing its greater desirability for establishing a universal bank says, "Universal bank is desirable from the point of view of efficiency of resource use."[73]

Universal banking would be of great advantage to Indian financial sector because in areas in which foreign banks enjoyed comparative advantage for decades, Indian universal banks are making serious inroads. As an example, three Indian universal banks have now crossed the two million card base, with ICICI bank leading the pack at four million cards (racing ahead of Citibank, which is at 2.8 million), while HDFC bank has a card base of 2.2 million, SBI cards have just crossed over 2 million.[74] In the process of universal banking, according to Bimal Jalan, "the overriding consideration should be the objectives and strategic interests of the financial institution concerned...subject to normal prudential norms applicable to banks. From the point of view of the regulatory framework, the movement towards universal banking should entrench stability of the financial system, preserve the safety of public deposits, improve efficiency in financial intermediation, ensure healthy competition, and impart transparent and equitable regulation."[75]

8.6. CONCLUSIONS

Last ten years have seen major improvements in the working of various financial market participants. For this the government and the regulatory authorities have followed a step-by-step approach. The entry of foreign players has assisted in the introduction of international practices and systems. Technology developments have improved customer service. Some gaps however remain. On the whole, the cumulative effect of the developments since 1991 has been quite encouraging. Problems related to South-East Asian crisis did not affect the financial system of India is an indication of the strength of the reformed Indian financial system.

"The Indian experience indicates that, *inter alia*, there are three important outcomes of financial liberalisation. First, increased financial fragility, which the irrational boom in India's stock market epitomises. Second, a deflationary macroeconomic stance, which adversely affects public capital formation and the objectives of promoting employment and reducing poverty. Finally, a credit squeeze for the commodity producing sectors and a decline in credit delivery to rural India and small scale industry. The belief that the financial deepening that results from liberalisation would in myriad way neutralise these effects has not been realised."[76] Banks and financial institutions thus should endeavour to "play a 'supply-leading' rather than 'demand-following' role in initiating the upturn by energizing the financial intermediation process. By virtue of a bird's eye view of the economy and their superior credit assessment of the investment proposals and the efficiency of capital, banks should endeavour to economize on 'search' costs in identifying and service producing sectors of the economy."[77]

It is widely acknowledged that India is the repository of the best of human skills, especially in the financial sector. The technological competence of the Indian workforce is perhaps presently very high. The present levels of growth optimism about the financial sector suggest that India is expected to remain one of the important growth drivers of the global economy in the near future. The financial infrastructure and regulatory framework in the country are broadly at par with those prevailing internationally. We are working towards evolving a globally competitive banking sector, stressing on banking services relevant to our socio-economic conditions and contributing to both growth and stability.

However, financial liberalization alone will not ensure stable economic growth. Some tough decisions need to be taken. For this sound economic policies and strong political support is necessary. Political support for sound economic management cannot come through exhortation by politicians rather it is necessary for politicians to perceive sound economics as good politics in the framework of democratic set-up.[78] The mere dilution of government equity in public sector banks cannot possibly contribute to any improvement in performance rather listing on the exchanges, a profit orientation and a measure of autonomy can together produce improvements in performance.[79] For which fiscal control, financial stability must be ensured and the political and legal structures over and above have to ensure that borrowers repay the loans on time. Above all, the various steps taken to improve the financial sector in India should make sure that the "Indian financial sector is emerging to culminate into a strong, transparent and resilient system"[80] so that the Indian financial sector is not only preserved but improved upon in its ability to withstand shocks and difficulties so that it may become stronger than ever before. It is also essential for India to adjust to the realities of globalization and play its part as a major economic player in a globalised world economy. M. Narasimham[81] strongly feels that India has the potential to be a major economic player in the world economy and it is up to us to realize that potential.

END NOTES

1. Rudra Sensarma, "Cost and Profit Efficiency of Indian Banks during 1986-2003: A Stochastic Frontier Analysis", *Economic and Political Weekly*, March 19, 2005, p. 1199.
2. Rakesh Mohan, "Financial Sector Reforms in India: Policies and Performance Analysis", *Economic and Political Weekly*, March 19, 2005, p. 1106.
3. *Ibid.*, p. 1106.
4. Y.V. Reddy, "Monetary and Financial Sector Reforms in India: A Practitioner's Perspective", at the Indian Economy Conference, Program on Comparative Economic Development (PCED) at Cornell University, USA, on April 19-20, 2002.
5. Y.V. Reddy, "Reforming India's Financial Sector: Changing Dimensions and Emerging Issues", address delivered by, Governor, RBI at the International Centre for Monetary and Banking Studies, Geneva on May 6, 2006.
6. V. Leeladhar, "Indian Banks and Global Challenges", Inaugural Address by Dy. Governor, Reserve Bank of India at the Joint Seminar on Indian Banks and the Global Challenges organized by Indian Merchants' Chamber and Indian Banks' Association on January 31, 2006 at Mumbai.

7. Dr. Manmohan Singh, Prime Minister of India's speech at Bicentennial Celebrations of State Bank of India, June 4, 2005, Mumbai, as given in http://www.banknetindia.com/banking/rbip3a.htm.
8. C.P. Chandrasekhar and Parthapratim Pal, "Financial Liberalisation in India: An Assessment of its Nature and Outcomes", *Economic and Political Weekly*, Vol. 41, No. 11, March 18, 2006, p. 985.
9. Y.V. Reddy, *op. cit.*
10. *Ibid.*
11. *Ibid.*
12. Rakesh Mohan, *op. cit.*, p. 1110.
13. As given by *Ibid.*, p. 1112.
14. *Ibid.*, p. 1110.
15. *Ibid.*
16. As given by *Ibid.*, p. 1112.
17. *Ibid.*, p. 1110.
18. S.K. Misra, "Development of Commercial Banking During the Post-Liberalisation Period – A Study in a Regional Dimension", *Post-Reform Leading Issues of Indian Economy*, A.D.N. Bajpai and others (eds.), Atlantic Publishers and Distributors (P) Ltd., New Delhi, 2002, p. 90.
19. *Ibid.*, p. 1112.
20. As given Rakesh Mohan, *op. cit.*, p. 1112.
21. As given by *Ibid.*, p. 1112.
22. Y.V. Reddy, *op. cit.*, Geneva on May 6, 2006.
23. Rudra Sensarma, *op. cit.*, p. 1204.
24. Abhiman Das, Ashok Nag and Subhash C. Ray, "Liberalisation, Ownership and Efficiency in Indian Banking: A Non-parametric Analysis", *Economic and Political Weekly March* 19, 2005, p. 1197.
25. *Ibid.*, p. 1197.
26. Quality Services means setting up of ALPM branches, upgradation of technology, flexible banking hours, online banking, etc.
27. Rudra Sensarma, *op. cit.*, p. 1205.
28. Y.V. Reddy, *op. cit.*, Geneva on May 6, 2006.
29. S.K. Misra, *op. cit.*, *Post-Reform Leading Issues of Indian Economy*, A.D.N. Bajpai and others (eds.), Atlantic Publishers and Distributors (P) Ltd., New Delhi, 2002, p. 87.
30. Y.V. Reddy, *op. cit.*, USA, on April 19-20, 2002.
31. www.unescap.org/drpad/publication/fin_2206/part4.pdf

32. Mainly Italy, Germany and France.
33. Y.V. Reddy, *op. cit.*, Geneva on May 6, 2006.
34. Reserve Bank of India, "Draft Technical Paper by the Internal Working Group on Priority Sector Lending", September, RBI, Rural Planning Credit Department, Mumbai, as given by C.P. Chandrasekhar and Parthapratim Pal, *op. cit.*, p. 987.
35. S.L. Shetty, "Distributional Issues in Bank Credit: Multi-Strategy for Correcting Past Neglect", *Economic and Political Weekly*, June 7, 2004.
36. C.P. Chandrasekhar and Parthapratim Pal, *op. cit.*, p. 987.
37. David C. Mulford, Economic Reform and Infrastructure, Remarks at FICCI's India Infrastructure Conference Federation House, New Delhi, March 28, 2005.
38. As given by Rakesh Mohan, "Agricultural Credit in India: Status, Issues and Future Agenda", *Economic and Political Weekly*, March 18, 2006, p. 1016.
39. *Ibid.*, p. 1017.
40. As given by *Ibid.*, p. 1017.
41. Rakesh Mohan, "Agricultural Credit in India: Status, Issues and Future Agenda", *Economic and Political Weekly*, March 18, 2006, p. 1019.
42. Based on 2001 population census.
43. Raj Kapila and Uma Kapila (eds.), *India's Economy in the 21st Century*, Academic Foundation, New Delhi, 2002, p. 308.
44. K.S. Rama Chandra Rao, Abhiman Das and Arvind Kumar Singh, "Commercial Bank Lending to Small-Scale Industry", *Economic and Political Weekly*, March 18, 2006, p. 1029.
45. As given by *Ibid.*, p. 1029.
46. *Ibid.*, p. 1033.
47. V. Leeladhar, *op. cit.*, on January 31, 2006 at Mumbai.
48. *Ibid.*
49. *Ibid.*
50. IMF, IMF survey, International Monetary Fund, Washington, DC, 1995. As given by Rakesh Mohan, *op. cit.*, March 19, 2005, p. 1118.
51. C.P. Chandrasekhar and Parthapratim Pal, *op. cit.*, p. 980.
52. S.L. Shetty, "Distributional Issues in Bank Credit: Multi-pronged Strategy for Correcting Past Neglect", *Economic and Political Weekly* July 17, 2004.

53. *Ibid.*, p. 986.

54. *Ibid.*

55. As given by C.P. Chandrasekhar and Parthapratim Pal, *op. cit.*, p. 987.

56. V. Leeladhar, *op. cit.*, On January 31, 2006 at Mumbai. Bimal Jalan, "Banking and Finance in India Managing New Challenges", Raj Kapila and Uma Kapila (eds.), *op. cit.*, p. 189. C.P. Chandrasekhar and Parthapratim Pal, *op. cit.*, p. 988. Bimal Jalan, "Banking and Finance in India: Managing New Challenges", Raj Kapila and Uma Kapila (eds.), *op. cit.*, p. 179. M. Narasimham, *op. cit.*, p. 107.

57. Y.V. Reddy, *op. cit.*, USA, on April 19-20, 2002.

58. The Indian Express, "Banking Reforms: Need to Walk the Talk", 25-9-2005 as found in http://iecolumnists.expressindia.com/full_column.php? content_id=78805

59. Dr. Y.V. Reddy, *op. cit.*, Geneva on May 6, 2006.

60. *Ibid.*

61. *Ibid.*

62. *Ibid.*

63. M. Narasimham, "Economic Reforms and Development and Finance", UBS Publishers' Distribution Ltd., New Delhi, 2002, p. 278.

64. R. Kannan (ed.), "Selected Essays on Indian Economy by C. Rangarajan", Academic Foundation, New Delhi, pp. 343-44.

65. Dr. Manmohan Singh, *op. cit.*, June 4, 2005, Mumbai.

66. M. Narasimham, *op. cit.*, p. 279.

67. *Ibid.*

68. Bimal Jalan, "Banking and Finance in India: Managing New Challenges", Raj Kapila and Uma Kapila (eds.), *India's Economy in the 21st Century, Academic Foundation*, New Delhi, 2002, p. 193.

69. Y.V. Reddy, *op. cit.*, USA, on April 19-20, 2002.

70. Montek S. Ahluwalia, "Economic Reforms: A Policy Agenda for the Future", Raj Kapila and Uma Kapila (eds.), *op. cit.*, p. 115.

71. Y.V. Reddy, *op. cit.*, USA, on April 19-20, 2002.

72. A.K. Khandelwal, "Universal Banking: Solution for Indian's Financial Challenges?" *Economic and Political Weekly*, March 18, 2006, p. 973.

73. RBI, *Annual Report, 1998-99*, p. 149, as quoted by N.A. Mujumdar, "Agenda for Financial Sector Reforms", Raj Kapila and Uma Kapila (eds.), *op. cit.*, p. 228.

74. A.K. Khandelwal, *op. cit.*, p. 972.
75. Bimal Jalan, "Banking and Finance in India: Managing New Challenges", Raj Kapila and Uma Kapila (eds.), *op. cit.*, p. 189.
76. C.P. Chandrasekhar and Parthapratim Pal, *op. cit.*, p. 988.
77. Bimal Jalan, "Banking and Finance in India: Managing New Challenges", Raj Kapila and Uma Kapila (eds.), *op. cit.*, p. 179.
78. M. Narasimham, *op. cit.*, p. 107.
79. T.T. Ram Mohan, "Long-run Performance of Public and Private Sector Bank Stocks", *Economic and Political Weekly*, February, 2003, p. 788.
80. Rohit Sarkar, "The Financial Sector: Vision 2020", *India Vision 2020: The Report plus Background Paper*", Planning Commission, Government of India, Academic Foundation, New Delhi, 2004, p. 909.
81. M. Narasimham, *op. cit.*, p. 117.

Conclusion and Policy Recommendations

9

9.1. INTRODUCTION

The study suggests that India's infrastructure is not up to the mark when compared to developed countries. But at the same time it is also true that India is upgrading its infrastructural facilities. India has a large and fairly well-developed infrastructure framework extending to all parts of the country. However, certain areas like power, telecommunications, transport and financial sector need further expansion and modernization. The public sector alone can no longer fully finance the requirements and the required developments. Infrastructure being an important element of development, there is an immediate need on the part of the Government and planning authorities to adopt an appropriate strategy simultaneously to develop, all sorts of infrastructural facilities. The public sector alone cannot bring about the desired development in the infrastructure sector. In the future, therefore, the private sector could be given a greater role in infrastructure sector to create additional capacity with quality and quantity specification. This does not mean that the Government should discontinue shouldering the responsibility of developing and investing in infrastructure rather the Government should continue to shoulder the major responsibility and burden of the economy.

In this connection, the Economic Survey 1996-97 rightly observed, "the process of deregulation and privatization of infrastructure services also needs to be supplemented by the establishment of statutory regulatory authorities for ensuring fair competition among public and private operators and protecting consumer interests, public safety, internal and external security, needs of vulnerable and weaker sections and environmental sustainability."[1] Growth in infrastructure sector is possible only with sincere, committed and competent Governments at all levels. It means a Government committed to the fight against corruption which is supported by an efficient and honest legal and judicial system. Development of infrastructure also requires a well supervised financial system that promotes transparency and sincerity. The Government should play the role of a facilitator in sensitizing various stakeholders about the efficient options available and the benefits arising from infrastructure sector efficiency. Unconventional approaches to infrastructure sector efficiency need to be integrated into an overall strategy. The concept of an integrated infrastructure strategy does not mean centralized action, rather it means a system and process of coordination, decision-making and actions that bring various infrastructure activities and decisions into a common framework. These minimum requirements are necessary to attain the projected growth in the infrastructure sector.

9.2. GENERAL STUDY ON THE INFRASTRUCTURAL DEVELOPMENT

9.2.1. Power Sector

Power is a key infrastructure, which is the backbone and prime mover of the economic development of any country because power is required for all the sectors of economy which include agriculture, industries, service, information and technology, transport and others. Energy sources play a vital role in the economic development of a nation, because energy facilitate to grow food; keep people alive; transport people and goods; fuel economic development and sustain the economic system. Energy is considered to be the prime mover of economic development and growth.

During post-reforms period the power sector in India to a certain extent succeeded in reducing power deficit by 9 per cent yet this cannot be considered as a considerable achievement during this period. The post-reforms have not succeeded in eradicating real problem of power shortage. We are still in a mistaken belief that somehow the growing gap between India's requirements of power and the supply of power will be made good without adopting significant energy management skills.

The financial performance of the power sector in India has not improved substantially even after reforms initiated in the power sector. Over the years the gap between user charges and the cost of supply has worsened despite reform efforts. The restoration of the financial health of SEBs and improvement in their operational performance continue to remain a critical issue even today in the power sector. Economic reforms introduced could not redeem the deteriorating financial health of the State Electricity Boards. However, certain awareness has come into the power sector that the deteriorating financial health of the State Electricity Boards should not continue to remain the same for ever. The processes of measurement of T&D losses have improved over the years and the earlier estimates are considered to be biased downwards. However, the high T&D loss figures clearly indicate the enormous scope for improvements in transmission and distribution even during post-reforms period. However, to restore the performance of power sector in India the following recommendations are suggested:

- Energy has an ever-increasing demand in the market. So, it must be generated as much as possible and supplied to the consumers at a fair price. The power sector should be corporatized and the concept of productivity—number of employees per 1000 consumers and per million units sold—should be applied.
- Compared to urban areas consumption of power is less in the villages, hence the use of sources of renewable energy such as solar-thermal, solar-photovoltaic, biomass based thermal power or mini and micro-hydropower system must be decentralized in villages where power consumption is less. This would eliminate a large part of the line loss, as also huge investment in setting up of transmission lines, meeting the administrative overheads.
- The entry of private investors must be encouraged wherever feasible and possible, this would ensure higher rate of return on investment.

- In India, the per capita power consumption is the lowest in the world but highest in wastage of energy, which is attributed to lack of modern fuel-efficient equipment, operations of energy management and culture of saving and conservation. Hence, the private enterprises must be offered and allowed to start power-generating availability.
- The efficient management and educational programmes like use of energy efficient bulbs, tube lights, agricultural pump sets and metering at differential tariff for peak and non-peak seasons are important measures to be implemented on the demand side.
- For tariff fixation only two slabs should be considered—agricultural and non-agricultural—in the present seven slabs. For agricultural purposes the tariff should be charged on the basis of cost of generation of hydropower projects while for non-agricultural purposes the tariff should be charged on the basis of average cost of generation of electricity from all other generating units. This would fulfill the Governments' obligation to agriculture on the one hand, and commercialization of power tariff for better revenue on the other. Over and above this, the Government should phase out subsidies in general and bring down subsidy given to agricultural sector within the next few years.
- "Modernization of the work through extensive computerization in power stations both for process control and general management and in distribution system planning, computers are also extensively used for commercial land establishment applications, in the head office. Over and above sufficient attention to human resource development and training for staff at all levels in job-related skills and modern technical and analytical skills and computers right from induction level and at all levels."[2] This statement emphasizes that computerization is the main contributory factor for the good performance of a number of Electricity Boards in the World. It is understood therefore that "the solution

to the power sector squarely lies on 'Prudent Management with Expertise'—know-how and do-how, which is a guiding and governing principle."[3]

- The provision with regards to the electricity bill payment by 'pay date' should strictly be implemented. If not paid by the due date, a penalty must be imposed at specific rate for the first time and permanent disconnection in case of subsequent instances.
- Loss in transmission is purely technical which should be brought down to ideal figures by proper planning of transmission at technical and commercial level. Commercial loss means un-metered consumption, which in other words is called power theft. This should be reduced totally through means of penalized provisions through anti-power theft Law.
- Energy Audit should be initiated at all sub-stations; penalty may be imposed for theft or loss on the erring person. Electricity thefts should be eliminated not gradually but speedily. For this a sense of accountability must be infused among the employees based on a well-devised system of incentives or disincentives. Bill readings of the consumers in the area of substation and reading at the substation through the check meter provided for the purpose should tally. If not the employee who is in-charge should be made responsible.
- India's power system is divided into five regional systems: eastern, northern, north-eastern, southern, and western. Weak or non-existent connections between these regions mean that there is little exchange of energy. The east cannot export much of its power surplus to other regions. The Government should plan to increase regional interchanges of power by developing the transmission system and creating the necessary pricing and grid rules for bulk power markets.
- The role of the Government should be focused and confined to policy-making and the regulatory bodies should monitor the regulation of generation, transmission and distribution, so that the functions of generation,

transmission and distribution of electricity can be segregated with accountability and transparency on the basis of power utility rate with business risk analysis.

- "The heavily subsidized farm and residential sectors should be targeted to achieve major energy savings through a judicious blend of agricultural demand side management and residential energy efficiency, which can be converted into utility flow."[4]
- Privatization of distribution should be done in a way that does not turn consumers away from reforms. For this we should set up a process which ensures that consumers are not required to pay any more for the inefficiency of the system. For this, it is necessary to create conditions for competition in the electricity industry, between producers, suppliers, transporters and traders so that the power tariff could be linked to the actual quality of power supplied. Consumer must pay a higher price if they want good quality power supply.
- "For the balance of the poor, the Government's effort should be directed towards facilitation rather than dole. For this purpose, India needs to start looking at a different set of mechanisms. The poor need to be able to choose from a specially designed set of services tailored to meet their end-use needs in quantities that they can afford."[5]
- We should work out the minimum cost at which an efficiently working power system without pilferage would supply power to different consumers.
- The private Distribution Companies should be asked to make a plan for eliminating pilferage over a given time period.
- Fundamental changes are required in the boards' management and operations. Improving their performance will require the introduction of private management, with a substantial financial incentive to cut losses and increase efficiency. Experience from

power privatizations in Latin America suggests that the private sector can minimize losses from theft, inadequate metering, and other factors in systems with high and low loss levels. Corporatization will be an important first step in introducing the private sector, and will require legislation to allow the transfer of State Electricity Board assets to successor companies.

- The distributors are free to purchase electricity at a mutually agreed price from generators. They are also free to set up their own generating plants. The generators may be permitted to sell power directly to consumers.
- Alternatively, the task of revenue collection can be handed over to the private sector. Prepaid cash system, advance payments or deposits, and remotely readable meters are some of the other new alternatives.
- Measures taken to improve the financial health of the SEBs should aim at efficiency gains and thereby, have efficiency pricing. For this the Government should aim at improvement in technical performance so that it could reduce fuel cost, auxiliary consumption, etc., and control the expenses on salary and wages.
- Political influence must be kept away from employment.
- SEBs should be unbundled and distribution must be privatized immediately. However, this need not be a pre-condition for taking measures aimed at efficiency gains and levy of economic user charges.
- It is necessary to grant a wide range of powers to regulatory agencies, so that in addition to setting of tariffs, the regulatory agencies could involve it in licensing, resolving disputes among service providers, and in regulating the quality of service.
- There is also a need to strengthen the regulatory body with extra powers so that it is free from political processes as much as possible. This will enable tariffs to track costs over time. These bodies will also facilitate the process of introducing tariffs that reflect costs and reducing current levels of cross-subsidies.

- In order to augment power availability in a short period, R&M works should be given priority. It is well known that 1 per cent improvement in plant load factor is equivalent to creation of 600 MW capacities. Similarly, 1 per cent reduction in T&D losses leads to additional revenue of about Rs. 600 crores. Recognizing the importance of R&M works[6] improvement in transmission/distribution system and 100 per cent metering works must be undertaken in a time-bound manner.
- There should be a growing interest in cross-border power trade. The benefits from trading power lie in addressing the mismatch between supply and demand in the region, while using regional natural resources better. India has large supply shortfalls and could be the main purchaser.
- Captive power generation must be encouraged.
- Decentralized energy production and supply systems, mostly through renewable sources, by private players like NGOs, cooperatives, PRIs, etc., must also be encouraged.

In India we are at the crossroad of development of the power sector. Since Independence tremendous strides have been made in this sector. Despite this much more remains to be done. Power has been one of the main drivers of growth of Indian economy. It is essential to ensure that lack of power does not become a drag on the accelerated growth which we are aiming at. For this, the power sector in India needs the concept of an integrated energy strategy. It means a system and process of coordinated decision-making and actions that bring various energy activities and decisions into a common framework. There is an urgent need for an institutional structure that allows integration of energy decision-making which rests on a system of integrated analysis, monitoring, coordinated decision-making, policy formulation and implementation.

The power sector today is in need of a holistic approach to reap the potential benefit which various reforms could render.

Thus there is a "need for a coordinated movement across all sectors linked to the provision of energy services."[7] This "will depend upon the existence of some sort of restraining or disciplining mechanism in the sector in the absence of which, efforts made will likely result in a transition from inefficient public ownership to profit-gouging monopolies or oligarchies."[8] Thus to enable competition, acceleration of economic growth and to raise the comfort level of the common man, the major challenge of the power sector is to continue with the reforms and improve the financial health of State Electricity Boards, so that quality power could be made available at an affordable price.

9.2.2. Telecommunication Sector

Telecommunications have played a critical role in shaping India's march towards progress and the importance they hold for the future of India cannot be overstated. "A new framework for infrastructure policy, consisting of competition between multiple players, under a regulatory framework defined by the State has made much headway in the area of telecom. The successful implementation of reforms since 1991 has resulted in unprecedented growth of the sector. It has enabled the adoption of latest available technologies. The perception about telecom services, until recently considered an elitist luxury, has changed to a preferred good of mass consumption with increasing usage of telecom and IT services. The benefits from increased market access for the masses, improved productivity and market efficiency, and unprecedented innovation in business models and organizational structures are now widely recognized."[9] However, to sustain the growth achieved over the years following policy recommendations are suggested for the telecommunication sector:

- Legislation should be amended so that TRAI has clear authority over interconnection and all tariffs for service provision in the sector.
- Clear policy guidelines must be developed by the Telecom Regulatory Authority of India (TRAI).

- TRAI's role in influencing opening of sector and introduction of new service providers must be strengthened by giving it a formal role in the licensing process and the introduction of new service providers.
- Long-distance voice and data services could be liberalized without delay.
- Standard qualification requirements for opening fixed services and allowing qualified new players to enter could be established.
- License fees for long-distance and local fixed services, could be set at low levels so as to recover the costs of regulation alone.
- Liberalization of international services could be initiated.
- What genuinely constitutes non-commercial service could be reassessed.
- The Department of Telecommunications could be reimbursed through the New Telecom Policy fund proposed to encourage expansion of telecommunication services into non-economic areas. This reimbursement must be based on the excess costs that the department is incurring to meet its universal service obligations and not on its cellular license fee.
- Defense and security use could be relocated from parts of the commercially attractive bands to provide suitable compensation. Auctioning the spectrum in areas where there are constraints on its availability can be considered.
- There could be an independent agency for overseeing concessions in order to insulate tariff and investment decisions from political interference.

Service of telecom sector too has improved in terms of phone faults during post-reforms period. For the year 1990-91, per 100 stations 18.5 phone faults were being registered per month. This has been reduced to 9.4 phone faults per month for 100 stations in the year 2003-04. However, there is every possibility to decrease the rate of phone faults over the years and to minimize it to the lowest level possible. The number of rural DELs in the country has increased from 122.72 lakh as on March 31, 2004 to 130.37 lakh as on December 31, 2004. But the share of rural areas DELs to the total DELs is comparatively very low to the urban areas share to the total DELs. As in December 2004, only 14 per cent of DELs were installed in the rural areas wherein the urban areas share in the total DELs is 86 per cent. Today in rural areas the growth and development is much slow in comparison with urban areas of India.

However, telecommunications have played a critical role in shaping India's march towards progress and the importance they hold for the future of India cannot be overstated. A new framework for infrastructure policy, consisting of competition between multiple players, under a regulatory framework defined by the State has made much headway in the area of telecom. The successful implementation of reforms since 1991 has resulted in unprecedented growth of the sector. It has enabled the adoption of latest available technologies. The perception about telecom services, until recently considered an elitist luxury, has changed to a preferred good of mass consumption with increasing usage of telecom and IT services. The benefits from increased market access for the masses, improved productivity and market efficiency, and unprecedented innovation in business models and organizational structures are now widely recognized.

9.2.3. Indian Transport Sector

It is universally recognized that an effective transport system is crucial for sustained economic growth and modernization. Today it is believed that transport innovations and developments influence the pace and growth of economic development. Many say thus transport sector runs parallel to the growth of GDP. Transport is also necessary for connecting villages with towns, market centres and in bringing together remote and developing regions closer to one another.

9.2.3.1. Road Transport

Transport being a key input for production processes, adequate provision of transport infrastructure and services helps in increasing productivity and lowering production costs.

Therefore, the need for improving the capacity and quality of the transportation system through technological upgradation and removing distortions in the inter-modal mix by evolving a national tariff and investment policy is stressed. Over and above this the need for ensuring an improved transport system to provide speedy, efficient, safe and economical carriage of goods and people too are given importance.

It was felt that an integrated policy would be necessary for the road development programmes. Various policy initiatives, decisions, adaptation of modern road construction technology, construction of modern high density corridors, establishment of central road fund revamped, development of State Highways and major district roads, incentives to attract private and foreign direct invest in the transport sector and regular maintenance of roads were undertaken to enhance the performance of transport sector during this period.

There has been an overall improvement in the performance indicators of SRTUs over the years. Vehicles productivity has increased from Rs. 257 revenue earning km per bus held per day in 1989-90 to Rs. 305 revenue earning km per bus held per day in 2001-02. Staff productivity has increased from 35.3 revenue kilometer per worker per day in 1989-90 to 47.8 revenue km per worker per day in 2001-02. Fuel efficiency improved from 4.35 kilometers per litre to 4.69 km per litre during the same period. Bus staff ratio to fleet operated has also improved from 1:7.63 in 1976-77 to 1:7.16 km in 2001-02. Despite the increasing number of high performance motor vehicles coming on public roads over the years, the road conditions more or less remained the same. Poor driving conditions, mixed traffic on the road and encroachment activities over the years are considered to be the main reasons for the growing number of road accidents. As a result in India number of persons killed in road accidents has been increasing even during post-reforms.

As far as the financial performance of the State Road Transport Undertaking is concerned, it has been reporting losses on a continual basis year after year. Economic reforms in no way could improve its financial performance. In spite of increase in the gross receipts of State Road Transport

Undertakings over the years the SRTUs have not succeeded in reducing their operating expenditure as well as total expenditure incurred over the years. As a result the reported losses have been on an increase. Therefore, it is essential to introduce qualitative and quantitative measures for the better functioning of the SRTUs.

In the liberalized era of Indian economy, transport system needs to be looked as an integrated structure in which various modes of transport complement each other. There is need of a structure in which each mode of transport sector is able to operate on a "level playing field" so that comparative advantages and economic efficiencies are properly reflected in the costs for users. Over the years large investments have been made for the development of the transport sector in India. This has resulted in the expansion of transport infrastructure and facilities. In spite of these impressive achievements, the transport infrastructure has not been developed to the extent that it can effectively address the problems of accessibility and mobility needs for the movement of people and goods. Today therefore along with increase in quantity, there is a need for appreciable development of qualitative nature such as emergence of a multi-modal system in the form of container transport, reduction in areas of obsolete assets, improvement in the self-financing capacity of the transport sector and the establishment of new centres of excellence for manpower development.

9.2.3.2. Indian Railways

There has been a continuous decline in the share of Railways in total traffic. Its share of the freight traffic came down from 89 per cent in 1951 to less than 40 per cent in 2000. Over the same period, the share of passenger traffic came down from 68 per cent to less than 20 per cent. This decline in the share of Railways has caused serious distortions and leading to various adverse consequences. In order to reverse the trend, it is necessary that the capacity of Indian Railways be augmented. Thus policy implementations were initiated during post-reforms period to improve the quality of rail services through technological upgradation and modernization.

There is constant increase in the freight loading performance of Railways from the year 1980-81 to 2003-04. But trends in the total revenue earning freight traffic for the period 1990-91 to 2000-01 reflect a slowing down as compared to the period 1980-81 to 1990-91. In the year 1980-81, the total revenue earning freight traffic was 195.9 million tonnes and it increased to 318 million tonnes for the year 1990-91. So the total revenue earning freight traffic during this period has increased by 1.6 fold. It works out to be 62.32 per cent increase over 1980-81. During the year 2000-01, the total revenue earning freight traffic was 473.5 million tonnes and its performance was only 1.4 fold as compared to the year 1990-91. It works out to be 48.89 per cent growth over 1990-91.

Over the years Railways has sustained improvement in the utilization of assets and productivity performance. The wagon utilization has registered a continuous improvement. It increased from 1,449 net tonnes km per wagon per day in the year 1987-88 to 2,554 net tonnes km per wagon per day in 2003-04. It is an increase of about 76.25 per cent. During post-liberalization period net tonne km per wagon per day growth is greater the pre-liberalization period. Passenger traffic originating too increased from 3,792 million in the year 1987-88 to 5,112 in the year 2003-04.

Over the years the Railways has shown a greater reliance and emphasize on the gross budgetary support and market borrowings rather than emphasizing the need for financing the Railway plan through internally created resources. In the initial stages of globalization period there has been decline in the sum total of budgetary support provided in the various annual plans. From the year 1999-2000, there has been an increase in the total budgetary support provided to the Railways. It indicates that the Railways is going back once again to pre-economic liberalization period. This is not a good sign because the Government objective of the role of the Government as 'owner' and 'sole provider' to that of a 'facilitator' and of safeguarding the interests of the vulnerable sections of the community by legal and institutional framework may not be achieved in the near future.

The financial performance of Indian Railways has been surplus during post-reforms period. However, the percentage of growth in the gross traffic receipts during post-globalization is considerably lower as compared to pre-globalization period. There has been a constant increase in various commodities and goods carried by Indian Railways from 1980-81 to 2003-04. In terms of goods carried by Indian Railways was concerned, ten years of growth achieved during pre-reforms period was much greater than the growth achieved during ten years of post-reforms period. Similar trend is also seen in earnings from goods carried by Indian Railways. Though the total earnings from goods carried by Railways increased to Rs. 23,045.4 crore as in 2000-01, yet percentage of change in total earning from goods carried during this period over 1990-91 was 179.43 per cent and this percentage is much less than the increased percentage achieved during 1980-81 to 1990-91. So the various policy directions undertaken during post-liberalization period did not succeed in stimulating the needed increase in total earnings from goods carried by Railways.

Though there has been a greater decline in the number of railway accidents, yet the damage caused due to accidents has been on increase. In the year 1980-81, cost of damage to rolling stock is only Rs. 705 lakh. But it increased to Rs. 3,873 lakh for the year 1990-91 and it further increased to Rs. 4,421 lakh for the year 1995-96. However, cost of damage to rolling stock declined to Rs. 3,571 lakh in the year 2000-01. What is interesting to note is over the years Railways has improved in reducing the number of hours of interruption through better communication system. In the year 1985-86 interruption hours accounted for 17,218, but it declined to 10,041 hours in the year 1990-91. It further declined to 5,031 hours for the year 2000-01. This goes to prove that over the years Railways has learned to handle accidents and crisis in an effective way. As a result it has succeeded in reducing hours of interruption to a considerable extent.

Passenger satisfaction and their growth constitute major component for evaluation of performance of Indian railways. The passengers originating percentage growth during post-reforms period has been much higher than the period during pre-reforms period. However, this is not true of passengers earning and average rate per passenger kilometer. Statistical evidence proves that the percentage of growth taken place in terms of average rate per passenger kilometer during pre-liberalization was much larger than the growth that has taken place during post-liberalization period. Other than originating, performance of operations of Indian Railways in passengers earning and average rate per passenger kilometer was not satisfactory during post-liberalization period.

Mixed performance of Indian Railways during post-reforms suggests that rail reforms must be based on proved principles derived from international experiences, and adjusted to fit the Indian environment because the challenges facing Indian Railways have much in common with the situations driving rail reforms elsewhere. The question as far as Indian Railway is concerned is not just the need for change rather, the question is how to define reform options, fit them to Indian conditions and objectives, and implement the decided reforms. For Railways to re-emerge as the dominant transport sector in India it requires to undertake some more efforts and these include:

- In the long run, it is necessary to encourage private parties to provide door-to-door services and end the monopoly of CONNOR. Private parties can own wagons in which they can transport containers and carry them through trucks to the warehouses of their customers.
- In spite of the flexibilities offered, it has been reported that the Own-Your-Wagon scheme has not attracted many private parties. Similarly, many of the projects proposed under the BOLT scheme have not received enthusiastic response from private entrepreneurs. Unnecessary delays due to procedural formalities and uncertain return on investment are the various reasons. Delays add to the cost, thus reducing the profitability of the projects. It may be necessary for the railway authorities to make the projects more profitable by offering the development of auxiliary facilities to private parties. If the profitability of the projects is still in

doubt, then Government-private partnerships may be created to instill confidence in the private parties. Once projects become sufficiently profitable Government may disinvest and reinvest the money on other risky projects.

- An important feature of the new strategy of Indian Railways is the encouragement given to private parties to partially take part in its functioning. Agreements with private parties should be framed without ambiguity to avoid difficulties later. For example, allocation of risks should be clearly specified. It may require framing of additional rules in due course depending upon the then emerging scenario.
- To capture growing road freight traffic, it is necessary to run train services punctually and according to pre-specified schedules. The marketing strategy proposes such special parcel services. These should be operated on a scheduled guaranteed time delivery basis. If the services are convenient, time guaranteed and profitable to private truck operators, they will prefer these trains to running the energy inefficient trucks for long distances. Using trains they can then provide door-to-door freight services with guaranteed time delivery. This will capture a lot of long distance road freight traffic. There will also be phenomenal savings in diesel as train consumes only one-ninth as much diesel as a truck per TKM. In the long run, competition should be encouraged by allowing private entry to operate such container trains.
- The excess of railway earnings over expenses is much smaller compared to the investment needs. Earnings of Indian Railways have to be improved. A major portion of the loss in earnings occurs due to the subsidized second class and season ticket passenger fares. Hence a more rationalized cost based fare structure, especially in the suburban train operations, should be attempted.
- At present, only two services are offered in suburban train services. It may be worthwhile to attempt to provide further differentiated services to cater to different

sections of the community. This will help Railways to best utilize the consumers surplus. These differential services can also be used to provide cross-subsidization in passenger fare structures. Similar attempts may also be made in non-suburban services.

- A nominal percentage may be charged in fares which may form part of a long-term fund for railway capacity additions. Charging an additional 20-25 per cent increase in fares can meet the investment requirements of railways, particularly when these can be supplemented by borrowings from the capital market.
- Encroachment of railway land near the railway lines by slum dwellers affects the profitability of railways. Railways are not being able to exploit the commercial value of these encroached lands. Augmentation of railway lines becomes difficult. To avoid these difficulties the land should be leased for commercial purposes or given on a long-term lease for the development of telephone or electric lines or roads, if feasible.
- In addition, to this one important policy direction for financing capacity augmentation in Indian Railways needs to be highlighted. This involves identifying the opportunities for joint implementation in the context of global climate change for attracting investments from developed countries in Indian Railways.

Indian Railways is in need of an effective restructuring strategy that focuses not only on developing a well thought out restructuring plan, but also on strategies for generating a momentum for change, and creating champions for change in the process. Indian Railways has performed well in several spheres. However, in order to exploit its potential much more investment is required from private as well as from the Government. In addition to these, stabilization of passenger and freight rates is essential. Above all good planning and timely implementation of the proposed projects is the need of the hour.

9.2.3.3. Indian Ports

Ports are the gateways for India's international trade by sea and about 95 per cent by volume and 70 per cent by value of the country's foreign trade is carried on through maritime transport. However, India's share in global merchandise trade was at around 0.75 per cent. Although there has been significant improvement in port performance due to a series of reform actions, performance is still far below in comparison to ports in Asia. The problem seems to be that real berth capacities have not been used efficiently. Equipment use on berths is extremely low and resulting in high turnaround times for vessels. In addition, low productivity of equipment and labor increases handling costs for cargo and containers. One of the important planks of the stabilization measures was the compression of public expenditure and to promote private investment in infrastructural sector from internal and external sources.

The growth rate of Indian overseas shipping tonnage achieved during post-globalization was much greater in comparison to the growth rate of Indian overseas shipping tonnage achieved during pre-globalization period. It is interesting to note that the average growth achieved in growth of traffic handled by all the ports during post-reforms was 8.72 per cent. This was just 0.57 per cent more than the growth achieved during pre-reforms. But the performance of major ports during post-globalization period is better in comparison to minor ports. So globalization has given the much needed boost to major ports in terms of total traffic handled in comparison to minor ports.

One can see a certain revival in terms of passengers during post-liberalization period. In 1991-92 numbers of passengers increased to 162.40 hundred and it further increased to 252.00 hundred as in 2001-02. The same trend was also seen in all minor ports. This achievement could be considered as a remarkable one because Indian ports have achieved an increase in number of passengers in spite of people's preference to travel by air. The performance of Indian ships in Indian overseas trade, the performance of foreign line has been much better during post-reform in comparison to the performance of Indian line. The percentage of growth achieved in terms of operating surplus in financial performance during pre-reforms period was much greater than the growth achieved during post-reforms period.

The trend of decline in employment opportunities available in Indian ports was in no way reversed even after various reform measures were undertaken during liberalization period. Despite decline in the number of persons employed there has been an increase in the total cargo traffic handled. It means that the work efficiency of staff working in Indian ports has increased during post-reforms period in comparison to the year 1990-91.

There has been considerable progress in bringing the private sector into port development and operation. However, reforms are still needed to provide greater commercial autonomy to all the port trusts. It is also necessary to enhance competition among ports, and provide the necessary institutional structure for a modernized ports sector. Indian ports require an immediate upgradation of handling technology, and modernization of equipment and management. For this the following suggestions are recommended:

- It is necessary to restructure the existing ports sector. There could be statutory authorities independent of political interests to deal with the policy of regulatory and commercial roles. This in turn will help to reduce conflict of interests of various organizations involved in the Ports Sector. Statutory authorities could be created at each major port and TAMP could continue to play the role of higher reference to other statutory organizations.
- MOST and the Ministry of Railways have shared interest in finding a common approach to creating inter-modal platforms that would reduce transport costs and increase trade competitiveness. In normal situations the cargo transfer between Indian Railways and the local port railways results in delays. Therefore, a common

approach is necessary to enhance the impact of such developments and integrate them into the inland transport network as a whole. Even at the port level, systematic cooperation between Indian Railways, Container Corporation of India, and the Central Warehousing Corporation would definitely improve the investment in the ports system.

- Rearrangement of the workforce consistent with modern traffic and cargo handling requirements cannot be avoided in the Ports sector. Before bringing the private sector into Ports sector it is necessary to introduce management skills and resolve problems related to workforce so that the existing social protection could ensure that the staff adjustment process is acceptable. These provisions could also include retraining, voluntary retirement, indemnity payments for voluntary departure, and creation of a temporary workers' pool. For better functioning of ports it is essential to develop a new institutional structure for the sector.
- It is essential to corporatise port trusts with private and public operating companies. So that the public and private operating companies could conduct commercial activities related to ship services and cargo traffic management and handling.
- National Ports Council could be entrusted with the duty to determine national port policy and strategic planning objectives, and define main sector regulations to be enforced by the Port Authorities. The council could comprise representatives from the Ministry of Surface Transportation (MOST), the Ministry of Railways, and the Ministry of Environment and Forests (MOEF), mayors of port cities, and Port Authority managers.
- When competition in the market is strong, the Government could take bids on the highest price paid for the assets or shares of the enterprise being privatized. When competition in the market is weak or non-existent, the Government would be alert to the risk of

rent-seeking behavior, and therefore take bids on the basis of the lowest tariff charged to consumers.

- Autonomous port authorities should be made to operate on commercial lines so that they can raise resources from the primary market by way of equity and debt and form financial institutions. They should also be allowed to fix tariffs so as to cover their debt obligations and earn a reasonable return on equity. Port authorities should be delegated powers to create new technical ports required for modernization.
- Training institutes should be set up to improve the technical skills of the existing labour in line with modernization of ports. Enhanced technical skills will help to minimize the unionized labour problems, because they would be capable of functioning in a new environment and privatization.

To implement these guidelines, the importance of private sector participation in bridging the resource gap and improvement in the operational and managerial efficiency has also been greatly recognized. As a result efforts could be made to make private participation models such as BOT. However, there is still a long way to go in this sector. Drawing lessons from experiences in the past, it is necessary to formulate new policies, offering more attractive incentive packages to develop mechanisms to ensure greater participation of the private sector, so that the overall environment becomes more conducive to the consumers with better infrastructure facilities in the port and shipping sector.

9.2.3.4. Indian Civil Aviation

As India modernizes rapidly, the Civil Aviation sector has acquired a vital role in the economic growth and development of the country. In India air transport plays an important role in places where industrial and commercial centers are located. The full potential of the Civil Aviation sector in India, however, has yet to be realized. This means an improvement and growth in the quality of services, competitive pricing, better airport infrastructure, etc. In the past, steps were taken to improve the quality of air transport services. The emphasis was on liberalization of the air transport sector in order to encourage private sector participation. Over the years, the Government has disengaged itself considerably from commercial airline operations. Private sector participation in domestic air services has been aimed at bridging the resource gap in investments to meet the growing demand and improve the managerial and operational efficiency of air services.

Private sector participation has registered a remarkable growth in terms of the number of passengers carried and total percentages of passengers handled and increase in volume of freights carried. Increase in private sector participation in the Civil Aviation sector has been a remarkable achievement during globalization period. However, to enlarge and upgrade airports and allied infrastructural facilities private investment should be encouraged. For this it is essential to minimize procedural formalities and removal of unnecessary confusions. The following recommendations are suggested to ensure future enhancement of infrastructure facilities in Civil Aviation sector:

- The process of disinvestment of Government equity in Indian Airlines and Air India could be accelerated.
- Increasing the share of foreign equity on both domestic and international carriers with a view to attracting new technology and management expertise must be considered.
- Bar on equity participation by foreign airlines in a company formed for domestic air transportation should be reconsidered.
- The process of long-term lease of the four metro airports in order to make them world class airports could be speeded up.
- The route dispersal guideline system that provides air services to northeast and other isolated areas could be replaced with a more transparent and efficient system.
- Private sector participation in the provision of infrastructure facilities as well as air services must be increased.

- Adequate security arrangements at various airports must be ensured in view of the increased threat perception.
- The Civil Aviation sector should aim at being financially self-sustaining. Efforts to generate larger internal resources could be made. It is necessary to encourage private sector to cater to the growing demand for air services on short haul routes. Air taxis could also be encouraged on tourist routes.
- Priority should be given to upgrading infrastructure and modernizing communication facilities to permit full utilization of aircraft capacity. Maintenance of infrastructure already created should receive immediate attention.
- Among the different modes of transport, Civil Aviation is closely linked with the development of tourism, as the vast majority of tourists coming to India, arrive and depart by air. Capacity constraints are often felt on air travel too and from India particularly during the peak tourist season. Tourist charters could be encouraged.
- Airborne trade has been increasing in importance and it now accounts for more than a quarter of the total foreign trade in terms of value. Upgrading airport infrastructure in terms of increased storage space, better handling capacities and augmentation of upliftment capacity for carriage of more cargo could be stressed on.
- It is necessary to undertake wide-ranging privatization of operations at the existing airports in addition to concessioning out Greenfield sites to the private sector for development.
- The very functioning of the Airport Authority of India could be reviewed and the functions of the Airports Authority of India could be shifted away from operations and could focus on policy, planning and statutory functions.

- It is essential also to create a separate independent authority to handle economic regulations for the sector. The authority's powers could be clearly defined to ensure that they concentrate on areas where competition is restricted.
- Any restriction on the import of specific type of aircrafts should be reduced considerably and real location of aircrafts from one domestic operator to another should also be freely allowed. An operator should have the freedom to choose aircraft which increases his profitability.
- Restrictions on the entry of private players in the industry should be made open to all operators so that there can be healthy competitive environment in the long run, which would improve the efficiencies of air operation and the overall quality of service.
- The existing training school could cater to the needs of both public and private operators equally. If needed the private sector should be free to build more training schools.
- To minimize the problems due to labour unrest in Indian Airlines, several strategies of employee participation should be experimented. These strategies could be making employees joint equity owners of the airlines and introducing an incentive scheme tied directly to the financial performance of the airlines, etc.
- To enable distribution of excess workforce from Indian Airlines to private operators, a voluntary retirement scheme in Indian Airlines should be initiated.
- The authority's powers could be clearly defined to ensure that it concentrates on areas where competition is restricted. This would include oversight of the terms and conditions of leases and concessions.
- The Directorate General of Civil Aviation could continue to handle technical and safety aspects.

In the globalized and liberalized era of Indian economy transport system needs to be looked at as an integrated structure in which various modes of transport complement each other. There is need for a structure in which each mode of transport is able to operate on a "level playing field" so that comparative advantages and economic efficiencies are properly reflected in the costs for users. Over the years large investments have been made for the development of the transport sector in India. This has resulted in the expansion of transport infrastructure and facilities. In spite of these impressive achievements, the transport infrastructure has not been developed to the extent that it can effectively address the problems of accessibility and mobility needs for the movement of people and goods.

9.2.4. Indian Finance Sector

A sound financial sector is considered to be a prerequisite for efficient macroeconomic management and the financial sector plays a crucial role in the development process of a country. The process of financial intermediation enhances capital accumulation through the institutionalization of savings and investment. How efficient a country's financial system is, depends to a large degree, on how efficient the banking system is. The financial reform initiated during early 90s has resulted in rapid growth and development. The financial reforms brought about a range of instruments in domestic and financial markets. In addition, the market in corporate bonds has been spurred with increased use of external credit ratings. Further banks have learnt to manage their risk exposures. The financial market has also grown significantly. Moreover, the access to credit has improved, through newly established domestic banks, foreign banks and bank-like intermediaries. There have also been significant improvements in the use of information technology in the entire bank transactions and financial transactions.

The accounting and auditing of intermediaries has strengthened. Availability of information on borrowers has improved. The technological infrastructure has developed in tandem with modern-day requirements in information technology and communication networking. Moreover, the concept of finance has permeated across various institutions. The quality of human capital involved in the financial sector has typically been of the highest genre. They have come to the realization that the consumer satisfaction and consumer oriented services alone will help them to sustain in the financial market. However, following are the points which the banking sector should seriously consider for its significant and sustainable growth and development:

- It is essential to improve the autonomy and efficiency of public sector banks by minimizing Government interference. This could be achieved by taking adequate steps for strengthening the quality of bank boards.
- High quality talent with domain knowledge cannot be attracted by the present salary structure. Therefore, market-oriented allurements need to be introduced in public sector banks.
- Most of the rural banks and cooperative banks credit structure is multi-layered and under-capitalized. It also suffers from being over-staffed and under-skilled. As a result it is often burdened with high level of delinquent loans. Therefore, it is necessary to revitalize rural banks and cooperative banks and urban cooperative banks in a medium-term framework so that they are able to sustain themselves in the financial transactions that are underway.
- Corporate planning combined with organizational restructuring are a necessary prerequisite to achieve desired results in terms of productivity and profitability. A properly designed management system needs to be introduced and must be clearly spelt out to improve productivity and to drive the employees in delivering quality service.
- In an increasingly open and integrated world economy, commercial banks will need to develop an ability to respond to a wide range of expectations from customers, seeking different kinds of products and services.

- Technology is considered to be a key driver in the banking industry, which creates new business models and processes, and also creates revolution in distribution channels. Strengthening of information technology in banks could improve the effectiveness of asset-liability management in banks. The banks thus have to take pro-active measures to strengthen the use of modern technology in the banking sector.
- Several legislative measures need to be undertaken to enable further progress in the financial sector. These could be related to ownership, regulatory focus, development of financial markets, and bankruptcy procedures.
- The concept of universal banking structure could be initiated to help in improving the competitive strength of Indian banking. A universal banking character would offer more options for penetrating more quickly, new segments within the financial services sector, as guided by the customer demands and for generating revenue synergies through the provision of multiple services.
- The gradual disappearance of development banks created a situation where by adequate long-term finance is not available to medium and more particularly small, industries. To provide adequate long-term finance to industry, two important changes are called for:
    (i) need to develop an active debt market in the country which will satisfy the long-term capital requirements of large and medium industries; and,
    (ii) banks should expand their credit portfolio to include increased provision of long-term finance to small scale industries.

The past ten years have seen major improvements in the working of various financial market participants. For this the Government and the regulatory authorities have followed a step-by-step approach. The entry of foreign players has assisted in the introduction of international practices and systems. Technology developments have improved customer service.

Some gaps however remain. On the whole, the cumulative effect of the developments since 1991 has been quite encouraging. The problems related to Southeast Asian Crisis did not affect the financial system of India and this is an indication of the strength of the reformed Indian financial system.

9.3. CONCLUSION

During the first four decades of India's Independence, economic policies of India have been highly protectionist and witnessed controlled restrictive economic regime. Such policies led to mediocre growth performance of the Indian economy. The restrictive regime in India protected vested interests. The socialist rhetoric regime in India failed to improve the lot of the masses. India felt the need to install a new economic regime which would be quite different from what was practiced before.[10]

The policies initiated since 1991 did succeed in bringing about radical changes in the infrastructure sector in India. "There is no support for sweeping claims that the 1990s have been a period of either 'unprecedented improvement' or 'widespread impoverishment'. This is as clear a message as one is likely to get on the impact of globalization on the Indian economy as a whole"[11] and in particular on the infrastructure sector. If the country is to achieve higher growth then its economic institutions and policies need to undergo major changes because globalization is beneficial and effective only when it is monitored by a countries own policies, strategies and priorities.

At the present juncture, the international pace of globalization is an important aspect which needs correct decision.[12] It means the need to have both the private and the Government sector in building up of infrastructure facilities so that an alternative system of public-private partnership is possible in infrastructure development in India. For this "rulers and administration would have to mend their ways to move forward. All State Governments have to realize that there is no alternative to competition and public-private partnership in infrastructure."[13] There is also the need to broaden the base for institutional investors for infrastructure investment by adding the insurance companies, pension funds and endowment funds with mutual funds and fills.

However, liberalization of Indian economy alone will not ensure stable economic growth rather certain tough decisions still need to be taken. For this, sound economic policies and strong political support is necessary so that the Indian economy can adjust itself to the realities of globalization and play its part as a major economic power in a globalised world economy. M. Narasimham strongly and rightly feels that with the initiation of the right set of economic policies India has the great potential to be a major economic player in the world economy.[14] It is up to us to realize our economic potential by giving greater emphasis to the development of infrastructure in India.

Above all it is also felt that the role of the Government has to diminish if the infrastructure sector is to see any improvement. Before that a strong regulatory body should be in place before any privatization takes major chunks of utilities and other infrastructure facilities. However, this does not mean that the public sector stop investing in infrastructure rather than public sector will have to continue to fund a greater part of fresh investments taking place in infrastructure. It is possible only if the Government manages to discipline its expenditures. The telecom sector has demonstrated that competition can do what regulation and State control cannot. For example deregulation brought cellular tariffs to nearly a tenth of what they were two years ago. In this given situation a monopoly situation is thus undesirable. It is necessary to have both the private and the Government sector in building up of infrastructure facilities so that an alternative system of public-private partnership is possible in infrastructure development in India.

END NOTES

1. *Economic Survey 1996-97*, p. 181.
2. T.L. Sankar, "Power Sector: Rise, Fall and Reform", *Economic and Political Weekly*, Vol. 38, Nos. 12 and 13, March 22, 2003, p. 1171.
3. C.R. Reddy and others, "Power Sector Reforms", *Southern Economist*, Vol. 42, No. 7, August 1, 2003, pp. 7-8.

4. R. Ponraj, "Power Sector Reforms: Need for Different Thinking", S. Ganesan (ed.), *Infrastructure Development and Financing*, Kanishka Publishers, New Delhi, 2001, p. 295.

5. TERI (Tata Energy Research Institute), "Defining an Integrated Energy Strategy for India", 2002, p. 38.

6. K.C. Pant, *India's Development Scenario Next Decade and Beyond...*, Academic Foundation, New Delhi, Vol. II, 2004, p. 158.

7. TERI (Tata Energy Research Institute), *op. cit.*, p. 41.

8. Amol Phadke and Sudhir Chella Rajan, "Electricity Reforms in India: Not Too Late to Go Back to the Drawing Board", *Economic and Political Weekly*, 2003, July 19-25, Vol. 38, No. 29, p. 3062.

9. *Economic Survey 2003-04*, p. 180.

10. Vijay Joshi and I.M.D. Little, "*India's Economic Reforms 1991-2001*", Oxford University Press, New Delhi, 1996.

11. Pulapre Balakrishnan, "Globalization, Growth and Justice", *Economic and Political Weekly*, July 26, 2003, Vol. 38, p. 3171.

12. S.A.R. Bilgrami, "Towards Globalization of Indian Economy: Opportunities and Challenges", *Post-Reform Leading Issues of Indian Economy*, A.D.N. Bajpai and others (eds.), Atlantic Publishers and Distributors, New Delhi, 2002, p. 25.

13. Anupam B. Rastogi, *The Infrastructure Sector in India, 2000-01*, 3iNetwork (2002), p. 54.

14. M. Narasimham, *Economic Reforms and Development and Finance*, UBS Publishers' Distribution Ltd., New Delhi, p. 117.

Bibliography

Abhinay Taneja: 'Rural Telecommunications in India: An Analysis', Delhi College of Engineering (University of Delhi), New Delhi.

Ahluwalia, Montek S. (2002): 'Economic Reforms: A Policy Agenda for the Future', *India's Economy in the 21st Century*, Raj Kapila and Uma Kapila (eds.), Academic Foundation, New Delhi.

Alling, G., E. Brazier, D. Burjorjee, A. Camoens and A. Webber (1997): 'Mainstreaming Gender in Transportation Projects: A Toolkit, Report to the Gender Analysis and Policy Group', The World Bank mimeo.

Ray, Alok, (1993): 'External Sector Liberalization in India', *Economic and Political Weekly*, October 2.

Amaladoss, Michael, ed. (2000): *Globalization and its Victims as Seen by its Victims,* ISPCK, New Delhi.

Anbumani, V. and K. Amuthavalli (1997): 'Development of Electric Power', *Infrastructure Development for Economic Growth*, M.V. Srinivasa Gowda and Susheela Subrahmanya ed., Deep & Deep Publications, New Delhi.

Annapoorani, R. and K. Nirmaladevi (2002): 'Impact of Globalization on Export Performance of Manufactured Goods in India', *The Indian Economic Association 85th Conference Volume*, Thiruvananthapuram.

Balakrishnan, Pulapre (2003): 'Globalization, Growth and Justice', *Economic and Political Weekly,* Vol. 38, July, 26.

Bajpai, A.D.N., S.K. Choubey, N.G. Pendse and S.K. Shrivastava (eds.) (1995): *Emerging Trends in Indian Economy*, Atlantic Publishers and Distributors (P) Ltd., New Delhi.

Bajpai, A.D.N. and S.K. Chaubey, Anjila Gupta, N.G. Pendse, P.K. Joshi (eds.) (2002): *Post-Reform Leading Issues of Indian Economy*, Atlantic Publishers and Distributors (P) Ltd., Vol. I, New Delhi.

Bajpai, Nirupam (2003): 'Ten Years of Indian Reforms: The Unfinished Agenda', *Infrastructure*, CMIE, Mumbai, February.

Bagchi, Amiya Kumar (1999): 'Globalization, Liberalization and Vulnerability: India and Third World', *Economic and Political Weekly*, Vol. 34, No. 45, November 6-12.

Banerjee, Bani P. (2005): *Handbook of Energy and the Environment in India*, Oxford University Press, New Delhi.

Banerjee, Debdas (2005): *Globalisation, Industrial Restructuring and Labour Standards: Where India Meets the Global*, Sage Publications India, New Delhi.

Baru, Sanjaya (1990): 'Fiscal Liberalism and Industrial Growth', *Economic Times*, September 22.

Bhagwati, Jagdish (2004): *In Defense of Globalization*, Oxford University Press, New Delhi.

Bhattacharya, Manas (2004): 'Telecom Sector in India: Vision 2020', *India Vision 2020*, Planning Commission, Government of India, New Delhi.

Bilgrami, S.A.R. (2002): 'Towards Globalization of Indian Economy: Opportunities and Challenges', *Post-Reform Leading Issues of Indian Economy*, A.D.N. Bajpai and others (eds.), Atlantic Publishers and Distributors (P) Ltd., New Delhi.

Brahmananda, P.R. (1996): *Indian Economy Crisis – Adjustment – Crisis*, Bodh Publications, Kanpur.

Business Line (2004): November 10.

Businessworld, *The Marketing Whitebook 2005*, New Delhi.

Central Electricity Authority (CEA) (1997): *Fourth National Power Plan 1997-2012*, New Delhi.

Centre for Monitoring Indian Economy (2003): *Infrastructure*, February, Mumbai.

Chandrasekhar, C.P (2005): 'What Pace Liberalization?', *The Week*, December 31.

Chandrasekhar, C.P. and Parthapratim Pal (2006): 'Financial Liberalisation in India: An Assessment of its Nature and Outcomes', *Economic and Political Weekly*, Vol. 41, No. 11, March 18.

Chakraborty, Chandana and C. Jayachandran (2001): 'Software Sector: Trends and Constraints', *Economic and Political Weekly*, Vol. 34, No. 34, August 25-31.

Chennappa, D. (2005): 'FDI in Telecom in India: A Study', *Southern Economist*, Vol. 44, No. 10, September, 15.

Chossudovsky, Michel (1991): 'Global Poverty and the New World Economic Order', *Economic and Political Weekly*, Vol. 26, No. 44, November 2, 1991.

Choudhary, T.H. (2001): 'Telecommunications in the Tenth Plan', *Economic and Political Weekly*, Vol. 34, No. 36, August 25-31.

Commander, S. and T. Killick (1988): 'Privatisation in Developing Countries: A Survey of the Issues', *Privatisation in Less Developed Countries*, Cook, P. and C. Kirkpatrick (eds.) Harvester Wheatsheaf, Hemel Hempstead.

Das, Abhiman, Ashok Nag, and Subhash C. Ray (2005): 'Liberalisation, Ownership and Efficiency in Indian Banking: A Nonparametric Analysis', *Economic and Political Weekly,* March 19.

Dasgupta, S., Somik Lall and David Wheeler (2001): 'Policy Reform, Economic Growth and the Digital Divide: An Econometric Analysis', *Working Paper No. 2567*, World Bank, March 28.

Dasgupta, Biplab (2005): *Globalization: India's Adjustment Experience*, Sage Publications India, New Delhi.

Dasgupta, Samir (ed.) (2004): *The Changing Face of Globalization*, Sage Publications India, New Delhi.

Datt, Ruddra (1993): 'New Economic Policy and Its Impact on Industrial Relations and Employment in India', *The Indian Journal of Labour Economies*, Vol. 36, No. 1.

Datt, Ruddra and K.P.M. Sundharam (1999): *Indian Economy*, S. Chand & Company, Ram Nagar, New Delhi.

Datt, Ruddra and K.P.M. Sundharam (2002): *Indian Economy*, S. Chand & Company, New Delhi.

Dhar, P.K. (2001): *Indian Economy: Its Growing Dimensions*, Kalyani Publishers, New Delhi.

Dubash, Navroz K. and Sudhir Chella Rajan (2001): 'Power Politics Process of Power Sector Reform in India', *Economic and Political Weekly*, September 1-7, Vol. 36, No. 35.

Economic Times (1994): 'Reforms': Negative Impact on Orissa', March 26.

European Communities – Commission (EC) (1996): 'Towards Sustainable Transport Infrastructure: A Sectoral Approach in Practice', European Commission, Directorate General for Development, *Sustainable Development and Natural Resources*, Brussels, Luxembourg, July.

Ganesan, S. (ed.) (2001): *Infrastructure Development and Financing*, Kanishka Publishers & Distributors, New Delhi.

Gandhi, Jagdish (2001): 'Dynamics of Global Economy', *Southern Economist*, Vol. 40, May.

Gandhi, P. Hegadish and G. John Gunaseelan (1994): *Indian Transport System: An Appraisal of Nationalised Bus Services*, Mittal Publications, New Delhi.

Ganesan, P. and S. Ratinavel (2001): 'Empowering India with Power Sector Development', *Infrastructure Development and Financing*, S. Ganesan (ed.), Kanishka Publishers & Distributors, New Delhi.

Gangopadhyay, Shubhashis (1997): 'Gram By Kilogram', *Outlook*, April 3.

George, Leena and M.S. Vijayakumari (1999): 'Reflection on the Globalization of Indian Economy', *Southern Economist,* Vol. 38, No. 14, November 15.

Ghosh, Buddhadeb and Prabir De (2001): 'Indian Ports and Globalization: Grounding Economics in Geography', *Economic and Political Weekly*, Vol. 36, No. 34, August 25-31.

Ghosh, Buddhadeb and Prabir De (2005): *Indian Infrastructure Database 2005*, Bookwell, New Delhi, Vol. II.

Ghosal, M.K (1993): 'Inflation Review and Outlook', *Yojana*, January.

Glyn, Ford (2000): 'To Tax Capital Movement', *Frontline,* August 18.

Godbole, Madhav (2002): 'Power Sector Reforms: If Wishes Were Horses', *Economic and Political Weekly*, Vol. 37, No. 7, February 16-22.

Godbole, Madhav (2002): 'Electricity Bill, 2001: Need for a Fresh Look', *Economic and Political Weekly*, Vol. 37, No. 20, May 18-24.

Godbole, Madhav (2002): 'Electricity Regulatory Commissions: The Jury is Still Out', *Economic and Political Weekly*, Vol. 37, No. 23, June 8.

Government of India (2001): *Annual Report, 2000-2001*, Department of Telecommunications, Ministry of Communications and Information Technology, New Delhi.

Government of India (2002): *Annual Report, 2001-2002*, Department of Telecommunications, Ministry of Communications and Information Technology, New Delhi.

Government of India (2003): *Annual Report, 2002-2003*, Department of Telecommunications, Ministry of Communications and Information Technology, New Delhi.

Government of India (2004): *Annual Report, 2003-2004*, Department of Telecommunications, Ministry of Communications and Information Technology, New Delhi.

Government of India (2005): *Annual Report, 2004-2005*, Department of Telecommunications, Ministry of Communications and Information Technology, New Delhi.

Government of India (1981): *Economic Survey 1980-1981,* Ministry of Finance, Economic Division, New Delhi.

Government of India (1991): *Economic Survey 1990-1991,* Ministry of Finance, Economic Division, New Delhi.

Government of India (1997): *Economic Survey 1996-1997*, Ministry of Finance, Economic Division, New Delhi.

Government of India (2001): *Economic Survey 2000-2001*, Ministry of Finance, Economic Division, New Delhi.

Government of India (2002): *Economic Survey 2001-2002*, Ministry of Finance, Economic Division, New Delhi.

Government of India (2003): *Economic Survey 2002-2003*, Ministry of Finance, Economic Division, New Delhi.

Government of India (2004): *Economic Survey 2003-2004*, Ministry of Finance, Economic Division, New Delhi.

Government of India (2005): *Economic Survey 2004-2005*, Ministry of Finance, Economic Division, New Delhi.

Government of India (2006): *Economic Survey 2005-2006*, Ministry of Finance, Economic Division, New Delhi.

Government of India (1980): *India 1980: A Reference Annual*, Ministry of Information and Broadcasting, New Delhi.

Government of India (1991): *India 1991: A Reference Annual*, Ministry of Information and Broadcasting, New Delhi.

Government of India (1995): *India 1995: A Reference Annual*, Ministry of Information and Broadcasting, New Delhi.

Government of India (1999): *India 1999: A Reference Annual*, Ministry of Information and Broadcasting, New Delhi.

Government of India (2000): *India 2000: A Reference Annual*, Ministry of Information and Broadcasting, New Delhi.

Government of India (2001): *India 2001: A Reference Annual*, Ministry of Information and Broadcasting, New Delhi.

Government of India (2002): *India 2002: A Reference Annual*, Ministry of Information and Broadcasting, New Delhi.

Government of India (2003): *India 2003: A Reference Annual*, Ministry of Information and Broadcasting, New Delhi.

Government of India (2004): *India 2004: A Reference Annual*, Ministry of Information and Broadcasting, New Delhi.

Government of India (2005): *India 2005: A Reference Annual*, Ministry of Information and Broadcasting, New Delhi.

Government of India (2006): *India 2006: A Reference Annual*, Ministry of Information and Broadcasting, New Delhi.

Government of India (1951): *First Five-Year Plan, 1951-56*, Planning Commission, New Delhi.

Government of India (1956): *Second Five-Year Plan, 1956-61*, Planning Commission, New Delhi.

Government of India (1961): *Third Five-Year Plan, 1961-66*, Planning Commission, New Delhi.

Government of India (1969): *Fourth Five-Year Plan, 1969-74*, Planning Commission, New Delhi.

Government of India (1974): *Fifth Five-Year Plan, 1974-79*, Planning Commission, New Delhi.

Government of India (1980): *Sixth Five-Year Plan, 1980-1985*, Planning Commission, New Delhi.

Government of India (1985): *Seventh Five-Year Plan, 1985-1990*, Planning Commission, New Delhi.

Government of India (1992): *Eighth Five-Year Plan, 1992-1997*, Planning Commission, New Delhi.

Government of India (1997): *Ninth Five-Year Plan, 1997-2002*, Planning Commission, New Delhi.

Government of India (2002): 'Infrastructure', *Tenth Five-Year Plan 2002-07*, Planning Commission, New Delhi, Vol. II.

Government of India (2005): *Annual Report, 2004-05*, Ministry of Non-Conventional Energy Resources, New Delhi, as in http://www.mnes.nic.in.

Government of India (2005): *Reports on Rural Development*, Ministry of Rural Development, New Delhi.

Government of India (2003): *Third All-India Census of Small-Scale Industries, 2001-02*, Ministry of Industries, New Delhi.

Government of India (2003): *Annual Report, 2002-03*, Ministry of Shipping, New Delhi.

Government of India (2004): *Annual Report, 2003-04*, Ministry of Shipping, New Delhi.

Government of India (2005): *Annual Report, 2004-05*, Ministry of Shipping, New Delhi.

Government of India (2003): *Annual Report, 2002-03*, Ministry of Civil Aviation, New Delhi, as given in www.civilaviation.nic.in.

Government of India (2003): *Annual Report, 2002-03*, Ministry of Civil Aviation, New Delhi, as given in civilaviation.nic.in.

Government of India (2004): *Annual Report, 2003-04*, Ministry of Civil Aviation, New Delhi, as given in www.civilaviation.nic.in.

Government of India (2005): *Annual Report, 2004-05*, Ministry of Civil Aviation, New Delhi, as given in www.civilaviation.nic.in.

Government of Orissa (2001): *Report of the Committee on Power Sector Reforms in Orissa*, October.

Gowda, M.V. Srinivasa and Susheela Subrahmanya (eds.) (1997): *Infrastructure Development for Economic Growth*, Deep & Deep Publications, New Delhi.

Gowad, J. Made (1997): 'Road network – A Critical Look', *Infrastructure Development for Economic Growth*, M.V. Srinivasa Gowda and Susheela Subrahmanya (eds.), Deep & Deep Publications, New Delhi.

Gupta, Anil and Rajya Shree Arora (1991): *Growth of Infrastructural Sectors in India*, Radha Publications, New Delhi.

Gupta, K.R. (ed.) (2005): *Studies in Indian Economy*, Atlantic Publishers & Distributors (P) Ltd., New Delhi.

Gupta, K.R. (ed.) (1997): *Liberalisation and Globalisation of Indian Economy*, Atlantic Publishers & Distributors (P) Ltd., New Delhi, Vol. I.

Gupta, K.R. (ed.) (1997): *Liberalisation and Globalisation of Indian Economy*, Atlantic Publishers & Distributors (P) Ltd., New Delhi, Vol. II.

Gupta, K.R. (ed.) (1999): *Liberalisation and Globalisation of Indian Economy*, Atlantic Publishers & Distributors (P) Ltd., New Delhi, Vol. III.

Gupta, K.R. (ed.) (2000): *Liberalisation and Globalisation of Indian Economy*, Atlantic Publishers & Distributors (P) Ltd., New Delhi, Vol. IV.

Gupta, K.R. (ed.) (2005): *Liberalisation and Globalisation of Indian Economy*, Atlantic Publishers & Distributors (P) Ltd., New Delhi, Vol. VI.

Gupta, K.R. (ed.) (2000): *Issues in Indian Economy,* Atlantic Publishers and Distributors (P) Ltd., New Delhi, Vol. III.

Haque, S.M. Imamul (1989): *Management of Indian Railways*, Mittal Publications, New Delhi.

Harriss, John (2001): 'Globalization and World's Poor Institutions, Inequality and Justice', *Economic and Political Weekly*, Vol. 36, No. 23, June 9-15.

Haseloff, Anikar M. (2005): 'Cybercafes and their Potential as Community Development Tools in India', *The Journal of Community Informatics*, Vol. 1, No. 3.

Heggade, Odeyar D. (2002): *Infrastructure Development under Economic Reforms*, Mohit Publications, New Delhi.

Heggie, I. (1991): 'Designing Major Policy Reform: Lessons from the Transport Sector', *World Bank Discussion Paper 115*, World Bank, Washington DC.

Heggie, I. (1995): 'Management and Financing of Roads: An Agenda for Reform', *World Bank Technical Paper No. 275*, World Bank, Washington DC.

The Indian Express (2000): 'Costs of Globalization', April 17.

The Indian Express (2005): 'Banking Reforms: Need to Walk the Talk', September 25.

IndianInfoline.com (2005): 'Telecom Sector Update', Feb. 2005. *India Infoline Feature,* March 11.

India Today (1991): August 15.

India Today (2001): January 22.

India Today (2001): January 8.

India Today (2001): February 5.

India Today (2001): February 19.

India Today (2001): July 9.

Jain, J.K. (1983): *Transport Economic*, Chaitanya Publishing House, Allahabad.

Jalan, Bimal (1996): *India's Economic Policy: Preparing for the Twenty-first Century,* Penguin Books, New Delhi.

Jalan, Bimal (2000): 'Finance and Development—Which Way Now?' *RBI Bulletin*, January.

Jalan, Bimal (2001): 'Banking and Finance in the New Millennium', *RBI Bulletin*, February.

Jalan, Bimal (2002): 'Banking and Finance in India: Managing New Challenges', *India's Economy in the 21st Century*, Raj Kapila and Uma Kapila (eds.), Academic Foundation, New Delhi.

Joshi, Vijay and I.M.D. Little (1996): *India's Economic Reforms 1991-2001,* Oxford University Press, New Delhi.

Joshi, Vijay (2000): *India's Economic Reforms 1991-2000*, Oxford University Press, New Delhi.

Joseph, K.J. and K.N. Harilal (2001): 'Structure and Growth of India's IT Exports Implications and an Export-Oriented Growth Strategy', *Economic and Political Weekly,* Vol. 36, No. 34, August 25-31.

Kalkodkar, Anil (2004): 'Fast Breeding Nuclear Energy', *Yojana,* Vol. 48, January, No. 1.

Kannan, R. (ed.) (2004): *Selected Essays on Indian Economy by Rangarajan C.*, Academic Foundation, New Delhi, Vol. I.

Kannan, R. (ed.) (2004): *Selected Essays on Indian Economy by Rangarajan C.*, Academic Foundation, New Delhi, Vol. II.

Kannan, K.P. and N. Vijayamohanan Pillai (2002): *Plight of the Power Sector in India: Inefficiency, Reform and Political Economy*, Centre for Development Studies, Thiruvananthapuram, Kerala.

Kapila, Raj and Uma Kapila (eds.) (2002): *India's Economy in the 21st Century*, Academic Foundation, New Delhi.

Kapila, Uma (ed.) (2002): *Indian Economy Since Independence*, Academic Foundation, New Delhi.

Kapoor, Mahesh (2004): 'Transport: Vision 2020', *India Vision 2020*, Planning Commission, Government of India, New Delhi.

Kaur, Arvinder (2000): 'Market for Green Technologies Fast opening up', *The Hitavada*, June 18.

Kothari, Pooja and Aditya Chatterjee (2001): 'Short-circuit at Ennore Power Project', *Economic Times*, 15 June.

Koyama, Ken (2000): 'Energy Strategies in China and India and Their Implications', This report is a part of a study project conducted in FY2000 on behalf of the Agency of Natural Resources and Energy.

Khandelwal, A.K. (2006): 'Universal Banking: Solution for Indian's Financial Challenges?' *Economic and Political Weekly*, March 18.

Kulshrestha, D.K. (1993): *Transport Management in India: In Special Reference to Bus Stations*, Mittal Publications, New Delhi.

Kulshrestha, D.K. (1989): *Management of State Road Transports in India*, Mittal Publications, New Delhi.

Kurien, C.T. (1993): 'Indian Economic Reforms in the Context of Emerging Global Economy', *Economic and Political Weekly*, 10 April.

Leeladhar, V. (2006): 'Indian Banks and Global Challenges', Inaugural address at the Joint Seminar on Indian Banks and the Global Challenges organized by Indian Merchants' Chamber & Indian Banks' Association on January 31, at Mumbai.

Lekhi, R.K. (2005): *Public Finance*, Kalyani Publishers, New Delhi.

Lynch, Richard (2003): 'An Energy Overview of India', *U.S. Department of Energy*, Washington, USA, in mailto:richard.lynch@hy.doe.gov

Magesh, R. and R. Duraipandian (2001): 'Infrastructure Development and India's Power Policies', *Infrastructure Development and Financing*, S. Ganesan (ed.), Kanishka Publishers, New Delhi.

Mahajan, V.S., S.K. Agnihotri, and R.P. Athparia (eds.) (1999): *Energy and Energy Resource Management*, Deep & Deep Publications, New Delhi.

Malcolm, S. Adiseshiah, (1992): 'Globalization of the Economy', *Indian Association of Social Science Institution*, Vol. 11, No. 1, July-September.

Mishra, P.C. (2002): 'Infrastructure Development and Economic Growth in India', *Post-Reform Leading Issues of Indian Economy*, A.D.N. Bajpai and others (eds.), Atlantic Publishers and Distributors (P) Ltd., New Delhi.

Mishra, R.S. (2002): 'Globalisation and Development of Indian Transport Sector', *The Indian Economic Association 85*th *Conference Volume*, Thiruvananthapuram.

Misra, S.K. and V.K. Puri (1999): *Indian Economy: Its Development Experience*, Himalaya Publishing House, Mumbai.

Misra, S.K. and V.K. Puri (2002): *Economic Environment of Business*, Himalaya Publishing House, Mumbai.

Misra, S.K. and V.K. Puri (2004): Indian *Economy: Its Development Experience*, Himalaya Publishing House, Mumbai.

Misra, S.K. (2002): 'Development of Commercial Banking During the Post-Liberalisation Period: A Study in a Regional Dimension', *Post-Reform Leading Issues of Indian Economy*, A.D.N. Bajpai and others (eds.), Atlantic Publishers and Distributors (P) Ltd., New Delhi.

Mody, Russi (1992): 'Globalization Efforts with Accent in Export', *The Economic Times,* April 21.

Mohan, Rakesh (1994): *India Infrastructure Report*, Rakesh Mohan Committee.

Mohan, Rakesh (2001): 'Small-Scale Industry Policy in India: A Critical Evaluation', *National Council of Applied Economic Research*, New Delhi.

Mohan, Rakesh (2005): 'Financial Sector Reforms in India: Policies and Performance Analysis', *Economic and Political Weekly,* March 19.

Mohan, Rakesh (2006): 'Agricultural Credit in India: Status, Issues and Future Agenda', *Economic and Political Weekly*, March 18.

Mohan, T.T. Ram (2003): 'Long-run Performance of Public and Private Sector Bank Stocks', *Economic and Political Weekly*, Vol. 48, February.

Morris, Sebastian (ed.) (2001): *India Infrastructure Report 2001*, 3iNetwork, Oxford University Press, New Delhi.

Morris, Sebastian (ed.) (2002): *India Infrastructure Report 2002*, 3iNetwork, Oxford University Press, New Delhi.

Morris, Sebastian (ed.) (2003): *India Infrastructure Report 2003*, 3iNetwork, Oxford University Press, New Delhi.

Morris, Sebastian (ed.) (2004): *India Infrastructure Report 2004*, 3iNetwork, Oxford University Press, New Delhi.

Morris, Sebastian (ed.) (2005): *India Infrastructure Report 2005*, 3iNetwork, Oxford University Press, New Delhi.

Mundle and Sudip (1993): 'Unemployment and Financing of Relief Employment in Period of Stabilization in India 1992-94', *Economic and Political Weekly*, January 30.

Munjal, S. (1999): *Survey of Indian Economy: Some Burning Issues*, Raj Publishing House, Jaipur.

Mujumdar, N.A. (2002): 'Agenda for Financial Sector Reforms', *India's Economy in the 21st Century*, Raj Kapila and Uma Kapila (eds.), Academic Foundation, New Delhi.

Mulford, David C. (2005): 'Economic Reform and Infrastructure', *Remarks at FICCI's India Infrastructure Conference Federation House*, New Delhi, March 28.

Murty, S. (2002): *Infrastructure and Social Sector Development for Economic Growth*, RBSA Publishers, Jaipur.

Nagresh, Kumar (2000): 'Economic Reforms and their Macro-Economic Impact', *Economic and Political Weekly*, Vol. 35, No. 10, March 4-10.

Nair, K.R.G. (1993): 'New Economic Policy and Development of Backward Regions: A Note on Orissa', *Economic and Political Weekly*, Vol. 28, No. 19, May 18.

Narasimham, M. (2002): *Economic Reforms and Development and Finance*, UBS Publishers' Distribution Ltd., New Delhi.

Nayar, Baldev Raj (2001): 'Opening Up and Openness of Indian Economy', *Economic and Political Weekly*, Vol. 36, No. 37, September 15-21.

Nayyar, Deepak (1996): 'Globalization: The Past in Our Present', *Indian Economic Journal*, Vol. 31, No. 3.

Noronha Frederic (2006): 'Internet for All: Indian Villagers to Get Access at Prices They can Afford', as in www.tenet.res.in.

Outlook (2001): *Special Issue*, June 25.

Panchamukhi, V.R. (1999): 'Globalization, Competition and Economic Stability', *Disarmament and Development*, Vol. 2, No. 2, March-April.

Pachauri, Shonali and Daniel Spreng (2004): 'Energy Use and Energy Access in Relation to Poverty', *Economic and Political Weekly*, Vol. 39, No. 3, January 17.

Pandey, Shridhar: 'Liberalization, Globalization and the State in Indian Economy', *Liberalisation and Globalisation of Indian Economy*, K.R. Gupta (ed.), Atlantic Publishers and Distribution (P) Ltd., New Delhi, Vol. II.

Pant, K.C. (2003): *India's Development Scenario Next Decade and Beyond ...*, Academic Foundation, New Delhi, Vol. I.

Pant, K.C. (2004): *India's Development Scenario Next Decade and Beyond...*, Academic Foundation, New Delhi, Vol. II.

Parikh, Kirit S. (ed.) (1999): *India Development Report 1999-2000*, Oxford University Press, New Delhi.

Parikh, Kirit S. and R. Radhakrishna (eds.) (2002): *India Development Report 2002*, Oxford University Press, New Delhi.

Patel, S.K. and R.C. Talati (1997): 'Globalization of the Indian Economy', *Liberalisation and Globalisation of Indian Economy*, K.R. Gupta (ed.), Atlantic Publishers and Distribution (P) Ltd., New Delhi, Vol. I.

Phadke, Amol and Sudhir Chella Rajan (2003): 'Electricity Reforms in India: Not Too Late to Go Back to the Drawing Board', *Economic and Political Weekly*, July 19-25, Vol. 38, No. 29.

Phadke, Amol (2001): 'Questionable Economics of LNG-based Power Generation Need for Rigorous Analysis', *Economic and Political Weekly*, Vol. 36, No. 20, May 19-25.

Ponraj, R. (2001): 'Power Sector Reforms: Need for Different Thinking', *Infrastructure Development and Financing*, S. Ganesan (ed.), Kanishka Publishers, New Delhi.

Pratibha, B. Munot (2002): *Email: Study of Telecommunications Structure in India*, Oklahoma State University, October, 10.

Prayas (2002): 'HT Energy Audit: The Crucial Starting Point for Curbing Revenue Loss', *Prayas Occasional Report*, February.

Purkayastha, Prabir (2001): 'Power Sector Policies and New Electricity Bill from Crisis to Disaster', *Economic and Political Weekly*, Vol. 36, No. 25, June 23-29.

Ramanathan, R. (1997): 'Transport: A Crucial Infrastructure', *India Development Report 1997*, Oxford University Press, New Delhi.

Ramanathan, A.R. (2001): 'Independence of Regulators under the Electricity Bill', *Economic and Political Weekly*, November 2-9, 2001, Vol. 36, No. 44.

Ramaswamy, S. and T. Tamizh Chelvam (1997): 'Energy and Economic Development', *Infrastructure Development for Economic Growth*, M.V. Srinivasa Gowda and Susheela Subrahmanya (ed.), Deep & Deep Publications, New Delhi.

Rama, K.S., Chandra Rao, Abhiman Das, and Arvind Kumar Singh (2006): 'Commercial Bank Lending to Small-Scale Industry', *Economic and Political Weekly*, March 18.

Rangarajan, C. (1998): Indian *Economy: Essays on Money and Finance*, UBS Publishers & Distributors, New Delhi.

Rangarajan, C. (2000): *Perspectives on Indian Economy: A Collection of Essays*, UBS Publishers & Distributors, New Delhi.

Rao, S.L. (2001): 'Electricity Bill 2001: What it Reflects of Power Policy', *Economic and Political Weekly*, Vol. 36, No. 38, September 22-28.

Rao, S.L. (2003): 'Electricity Bill, 2001: Many Shortcomings, but a Step Forward', *Economic and Political Weekly*, Vol. 38, No. 5, February 1.

Rao, Suneeti (2001): 'Information Technology Act: Consumers' Perspective', *Economic and Political Weekly*, Vol. 36, No. 37, September 15-21.

Rao, V.D.R.V (1981): 'Infrastructure and Economic Development', *Commerce Annual*, 1981.

Rath, Nilakantha (2001): 'Data on Employment, Unemployment and Education: Where to Go from Here?', *Economic and Political Weekly*, Vol. 36, No. 23, June 9-15.

Rastogi, Anupam B. (2003): 'The Infrastructure Sector in India, 2001-02' *India Infrastructure Report 2003*, 3iNetwork, Oxford University Press, New Delhi.

Reddy, C.R. and others (2003): 'Power Sector Reforms', *Southern Economist*, Vol. 42, No. 7, August 1.

Reddy, D. Narasimha, (2002): 'Globalisation and Decentralised Development: Bringing Back the Nation-State', an invited paper at *The Indian Economic Association 85*th *Conference Volume*, Thiruvananthapuram.

Reddy, Justice B.P. Jeevan (1999): 'The Perils of Globalization', *Disarmament and Development*, Vol. 2, No. 2, March-April.

Reddy, Y.V. (2000): *Monetary and Financial Sector Reforms in India, A Central Banker's Perspective*, UBS Publishers & Distributors, New Delhi.

Reddy, Y.V. (2000): 'Fiscal and Monetary Policy Interface: Recent Developments in India', *Reserve Bank of India Bulletin*, November.

Reddy, Y.V. (2001): 'Developments in Monetary Policy and Financial Markets in India', *Reserve Bank of India Bulletin.*

Reddy, Y.V. (2001): 'Autonomy of the Central Bank: Changing Contours in India', *Reserve Bank of India Bulletin*, November.

Reddy, Y.V. (2002): 'Monetary and Financial Sector Reforms in India: A Practitioner's Perspective', address delivered at the *Indian Economy Conference*, "Program on Comparative Economic Development" (PCED) at Cornell University, USA, on April 19-20.

Reddy, Y.V. (2006): 'Reforming India's Financial Sector: Changing Dimensions and Emerging Issues', address delivered at the *International Centre for Monetary and Banking Studies*, Geneva, on May 6.

Reserve Bank of India (2004): *Report on the Trend and Progress of Banking in India, 2003-04*, Reserve Bank of India, Mumbai.

Reserve Bank of India (1999): 'Annual Report for the Year 1998-99', Reserve Bank of India, Mumbai.

Reserve Bank of India (2000): 'Annual Report for the Year 1999-2000', Reserve Bank of India, Mumbai.

Reserve Bank of India (2001): 'Annual Report for the Year 2000-02', Reserve Bank of India, Mumbai.

Reserve Bank of India (2002): 'Annual Report for the Year 2001-02', Reserve Bank of India, Mumbai.

Saikia, Kula (1999): 'Energy Planning: Relevant Issues', *Energy and Energy Resource Management*, V.S. Mahajan, S.K. Agnihotri and R.P. Athparia (eds.), Deep & Deep Publications, New Delhi.

Salam, Md. Abdus (2002): 'Globalization: A Myth of the Indian States', *The Indian Economic Association 85*th *Conference Volume*, Thiruvananthapuram.

Samuel, John, 'The Deceptive Globalization', *Caritas India Quarterly*, Vol. 49, No. 1, January-March.

Sankar, T.L. (2003): 'Power Sector: Rise, Fall and Reform', *Economic and Political Weekly*, Vol. 38, Nos. 12 and 13, March 22.

Sarkar, Rohit (2004): 'The Financial Sector: Vision 2020' *India Vision 2020: The Report plus Background Paper*, Planning Commission, Government of India, Academic Foundation, New Delhi.

Sasikumar, John K.C. (2001): 'Present Status and Challenges of Rural Telecommunications in India', as in S. Ganesan (ed.), *Infrastructure Development and Financing*, Kanishka Publishers & Distributors, New Delhi.

Sengupta, Chandan (2001): 'Conceptualizing Globalization: Issues and Implications', *Economic and Political Weekly*, Vol. 36, No. 33, August 18-24.

Sensarma, Rudra (2005): 'Cost and Profit Efficiency of Indian Banks during 1986-2003: A Stochastic Frontier Analysis', *Economic and Political Weekly*, March 19.

Shah, Ajay (1997): 'Telecommunication: Monopoly vs. Competition', *India Development Report 1997*, Oxford University Press, New Delhi.

Shetty, S.L. (2001): 'Reviving the Economy: Some Explorations', *Economic and Political Weekly,* Vol. 36, No. 30, July 28-August 3.

Shetty, S.L. (2004): 'Distributional Issues in Bank Credit: Multi-Strategy for Correcting Past Neglect', *Economic and Political Weekly*, Vol. 49, June 7.

Ghosh, Shyamal, (2004): 'Indian Telecom Scenario', *Yojana*, Vol. 48, January.

Singh, Bishwa Nath, Mohan Prasad Shrivastava, and Narendra Prasad (2003): *Economic Reforms in India*, APH Publishing Corporation, New Delhi.

Singh, Charan (2006): 'Should India Use Foreign Exchange Reserves to Finance Infrastructure?' *Economic and Political Weekly*, Vol. 41, February 11.

Singh, J.P. (1998): 'Evaluating Telecommunication Privatization and Liberalization in India and the Far East', Paper presented at the *Conference on "Has Privatization Worked? The International Experience"*, Columbia Institute of TeleInformation, Columbia University, New York, June 12.

Singh, Manmohan (2005): Speech at Bicentennial Celebrations of State Bank of India, June 4, Mumbai.

Singh, Manmohan: 'Well Begun, but Half Done: A Look Back at Liberalization', *Times of India*, July 28.

Sood, Aditya Dev (2001): 'How to Wire Rural India: Problems and Possibilities of Digital Development', *Economic and Political Weekly*, October 27.

Subrahmanaya, Susheela (1999): 'Multinationals in India: Boon or Bane?', *Southern Economists*, Vol. 38, No. 14, November 15.

Swamy, Dalip S. (1994): *The Political Economy of Industrialization*, New Delhi.

Swamy, Subramanian (2000): *Indian's Economic Performance and Reforms: A Perspective for the New Millennium*, Konark Publishers, New Delhi.

Tarapore S.S. (2000): *Issues in Financial Sector Reforms*, UBS Publishers & Distributors, New Delhi.

Tarapore, S.S. (2002): Twists *and Turns in Financial Reforms*, UBS Publishers & Distributors, New Delhi.

TERI (Tata Energy Research Institute) (2002): *Defining an Integrated Energy: A Document for Discussion, Debate, and Action,* New Delhi.

TERI (Tata Energy Research Institute): 'Road Transport in India', Kaushik Deb, New Delhi.

Tiwari, G. (2001): 'Transportation Safety Issues: Institutional Restructuring Proposed for India', IIT, Delhi.

Tichy, Nowel M. (1999): 'Glee and Gloom of Globalization', *Indian Currents*, July 12-18.

Trivedi, I.V. (2002): *Commerce Education in the New Millennium,* RBAS Publishers, Jaipur.

Uday Lal Pai (2005), 'India Tops Internet Reliability in Asia', as given in http://asia.internet.com/cyberatlas/0913-india.html

UNI, (2006): 'Indians becoming more Net Savvy: A Study", *The Hitavada*, September 21.

Venkatapathey, R. and R. Rani Geetha Priyadarshini (2001): 'Current Status of Power, the Key Infrastructure India', *Infrastructure Development and Financing*, S. Ganesan (ed.), Kanishka Publishers & Distributors, New Delhi.

Verma, V.S. (2004): 'Power Reforms: Overview of Power Sector', *Yojana*, Vol. 48, No. 1, January.

Vaidyanathan, V.S. (2000): 'The Failed Globalization: Need for Alternative Policies', *The Hitavada*, June 4.

Warrior, Shoba (2002): 'Telecom Sector Offers big Growth Opportunity', Rediff.com, as given by Rediff Report, May 18.

World Bank and Public-Private Infrastructure Advisory Facility (2000): *India: Country Framework Report for Private Participation in Infrastructure*, Washington, DC.

World Bank (1996): *Sustainable Transport: Priorities for Policy Reform*, Washington, DC.

World Bank (1997): *Country Study on India*, Washington, DC.

World Bank (2002): 'Competition Policy in Telecommunication: The Case of India', *International Telecommunication Union,* November as in sidharth @iimahd.ernet.in

World Bank (2001): *World Employment Report 2001: Life at Work in the Information Economy*, ILO, Geneva.

World Bank (2002): *World Telecommunication Development Report 2002*, ITU, Geneva.

Yoganand, Kale (2000): 'Sustainable Development: An Indian View Point', The *Hitavada,* August 13.

Websites:

http://www.indiabandwidth.com/

http://www.indiainfoline.com/nevi/vsmt.html

http://www.analysys.com/default.asp?Mode=article&iLeftArticle=838

http://www.budde.com.au/Cat/Cat100.html

http://www.commercialdiplomacy.org/ma_projects/ma_india1.htm

http://www.phoneplusinternational.com/hotnews/24h15161123.html

http://www.igigroup.com/st/pages/indiav1.html

http://www.businessweek.com/magazine/content/02_06/b3769124.htm

http://www.businessworldindia.com/archive/201211/cover1.htm

http://www.oecd.org/pdf/M00025000/M00025199.pdf

http://www.india-cellular.com/News-July-2002.html

http://www.indiateleservices.com/callcenreport.html

http://www.ibc-asia.com/Voice-Over-IP-India/indiaVoIPIntro.htm

http://aol.businessweek.com/magazine/content/02_06/b3769124.htm

http://www.dayafterindia.com/jan1/more.html

http://www.nasscom.org.

http://www.indiabandwidth.com/dir1/longdist32.html.

http://www.indiainfoline.com/nevi/vsmt.html.

http://www.india-cellular.com/News-July-2002.html.

http://www.indiainfoline.com/nevi/vsmt.html

http://www.indiabandwidth.com/dir1/longdist21.html.

http://network.realmedia.com/RealMedia/ads/click_lx.ads/lycostripod/ros/1x1/wp/ss/a/805011057/Position3/OasDefault/DEF2004020008_Lycos_1x1a/1x1.gif/336430313039343634313539383931 30?

http://www.pfcindia.com, comparative performance during last five years (1998-2003).

http://www.pfcindia.com, growth of power sector in India.

http://www.5paisa.com/cgi-bin/login/login.pl?Goto=http://regi.5paisa.com/5paisatrade/asp/InvRegistration.asp.http://www.windpowerindia.com/statyear/asp.

http://www.energylineindia.com.

http://www.Indiastat.com.

http://www.banknetindia.com/banking/rbip3a.htm

http://www.arts.cornell.edu/econ/ indiaconf/Y.V.%20Reddy%20Paper.pdf

http://www.unescap.org/drpad/publication/fin_2206/part4.pdf

http://www.sba.muohio.edu/abas/2003/vancouver/rishi_indianbanksabas2003.pdf

http://www.bis.org/review/r050519b.pdf

http://www.iecolumnists.expressindia.com/full_column.php?content_id=78805